SCIENCE

Mc
Graw
Hill
Education

These safety symbols are used in laboratory and field investigations in this book to indicate possible hazards. Learn the meaning of each symbol and refer to this page often. *Remember to wash your hands thoroughly after completing lab procedures.*

PROTECTIVE EQUIPMENT   Do not begin any lab without the proper protection equipment.

GOGGLES	Proper eye protection must be worn when performing or observing science activities that involve items or conditions as listed below.	APRON	Wear an approved apron when using substances that could stain, wet, or destroy cloth.	SOAP	Wash hands with soap and water before removing goggles and after all lab activities.	GLOVES	Wear gloves when working with biological materials, chemicals, animals, or materials that can stain or irritate hands.

LABORATORY HAZARDS

Symbols	Potential Hazards	Precaution	Response
DISPOSAL	contamination of classroom or environment due to improper disposal of materials such as chemicals and live specimens	• DO NOT dispose of hazardous materials in the sink or trash can. • Dispose of wastes as directed by your teacher.	• If hazardous materials are disposed of improperly, notify your teacher immediately.
EXTREME TEMPERATURE	skin burns due to extremely hot or cold materials such as hot glass, liquids, or metals; liquid nitrogen; dry ice	• Use proper protective equipment, such as hot mitts and/or tongs, when handling objects with extreme temperatures.	• If injury occurs, notify your teacher immediately.
SHARP OBJECTS	punctures or cuts from sharp objects such as razor blades, pins, scalpels, and broken glass	• Handle glassware carefully to avoid breakage. • Walk with sharp objects pointed downward, away from you and others.	• If broken glass or injury occurs, notify your teacher immediately.
ELECTRICAL	electric shock or skin burn due to improper grounding, short circuits, liquid spills, or exposed wires	• Check condition of wires and apparatus for fraying or uninsulated wires, and broken or cracked equipment. • Use only GFCI-protected outlets.	• DO NOT attempt to fix electrical problems. Notify your teacher immediately.
CHEMICAL	skin irritation or burns, breathing difficulty, and/or poisoning due to touching, swallowing, or inhalation of chemicals such as acids, bases, bleach, metal compounds, iodine, poinsettias, pollen, ammonia, acetone, nail polish remover, heated chemicals, mothballs, and any other chemicals labeled or known to be dangerous	• Wear proper protective equipment such as goggles, apron, and gloves when using chemicals. • Ensure proper room ventilation or use a fume hood when using materials that produce fumes. • NEVER smell fumes directly. • NEVER taste or eat any material in the laboratory.	• If contact occurs, immediately flush affected area with water and notify your teacher. • If a spill occurs, leave the area immediately and notify your teacher.
FLAMMABLE	unexpected fire due to liquids or gases that ignite easily such as rubbing alcohol	• Avoid open flames, sparks, or heat when flammable liquids are present.	• If a fire occurs, leave the area immediately and notify your teacher.
OPEN FLAME	burns or fire due to open flame from matches, Bunsen burners, or burning materials	• Tie back loose hair and clothing. • Keep flame away from all materials. • Follow teacher instructions when lighting and extinguishing flames. • Use proper protection, such as hot mitts or tongs, when handling hot objects.	• If a fire occurs, leave the area immediately and notify your teacher.
ANIMAL SAFETY	injury to or from laboratory animals	• Wear proper protective equipment such as gloves, apron, and goggles when working with animals. • Wash hands after handling animals.	• If injury occurs, notify your teacher immediately.
BIOLOGICAL	infection or adverse reaction due to contact with organisms such as bacteria, fungi, and biological materials such as blood, animal or plant materials	• Wear proper protective equipment such as gloves, goggles, and apron when working with biological materials. • Avoid skin contact with an organism or any part of the organism. • Wash hands after handling organisms.	• If contact occurs, wash the affected area and notify your teacher immediately.
FUME	breathing difficulties from inhalation of fumes from substances such as ammonia, acetone, nail polish remover, heated chemicals, and mothballs	• Wear goggles, apron, and gloves. • Ensure proper room ventilation or use a fume hood when using substances that produce fumes. • NEVER smell fumes directly.	• If a spill occurs, leave area and notify your teacher immediately.
IRRITANT	irritation of skin, mucous membranes, or respiratory tract due to materials such as acids, bases, bleach, pollen, mothballs, steel wool, and potassium permanganate	• Wear goggles, apron, and gloves. • Wear a dust mask to protect against fine particles.	• If skin contact occurs, immediately flush the affected area with water and notify your teacher.
RADIOACTIVE	excessive exposure from alpha, beta, and gamma particles	• Remove gloves and wash hands with soap and water before removing remainder of protective equipment.	• If cracks or holes are found in the container, notify your teacher immediately.

Alton Biggs
Biggs Educational Consulting
Commerce, TX

Ralph M. Feather, Jr., Ph.D.
Associate Professor
  Chair, Dept. of Educational
  Studies and Secondary Education
Bloomsburg University
Bloomsburg, PA

Douglas Fisher, Ph.D.
Professor of Teacher Education
San Diego State University
San Diego, CA

S. Page Keeley, M.Ed.
Maine Mathematics and
  Science Alliance
Augusta, ME

Margaret Kilgo
Educational Consultant
Kilgo Consulting, Inc.
Austin, TX

Michael Manga, Ph.D.
University of California, Berkeley
Berkeley, CA

Edward Ortleb
Science/Safety Consultant
St. Louis, MO

Dinah Zike, M.Ed.
Author, Consultant,
  Inventor of FOLDABLES
Dinah Zike Academy;
  Dinah Might Adventures, LP
San Antonio, TX

AMERICAN MUSEUM
ᴼ NATURAL HISTORY
New York, NY

Texas Advisory Board

Nedaro Bellamy, M.Ed.
Teacher Development Specialist
Houston ISD
Houston, TX

Rocio Munoz
Secondary Science Coordinator
Galena Park ISD
Houston, TX

Teresa Bosworth-Green
Director of Science
Spring ISD
Spring, TX

Cara Nanez
District Science Facilitator
Garland ISD
Garland, TX

Dean Boykin
Teacher/Academic Leader
Coppell Middle School North
Coppell, TX

Anita Snell de la Isla
Pre-K–12 Staff Development
Irving ISD
Irving, TX

Donald Burken
District Instructional Specialist
Spring Branch ISD
Houston, TX

Sandra West, Ph.D.
Associate Professor of
Biology and Science Education
Texas State University – San Marcos
San Marcos, TX

Yolanda Smith-Evans
Secondary Science Coordinator
Houston ISD
Houston, TX

Sharon Wilder, Ph.D.
K–12 Science Coordinator
Wallen ISD
Wallen, TX

Kevin Fisher
Secondary Science Coordinator
Lewisville ISD
Lewisville, TX

Omah Williams, M.Ed.
Education Consultant
Catalyst Science Consulting
Houston, TX

Julie Garner
Science Teacher
Lamar Middle School
Irving, TX

Tony Zahn
Pre-K–12 Science Coordinator
Grapevine-Colleyville ISD
Grapevine, TX

Roman Gomez
Pre-K–12 Science Curriculum
Specialist
Brownsville ISD
Brownsville, TX

Lead Consultants:

Lisa K. Felske
Science Specialist
Harris County Department of
    Education
Houston, Texas

Ann C. Mulvihill
Pre-K–12 Science Coordinator
Irving ISD
Irving, Texas

Tracy Ake
7th Grade Science Teacher
Fortbend ISD

Felecia Joiner
Stony Point Ninth Grade Center
Round Rock, TX

Carlos E. Salinas
7th Grade Science Teacher
East Central ISD

Meg Choate
6th Grade Science
    Teacher
Northside ISD

Joseph L. Kowalski, MS
Lamar Academy
McAllen, TX

Toni D. Sauncy
Associate Professor of Physics
Dept. of Physics
Angelo State University
St Angelo, TX

Tripp Givens
7th Grade Science Teacher
Mesquite ISD

Ginger Meeks
8th Grade Science Teacher
Austin, TX

Alison Welch
Wm. D. Slider Middle School
El Paso, TX

Jose Miguel Hurtado
    Jr., Ph.D.
Associate Professor
Dept. of Geological Sciences
University of Texas at El Paso
El Paso, TX

Paula Noe, M.Ed.
Science Specialist
Austin ISD
Austin, TX

Contributing Writers

Michelle Anderson, MS
Lecturer
The Ohio State University
Columbus, OH

Juli Berwald, Ph.D.
Science Writer
Austin, TX

John E. Bolzan, Ph.D.
Science Writer
Columbus, OH

Rachel Clark, MS
Science Writer
Moscow, ID

Patricia Craig, MS
Science Writer
Moscow, ID

Randall Frost, Ph.D
Science Writer
Pleasanton, CA

Lisa S. Gardiner, Ph.D.
Science Writer
Denver, CO

Jennifer Gonya, Ph.D.
The Ohio State University
Columbus, OH

Mary Ann Grobbel, MD
Science Writer
Grand Rapids, MI

**Whitney Crispen Hagins,
MA, MAT**
Biology Teacher
Lexington High School
Lexington, MA

Carole Holmberg, BS
Planetarium Director
Calusa Nature Center and
 Planetarium, Inc.
Fort Myers, FL

Tina C. Hopper
Science Writer
Rockwall, TX

Jonathan D. W. Kahl, Ph.D.
**Professor of Atmospheric
 Science**
University of Wisconsin–
 Milwaukee
Milwaukee, WI

Nanette Kalis
Science Writer
Athens, OH

Cindy Klevickis, Ph.D.
**Professor of Integrated
 Science and Technology**
James Madison University
Harrisonburg, VA

Kimberly Fekany Lee, Ph.D.
Science Writer
La Grange, IL

Devi Ried Mathieu
Science Writer
Sebastopol, CA

William D. Rogers, DA
Professor of Biology
Ball State University
Muncie, IN

Donna L. Ross, Ph.D.
Associate Professor
San Diego State University
San Diego, CA

Marion B. Sewer, Ph.D.
**Assistant Professor
 School of Biology**
Georgia Institute of
 Technology
Atlanta, GA

Julia Meyer Sheets, Ph.D.
Lecturer
School of Earth Sciences
The Ohio State University
Columbus, OH

Michael J Singer, Ph.D.
Professor of Soil Science
Department of Land, Air and
 Water Resources
University of California
Davis, CA

Karen S. Sottosanti, MA
Science Writer
Pickerington, OH

Paul K. Strode, Ph.D.
I.B. Biology Teacher
Fairview High School
Boulder, CO

Jan M. Vermilye, Ph.D.
Research Geologist
Seismo-Tectonic Reservoir
Monitoring (STRM)
Boulder, CO

Judith A. Yero, MA
Director
Teacher's Mind Resources
Hamilton, MT

Margaret Zorn, MS
Science Writer
Yorktown, VA

Your assignment's due tomorrow...

but your book is in your locker!

NOW WHAT?

Even in crunch time, with ConnectED, we've got you covered!

With ConnectED, you have instant access to all of your study materials—anytime, anywhere. From homework materials to study guides—it's all in one place and just a click away. ConnectED even allows you to collaborate with your classmates and use mobile apps to make studying easy.

Resources built for you—available 24/7:

- Your eBook available wherever you are

- Personal Tutors and Self-Check Quizzes to help your learning

- An Online Calendar with all of your due dates

- eFlashcard App to make studying easy

- A message center to stay in touch

Reimagine Learning

Go Online!

connectED.mcgraw-hill.com

Vocab
Learn about new vocabulary words.

Watch
Watch animations and videos.

Tutor
See and hear a teacher explain science concepts.

Tools
Find tools to help you study.

Check
Check your progress.

Lab
Get all of your labs and lab worksheets.

Resources
Access practice worksheets.

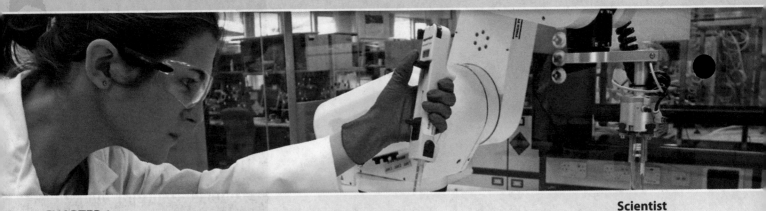

Scientist working in a lab

CHAPTER 1

Methods of Scientific Investigation

⚐ LAB Manager

Go to your Lab Manual or visit connectED.mcgraw-hill.com to perform the labs for this lesson.

Lesson 1.1
Skill Practice: *What can you learn by collecting and analyzing data?* **TEKS** 6.1(A); 6.2(A), (C), (D), (E); 6.4(A), (B)

Lesson 1.2
Lab: *Can one bad apple spoil the bunch?* **TEKS** 6.1(A); 6.2(B), (C); 6.4(B)

Lab: *Inferring from Indirect Evidence* **TEKS** 6.1(A), (B); 6.2(A), (C), (E); 6.4(A), (B)

Go Online! connectED.mcgraw-hill.com

Watch   Resources   Vocab   Tutor   IWB   Check   Lab
▶   📄   abc   💬   📈   ✓   ⬈

BrainPOP®: Scientific Methods

Strand 2: Matter and Energy

CHAPTER 2
Matter and Its Changes

Fireworks over Houston, Texas

☑ LAB Manager

Go to your Lab Manual or visit connectED.mcgraw-hill.com to perform the labs for this lesson.

Lesson 2.1
MiniLAB: *How do elements, compounds, and mixtures differ?*
TEKS 6.1(A); 6.2(A), (C), (E); 6.4(A), (B); 6.5(A), (C)

LAB: *Balloon Molecules*
TEKS 6.1(A); 6.2(A), (E); 6.3(B); 6.4(B); 6.5(C)

Lesson 2.2
MiniLAB: *Is mass conserved during a chemical reaction?*
TEKS 6.1(A); 6.2(A), (C); 6.4(A); 6.5(D)

BrainPOP®: Property Changes

Go Online! connectED.mcgraw-hill.com

Watch   Resources   Vocab   Tutor   IWB   Check   Lab

CHAPTER 3
Classifying Matter

Cadillac Ranch in Amarillo, Texas

✓ LAB Manager
Go to your Lab Manual or visit
connectED.mcgraw-hill.com to
perform the labs for this lesson.

Lesson 3.1
MiniLab: *How can you find an
object's mass and volume?*
TEKS 6.1(A); 6.2(A), (C); 6.4(A), (B);
6.6(B)

Skill Practice: *How can you
calculate density?*
TEKS 6.1(A); 6.2(A), (C); 6.4(A), (B);
6.6(B)

LAB: *Identifying Unknown
Minerals*
TEKS 6.1(A); 6.2(A), (C), (E);
6.4(A), (B); 6.6(B), (C)

Lesson 3.2
MiniLAB: *How well do materials
conduct thermal energy?*
TEKS 6.1(A); 6.2(A), (C), (E);
6.4(A), (B); 6.6(A)

Lesson 3.3
MiniLAB: *Which insulates better?*
TEKS 6.1(A); 6.2(A), (C), (E); 6.4(A);
6.6(A)

BrainPOP®: Matter Changing State

Go Online! connectED.mcgraw-hill.com

Watch Resources Vocab Tutor IWB Check Lab

CHAPTER 4
Earth's Energy Resources

An oil derrick at sunset in the Panhandle Plains region of Texas

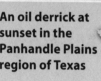

☑ LAB Manager

Go to your Lab Manual or visit connectED.mcgraw-hill.com to perform the labs for this lesson.

Lesson 4.1
MiniLAB: *What is your reaction?*
TEKS 6.1(A); 6.2(A), (E); 6.3(B); 6.4(B); 6.7(A)

Lesson 4.2
MiniLAB: *How are renewable energy resources used at your school?*
TEKS 6.2(A), (E); 6.4(A); 6.7(B)

Skill Practice: *How can you analyze energy use data for information to help conserve energy?* *TEKS* 6.2(A), (E); 6.7(B)

Skill Practice: *What color is best for solar panels?*
TEKS 6.1(A); 6.2(B), (C), (D), (E); 6.3(A); 6.4(A), (B); 6.7(A)

LAB: *Pinwheel Power*
TEKS 6.1(A); 6.2(A), (C), (D), (E); 6.3(B); 6.4(A), (B); 6.7(A)

Animation: Coal

Go Online! connectED.mcgraw-hill.com

Watch   Resources   Vocab   Tutor   IWB   Check   Lab

CHAPTER 5

Force and Motion

Historic Pleasure Pier in Galveston, Texas

◀ LAB Manager

Go to your Lab Manual or visit connectED.mcgraw-hill.com to perform the labs for this lesson.

Lesson 5.1
MiniLAB: *How can you determine average speed?*
TEKS 6.1(A); 6.2(A), (C), (E); 6.4(A), (B); 6.8(C)

Skill Practice: *How can you test and describe an object's motion?*
TEKS 6.1(A); 6.2(A), (C), (D), (E); 6.4(A), (B); 6.8(C)

Lesson 5.2
MiniLAB: *How can you make a speed-time graph?*
TEKS 6.2(E); 6.4(A); 6.8(D)

Lesson 5.3
MiniLAB: *Does a ramp make it easier to lift a load?* *TEKS* 6.1(A); 6.2(A), (C), (E); 6.4(A), (B); 6.8(E)

MiniLAB: *Can you increase mechanical advantage?*
TEKS 6.1(A); 6.2(A), (C), (E); 6.8(E)

MiniLAB: *How do forces affect motion?* *TEKS* 6.1(A); 6.2(A), (C), (E); 6.4(A), (B); 6.8(B)

LAB: *Comparing Two Simple Machines* *TEKS* 6.1(A); 6.2(B), (C), (D), (E); 6.4(A); 6.8(E)

LAB: *Design a Safe Vehicle* *TEKS* 6.1(A), (B); 6.2(B), (C), (E); 6.4(A), (B); 6.8(B)

Lesson 5.4
MiniLAB: *Can a moving object do work?* *TEKS* 6.1(A); 6.2(A), (C), (E); 6.4(A), (B)

Animation: Distance v. Time Graph

2:25 Time

Distance

Go Online! connectED.mcgraw-hill.com

Watch Resources Vocab Tutor IWB Check Lab

CHAPTER 6
Energy and Energy Transformations

Waves crashing onto
the rocks of Mustang
Island, Texas

☑ LAB Manager

Go to your Lab Manual or visit connectED.mcgraw-hill.com to perform the labs for this lesson.

Lesson 6.1
 MiniLAB: *How does a flashlight work?* **TEKS** 6.1(A); 6.2(A), (C), (E); 6.4(A), (B); 6.9(C)

 MiniLAB: *How does energy change form?*
 TEKS 6.1(A); 6.2(A), (C), (E); 6.4(A), (B); 6.9(C)

 Skill Practice: *Can you identify energy transformations?*
 TEKS 6.1(A); 6.2(A), (C), (D), (E); 6.4(A), (B); 6.9(C)

Lesson 6.2
 MiniLAB: *How does thermal energy move?*
 TEKS 6.1(A); 6.2(A), (C), (E); 6.4(A), (B); 6.9(B)

 MiniLAB: *How do the particles in a liquid move when heated?*
 TEKS 6.1(A); 6.2(A), (C), (E); 6.4(A), (B); 6.9(A)

 MiniLAB: *What affects the transfer of thermal energy?*
 TEKS 6.1(A); 6.2(A), (C), (E); 6.3(A); 6.4(A), (B); 6.9(A)

 LAB: *Design an Insulated Container*
 TEKS 6.1(A); 6.2(B), (C), (E); 6.3(A); 6.4(A), (B); 6.9(A)

Animation: Energy Transformation

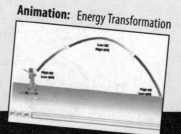

Go Online! connectED.mcgraw-hill.com

Watch Resources Vocab Tutor IWB Check Lab

CHAPTER 7
Earth's Structure

256   **The BIG Idea**

257   **Page Keeley SCIENCE PROBES**

Prickly pear cacti in the Guadalupe Mountains National Park

🔷 LAB Manager

Go to your Lab Manual or visit connectED.mcgraw-hill.com to perform the labs for this lesson.

Lesson 7.1
MiniLAB: *Which materials will sink?*
TEKS 6.1(A); 6.2(A); 6.4(A), (B)

Lesson 7.2
MiniLAB: *Which liquid is densest?*
TEKS 6.1(A); 6.2(A), (E); 6.3(B), (C); 6.4(A), (B); 6.10(A)

LAB: *Modeling Earth and Its Layers* *TEKS* 6.1(A); 6.2(A), (C), (E); 6.3(B), (C); 6.4(B); 6.10(A)

Lesson 7.3
MiniLAB: *How can you model convection currents?*
TEKS 6.1(A); 6.2(A), (C), (E); 6.3(B); 6.4(A), (B)

LAB: *Movement of Plate Boundaries*
TEKS 6.1(A), (B); 6.2(A), (C), (E); 6.3(B); 6.4(B); 6.10(D)

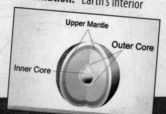

Animation: Earth's Interior

Upper Mantle
Outer Core
Inner Core

Go Online! connectED.mcgraw-hill.com

Watch Resources Vocab Tutor IWB Check Lab

Strand 4 *Continued*

✈ LAB Manager

Go to your Lab Manual or visit
connectED.mcgraw-hill.com to
perform the labs for this lesson.

Lesson 8.1
 MiniLAB: *Can you model the
rock cycle?*
 TEKS 6.1(A); 6.2(A), (C), (E); 6.3(B);
6.4(A), (B); 6.10(B)

Lesson 8.2
 MiniLAB: *How are cooling rate
and crystal size related?*
 TEKS 6.1(A); 6.2(A), (C), (E); 6.3(B);
6.4(A), (B); 6.10(B)

 Skill Practice: *How do you
identify igneous rocks?*
 TEKS 6.1(A); 6.2(A), (C), (E); 6.4(A);
6.10(B)

Lesson 8.3
 MiniLAB: *Where did these rocks
form?*
 TEKS 6.1(A); 6.2(A), (C), (E); 6.10(B)

 Skill Practice: *How are
sedimentary rocks classified?*
 TEKS 6.1(A); 6.2(A), (C), (E);
6.4(A), (B); 6.10(B)

Lesson 8.4
 MiniLAB: *Can you model
metamorphism?*
 TEKS 6.1(A); 6.2(A), (C); 6.3(B), (C);
6.4(B); 6.10(B)

 LAB: *Identifying the Type of Rock*
 TEKS 6.1(A); 6.2(A), (C), (E);
6.4(A), (B); 6.10(B)

Go Online! connectED.mcgraw-hill.com

Watch   Resources   Vocab   Tutor   IWB   Check   Lab

BrainPop®: Types of Rocks

TYPES OF ROCKS
MOVIE

Contents   **xv**

CHAPTER 9
The Solar System

Hobby-Eberly Telescope in the Davis Mountains

346 **The BIG Idea**

347 **Page Keeley SCIENCE PROBES**

Science Video: Blast Off

🔷 LAB Manager

Go to your Lab Manual or visit connectED.mcgraw-hill.com to perform the labs for this lesson.

Lesson 9.1
MiniLAB: *Sunspots*
TEKS 6.11(A)

MiniLAB: *How can you model an elliptical orbit?*
TEKS 6.1(A); 6.2(A), (C); 6.11(A)

Lesson 9.2
MiniLAB: *How can you model the inner planets?*
TEKS 6.2(A), (C); 6.3(B); 6.4(A), 6.11(A)

Skill Practice: *What can we learn about planets by graphing their characteristics?*
TEKS 6.2(A), (E); 6.11(A)

Lesson 9.3
MiniLAB: *How do Saturn's moons affect its rings?*
TEKS 6.1(A); 6.2(A), (C), (E); 6.3(B); 6.4(A), (B)

Lesson 9.4
MiniLAB: *How do impact craters form?* **TEKS** 6.2(A), (C); 6.3(B); 6.4(B); 6.11(A)

LAB: *Scaling down the Solar System* **TEKS** 6.2(A), (C), (E); 6.3(B), (C); 6.4(A), (B); 6.11(A)

CHAPTER 10
Space Exploration

Planetary exploration rover at the Johnson Space Center in Houston, Texas

TEKS 6.11(C); Also covers 6.1(A); 6.2(A), (C), (E); 6.3(B), (D); 6.4(A), (B)

TEKS 6.11(C); Also covers 6.1(A); 6.2(A), (C), (E); 6.3(B); 6.4(A), (B)

✈ LAB Manager

Go to your Lab Manual or visit connectED.mcgraw-hill.com to perform the labs for this lesson.

Lesson 10.1
MiniLAB: *How does lack of friction in space affect simple tasks?*
TEKS 6.1(A); 6.2(A), (C), (E); 6.4(B)

Lesson 10.2
MiniLAB: *What conditions are required for life on Earth?*
TEKS 6.2(A), (C), (E); 6.4(A); 6.11(C)

LAB: *Design and Construct a Moon Habitat*
TEKS 6.1(A); 6.2(A), (C), (E); 6.3(B); 6.4(B); 6.11(C)

Science Video: Living in Space

Go Online! connectED.mcgraw-hill.com

Watch   Resources   Vocab   Tutor   IWB   Check   Lab

CHAPTER 11
Interactions of Life

Yellow belly blue tang in the Dallas Aquarium, Dallas, Texas

⊲ LAB Manager

Go to your Lab Manual or visit connectED.mcgraw-hill.com to perform the labs for this lesson.

Lesson 11.1
MiniLAB: *How do eukaryotic and prokaryotic cells compare?*
TEKS 6.1(A); 6.2(A), (C), (E); 6.3(B); 6.12(B)

Lesson 11.2
MiniLAB: *Whose shoe is it?*
TEKS 6.1(A); 6.2(A), (C), (E); 6.12(D)

LAB: *How can living things be classified?*
TEKS 6.1(A); 6.2(A), (C), (E); 6.4(A), (B); 6.12(C), (D)

Lesson 11.3
MiniLAB: *How do you describe an ecosystem?*
TEKS 6.1(A); 6.2(A), (C), (E); 6.12(E), (F)

Skill Practice: *What can analyzing data reveal about predator-prey populations?*
TEKS 6.2(A), (E); 6.12(F)

LAB: *Design an Ecosystem*
TEKS 6.1(A); 6.2(A), (C), (E); 6.4(A), (B); 6.12(E), (F)

Animation: Plant Cell

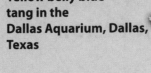

Plant Cell
Vacuole
Chloroplast

Go Online! connectED.mcgraw-hill.com

Watch Resources Vocab Tutor IWB Check Lab

Copyright © McGraw-Hill Education McGraw-Hill Education

TEKS Strand 1
Scientific Investigation and Reasoning

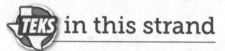 **in this strand**

✓ **6.1** The student, for at least 40% of instructional time, conducts laboratory and field investigations following safety procedures and environmentally appropriate and ethical practices.

✓ **6.2** The student uses scientific inquiry methods during laboratory and field investigations.

✓ **6.3** The student uses critical thinking, scientific reasoning, and problem solving to make informed decisions and knows the contributions of relevant scientists.

✓ **6.4** The student knows how to use a variety of tools and safety equipment to conduct science inquiry.

Did You Know? Fixing typing mistakes wasn't always as easy as hitting the backspace key. Making a mistake while using a typewriter meant having to re-type the entire document. Fortunately, Dallas, TX, native Bette Nesmith Graham invented Liquid Paper™ in 1958. Her invention has helped correct the mistakes of millions of typists.

1

Methods of Scientific Investigation

The **BIG** Idea

Scientists use the process of scientific inquiry to perform scientific investigations.

1.1 Understanding Science

Scientific inquiry is a process that uses a set of skills to answer questions or to test ideas about the natural world.

TEKS 6.1(A); 6.2(A), (B), (C), (D), (E); 6.4(A), (B)

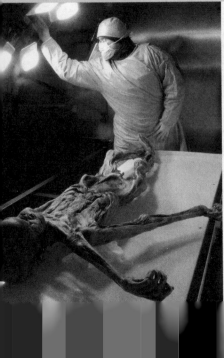

1.2 Case Study: The Iceman's Last Journey

Scientific inquiry is used in real-life investigation.

TEKS 6.1(A), (B); 6.2(A), (B), (C), (E); 6.3(A), (D); 6.4(A), (B)

The Scientific Method

Rita claims that scientists conduct scientific investigations using the scientific method. She says that even though there are many different kinds of investigations, scientists follow the same series of steps.

Do you agree or disagree with Rita? Explain your reasoning.

INQUIRY

Ice cubes? This scientist is removing ice core samples from the ground. The scientist uses the samples to determine what Earth's climate was like in the past and to make a hypothesis about how climate could affect Earth in the future. What is a hypothesis?

Write your response in your interactive notebook.

LAB Manager

Go to your Lab Manual or visit connectED.mcgraw-hill.com to perform the labs for this lesson.

Skill Practice: *What can you learn by collecting and analyzing data?*

TEKS 6.1(A); 6.2(A), (C), (D), (E); 6.4(A), (B)

Ragnar Th. Sigurdsson/age fotostock

Copyright © McGraw

Explore Activity

TEKS 6.1(A); 6.2(A), (C); 6.4(A), (B)

Does color affect temperature?

Suppose it is your job to pick out new uniforms for your school band. Other students have expressed their concern about how hot their uniforms are during football games and parades. You suspect that some colors of uniforms will be warmer than others, so you decide to design an experiment to determine which color absorbs the most amount of heat.

Procedure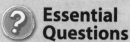

1. Read and complete a lab safety form.

2. Obtain **fabric** samples in five different colors. Using **scissors**, cut the samples to the same size and fold them into pockets.

3. Design a data table in your Lab Manual or interactive notebook to collect temperature data.

4. Place a **thermometer** in each pocket and place the fabric samples in the Sun.

5. Record a temperature for each sample every minute for ten minutes. Record your data in your data table.

Think About This

1. Rank the fabric samples in order of biggest difference between starting temperature and ending temperature to the least difference. What kind of pattern can you observe?

_____

_____

_____

2. Hypothesize whether using different sizes of fabric samples affects the results of the experiment.

_____

_____

_____

_____

TEKS in this Lesson

6.1(A) Demonstrate safe practices during laboratory and field investigations as outlined in the Texas Safety Standards

6.2(B) Design and implement experimental investigations by making observations, asking well-defined questions, formulating testable hypotheses, and using appropriate equipment and technology

Also covers Process Standards: 6.2(A), (C), (D), (E); 6.4(A), (B)

? Essential Questions

• What are the parts of a scientific investigation?

• What safety precautions need to be taken when working on lab and field investigations?

• How is scientific inquiry different from other forms of inquiry?

abc Vocabulary

science
observation
inference
hypothesis
prediction
technology
scientific theory
scientific law
critical thinking

What is science?

Did you ever hear a bird sing and then look in nearby trees to find the singing bird? Have you ever noticed how the Moon changes from a thin crescent to a full moon each month? When you do these things, you are doing science. **Science** *is the investigation and exploration of natural events and of the new information that results from those investigations.*

People use science in their everyday lives and careers. For example, firefighters, as shown in **Figure 1**, wear clothing that has been developed and tested to withstand extreme temperatures without burning. Parents use science when they set up an aquarium for their children's pet fish. Athletes use science when they use high-performance gear or wear high-performance clothing. Without thinking about it, you use science or the results of science in almost everything you do. Your clothing, food, hair products, electronic devices, athletic equipment, and almost everything else you use are results of science.

Figure 1 Firefighters' clothing, oxygen tanks, and equipment are results of science.

Branches of Science

There are many different parts of the natural world. Because there is so much to study, scientists often focus their work in one branch of science or on one topic within that branch of science. As shown below, there are three main branches of science—Earth science, life science, and physical science.

Word Origin

physical from Latin *physica*; means "study of nature"

Earth Science

The study of Earth, including rocks, soils, oceans, and the atmosphere is Earth science. The Earth scientist to the right is collecting lava samples for research. Earth scientists might ask other questions such as

- How do different shorelines react to tsunamis?
- Why do planets orbit the Sun?
- What is the rate of climate change?

Life Science

The study of living things is life science, or biology. These biologists are attaching a radio collar to a caribou. The collar on a caribou's neck can be tracked from the air. Biologists also ask questions such as

- Why do some trees lose their leaves in winter?
- How do birds know which direction they are going?
- How do mammals control their body temperatures?

Physical Science

The study of matter and energy is physical science. It includes physics and chemistry. This research chemist is preparing samples of possible new medicines. Physicists and chemists ask other questions such as

- Which chemical reactions must take place to launch a spaceship into space?
- Is it possible to travel faster than the speed of light?
- What makes up matter?

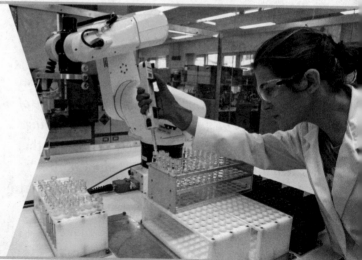

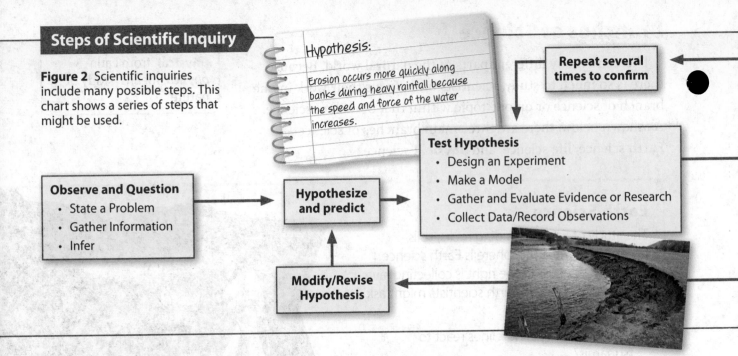

Figure 2 Scientific inquiries include many possible steps. This chart shows a series of steps that might be used.

Hypothesis:

Erosion occurs more quickly along banks during heavy rainfall because the speed and force of the water increases.

Repeat several times to confirm

Test Hypothesis
- Design an Experiment
- Make a Model
- Gather and Evaluate Evidence or Research
- Collect Data/Record Observations

Observe and Question
- State a Problem
- Gather Information
- Infer

Hypothesize and predict

Modify/Revise Hypothesis

Scientific Inquiry ⬛TEKS 6.2(A), (B), (E)

When scientists conduct scientific investigations, they use scientific inquiry. Scientific inquiry is a process that uses a set of skills to answer questions or to test ideas about the natural world. There are many kinds of scientific investigations and ways to conduct them. The steps used in each investigation often vary. The flowchart in **Figure 2** shows an example of the skills used in scientific inquiry.

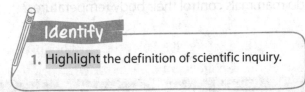

Identify

1. Highlight the definition of scientific inquiry.

Ask Questions

One way to begin a scientific inquiry is to observe the natural world and ask questions. **Observation** *is the act of using one or more of your senses to gather information and taking note of what occurs.* Suppose you observe that the banks of a river have eroded more this year than in the previous year and you want to know why. You also note that there was an increase in rainfall this year. You make an inference based on these observations.

An **inference** *is a logical explanation of an observation that is drawn from prior knowledge or experience.* You infer that the increase in rainfall caused the increase in erosion. You decide to investigate by developing a hypothesis and test method.

Hypothesize and Predict

A **hypothesis** *is a possible explanation for an observation that can be tested by scientific investigations.* A hypothesis states an observation and provides an explanation. You might make the following hypothesis: More of the riverbank eroded this year because the amount, speed, and force of the river water increased.

Scientists often use a hypothesis to make predictions to help test their hypothesis. *A* **prediction** *is a statement of what will happen next in a sequence of events.* Scientists make predictions based on information they think they will find when testing their hypothesis. Predictions for the hypothesis above could be: If rainfall increases, then the amount, speed, and force of river water will increase. If the amount, speed, and force of river water increase, then there will be more erosion.

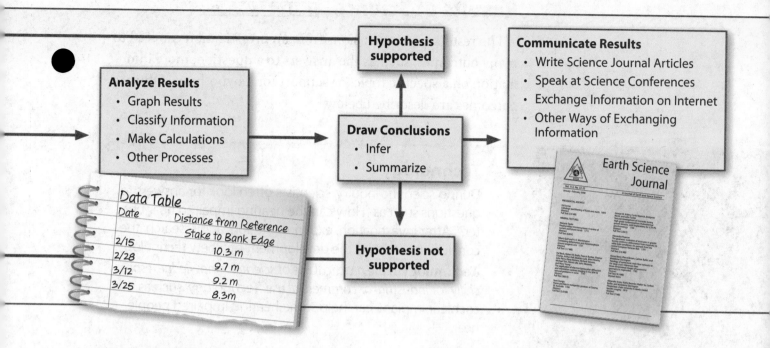

Test Hypothesis

When you test a hypothesis, you often test whether your predictions are true. If a prediction is confirmed, then it supports your hypothesis. If your prediction is not confirmed, you might need to modify your hypothesis and retest it.

There are several ways to test a hypothesis when performing a scientific investigation. Four possible ways are shown in **Figure 2.** For example, you might make a model of a riverbank in which you change the speed and the amount of water and record results and observations.

Analyze Results

After testing your hypothesis, you analyze your results using various methods, as shown in **Figure 2.** Often, it is hard to see trends or relationships in data while collecting it. Data should be sorted, graphed, or classified in some way. After analyzing the data, additional inferences can be made.

Draw Conclusions

Once you find the relationships among data and make several inferences, you can draw conclusions.

A conclusion is a summary of the information gained from testing a hypothesis. Scientists study the available information and draw conclusions based on that information.

Communicate Results

An important part of the scientific inquiry process is communicating results. Several ways to communicate results are listed in **Figure 2.** Scientists might share their information in other ways, too. Scientists communicate results of investigations to inform other scientists about their research and the conclusions of their research. Scientists might apply each other's conclusions to their own work to help support their hypotheses.

Further Scientific Inquiry

Scientific inquiry is not completed once one scientific investigation is completed. If predictions are correct and the hypothesis is supported, scientists will retest the predictions several times to make sure the conclusions are the same. If the hypothesis is not supported, then any new information gained can be used to revise the hypothesis. Hypotheses can be revised and tested many times.

Results of Science   **TEKS** TEKS 6.2.(B), (E)

The results and conclusions from an investigation can lead to many outcomes, such as the answers to a question, more information on a specific topic, or support for a hypothesis. Other outcomes are described below.

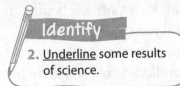

Technology

During scientific inquiry, scientists often look for answers to questions such as "How can the hearing impaired hear better?" After investigation, experimentation, and research, the conclusion might be the development of a new technology. **Technology** *is the practical use of scientific knowledge, especially for industrial or commercial use.* Technology, such as the cochlear implant, can help some hearing impaired people hear.

New Materials

Space travel has unique challenges. Astronauts must carry oxygen to breathe. They also must be protected against temperature and pressure extremes, as well as small, high-speed flying objects. Today's spacesuit, which is the result of research, testing, and design changes, consists of 14 layers of material. The outer layer is made of a blend of three materials. One material is waterproof and another is heat and fire-resistant.

Possible Explanations

Scientists often perform investigations to find explanations as to why or how something happens. NASA's *Spitzer Space Telescope,* which has aided in our understanding of star formation, shows a cloud of gas dust with newly formed stars.

Scientific Theory and Scientific Law

Identify

2. Underline some results of science.

Another outcome of science is the development of scientific theories and laws. Recall that a hypothesis is a possible explanation about an observation that can be tested by scientific investigations. What happens when a hypothesis or a group of hypotheses have been tested many times and have been supported by repeated scientific investigations? The hypothesis can become a scientific theory.

Scientific Theory

Often, the word theory is used in casual conversations to mean an untested idea or an opinion. However, scientists use theory differently. *A* **scientific theory** *is an explanation of observations or events that is based on knowledge gained from many observations and investigations.*

Scientists regularly question scientific theories and test them for validity. A scientific theory generally is accepted as true until it is disproved. An example of a scientific theory is the theory of plate tectonics. The theory of plate tectonics explains how Earth's crust moves and why earthquakes and volcanoes occur. Another example of a scientific theory is discussed in **Figure 3.**

Scientific Law

A scientific law is different from a social law, which is an agreement among people concerning a behavior. *A* **scientific law** *is a rule that describes a pattern in nature.* Unlike a scientific theory that explains why an event occurs, a scientific law only states that an event will occur under certain circumstances. For example, Newton's law of gravitational force implies that if you drop an object, it will fall toward Earth. Newton's law does not explain why the object moves toward Earth when it is dropped, only that it will.

Figure 3 Scientists once believed that the Earth was the center of the solar system. In the 16th century, Nicolaus Copernicus hypothesized that the Earth and the other planets revolve around the Sun.

Infer

3. How do scientific laws and theories differ?

_____

_____

_____

_____

New Information TEKS 6.3(A)

Scientific information constantly changes as new information is discovered or as previous hypotheses are retested. New information can lead to changes in scientific theories, as explained in **Figure 4.** When new facts are revealed, a current scientific theory might be revised to include the new facts, or it might be disproved and rejected.

If new information supports a current scientific theory, then the theory is not changed. The information might be published in a scientific journal to show further support of the theory. The new information might also lead to advancements in technology or spark new questions that lead to new scientific investigations.

If new information opposes, or does not support a current scientific theory, the theory might be modified or rejected altogether. Often, new information will lead scientists to look at the original observations in a new way. This can lead to new investigations with new hypotheses. These investigations can lead to new theories.

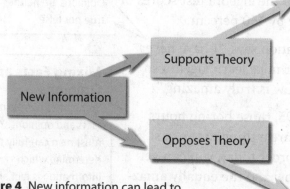

Figure 4 New information can lead to changes in scientific theories.

Evaluating Scientific Evidence

Did you ever read an advertisement, such as the one below, that made extraordinary claims? If so, you probably practice **critical thinking**—*comparing what you already know with the information you are given in order to decide whether you agree with it.* To determine whether information is true and scientific or pseudoscience (information incorrectly represented as scientific), you should be skeptical and identify facts and opinions. This helps you evaluate the strengths and weaknesses of information and make informed decisions. Critical thinking is important in all decision making—from everyday decisions to community, national, and international decisions.

Skepticism
To be skeptical is to doubt the truthfulness or accuracy of something. Because of skepticism, science can be self-correcting. If someone publishes results or if an investigation gives results that don't seem accurate, a skeptical scientist usually will challenge the information and test the results for accuracy.

Identifying Facts
The prices of the pillows and the savings are facts. A fact is a measurement, observation, or statement that can be strictly defined. Many scientific facts can be evaluated for their validity through investigations.

Learn Algebra While You Sleep!

Have you struggled to learn algebra? Struggle no more.

Math-er-ific's new algebra pillow is scientifically proven to transfer math skills from the pillow to your brain while you sleep. This revolutionary scientific design improved the algebra test scores of laboratory mice by 150 percent.

Dr. Tom Equation says, "I have never seen students or mice learn algebra so easily. This pillow is truly amazing."

For only $19.95, those boring hours spent studying are a thing of the past. So act fast! If you order today, you can get the algebra pillow and the equally amazing geometry pillow for only $29.95. That is a $10 savings!

Identifying Opinion
An opinion is a personal view, feeling, or claim about a topic. Opinions are neither true nor false.

Mixing Facts and Opinions
Sometimes people mix facts and opinions. You must read carefully to determine which information is fact and which is opinion.

Science cannot answer all questions.

Scientists recognize that some questions cannot be studied using scientific inquiry. Questions that deal with opinions, beliefs, values, and feelings cannot be answered through scientific investigation. For example, questions that cannot be answered through scientific investigation might include: Are comedies the best kinds of movies? Is it ever okay to lie? Which food tastes best?

The answers to all these questions are based on opinions, not facts.

Safety in Science   **TEKS** 6.1(A); 6.4(B)

It is very important for anyone performing scientific investigations to use safe practices, such as the student shown in **Figure 5.** You should always follow your teacher's instructions. If you have questions about potential hazards, use of equipment, or the meaning of safety symbols, ask your teacher. Always wear protective clothing and equipment while performing scientific investigations. You should also have proper safety equipment easily accessible in the lab in case an accident occurs. For example, fire extinguishers and fire blankets are necessary safety equipment when open flames or flammable materials are used. If you are using live animals in your investigations, provide appropriate care and ethical treatment to them.

Figure 5 Always use safe lab practices when doing scientific investigations.

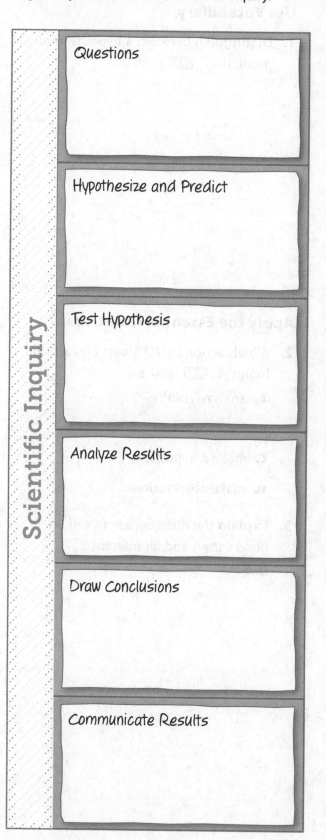

Cut out the Lesson 1.1 Foldable in the back of the book. Use it to make a six-tab book and to organize your notes about scientific inquiry.

Scientific Inquiry

Questions

Hypothesize and Predict

Test Hypothesis

Analyze Results

Draw Conclusions

Communicate Results

Use Vocabulary

1. **Distinguish** between a hypothesis and a prediction. *TEKS* TEKS 6.2(B)

_____

_____

_____

_____

Apply the Essential Questions

2. Which action is NOT part of scientific inquiry? *TEKS* TEKS 6.2(B)
   A. analyze results
   B. falsify results
   C. make a hypothesis
   D. make observations

3. **Explain** the difference between an observation and an inference. *TEKS* TEKS 6.2(B)

_____

_____

_____

_____

_____

4. Which action is NOT an example of a safe lab practice? *TEKS* TEKS 6.4(B)
   A. sniffing chemical bottles
   B. using an eye wash station
   C. wearing chemical splash goggles
   D. wearing gloves

5. Which items help scientists identify potential laboratory hazards? *TEKS* TEKS 6.4(B)
   A. inferences
   B. predictions
   C. safety symbols
   D. scientific theories

 H.O.T. Questions (Higher Order Thinking)

6. **Identify** a problem from your home, community, or school that could be investigated scientifically. *TEKS* TEKS 6.2(B)

_____

_____

_____

7. **Design** a scientific investigation to test one possible solution to the problem you identified in the previous question. *TEKS* TEKS 6.2(B)

_____

_____

_____

_____

Science and ENGINEERING

The Design Process

Create a Solution to a Problem

Scientists investigate and explore natural events. Then they interpret data and share information learned from those investigations. How do engineers differ from scientists? Engineers design, construct, and maintain the designed world. Look around you and notice things that do not occur in nature. Schools, roads, submarines, toys, microscopes, medical equipment, amusement park rides, computer programs, and video games are the result of engineering. Science involves the practice of scientific inquiry, but engineering involves the design process—a set of methods used to create a solution to a problem or need.

From the first snowshoes to modern ski lifts, people have designed solutions to effectively travel in the snow. The term *engineer* might not have existed when the first snowshoes were made. However, The design process and the goals of the people who developed snowshoes and ski lifts are similar.

1. Identify a Problem or Need
- Determine a problem or need.
- Document all questions, research, and procedures throughout the process.

2. Research and Develop Solutions
- Brainstorm possible solutions.
- Research any existing solutions that address the problem or need.
- Suggest limitations of the solutions.

5. Communicate Results and Redesign
- Communicate your design process and results to others.
- Redesign and modify the solution.
- Construct the final solution.

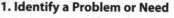

The Design Process

3. Construct a Prototype
- Develop possible solutions.
- Estimate materials, costs, resources, and time to develop the solutions.
- Select the best possible solution.
- Construct a prototype.

4. Test and Evaluate Solutions
- Use models to test the solutions.
- Use graphs, charts, and tables to evaluate results.
- Analyze the process and evaluate strengths and weaknesses of the solution.

Design a Zipline You are a guide for an adventure tour company that specializes in physically challenging activities in natural environments. You have been hired to design an exciting zipline ride near your town.

Identify the Problem

You know nothing about zipline rides or the requirements to construct a fast and safe zipline course. Consider the best location, platform design and construction, maximum angle of descent, length of ride, and materials required. Is it possible to zip too quickly or too slowly? Record your problem and questions with possible solutions in your interactive notebook.

Research Existing Solutions

Begin answering your questions by researching existing ziplines, roller coasters, and other similar thrill rides. Note possible limitations to your solutions, such as cost, size, materials, location, time, or other restraints.

Brainstorm Possible Solutions

Continue recording ideas for your zipline.

Include possible locations for it in your environment, sites for launching and safe-landing platforms, length of the zipline, materials and equipment needed for the zipline and rider, estimated costs, and time for development and construction.

Construct a Prototype

Draw several plans to answer your problems. Use simple materials to construct a scale model of your zipline. Check for accurate scale of dimensions and weight for each element to guarantee a fun, fast, and safe ride.

Test and Evaluate Solutions

Test your model many times to guarantee weight, speed, distance, and safe solutions. Use graphs, charts, and tables to evaluate the process and identify strengths and weaknesses in your solutions.

Communicate Your Results and Redesign Your Zipline

Communicate your design process and solution to peers using your visual displays and model. Discuss and critique your working solution. Do further research and testing, if necessary. Redesign and modify your solution to meet design objectives. Finally, construct a model of your solution.

1.2 Case Study: The Iceman's Last Journey

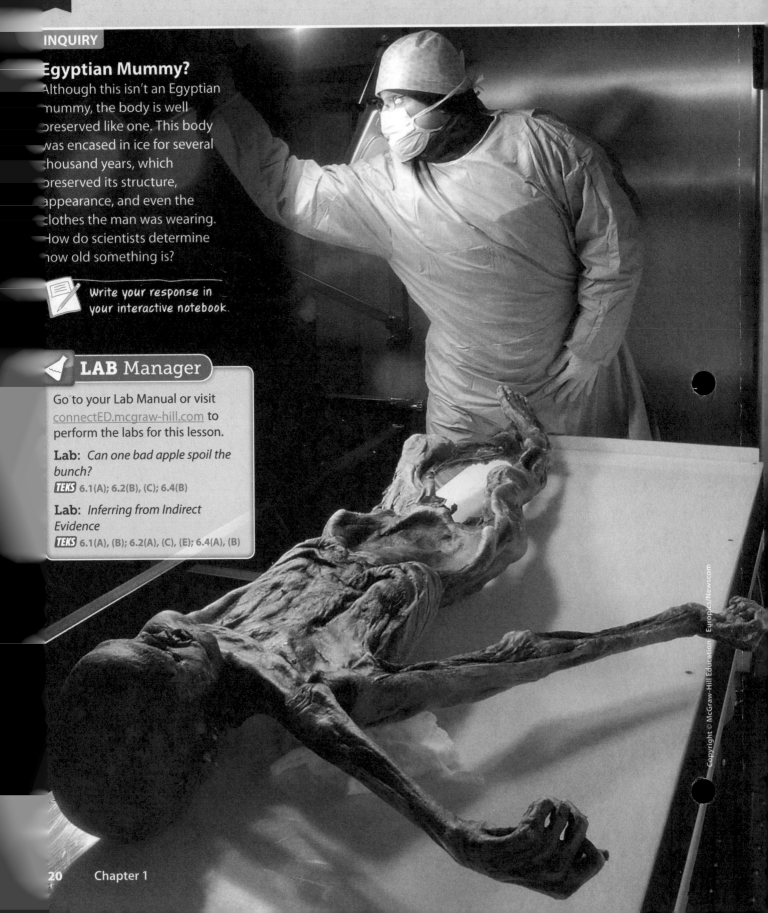

INQUIRY

Egyptian Mummy?

Although this isn't an Egyptian mummy, the body is well preserved like one. This body was encased in ice for several thousand years, which preserved its structure, appearance, and even the clothes the man was wearing. How do scientists determine how old something is?

Write your response in your interactive notebook.

LAB Manager

Go to your Lab Manual or visit connectED.mcgraw-hill.com to perform the labs for this lesson.

Lab: *Can one bad apple spoil the bunch?*
TEKS 6.1(A); 6.2(B), (C); 6.4(B)

Lab: *Inferring from Indirect Evidence*
TEKS 6.1(A), (B); 6.2(A), (C), (E); 6.4(A), (B)

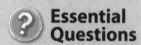

Paleozoic Puzzle

Suppose that there are many different and interesting fossils displayed around your classroom. Many of the fossil samples have been collected by other students and your teacher. Your teacher tells you that she studied some exposed rocks in the city where she attended college. It was at this time that she began her collection of fossils from that area, which is displayed in your room. Her favorite fossil was a particular species of brachiopod known as *Mucrospirifer*. She identified this fossil from pictures and descriptions in books about Paleozoic fossils.

When your teacher went on a fossil collecting trip last summer, she found what seemed to be the same type of *Mucrospirifer* fossil in a rock formation located hundreds of kilometers from her college.

Think About This

1. Is it possible that both fossils found by your teacher are *Mucrospirifer*?

   _____

   _____

2. Which fact should your teacher know about *Mucrospirifer* before using her fossils to date the rock layers in which they were found?

   _____

   _____

   _____

   _____

3. After your teacher determined that both samples she found were *Mucrospirifer*, what could she have concluded about the rock layers near her college and those she studied on her more recent fossil-collection trip?

   _____

   _____

   _____

TEKS in this Lesson

6.3(A) In all fields of science, analyze, evaluate, and critique scientific explanation by using empirical evidence, logical reasoning, and experimental and observational testing, including examining all sides of scientific evidence of those scientific explanations, so as to encourage critical thinking by the student

6.3(D) Relate the impact of research on scientific thought and society, including the history of science and contributions of scientists as related to the content.

Also covers Process Standards: 6.1(A), (B); 6.2(A), (B), (C), (E); 6.4(A), (B)

? Essential Questions

- How are independent variables and dependent variables related?
- How is scientific inquiry used in a real-life scientific investigation?

abc Vocabulary

variable
independent variable
dependent variable

Case Study: The Iceman's Last Journey

TEKS 6.3(A), (D)

The Tyrolean Alps border western Austria, northern Italy, and eastern Switzerland, as shown in **Figure 1**. They are popular with tourists, hikers, mountain climbers, and skiers. In 1991, two hikers discovered the remains of a man, also shown in **Figure 1**, in a melting glacier on the border between Austria and Italy. They thought the man had died in a hiking accident. They reported their discovery to the authorities.

Initially authorities thought the man was a music professor who disappeared in 1938. However, they soon learned that the music professor was buried in a nearby town. Artifacts near the frozen corpse indicated that the man died long before 1938. The artifacts, as shown in **Figure 2**, were unusual. The man, nicknamed the Iceman, was dressed in leggings, a loincloth, and a goatskin jacket. A bearskin cap lay nearby. He wore shoes made of red deerskin with thick bearskin soles. The shoes were stuffed with grass for insulation. In addition, investigators found a copper ax, a partially constructed longbow, a quiver containing 14 arrows, a wooden backpack frame, and a dagger at the site.

Figure 1 Excavators used jackhammers to free the man's body from the ice, which caused serious damage to his hip. Part of a longbow also was found nearby.

A Controlled Experiment

The identity of the corpse was a mystery. Several people hypothesized about his identity, but controlled experiments were needed to unravel the mystery. Scientists and the public wanted to know the identity of the man, why he had died, and when he had died.

Identifying Variables and Constants

When scientists design a controlled experiment, they have to identify factors that might affect the outcome of the experiment. *A variable is any factor that can have more than one value.* In controlled experiments, there are two kinds of variables. The **independent variable** *is the factor that you want to test.* It is changed by the investigator to observe how it affects a dependent variable. The **dependent variable** *is the factor you observe or measure during an experiment.* When the independent variable is changed, it causes the dependent variable to change.

A controlled experiment has two groups—an experimental group and a control group. The experimental group is used to study how a change in the independent variable changes the dependent variable. The control group contains the same factors as the experimental group, but the independent variable is not changed. Without a control, it is difficult to know if your experimental observations result from the variable you are testing or from another factor.

Scientists used inquiry to investigate the mystery of the Iceman. As you read, notice how scientific inquiry was used throughout the investigation. The blue boxes in the margins point out examples of the scientific inquiry process. The notebooks in the margin identify what a scientist might have written in a journal.

Figure 2 These models show what the Iceman and the artifacts found with him might have looked like.

Scientific investigations often begin when someone asks a question about something.

Observation: A corpse was found buried in ice in the Tyrolean Alps.

Hypothesis: The corpse is the body of a missing music professor, because he disappeared in 1938 and had not been found.

Observation: Artifacts near the corpse suggested that it was much older than the music professor would have been.

Revised Hypothesis: The person was dead long before 1938, because the artifacts found near him appear to date before the 1930s.

Prediction: If the artifacts belong to the corpse and they date before 1930, then the corpse is not the music professor.

An inference is a logical explanation of observations based on past experiences.

Inference: Based on its construction, the ax is at least 4,000 years old.

Prediction: If the ax is at least 4,000 years old, then the body found near it is also at least 4,000 years old.

Test Results: Radiocarbon dating showed the man to be 5,300 years old.

After many observations, revised hypotheses, and tests, conclusions can often be made.

Conclusion: The Iceman is about 5,300 years old. He was a seasonal visitor to the high mountains. He died in autumn. When winter came, the Iceman's body became buried and frozen in the snow, which preserved his body.

Figure 3 This ax, bow and quiver, and dagger and sheath were found with the Iceman's body.

An Early Conclusion

Konrad Spindler was a professor of archaeology at the University of Innsbruck in Austria when the Iceman was discovered. Spindler estimated that the ax, shown in **Figure 3,** was at least 4,000 years old based on its construction. If the ax was that old, then the Iceman was also at least 4,000 years old. Later, radiocarbon dating showed that the Iceman lived about 5,300 years ago.

The Iceman's body was in a mountain glacier 3,210 m above sea level. What was he doing so high in the snow- and ice-covered mountains? Was he hunting for food, shepherding his animals, or looking for metal ore?

Spindler noted that some of the wood used in the artifacts was from trees that grew at lower elevations. He concluded that the Iceman was probably a seasonal visitor to the high mountains.

Spindler also hypothesized that shortly before the Iceman's death, the Iceman had driven his herds from their summer high mountain pastures to the lowland valleys. However, the Iceman soon returned to the mountains where he died of exposure to the cold, wintry weather.

The Iceman's body was extremely well preserved. Spindler inferred that ice and snow covered the Iceman's body shortly after he died. Spindler concluded that the Iceman died in autumn and was quickly buried and frozen, which preserved his body and his possessions.

More Observations and Revised Hypotheses

When the Iceman's body was discovered, Klaus Oeggl was an assistant professor of botany at the University of Innsbruck. His area of study was plant life during prehistoric times in the Alps. He was invited to join the research team studying the Iceman.

Upon close examination of the Iceman and his belongings, Professor Oeggl found three plant materials—grass from the Iceman's shoe, as shown in **Figure 4**, a splinter of wood from his longbow, and a tiny fruit called a sloe berry.

Over the next year, Professor Oeggl examined bits of charcoal wrapped in maple leaves that had been found at the discovery site. Examination of the samples revealed the charcoal was from the wood of eight different types of trees. All but one of the trees grew only at lower elevations than where the Iceman's body was found. Like Spindler, Professor Oeggl suspected that the Iceman was at a lower elevation shortly before he died. Using Oeggl's observations, he formed a hypothesis and made some predictions.

Oeggl realized that he would need more data to support his hypothesis. He requested that he be allowed to examine the contents of the Iceman's digestive tract. If all went well, the study would show what the Iceman had swallowed just hours before his death.

> Scientific investigations often lead to new questions.

Observations: Plant matter near body to study—grass on shoe, splinter from longbow, sloe berry fruit, charcoal wrapped maple leaves, wood in charcoal from 8 different trees—7 of 8 types of wood in charcoal grow at lower elevations.

Hypothesis: The Iceman recently had been at lower elevations before he died, because the plants identified near him grow only at lower elevations.

Prediction: If the identified plants are found in the digestive tract of the corpse, then the man was at lower elevations just before he died.

Question: What did the Iceman eat the day before he died?

Figure 4 Professor Oeggl examined the Iceman's belongings along with the leaves and grass that were stuck to his shoe.

Test Plan:

• Divide a sample of the Iceman's digestive tract into four sections.

• Examine the pieces under microscopes.

• Gather data from observations of the pieces and record observations.

Experiment to Test Hypothesis

The research teams provided Professor Oeggl with a tiny sample from the Iceman's digestive tract. He was determined to study it carefully to obtain as much information as possible. Oeggl carefully planned his scientific inquiry. He knew that he had to work quickly to avoid the decomposition of the sample and to reduce the chances of contaminating the samples.

His plan was to divide the material from the digestive tract into four samples. Each sample would undergo several chemical tests. Then, the samples would be examined under an electron microscope to see as many details as possible.

Professor Oeggl began by adding a saline solution to the first sample. This caused it to swell slightly, making it easier to identify particles using the microscope at a relatively low magnification. He saw particles of a wheat grain known as einkorn, which was a common type of wheat grown in the region during prehistoric times. He also found other edible plant material in the sample.

Oeggl noticed that the sample also contained pollen grains, as shown in the inset of **Figure 5.** To see the pollen grains more clearly, he used a chemical that separated unwanted substances from the pollen grains. He washed the sample a few times with alcohol. After each wash, he examined the sample under a microscope at a high magnification. The pollen grains became more visible. Many more microscopic pollen grains could now be seen. Professor Oeggl identified these pollen grains as those from a hop-hornbeam tree.

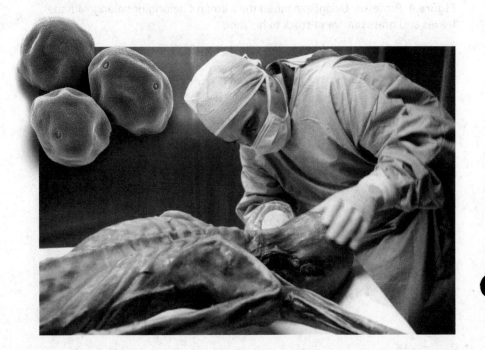

Figure 5 Eventually, Professor Oeggl identified pollen grains from hop-hornbeam trees.

Analyzing Results

Professor Oeggl observed that the hop-hornbeam pollen grains had not been digested. Therefore, the Iceman must have swallowed them shortly before his death. But, hop-hornbeam trees only grow in lower valleys. Oeggl was confused. How could pollen grains from trees at low elevations be ingested within few hours of this man dying in high, snow-covered mountains? Perhaps the samples from the Iceman's digestive tract had been contaminated. Oeggl knew he needed to investigate further.

Further Experimentation

Oeggl realized that the most likely source of contamination would be his own laboratory. He decided to test whether his lab equipment or saline solution contained hop-hornbeam pollen grains. To do this, he prepared two identical, sterile slides with saline solution. On one slide, he placed a sample from the Ice-man's digestive tract. The slide with the sample was the experimental group. The slide without the sample was the control group.

The independent variable, or the variable that Oeggl changed, was the presence of the sample on the slide. The dependent variable, or the variable Oeggl tested, was whether hop-hornbeam pollen grains showed on the slides. Oeggl examined the slides carefully.

Analyzing Additional Results

The experiment showed that the control group (the slide without the digestive tract sample) contained no pollen grains. Therefore, the pollen grains had not come from his lab equipment or solutions. Each sample from the Iceman's digestive tract was reexamined. All the samples contained the same hop-hornbeam pollen grains. The Iceman had swallowed the hop-hornbeam pollen grains.

Error is unavoidable in scientific research. Scientists are careful to document procedures and any unanticipated factors or accidents. They also are careful to document possible sources of error in their measurements.

Procedure:

• Sterilize laboratory equipment.

• Prepare saline slides.

• View saline slides under electron microscope. Results: no hop-hornbeam pollen grains

• Add digestive tract sample to one slide.

• View this slide under electron microscope. Results: hop-hornbeam pollen grains present

Controlled experiments contain two types of variables.

Dependent Variables: amount of hop-hornbeam pollen grains found on slide

Independent Variable: digestive tract sample on slide

Without a control group, it is difficult to determine the origin of some observations.

Control Group: sterilized slide

Experimental Group: sterilized slide with digestive tract sample

Observation: The Iceman's digestive tract contains pollen grains from the hop-hornbeam tree and other plants that bloom in spring.

Inference: Knowing the rate at which food and pollen decompose after swallowed, it can be inferred that the Iceman ate three times on the day that he died.

Prediction: The Iceman died in the spring within hours of digesting the hop-hornbeam pollen grains.

LAB Manager

Lab: *Can one bad apple spoil the bunch?*
TEKS 6.1(A); 6.2(B), (C); 6.4(B)

Lab: *Inferring from Indirect Evidence.*
TEKS 6.1(A), (B); 6.2(A), (C), (E); 6.4(A), (B)

Mapping the Iceman's Journey

The hop-hornbeam pollen grains were helpful in determining the season the Iceman died. Because the pollen grains were whole, Professor Oeggl inferred that the Iceman swallowed the pollen grains during their blooming season. Therefore, the Iceman must have died between March and June.

After additional investigation, Professor Oeggl was ready to map the Iceman's final trek up the mountain. Because Oeggl knew the rate at which food travels through the digestive system, he inferred that the Iceman had eaten three times in the final day and a half of his life. From the digestive tract samples, Oeggl estimated the Iceman's location when he ate.

First, the Iceman ingested pollen grains native to higher mountain regions. Then he swallowed hop-hornbeam pollen grains from the lower mountain regions several hours later. Last, the Iceman swallowed other pollen grains from trees of higher mountain areas again. Oeggl proposed the Iceman traveled from the southern region of the Italian Alps to the higher, northern region as shown in **Figure 6**, where he died suddenly. He did this all in a period of about 33 hours.

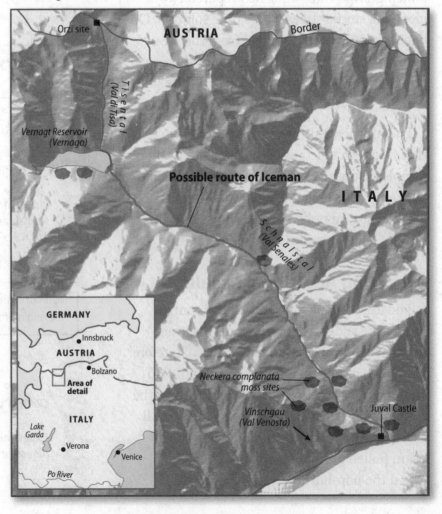

Figure 6 By examining the contents of the Iceman's digestive tract, Professor Oeggl was able to reconstruct the Iceman's last journey.

Copyright © McGraw-Hill Education

Conclusion

Researchers from around the world worked on different parts of the Iceman mystery and shared their results. Analysis of the Iceman's hair revealed that his diet usually contained vegetables and meat. Examining the Iceman's one remaining fingernail, scientists determined that he had been sick three times within the last six months of his life. X-rays revealed an arrowhead under the Iceman's left shoulder. This suggested that he died from that serious injury rather than from exposure.

Finally, scientists concluded that the Iceman traveled from the high alpine region in spring to his native village in the lowland valleys. There, during a conflict, the Iceman sustained a fatal injury. He retreated back to the higher elevations, where he died. Scientists recognize their hypotheses can never be proved, only supported or not supported. However, with advances in technology, scientists are able to more thoroughly investigate mysteries of nature.

Scientific investigations may disprove early hypotheses or conclusions. However, new information can cause a hypothesis or conclusion to be revised many times.

Revised Conclusion: In spring, the Iceman traveled from the high country to the valleys. After he was involved in a violent confrontation, he climbed the mountain into a region of permanent ice where he died of his wounds.

Analyze

1. Describe how an early hypothesis in the scientific investigation of the Iceman was not supported by evidence.

_____

_____

_____

_____

_____

_____

_____

_____

_____

_____

_____

_____

Copyright © McGraw-Hill Education

Use Vocabulary

1. A factor that can have more than one value is a(n)

_____

Apply the Essential Question

2. **Differentiate** between independent and dependent variables.

_____

_____

_____

_____

_____

_____

3. Which part of scientific inquiry was NOT used in this case study? **TEKS** 6.3(A)

  A. Draw conclusions.

  B. Make observations.

  C. Hypothesize and predict.

  D. Make a computer model.

4. Which sentence best describes an independent variable?

  A. It is a factor that is not in every test.

  B. It is a factor the investigator changes.

  C. It is a factor you measure during a test.

  D. It is a factor that stays the same in every test.

🔥 **H.O.T. Questions** (Higher Order Thinking)

5. **Formulate** more questions about the Iceman. What would you want to know next? **TEKS** 6.3(A)

_____

_____

_____

_____

6. **Evaluate** the importance of having a control group in a scientific investigation. **TEKS** 6.3(A)

_____

_____

_____

_____

7. **Relate** the impact of research on the original hypothesis about the Iceman's death. **TEKS** 6.3(D)

_____

_____

_____

_____

_____

_____

My Notes

Test-Taking Strategy

Interpret an Experiment Data from an experiment is often presented in graphics such as tables, graphs, photos, and diagrams. By reading the data in the graphic, you can learn about the results of an experiment and use them to answer the question.

Example

Use the table to answer question 2.

Paper Shape	Time to Fall to the Ground (seconds)
	5
	14
	8
	3

1 Identify the variables and constants in the experiment. In this experiment, the student changed the shape of the paper, which is the independent variable. She measured the time it took for the paper to hit the ground, which is the dependent variable.

2 Determine how those variables changed in relation to one another. In this experiment, the time it took the paper to fall to the ground decreased as the shape of the paper shape became more compact.

3 Examine the answer choices to find the one that matches the trend that you found. Eliminate choices with the wrong variables identified. The first two choices can be eliminated. Read the remaining answers to identify the one describing the correct trend. Choice C correctly describes the trend shown by the table.

2 A student folded a piece of paper into four shapes. She dropped each shape from the same height and timed how long it took the paper to hit the ground. Which conclusion is best supported by the data? **TEKS** 6.2E

A The time the paper took to fall to the ground did not change as the weight of the paper increased.

B The time the paper took to fall to the ground decreased as the weight of the paper increased.

C The time the paper took to fall to the ground increased as the shape became broader.

D The time the paper took to fall to the ground decreased as the shape became broader.

Multiple Choice

1 Scientists use a variety of tools to make observations. They choose tools and technology based on what they are studying and the questions they are trying to answer. Which question would a scientist ask when using this tool to make observations? **TEKS** 6.2(A)

A Are there organisms in the local well water that could make you sick?

B How does an elk population change over one year?

C How does cloud formation occur?

D What type of soil grows the largest tomatoes?

2 In 2001, scientists used X-rays and a CAT scan to examine the Iceman. They found an arrowhead buried in his left shoulder. They concluded that the Iceman was wounded by an arrow and quickly died of blood loss. In 2012, scientists examined the Iceman again. This time they used a laser-based tool called a Raman microscope. It showed that a blood clot had formed to stop blood loss from the shoulder wound. The scientists now concluded the Iceman likely died from a head injury. This new explanation of the Iceman's death is an example of _____.
TEKS 6.3(A)

A how scientific explanations differ from other kinds of explanations

B how scientific explanations can change when new evidence is found

C how scientists find ways to work together in groups

D how scientists ignore the work of earlier scientists

3 Anna has a potted plant with healthy leaves and three straight stems. The plant sits by her kitchen window and she waters it regularly. After one month, Anna's plant looks like the one in the drawing below. Which hypothesis best explains her observation and how it can be tested? **TEKS** 6.2(B)

A Hypothesis: The plant bent toward the light because the plant collected too much water at the top.

Test: Stop watering the plant and see if the stems straighten out.

B Hypothesis: The plant bent toward the light because the plant is undernourished, making the stems weak.

Test: Add fertilizer to the plant to see if the stems grow stronger.

C Hypothesis: The plant bent toward the light because the plant turned toward the light as it grew.

Test: Turn the plant away from the light and see how it grows.

D Hypothesis: The plant bent toward the light because the plant needs water, making the stems weak.

Test: Give the plant more water and see if the plant grows straight.

4

> In the 1860s, French scientist Louis Pasteur performed a series of experiments in which he boiled broth in glass vessels. Each vessel had a long twisted tube on one side. This allowed air to reach the broth, but prevented dust particles from reaching the broth. Nothing grew in the broth as long as the tubes were in place. When the tubes were broken off, living organisms rapidly grew in the broth.

Which idea did Pasteur's experiment disprove? **TEKS** 6.3(D)

A Life can appear with no apparent source.

B Life comes from other living things.

C Microorganisms are the cause of diseases.

D Organisms are made of cells.

5   Polio is a disease caused by a virus. A polio vaccine began being used in 1955. The graph shows how the number of polio cases changed over the years from 1930 to 1970.   *TEKS* 6.2(E)

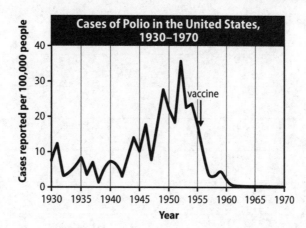

Before the use of the vaccine, what was the highest number of polio cases per 100,000 people? Round your answer to the nearest ten. Record and bubble your answer in the answer grid below.

My Notes

TEKS Strand 2
Matter and Energy

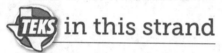 **in this strand**

✓ **6.5** The student knows the difference between elements and compounds.

✓ **6.6** The student knows matter has physical properties that can be used for classification.

✓ **6.7** The student knows that some of Earth's energy resources are available on a nearly perpetual basis, while others can be renewed over a relatively short period of time. Some energy resources, once depleted, are essentially nonrenewable.

✓ Also includes the following Scientific Investigation and Reasoning strand TEKS: **6.1; 6.2; 6.3; 6.4**

Texas Fun Fact

Did You Know? Texas is the top crude-oil producing state in the United States. Currently, there are 26 petroleum refineries in Texas. These refineries account for more than 25 percent of the total U.S. crude-oil production.

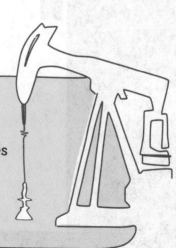

2

Matter and Its Changes

The **BIG** Idea
Matter can be classified by the type and arrangement of atoms from which it is made.

LESSON

2.1 Substances and Mixtures

Matter is made up of small particles called atoms. An element is matter made up of only one type of atom. Elements combine to form compounds.

TEKS 6.5(A), (B), (C); Also covers 6.1(A); 6.2(A), (C), (E); 6.3(B); 6.4(A), (B)

LESSON

2.2 Changes in Matter

Matter can undergo physical and chemical changes.

TEKS 6.5(D); Also covers 6.1(A); 6.2(A), (C), (E); 6.4(A), (B)

Does amount matter?

Some properties of matter depend on how much matter there is. Put an *X* next to all of the statements you think are true about properties of matter.

☐ **A.** The more you have of a substance, the greater its density is.

☐ **B.** The more you have of a substance, the greater its volume is.

☐ **C.** The more you have of a substance, the higher the temperature needed to reach its boiling point.

☐ **D.** The more you have of a substance, the greater its mass is.

☐ **E.** The more you have of a substance, the lower the temperature needed to freeze it.

☐ **F.** The more you have of a substance, the less its electrical conductivity.

Explain your thinking. What rule or reasoning did you use to decide whether the amount of matter made a difference in its properties?

Copyright © McGraw-Hill Education David McNew/Getty Images

INQUIRY

Is it pure? This worker is making a trophy by pouring hot, liquid metal into a mold. The molten metal is bronze, which is a mixture of several metals blended to make the trophy stronger. Why do you think a bronze trophy would be stronger than a pure metal trophy?

Write your response in your interactive notebook.

LAB Manager

Go to your Lab Manual or visit connectED.mcgraw-hill.com to perform the labs for this lesson.

MiniLAB: *How do elements, compounds, and mixtures differ?*

TEKS 6.1(A); 6.2(A), (C), (E); 6.4(A), (B); 6.5(A), (C)

LAB: *Balloon Molecules*

TEKS 6.1(A), 6.2(A), (E); 6.3(B); 6.4(B); 6.5(C)

Explore Activity

TEKS 6.1(A); 6.2(A), (C), (E); 6.4(A), (B); 6.5(C)

Can you always see the parts of materials?

If you eat a pizza, you can see the cheese, the pepperoni, and the other parts it is made from. Can you always see the individual parts when you mix materials?

Procedure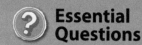

1. Read and complete a lab safety form.

2. Observe the materials at the eight stations your teacher has set up.

3. Record the name and a short description of each material in your Lab Manual or interactive notebook.

Think About This

1. How are you able to differentiate between the materials at each station?

_____

_____

_____

2. Is it always easy to see the parts of materials that are mixed? Explain.

_____

_____

_____

TEKS in this Lesson

6.5(A) Know that an element is a pure substance and is represented by chemical symbols

6.5(B) Recognize that a limited number of the many known elements comprise the largest portion of solid Earth, living matter, oceans, and the atmosphere

6.5(C) Differentiate between elements and compounds on the most basic level

Also covers Process Standards: 6.1(A); 6.2(A), (C), (E); 6.3(B); 6.4(A), (B)

Essential Questions

- What is the relationship among atoms, elements, and compounds?
- How do elements and compounds differ?
- What elements comprise Earth's surface, oceans, atmosphere, and living matter?

Vocabulary

matter
atom
substance
element
molecule
compound
mixture
heterogeneous mixture
homogeneous mixture

Figure 1 Everything around you is made of matter.

What is matter?

Imagine how much fun it would be to go windsurfing! As the force of the wind pushes the sail, you lean back to balance the board, as shown in **Figure 1.** You feel the wind in your hair and the spray of water against your face. Whether you are windsurfing on a lake or sitting at your desk in a classroom, everything around you is made of matter. **Matter** *is anything that has mass and takes up space.* Matter is everything you can see, such as water and trees. It is also some things you cannot see, such as air. You know that air is matter because you can feel its mass when it blows against your skin. You can see that it takes up space when it inflates a sail or a balloon.

Anything that does not have mass or volume is not matter. Types of energy, such as heat, sound, and electricity, are not matter. Forces, such as magnetism and gravity, also are not forms of matter.

What is matter made of?

The matter around you, including all solids, liquids, and gases, is made of atoms. *An* **atom** *is a small particle that is the building block of matter.* There are many types of atoms. Atoms can combine with each other in many ways. It is the many kinds of atoms and the ways they combine that forms different types of matter.

Copyright © McGraw-Hill Education   Design Pics/Ben Welsh

Word Origin

atom   from Greek *atomos*, means "uncut"

Identify

1. What two characteristics make up matter?

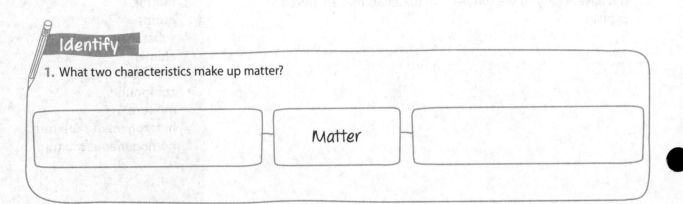

Matter

Classifying Matter

Because all the different types of matter around you are made of atoms, they must have characteristics in common. But why do all types of matter look and feel different? How is the matter that makes up a pure gold ring similar to the matter that makes up your favorite soda or the matter that makes up your body? How are these types of matter different?

As the chart in **Figure 2** shows, scientists place matter into one of two groups—substances or mixtures. Pure gold is in one group. Soda and your body are in the other. What determines whether a type of matter is a substance or a mixture? The difference is in the composition.

What is a substance? TEKS 6.5(A), (C)

What is the difference between a gold ring and a can of soda? What is the difference between table salt and trail mix? Pure gold is always made up of the same type of atom, but soda is not. Similarly, table salt, or sodium chloride, is always made up of the same types of atoms, but trail mix is not. This is because sodium chloride and gold are substances. A **substance** *is matter with a composition that is always the same.* A certain substance always contains the same kinds of atoms in the same combination. Soda and trail mix are another type of matter that you will read about later in this lesson.

Because gold is a substance, anything that is pure gold will have the same composition. Bars of gold are made of the same atoms as those in a pure gold ring, as shown in **Figure 3**. Because sodium chloride is a substance, if you add salt to your food in Alaska or Texas, the atoms that make up salt will be the same. If the composition of a substance changes, you will have a new substance.

Figure 2 You can classify matter as a substance or a mixture.

Matter
- Anything that has mass and takes up space
- Matter is made up of atoms.

Substances
- Matter with a composition that is always the same

Mixtures
- Matter that can vary in composition

Classify

2. **Highlight** why gold is classified as a substance.

Figure 3 A substance always contains the same kinds of atoms bonded in the same way.

Salt (NaCl)

Gold (Au)

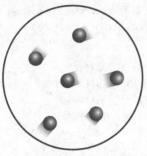

Individual atoms

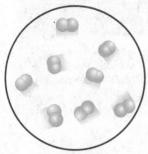

Molecules

Figure 4 The smallest part of all elements is an atom. In some elements, the atoms are grouped into molecules.

Figure 5 Element symbols have either one or two letters. Temporary symbols have three letters.

Elements

Some substances, such as gold, are made of only one kind of atom. Others, such as sodium chloride, are made of more than one kind. *An* **element** *is a pure substance made of only one kind of atom.* All atoms of an element are alike, but atoms of one element are different from atoms of other elements. For example, the element gold is made of only gold atoms, and all gold atoms are alike. But gold atoms are different from silver atoms, oxygen atoms, and atoms of every other element.

What is the smallest part of an element? If you could break down an element into its smallest part, that part would be one atom. Most elements, such as carbon and silver, consist of a large group of individual atoms. Some elements, such as hydrogen and bromine, consist of molecules. *A* **molecule** (MAH lih kyewl) *is two or more atoms that are held together by chemical bonds and act as a unit.* Examples of elements made of individual atoms and molecules are shown in **Figure 4**.

Elements on the Periodic Table You probably can name many elements, such as carbon, gold, and oxygen. Did you know that there are about 115 elements? As shown in **Figure 5**, each element has a symbol, such as C for carbon, Au for gold, and O for oxygen. The periodic table, printed in the back of this book, gives other information about each element.

Watch
Go Online!

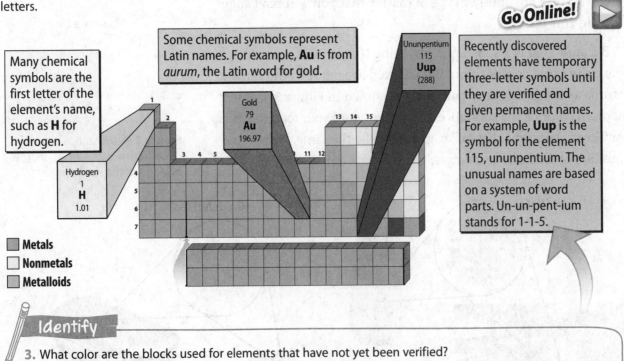

Many chemical symbols are the first letter of the element's name, such as **H** for hydrogen.

Some chemical symbols represent Latin names. For example, **Au** is from *aurum*, the Latin word for gold.

Recently discovered elements have temporary three-letter symbols until they are verified and given permanent names. For example, **Uup** is the symbol for the element 115, ununpentium. The unusual names are based on a system of word parts. Un-un-pent-ium stands for 1-1-5.

■ Metals
□ Nonmetals
■ Metalloids

Identify

3. What color are the blocks used for elements that have not yet been verified?

Compounds

Does it surprise you to learn that there are only about 115 different elements? After all, if you think about all the different things you see each day, you could probably name many more types of matter than this. Why are there so many kinds of matter when there are only about 115 elements? Most matter is made of atoms of different types of elements bonded together.

A **compound** *is a substance made of two or more elements that are chemically joined in a specific combination.* Because each compound is made of atoms in a specific combination, a compound is a substance. Pure water (H_2O) is a compound because every sample of pure water contains atoms of hydrogen and oxygen in the same combination—two hydrogen atoms to every oxygen atom. There are many types of matter because elements can join to form compounds.

Molecules Recall that a molecule is two or more atoms that are held together by chemical bonds and that act as a unit. Is a molecule the smallest part of a compound? For many compounds, this is true. Many compounds exist as molecules. An example is water. In water, two hydrogen atoms and one oxygen atom always exist together and act as a unit. Carbon dioxide (CO_2) and table sugar ($C_6H_{12}O_6$) are also examples of compounds that are made of molecules.

However, as shown in **Figure 6,** some compounds are not made of molecules. In some compounds, such as table salt, or sodium chloride, no specific atoms travel together as a unit. However, table salt (NaCl) is still a substance because it always contains only sodium (Na) and chlorine (Cl) atoms.

Sugar

Salt

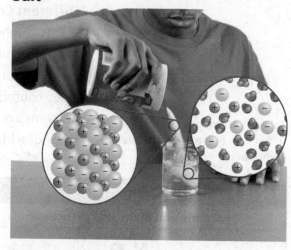

Figure 6 Sugar particles are molecules because they always travel together as a unit. Salt particles do not travel together as a unit.

Differentiate

4. How do elements and compounds differ?

_____

_____

_____

_____

_____

Properties of Compounds How would you describe sodium chloride, or table salt? The properties of a compound, such as table salt, are usually different from the properties of the elements from which it is made. Table salt, for example, is made of the elements sodium and chlorine. Sodium is a soft metal, and chlorine is a poisonous green gas. These properties are much different from the table salt you sprinkle on food!

Chemical Formulas Just as elements have chemical symbols, compounds have chemical formulas. A formula includes the symbols of each element in the compound. It also includes numbers, called subscripts, that show the ratio of the elements in the compound. You can see the formulas for some compounds in **Table 1**.

Different Combinations of Atoms Sometimes the same elements combine to form different compounds. For example, nitrogen and oxygen can form six different compounds. The chemical formulas are N_2O, NO, N_2O_3, NO_2, N_2O_4, and N_2O_5. They contain the same elements, but because the combinations of atoms are different, each compound has different properties, some of which are shown in **Table 1**.

Table 1 Atoms can combine in different ways and form different compounds.

Go Online!

Tutor

Table 1	
Formula and Molecular Structure	**Properties/Functions**
N_2O Nitrous oxide	colorless gas used as an anesthetic
NO_2 Nitrogen dioxide	brown gas, toxic, air pollutant
N_2O_3 Dinitrogen trioxide	blue liquid

Cut out the Lesson 2.1 Foldable in the back of the book. Use it to review properties of elements and compounds. Discuss the content of your Foldable with a partner.

Tape here

Classifying Matter

Properties of elements	Properties of compounds

Connect It! **Choose** an element to analyze. **Research** the properties of the specific element and its chemical symbol. Find out which kinds of compounds, solutions, or mixtures the element occurs in and how they are used. Record your findings below. Then, make an online poster about your element to present to the class. *TEKS* 6.5(A)

_____

_____

_____

_____

_____

_____

_____

_____

Elements of Earth

You have learned that there are about 115 elements represented on the current periodic table. Of these elements, 92 occur naturally on Earth. The others have been made in laboratories. The natural elements exist in Earth's crust, atmosphere, ocean, and living matter. However, the elements are not evenly distributed. Which elements are most abundant in Earth's crust? Which elements compose Earth's atmosphere and the oceans? Which elements make up living matter?

Elements in Earth's Crust

Of the 92 elements that exist naturally on Earth, only a few make up Earth's solid crust. **Table 2** shows the most abundant elements in Earth's crust. Earth's upper mantle contains mostly oxygen, silicon, and magnesium. Earth's core is made mostly of iron and nickel.

Earth's geology is related to its chemical makeup. Most rock-forming minerals are silicates, or minerals made of silicon and oxygen. Silicates are in all rock types—sedimentary, igneous, and metamorphic. The mineral quartz (SiO_2), shown in **Figure 7**, can be found in many types of rock. Another common type of mineral is feldspar, which is found in continental crust. Different types of feldspar can contain varying amounts of potassium (K), calcium (Ca), sodium (Na), and aluminum (Al), as well as silicon (Si) and oxygen (O). The minerals olivine, pyroxene, amphibole, and biotite are typically found in oceanic crust. These minerals contain iron (Fe) and magnesium (Mg), as well as K, Ca, Na, Al, Si, and O.

Figure 7 Quartz can vary in color. The quartz in this rock sample is white.

Table 2	Elements of Earth's Crust
Element	**Percent (by mass)**
Oxygen (O)	46.1
Silicon (Si)	28.2
Aluminum (Al)	8.2
Other	7.7
Iron (Fe)	5.6
Calcium (Ca)	4.2

Table 2 Oxygen is the most abundant element found in Earth's crust.

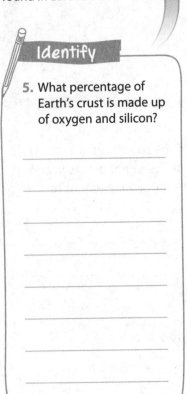

Identify

5. What percentage of Earth's crust is made up of oxygen and silicon?

_____

_____

_____

_____

_____

_____

_____

Elements in Earth's Oceans

As shown in **Figure 8,** water that flows over Earth's surface weathers and erodes rocks and soil and washes sediment into the ocean. Other minerals enter ocean water from Earth's interior through underwater volcanic eruptions. Seventy percent of Earth's surface is covered by water, and most of that water is in the ocean. About 96.5 percent of the ocean is water, a molecule of hydogen and oxygen (H_2O). The other 3.5 percent is made up of dissolved substances. Of the dissolved substances in ocean water, chlorine (Cl) makes up 58.3 percent and sodium (Na) makes up 32.4 percent. This is why ocean water tastes salty—the compound sodium chloride (NaCl), which geologists call halite, is table salt. Ocean water also contains the other elements listed in **Table 3**.

Table 3	Elements Dissolved in Earth's Oceans
Element	**Percent** (by mass)
Chlorine (Cl)	58.3
Sodium (Na)	32.4
Magnesium (Mg)	3.9
Sulfur (S)	2.7
Other	1.5
Calcium (Ca)	1.2

Table 3 Water (hydrogen and oxygen) accounts for 96.5% of Earth's oceans.

Identify

6. Highlight in the text the compound that makes ocean water salty. Circle, in **Table 3**, the elements that make up the compound.

Figure 8 Water from the Gulf of Mexico washes over rocks on Mustang Island, Texas.

Elements in Earth's Atmosphere

Although humans rely on the oxygen in the air we breathe, most of Earth's atmosphere—78.1 percent—is nitrogen (N). Only 21.0 percent of the atmosphere is oxygen (O). The remaining fraction of the atmosphere consists of argon and other trace elements. Molecules such as water vapor and carbon dioxide (CO_2) also are present in the atmosphere. You might be surprised to know that CO_2 makes up only 0.03 percent of the atmosphere. However, this greenhouse gas has a huge impact on Earth. As the amount of CO_2 in the atmosphere increases, the atmosphere traps more thermal energy. This thermal energy increases the surface temperature of Earth.

Construct

7. Using the percentages of each element and compound listed above, create a table organizing the elements of Earth's atmosphere.

Using the data in your table, create a circle graph. Be sure to color and label the graph.

Elements in Living Matter

Living matter (plants and animals) is made mostly of oxygen (O), carbon (C), and hydrogen (H). In fact, almost 75 percent of the human body is water. **Table 4** lists the elements that make up the human body.

Where can you find these elements in the human body? If all the water in your body were removed, most of the remaining mass would come from calcium (Ca). Calcium makes up most of your skeletal system, including your bones and teeth. Some of the elements in the body combine and form some of the basic chemicals that your body needs to function, such as proteins, lipids, and carbohydrates. Proteins are compounds of carbon, hydrogen, oxygen, and nitrogen that make up your hair, blood, muscles, organs, and fingernails. Lipids, which are made mostly of carbon and hydrogen, are a source of energy and make up cell membranes. Carbohydrates are also a source of energy for cells and contain the elements carbon, hydrogen, and oxygen.

Table 4	Elements in Humans
Element	**Percent**
Oxygen (O)	65.0
Carbon (C)	18.0
Hydrogen (H)	10.0
Nitrogen (N)	3.0
Calcium (Ca)	1.5
Other	1.5
Phosphorus (P)	1.2

Table 4 The majority of the human body contains oxygen, carbon, and hydrogen.

As you can see, only a small number of the many known elements comprise the largest portion of Earth and living things. Most elements do not exist alone. They combine to form compounds and the world around us.

TEKS 6.4(A); 6.5(B)

Comparing Elements Of all the known elements, only a limited number of elements make up Earth's crust, ocean, atmosphere, and living matter.

1. Using a computer spreadsheet program, make a bar graph to compare the relative amounts of the elements in Earth's crust, the ocean, the atmosphere, and living matter. Place the bar graph in your interactive notebook.

2. Which elements are common to these locations?

_____

_____

_____

_____

_____

_____

Apply it!

Figure 9 It's hard to tell which is in the glass—pure water (a substance) or lemon-lime soda (a mixture).

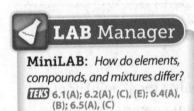

LAB Manager

MiniLAB: *How do elements, compounds, and mixtures differ?*

TEKS 6.1(A); 6.2(A), (C), (E); 6.4(A), (B); 6.5(A), (C)

What is a mixture?

By looking at the glass of clear liquid in **Figure 9**, can you tell whether it is lemon-lime soda or water? Lemon-lime soda is almost clear, and someone might confuse it with water, which is a substance. Recall that a substance is matter with a composition that is always the same. However, sodas are a combination of substances such as water, carbon dioxide, sugar, and other compounds. In fact, most solids, liquids, and gases you see each day are mixtures. *A* **mixture** *is matter that can vary in composition.* It is made of two or more substances that are blended but are not chemically bonded.

What would happen if you added more sugar to a glass of soda? You would still have soda, but it would be sweeter. Changing the amount of one substance in a mixture does not change the identity of the mixture or its individual substances.

Air and tap water are also mixtures. Air is a mixture of nitrogen, oxygen, and other substances. However, the composition of air can vary. Air in a scuba tank usually contains more oxygen and less of the other substances. Tap water might look like pure water, but it is a mixture of pure water (H_2O) and small amounts of other substances. Because the substances that make up tap water are not bonded together, the composition of tap water can vary. This is true for all mixtures.

Illustrate

8. Using □, ○, and △ to represent matter, draw a substance (pure water) and a mixture (tap water) in the circles below.

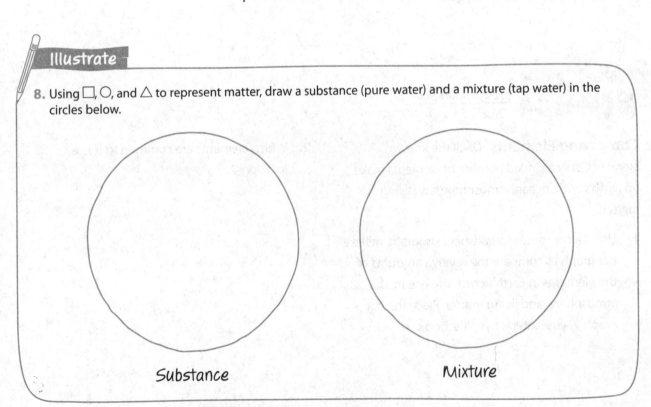

Substance   Mixture

Types of Mixtures

How do trail mix, soda, and air differ? One difference is that trail mix is a solid, soda is a liquid, and air is a gas. This tells you that a mixture can be any state of matter. Another difference is that you can see the individual parts that make up trail mix, but you cannot see the parts that make up soda or air. This is because trail mix is a different type of mixture than soda and air. There are two types of mixtures—heterogeneous (he tuh roh JEE nee us) and homogeneous (hoh muh JEE nee us). The prefix *hetero-* means "different," and the prefix *homo-* means "the same." Heterogeneous and homogeneous mixtures differ in how evenly the substances that compose them are mixed.

Heterogeneous Mixtures

Suppose you take a bag of trail mix and pour it into two identical bowls. What might you notice? At first glance, each bowl appears the same. However, if you look closely, you might notice that one bowl has more nuts and the other bowl has more raisins. The contents of the bowls differ because trail mix is a heterogeneous mixture. *A* **heterogeneous mixture** *is a mixture in which the substances are not evenly mixed.* Therefore, if you take two samples from the same mixture, such as trail mix, the samples might have different amounts of the individual substances. The mixtures shown in **Figure 10** are examples of heterogeneous mixtures.

Copyright © McGraw-Hill Education   (l)imagebroker/Alamy, (c)Mark Steinmetz, (r)Conny Fridh/Getty Images

Describe

9. Why is vegetable soup classified as a heterogeneous mixture?

_____

_____

_____

_____

_____

_____

_____

_____

Heterogeneous Mixtures

Figure 10 The different parts of a heterogeneous mixture are not evenly mixed.

The number of peanuts, pretzels, raisins, and other types of food in trail mix could change, and it still would be trail mix.

You know that granite is a heterogeneous mixture because you can see the different minerals from which it is made.

With a microscope, you would be able to see that smoke is a heterogeneous mixture of gas and solid particles.

Figure 11 Salt is soluble in water. Pepper is insoluble in water. The pepper and water is a mixture, but it is not a solution.

Homogeneous Mixtures

If you pour soda into two glasses, the amounts of water, carbon dioxide, sugar, and other substances in the mixture would be the same in both glasses. Soda is an example of a **homogeneous mixture**—*a mixture in which two or more substances are evenly mixed but not bonded together.*

Evenly Mixed Parts In a homogeneous mixture, the substances are so small and evenly mixed that you cannot see the boundaries between substances in the mixture. Brass, a mixture of copper and zinc, is a homogeneous mixture because the copper atoms and the zinc atoms are evenly mixed. You cannot see the boundaries between the different types of substances, even under most microscopes. Lemonade and air are also examples of homogeneous mixtures for the same reason.

Solution Another name for a homogeneous mixture is a solution. A solution is made of two parts—a solvent and one or more solutes. The solvent is the substance that is present in the largest amount. The solutes dissolve, or break apart, and mix evenly in the solvent. In **Figure 11,** water is the solvent, and salt is the solute. Salt is soluble in water. Notice also in the figure that pepper does not dissolve in water. No solution forms between pepper and water. Pepper is insoluble in water.

Other examples of solutions are described in **Figure 12.** Note that all three states of matter—solid, liquid, and gas—can be a solvent or a solute in a solution.

Figure 12 Solids, liquids, and gases can combine to make solutions.

Record

10. Highlight the two parts of a solution. Circle the part that is present in the largest amount.

Homogeneous Mixtures

A trumpet is made of brass, which is a solution of solid copper and solid zinc.

The natural gas used in a gas stove is a solution of methane, ethane, and other gases.

This ammonia cleaner is a solution of water and ammonia gas.

Compounds v. Mixtures

Think again about putting trail mix into two bowls. If you put more peanuts in one of the bowls, you still have trail mix in both bowls. Because the substances that make up a mixture are not bonded, adding more of one substance does not change the identity or the properties of the mixture. It also does not change the identity or the properties of each individual substance. In a heterogeneous mixture of peanuts, raisins, and pretzels, the properties of the individual parts don't change if you add more peanuts. The peanuts and the raisins do not bond and become something new.

Similarly, in a solution such as soda or air, the substances do not bond and form something new. Carbon dioxide, water, sugar, and other substances in soda are mixed together. Nitrogen, oxygen, and other substances in air also keep their separate properties because air is a mixture. If it were a compound, the parts would be bonded and would not keep their separate properties.

Compounds and Solutions Differ

Compounds and solutions are alike in that they look like pure substances. Look at the lemon-lime soda and the water in **Figure 9**. The soda is a solution. A solution might look like a substance because the elements and the compounds that make up a solution are evenly mixed. However, compounds and solutions differ in one important way. The atoms that make up a given compound are bonded. Therefore, the composition of a given compound is always the same. Changing the composition results in a new compound.

However, the substances that make up a solution, or any other mixture, are not bonded. Therefore, adding more of one substance will not change the composition of the solution. It will change the ratio of the substances in the solution. These differences are described in **Table 5.**

Table 5	Differences Between Solutions and Compounds	
	Solutions	**Compounds**
Composition	Made up of substances (elements and compounds) evenly mixed together; the composition can vary in a given mixture.	Made up of atoms bonded together; the combination of atoms is always the same in a given compound.
Changing the composition	The solution is still the same with similar properties. However, the relative amounts of substances might be different.	Changing the composition of a compound changes it into a new compound with new properties.
Properties of parts	The substances keep their own properties when they are mixed.	The properties of the compound are different from the properties of the atoms that make it up.

Separating Mixtures

Have you ever picked something you did not like off a slice of pizza? If you have, you have separated a mixture. Because the parts of a mixture are not combined chemically, you can use a physical process, such as removing them by hand, to separate the mixture. The identity of the parts does not change. Separating the parts of a compound is more difficult. The elements that make up a compound are combined chemically. Only a chemical change can separate them.

Separating Heterogeneous Mixtures Separating the parts of a pizza is easy because the pizza has large, solid parts. Two other ways to separate heterogeneous mixtures are shown in **Figure 13.** The strainer in the figure filters larger rocks from the mixture of rocks and dirt. The oil and vinegar photo also shows a heterogeneous mixture because the oil floats on the vinegar. You can separate this mixture by carefully removing the floating oil.

Other properties also might be useful for separating the parts. For example, if one of the parts is magnetic, you could use a magnet to remove it. In a mixture of solid powders, you might dissolve one part in water and then pour it out, leaving the other part behind. In each case, to separate a heterogeneous mixture, you use differences in the physical properties of the parts.

Figure 13 You can separate heterogeneous and homogeneous mixtures.

Separating Mixtures

A strainer removes large parts of the heterogeneous mixture of rocks and sediment. Only small rocks and dirt fall through.

In this heterogeneous mixture of oil and vinegar, the oil floats on the vinegar. You can separate them by removing the oil.

Making rock candy is a way of separating a solution. Solid sugar crystals form as a mixture of hot water and sugar cools.

Predict

11. How could you separate the small rocks and dirt that passed through the strainer on the left?

_____

_____

Separating Homogeneous Mixtures Imagine trying to separate soda into water, carbon dioxide, sugar, and other substances it is made from. Because the parts are so small and evenly mixed, separating a homogeneous mixture such as soda can be difficult. However, you can separate some homogeneous mixtures by boiling or evaporation. For example, if you leave a bowl of sugar water outside on a hot day, the water will evaporate, leaving the sugar behind. An example of separating a homogeneous mixture by making rock candy is shown in **Figure 13.**

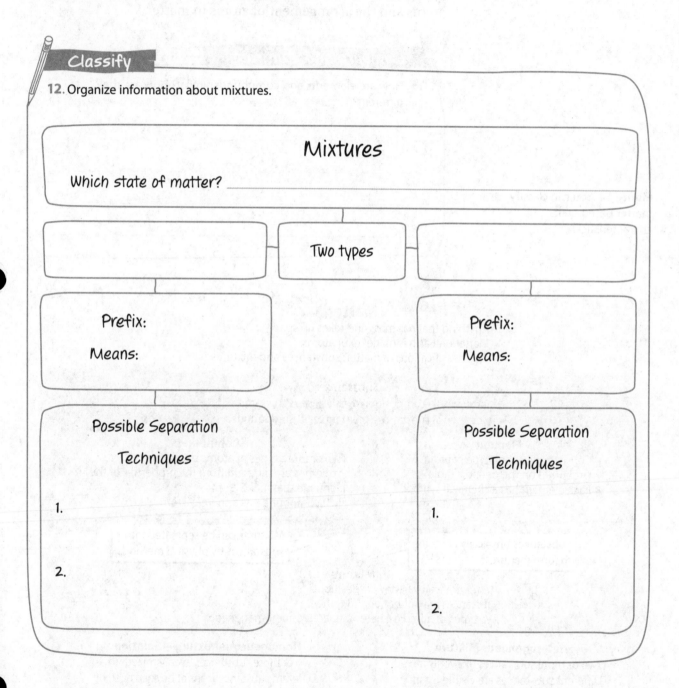

Classify

12. Organize information about mixtures.

Mixtures

Which state of matter? _____

Two types

Prefix:

Means:

Prefix:

Means:

Possible Separation Techniques

1.

2.

Possible Separation Techniques

1.

2.

Visualizing Classification of Matter TEKS 6.5(A), (C)

Think about all the types of matter you have read about in this lesson. As shown in **Figure 14,** matter can be classified as a substance or a mixture. Substances are elements or compounds. The two kinds of mixtures are homogeneous mixtures and heterogeneous mixtures. Notice that all substances and mixtures are made of atoms. Matter is classified according to the types of atoms and the arrangement of atoms in matter.

Compare and Contrast

13. How are elements and compounds similar? How are they different?

_____

_____

_____

_____

Figure 14 You can classify matter based on its characteristics.

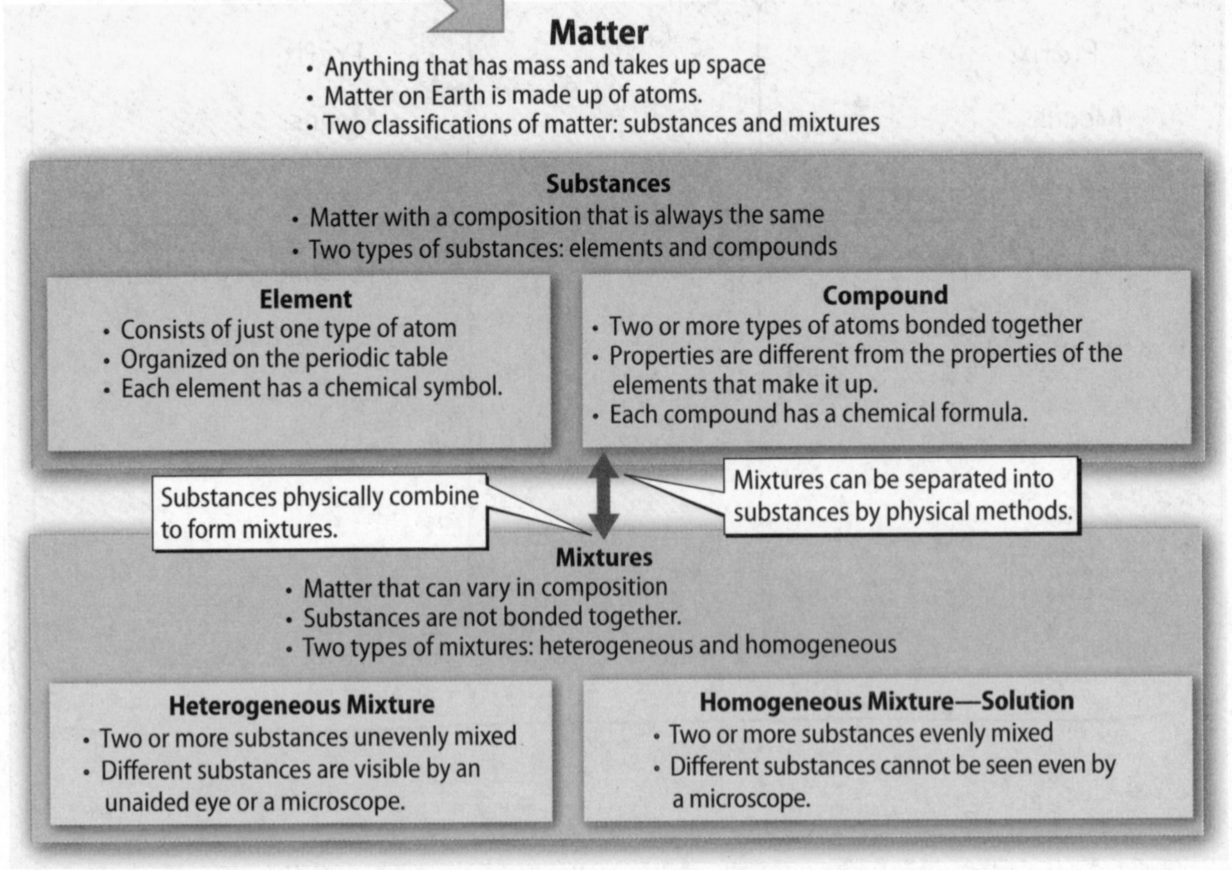

Matter
- Anything that has mass and takes up space
- Matter on Earth is made up of atoms.
- Two classifications of matter: substances and mixtures

Substances
- Matter with a composition that is always the same
- Two types of substances: elements and compounds

Element
- Consists of just one type of atom
- Organized on the periodic table
- Each element has a chemical symbol.

Compound
- Two or more types of atoms bonded together
- Properties are different from the properties of the elements that make it up.
- Each compound has a chemical formula.

Substances physically combine to form mixtures.

Mixtures can be separated into substances by physical methods.

Mixtures
- Matter that can vary in composition
- Substances are not bonded together.
- Two types of mixtures: heterogeneous and homogeneous

Heterogeneous Mixture
- Two or more substances unevenly mixed
- Different substances are visible by an unaided eye or a microscope.

Homogeneous Mixture—Solution
- Two or more substances evenly mixed
- Different substances cannot be seen even by a microscope.

Review the types of matter that you have learned about in this lesson.
Differentiate among the types of matter.

Matter	Description
Atom	
Substance	
Element	
Molecule	
Compound	
Mixture	

Connect it! **Apply** The element oxygen is a gas that makes up about 20 percent of Earth's atmosphere. Oxygen also is the most abundant element in Earth's crust, yet Earth's crust is not a gas. Explain the apparent conflict in your interactive notebook. *TEKS* 6.5(B), (C)

Summarize it!

Apply the Essential Questions

1. **List** the chemical symbols for the following elements. Use the periodic table in the back of the book, as needed.
   TEKS 6.5(A)

   Bromine _____

   Silver _____

   Sodium _____

   Iron _____

2. **List** the names of the following elements. Use the periodic table in the back of the book, as needed. **TEKS** 6.5(A)

   W _____

   Mg _____

   O _____

   He _____

3. **Recall** the most abundant element in each of the following: **TEKS** 6.5(B)

   Earth's crust _____

   Earth's atmosphere _____

   Dissolved in Earth's oceans _____

   Living matter _____

Writing in Science

4. **Analyze** The elements in Earth's crust affect the types of minerals and rocks that form in an area. Research the mineral resources of Texas and relate them to their chemical makeup. Write your research findings on a separate piece of paper. **TEKS** 6.5(B)

 **H.O.T. Questions** (Higher Order Thinking)

5. **Assess** During a science investigation, a sample of matter breaks down into two kinds of atoms. Was the original sample an element or a compound? Explain.
   TEKS 6.5(C) *supporting*

   _____

   _____

   _____

   _____

   _____

6. **Generalize** Consider the substances N_2O_5, H_2, CH_4, H_2O, KCl, and O_2. Is it possible to tell just from the symbols and the numbers which ones are elements and which ones are compounds? Explain.
   TEKS 6.5(C) *supporting*

   _____

   _____

   _____

   _____

   _____

7. **Critique** this statement: Substances are made of two or more types of elements.
   TEKS 6.5(C) *supporting*

   _____

   _____

   _____

Crude Oil

Separating Out Gasoline

Have you ever wondered where the gasoline used in automobiles comes from? Gasoline is part of a mixture of fuels called crude oil. How can workers separate gasoline from this mixture?

One way to separate a mixture is by boiling it. Crude oil is separated by a process called fractional distillation. First, the oil is boiled and allowed to cool. As the crude oil cools, each part changes from a gas to a liquid at a different temperature. Workers catch each fuel just as it changes back to a liquid. Eventually the crude oil is refined into all its useful parts.

1 **Crude oil** often is taken from liquid deposits deep underground. It might also be taken from rocks or deposits mixed in sand. The crude oil is then sent to a furnace.

Crude oil

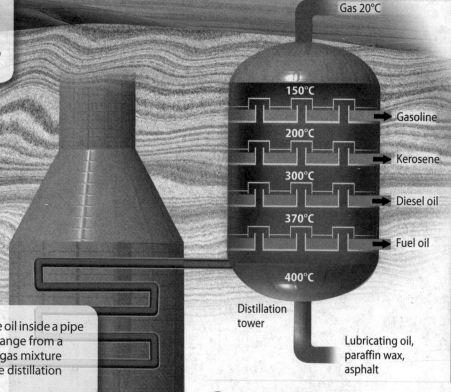

Gas 20°C

150°C → Gasoline

200°C → Kerosene

300°C → Diesel oil

370°C → Fuel oil

400°C

Distillation tower

Lubricating oil, paraffin wax, asphalt

Furnace

2 **A furnace** heats the oil inside a pipe until it begins to change from a liquid to a gas. The gas mixture then moves into the distillation tower.

3 **The distillation tower** is hot at the bottom and cooler higher up. As the gas mixture rises to fill the tower, it cools. It also passes over trays at different levels. Each fuel in the mixture changes to a liquid when it cools to a temperature that matches its boiling point. Gasoline changes to a liquid at the level in the tower at 150°C. A tray then catches the gasoline and moves it away.

It's Your Turn!

CREATE A POSTER Blood is a mixture, too. Donated blood often is refined in laboratories to separate it into parts. What are those parts? What are they used for? How are they separated? Find the answers and create a poster based on your findings.

INQUIRY

Why is it orange? Streams are usually filled with clear freshwater. However, this water has turned orange. What hypothesis can you make to explain what happened to the water?

Write your response in your interactive notebook.

LAB Manager

Go to your Lab Manual or visit connectED.mcgraw-hill.com to perform the labs for this lesson.

MiniLAB: *Is mass conserved during a chemical reaction?*
TEKS 6.1(A); 6.2(A), (C); 6.4(A); 6.5(D)

Explore Activity

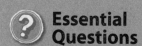

What does a change in the color of matter show?

Matter has many different properties. Chemical properties can only be observed if the matter changes from one type to another. How can you tell if a chemical property has changed? Sometimes a change in the color of matter shows that its chemical properties have changed.

Procedure

1. Read and complete a lab safety form.

2. Obtain the **red indicator sponge** and the **red acid solution** from your teacher. Predict what will happen if the red acid solution touches the red sponge.

3. Use a **dropper** to remove a few drops of acid solution from the **beaker**. Place the drops on the sponge.

⚠ *Be careful not to splash the liquid onto yourself or your clothing.*

4. Record your observations in your Lab Manual or interactive notebook.

Think About This

1. Compare the properties of the sponge before and after you placed the acid solution onto the sponge. Was your prediction correct?

_____

_____

_____

_____

2. What evidence from the activity helps you identify that a new substance may have formed?

_____

_____

_____

_____

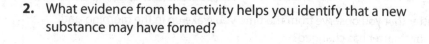

TEKS in this Lesson

6.5(D) Identify the formation of a new substance by using the evidence of a possible chemical change such as production of a gas, change in temperature, production of a precipitate, or color change

Also covers Process Standards: 6.1(A); 6.2(A), (C), (E); 6.4(A), (B)

? Essential Questions

- How are physical changes different from chemical changes?
- What evidence indicates a chemical change is occurring?

abc Vocabulary

physical change
chemical change
law of conservation of mass

Figure 1 The physical and chemical properties of matter change in a park throughout the year.

Changes of Matter TEKS 6.5(D)

Imagine going to a park in the spring and then going back to the same spot in the fall. What changes do you think you might see? The changes would depend on where you live. An example of what a park in the fall might look like in many places is shown in **Figure 1.** Leaves that are green in the spring might turn red, yellow, or brown in the fall. The air that was warm in the spring might be cooler in the fall. If you visit the park early on a fall morning, you might notice a thin layer of frost on the leaves. Matter, such as the things you see at a park, can change in many ways. These changes can be physical or chemical.

Describe

1. Give an example of a change in matter that you observe from the time you wake up in the morning until you arrive at school. How do you know matter has changed?

_____

_____

_____

_____

What are physical changes?

A change in the size, shape, form, or state of matter that does not change the matter's identity is a **physical change.** You can see an example of a physical change in **Figure 2.** Recall that mass is an example of a physical property. Notice that the mass of the modeling clay is the same before and after its shape was changed. When a physical change occurs, the chemical properties of the matter stay the same. The substances that make up matter are exactly the same before and after a physical change.

Figure 2 Changing the shape of the modeling clay does not change its mass.

Dissolving

One physical property is solubility—the ability of one material to dissolve, or mix evenly, in another. Dissolving is a physical change because the identities of the substances do not change when they are mixed. As shown in **Figure 3,** the identities of the water molecules and the sugar molecules do not change when sugar crystals dissolve in water.

> ✏️ Identify
>
> **2.** <u>Underline</u> why dissolving is classified as a physical change.

Dissolving—A Physical Change

Figure 3 The sugar crystals dissolve because they are soluble in water.

Key

Sugar crystal

1 Sugar molecule

$C_{12}H_{22}O_{11}$

1 Water molecule

H_2O

Crystals of sugar are made up of many sugar molecules. The crystals are surrounded by molecules of water.

As the sugar begins to dissolve, the crystals break apart.

Individual sugar and water molecules remain unchanged even after all sugar crystals have dissolved.

Figure 4 The particles that make up ice (solid water), liquid water, and water vapor (water in the gaseous state) are the same. Changing from one state to another changes only the amount of energy of the particles and the distances between the particles.

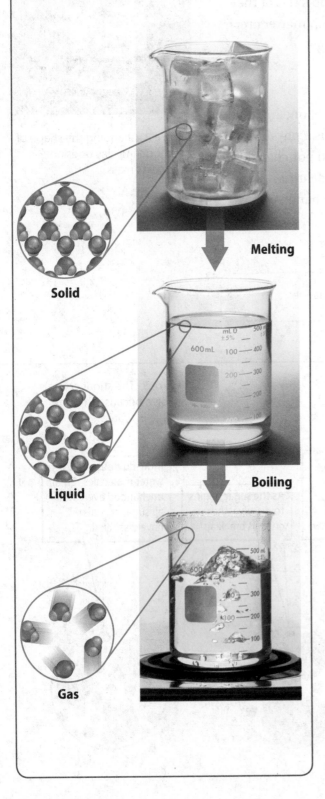

Melting

Solid

Boiling

Liquid

Gas

Changing State

You have read about three states of matter—solid, liquid, and gas. Can you think of examples of matter changing from one state to another? A layer of ice might form on a lake in the winter. A glassblower melts glass into a liquid so it can be formed into shapes. Changes in the state of matter are physical changes.

Melting and Boiling If you heat ice cubes in a pot on the stove, the ice will melt, forming water that soon begins to boil. When a material melts, it changes from a solid to a liquid. When it boils, it changes from a liquid to a gas. The substances that make up the material do not change during a change in the state of matter, as shown in **Figure 4.** The particles that make up ice (solid water) are the same as the particles that make up water as a liquid or as a gas.

Energy and Change in State The energy of the particles and the distances between the particles are different for a solid, a liquid, and a gas. Changes in energy cause changes in the state of matter. For example, energy must be added to a substance to change it from a solid to a liquid or from a liquid to a gas. Adding energy to a substance can increase its temperature. When the temperature reaches the substance's melting point, the solid changes to a liquid. At the boiling point, the liquid changes to a gas.

What would happen if you changed the rate at which you add energy to a substance? For example, what would happen if you heated an ice cube in your hand instead of in a pot on the stove? The ice would reach its melting point more slowly in your hand. The rate at which one state of matter changes to another depends on the rate at which energy is added to or taken away from the substance.

What are chemical changes? TEKS 6.5(D)

Some changes in matter involve more than just changing physical properties. *A chemical change is a change in matter in which the substances that make up the matter change into other substances with different chemical and physical properties.* Recall that a chemical property is the ability or inability of a substance to combine with or change into one or more new substances. During a physical change, only the physical properties of matter change. However, the new substance produced during a chemical change has different chemical and physical properties. Another name for a chemical change is a chemical reaction. The particles that make up two or more substances react, or combine, with each other and form a new substance.

Signs of a Chemical Change

How can you tell that the burning of the trees in **Figure 5** is a chemical change? The reaction produces two gases—carbon dioxide and water vapor—even though you cannot see them. After the fire, you can see that any part of the trees that remains is black, and you can see ash—another new substance. But with some changes, the only new substance formed is a gas that you cannot see. As trees burn in a forest fire, light and heat are signs of a chemical change. For many reactions, changes in physical properties, such as color or state of matter, are signs that a chemical change has occurred. However, the only sure sign of a chemical change is the formation of a new substance.

Identify

3. Highlight which properties change in a physical change and in a chemical change.

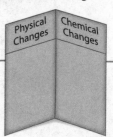

FOLDABLES®

Make a half book from a sheet of paper. Use it to record and compare information about physical and chemical changes.

Physical Changes | Chemical Changes

Chemical Change

Go Online!

Watch

Figure 5 A forest fire causes a chemical change in the trees, producing new substances.

Light and heat during a forest fire are signs that a chemical change is occurring.

After the fire, the formation of new substances shows that a chemical change has taken place.

Figure 6 Formation of a gas, formation of a precipitate, and color change are signs of a chemical change.

Formation of gas bubbles

Formation of a precipitate

Color Change

Formation of Gas Bubbles of gas can form during a physical change and a chemical change. When you heat a substance to its boiling point, the bubbles show that a liquid is changing to a gas—a physical change. When you combine substances, such as the medicine tablet and the water in **Figure 6,** gas bubbles show that a chemical change is occurring. Sometimes you cannot see the gas produced, but you might be able to smell it. The aroma of freshly baked bread, for example, is a sign that baking bread causes a chemical reaction that produces a gas.

Formation of a Precipitate Some chemical reactions result in the formation of a precipitate (prih SIH puh tut). As shown in the middle photo in **Figure 6,** a precipitate is a solid that sometimes forms when two liquids combine. When a liquid freezes, the solid formed is not a precipitate. A precipitate is not a state change from a liquid to a solid. Instead, the particles that make up two liquids react and form the particles that make up the solid precipitate, a new substance.

Color Change Suppose you want your room to be a different color. You would simply apply paint to the walls. The change in color is a physical change because you have only covered the wall. A new substance does not form. But notice the color of the precipitate in the middle photo of **Figure 6**. In this case, the change in color is a sign of a chemical change. The photo in the bottom of the figure shows that marshmallows change from white to brown when they are toasted. The change in the color of the marshmallows is also a sign of a chemical change.

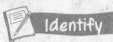 Identify

4. Describe two chemical changes that have happened in your home this week. What evidence of a chemical change did you see? Write a response in your interactive notebook.

Energy and Chemical Change

Think about a fireworks show. Repeatedly, you hear loud bangs as the fireworks burst into a display of colors, as in **Figure 7.** The release of thermal energy, light, and sound are signs that the fireworks result from chemical changes. All chemical reactions involve energy changes.

Thermal energy is often needed for a chemical reaction to take place. Suppose you want to bake pretzels, as shown in **Figure 8.** What would happen if you placed one pan of unbaked pretzel dough in a hot oven and another pan of unbaked pretzel dough on the kitchen counter? Only the dough in the oven would become pretzels. The thermal energy that bakes the pretzels is needed for the chemical reactions to occur.

Energy in the form of light is needed for other chemical reactions. Photosynthesis is a chemical reaction by which plants and some unicellular organisms produce sugar and oxygen. This process only occurs if the organisms are exposed to light. Many medicines also undergo chemical reactions when exposed to light. You might have seen some medicines stored in orange bottles. If the medicines are not stored in these light-resistant bottles, the ingredients can change into other substances.

Figure 7
The fireworks display over Houston, Texas, shows signs of a chemical change.

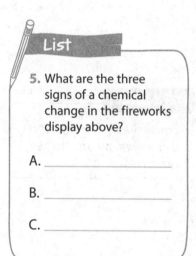

List

5. What are the three signs of a chemical change in the fireworks display above?

A. _____

B. _____

C. _____

Figure 8 Thermal energy provides the chemical reactions that occur when pretzels are baked.

Can changes be reversed?

Think again about the way matter changes form during a fireworks display. After the chemicals combine and cause the explosions, you cannot get back the original chemicals. Like most chemical changes, the fireworks display cannot be reversed.

Grating a carrot and cutting an apple are physical changes, and you cannot reverse these changes either. Making a mixture by dissolving salt in a pan of water is also a physical change. You can reverse this change by boiling the mixture. The water will change to a gas, leaving the salt behind in the pan. Some physical changes can be easily reversed, but others cannot.

Conservation of Mass

Physical changes do not affect the mass of substances. When ice melts, for example, the mass of the ice equals the mass of the resulting liquid water. If you cut a piece of paper into strips, the total mass of the paper remains the same. Mass is conserved, or unchanged, during a physical change.

Mass is also conserved during a chemical change. Antoine Lavoisier (AN twon • luh VWAH zee ay) (1743–1794), a French chemist, made this discovery. Lavoisier carefully measured the masses of materials before and after chemical reactions. His discovery is now a scientific law. *The **law of conservation of mass** states that the total mass before a chemical reaction is the same as the total mass after the chemical reaction.* Weight also is the same because it depends on mass. For example, the mass of an unburned match plus the mass of the oxygen it reacts with equals the mass of the ashes plus the masses of all the gases given off when the match burns.

Word Origin

conservation from Latin *conservare*, means "to keep, preserve"

Predict

6. Predict the effect of each event. Circle the effect that can be reversed.

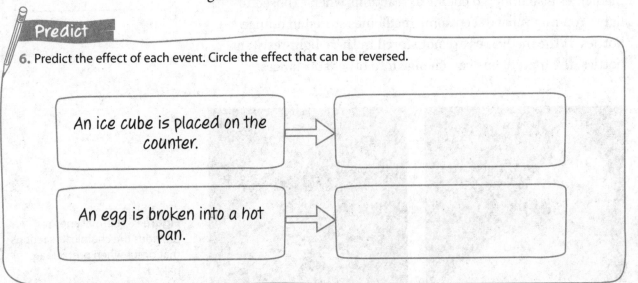

An ice cube is placed on the counter.

An egg is broken into a hot pan.

Comparing Physical and Chemical Changes TEKS 6.5(D)

Suppose you want to explain to a friend the difference between a physical change and a chemical change. What would you say? You could explain that the identity of matter does not change during a physical change, but the identity of matter does change during a chemical change. However, you might not be able to tell just by looking at a substance whether its identity changed. You cannot tell whether the particles that make up the matter are the same or different.

Sometimes deciding whether a change is physical or chemical is easy. Often, however, identifying the type of change is like being a detective. You have to look for clues that will help you figure out whether the identity of the substance has changed. For example, look at the summary of physical changes and chemical changes in **Table 1.** A change in color can occur during a chemical change or when substances are mixed (a physical change). Bubbles might indicate boiling (a physical change) or the formation of gas (a chemical change). You must consider many factors when comparing physical and chemical changes.

Apply

7. Is making toast in a toaster a physical or chemical change? How do you know? Is it reversible?

_____
_____
_____
_____
_____
_____
_____
_____

Table 1 Chemical changes produce a new substance, but physical changes do not.

Watch

Table 1 Comparing Physical and Chemical Changes		Go Online!
Type of Change	**Examples**	**Characteristics**
Physical Change	• melting • boiling • changing shape • mixing • dissolving • increasing or decreasing in temperature	• Substance is the same before and after the change. • Only physical properties change. Physical change
Chemical Change	• changing color • burning • rusting • formation of gas • formation of a precipitate • spoiling food • tarnishing silver • digesting food	Chemical change • Substance is different after the change. • Both physical and chemical properties change.

2.2 Review

Compare and contrast information about physical changes and chemical changes. Then, **identify** the five types of physical changes and five signs of a chemical change. *TEKS* 6.5(D)

Physical Changes	Chemical Changes
• substance _____	• _____ substance formed
• substance _____ change	• both _____ change

Five Types of Physical Changes	Five Signs of a Chemical Change
1.	1.
2.	2.
3.	3.
4.	4.
5.	5.

Connect it! **Analyze** A classmate shows you the remnants of a campfire. He tries to convince you that the ashes in the fire pit are all that remains of the wood that burned. What can you tell your friend about chemical changes that will help him understand what happened to the matter that made up the wood? *TEKS* 6.5(D)

_____

_____

_____

_____

Apply the Essential Questions

1. **Describe** how physical changes are different from chemical changes.
   TEKS 6.5(D)

   _____

   _____

   _____

   _____

2. **Create** a list of five chemical changes you observe each day. For each, identify the formation of a new substance by using evidence of a chemical change.
   TEKS 6.5(D)

   _____

   _____

   _____

   _____

   _____

   _____

H.O.T. Questions (Higher Order Thinking)

3. **Assess** Suppose you mix baking soda and white vinegar. What signs might indicate that a chemical change occurs?
   TEKS 6.5(D)

   _____

   _____

   _____

4. **Critique** A scientist measures the mass of two liquids before and after combining them. The mass after combining the liquids is less than the sum of the masses before. Where is the missing mass? What type of change occurred? How do you know? **TEKS** 6.5(D)

   _____

   _____

   _____

   _____

5. **Identify** Think of a burning candle. What evidence do you have that there are chemical changes and physical changes in the candle as it burns? **TEKS** 6.5(D)

   _____

   _____

   _____

   _____

6. **Evaluate** Is the process of bananas ripening a chemical or physical change? Explain. **TEKS** 6.5(D)

   _____

   _____

   _____

   _____

Freeze-Drying Foods

Have you noticed that the berries you find in some breakfast cereals are lightweight and dry—much different from the berries you get from the market or the garden?

Fresh fruit would spoil quickly if it were packaged in breakfast cereal, so fruits in cereals are often freeze-dried. When liquid is returned to the freeze-dried fruit, its physical properties more closely resemble fresh fruit. Freeze-drying, or lyophilization (li ah fuh luh ZAY shun), is the process in which a solvent (usually water) is removed from a solid. During this process, a frozen solvent changes to a gas without going through the liquid state. Freeze-dried foods are lightweight and long-lasting. Astronauts have been using freeze-dried food during space travel since the 1960s.

How Freeze-Drying Works

1. Machines called freeze-dryers are used to freeze-dry foods and other products. Fresh or cooked food is flash-frozen, changing moisture in the food to a solid.

2. The frozen food is placed in a large vacuum chamber, where moisture is removed. Heat is applied to accelerate moisture removal. Condenser plates remove vaporized solvent from the chamber and convert the frozen food to a freeze-dried solid.

3. Freeze-dried food is sealed in oxygen- and moisture-proof packages to ensure stability and freshness. When the food is rehydrated, it returns to its near-normal state of weight, color, and texture.

It's Your Turn!

PREDICT/DISCOVER What kinds of products besides food are freeze-dried? Use library or Internet resources to learn about other products that undergo the freeze-drying process. Discuss the benefits or drawbacks of freeze-drying.

Test-Taking Strategy

Key Words Circle the key words in a multiple choice question such as *most likely* and *best*. These words are very important in determining what the question is asking.

Example

Use the diagrams to answer question 6.

Substance A

Substance B

> **1** The key word *best* indicates that there might be multiple correct answers. When *best* is used, it is very important to read through all of the answer choices and compare them to determine which best answers the question.

6. Students modeled several common substances. Now they want to classify the substances. Which best classifies the substances shown above?

TEKS 6.5(C) *supporting*

> **2** After carefully reading the question and examining the diagrams, eliminate the answer choices that are incorrect. Choice B and choice D are incorrect.

A Substance A is a compound and substance B is an element.

B Substance A is an element and substance B is a compound.

C Substance A contains 2 elements and substance B contains 1 element.

> **3** Carefully examine the remaining choices to decide which one better answers the question. Go back and reread the question. Choice A correctly classifies the substances. Though choice C is correct, it is a description, not a classification.

D Substance A contains 1 element and substance B contains 2 elements.

TIP: Make flashcards to review key concepts, vocabulary words, and equations.

Multiple Choice

1 Four groups of students were each asked to create a table listing two elements and two compounds. Only one group's table was correct. **TEKS** 6.5(C) *supporting;* 6.2(E)

Group 1

Al
Al_2O_3
C
Fe

Group 3

Al
C
Fe
FeO

Group 2

Al
Al_2O_3
C
FeO

Group 4

Al
Al_2O_3
FeO
NaCl

Which group's table is correct?

A Group 1

B Group 2

C Group 3

D Group 4

2

> Mr. Torrez did a demonstration for his science class. He had two beakers each containing 10 mL of a clear liquid. He carefully poured the contents of these two beakers into a third empty beaker. He stirred the combined substances in the third beaker with a glass rod. After 3 minutes, a white substance began to collect at the bottom of the beaker.

What is the best explanation for what happened when the two substances were mixed together? **TEKS** 6.5(D)

A A precipitate formed, but no change took place because there was no color change.

B A precipitate formed, indicating a chemical change took place.

C A precipitate formed, indicating a physical change took place.

D A precipitate formed, indicating the two substances went into solution.

3 The table below shows the percentage of major elements found in the crust of Earth, living matter, the oceans and the atmosphere. **TEKS** 6.5(B); 6.2(E)

Element	Earth's Crust	Living Matter	Oceans	Atmosphere
aluminum	8.2	----	----	----
carbon	----	18.0	----	----
chlorine	----	----	58.3	----
hydrogen	----	10.0	----	----
magnesium	----	----	3.9	----
nitrogen	----	----	----	78.1
oxygen	46.1	65.0	----	21.0
silicon	28.2	----	----	----
sodium	----	----	32.4	----
others	17.5	7.0	5.4	0.9

Which elements comprise the largest portion of solid Earth, living matter, oceans, and the atmosphere?

    A oxygen, chlorine, silicon, carbon

    B carbon, hydrogen, oxygen, nitrogen

    C oxygen, chlorine, sodium, carbon

    D nitrogen, oxygen, sodium, chlorine

---

4 According to the chemical formula shown below, all of the following elements are found in phosphoric acid EXCEPT _____. **TEKS** 6.5(A)

Phosphoric Acid H_3PO_4

    A hydrogen

    B oxygen

    C phosphorus

    D potassium

5 When zinc is added to a hydrochloric acid solution, the zinc combines with the chlorine to form zinc chloride. The zinc chloride dissolves in water. In addition to zinc chloride, bubbles form in the water. What evidence indicates that a chemical change might have occurred? **TEKS** 6.5(D)

A Zinc chloride is dissolved in water.

B Zinc is added to hydrochloric acid.

C Bubbles formed in the water.

D The solution is boiling.

6

The composition of Earth's crust is different than that of the universe. The universe is largely hydrogen and helium with a small percentage of oxygen. Earth's crust, however, is about 47 percent oxygen. Silicon makes up about 28 percent of Earth's crust. The next most abundant elements in Earth's crust are aluminum, iron, calcium, sodium, potassium, and magnesium. The remaining elements account for less than two percent of Earth's crust.

Of the eight most abundant elements in Earth's crust, what percentage does the six next most abundant elements of Earth's crust make up? Record and bubble in your answer in the answer grid below. **TEKS** 6.5(B)

Classifying Matter

 The BIG Idea

Matter has physical properties that can be used for classification.

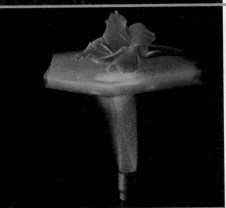

Ball of Clay

Jenna placed a ball of clay on a table. She flattened it into the shape of a pancake. Which row in the chart best describes the properties of the clay after it was flattened?

	Weight	Mass
A	Stays the same	Increases
B	Stays the same	Decreases
C	Stays the same	Stays the same
D	Increases	Increases
E	Increases	Decreases
F	Increases	Stays the same
G	Decreases	Increases
H	Decreases	Decreases
I	Decreases	Stays the same

Explain your thinking about what happens to the mass and weight and why.

3.1 Matter and Its Properties

INQUIRY

What makes this possible? Scuba diving is a lot of fun, but you have to be prepared. Exploring below the water's surface can be dangerous, and you need proper equipment. Discuss with a partner what properties must a diver's wet suit, mask, flippers, and breathing apparatus have to make a safe dive possible.

Write your responses in your interactive notebook.

LAB Manager

Go to your Lab Manual or visit connectED.mcgraw-hill.com to perform the labs for this lesson.

MiniLAB: *How can you find an object's mass and volume?*
TEKS 6.1(A); 6.2(A), (C); 6.4(A), (B); 6.6(B)

Skill Practice: *How can you calculate density?*
TEKS 6.1(A); 6.2(A), (C); 6.4(A), (B); 6.6(B)

LAB: *Identifying Unknown Minerals*
TEKS 6.1(A); 6.2(A), (C), (E); 6.4(A), (B); 6.6(B), (C)

Explore Activity

TEKS 6.1(A); 6.2(A), (C); 6.4(B)

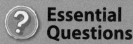

How can you describe a substance?

Think about the different ways you can describe a type of matter. Is it hard? Can you pour it? What color is it? Answering questions like these can help you describe the properties of a substance. In this activity, you will observe how the properties of a mixture can be very different from the properties of the substances it is made from.

Procedure

1. Read and complete a lab safety form.

2. Using a **small plastic spoon**, measure two spoonfuls of **cornstarch** into a **clear plastic cup**. What does the cornstarch look like? What does it feel like? Record your observations in your Lab Manual or interactive notebook.

3. Slowly stir one spoonful of **water** into the cup containing the cornstarch. Gently roll the new substance around in the cup with your finger. Record your observations.

Think About This

1. Describe some properties of the cornstarch and water before they were mixed.

   _____

   _____

2. Describe how the properties of the mixture differ from the original properties of the cornstarch and water.

   _____

   _____

   _____

TEKS in this Lesson

6.6(B) Calculate density to identify an unknown substance

6.6(C) Test the physical properties of minerals, including hardness, color, luster, and streak

Also covers Process Standards:
6.1(A); 6.2(A), (C), (E); 6.4(A), (B)

? Essential Questions

- What are physical and chemical properties?
- What is density and how is it used to identify an unknown substance?
- How are physical properties used to identify a mineral?

abc Vocabulary

volume
solid
liquid
gas
physical property
mass
density
solubility
chemical property

What is matter?

Figure 1 The different properties of matter keep you safe on a white-water-rafting trip.

Imagine the excitement of white-water rafting through a mountain pass, as shown in **Figure 1**. As your raft moves up and down through the rushing water, you grip your oar. You hope that the powerful current will lead you safely past the massive boulders. Only after you reach a quiet pool of water can you finally take a breath and enjoy the beautiful surroundings.

Imagine looking around and asking yourself, "What is matter?" Trees, rocks, water, and all the things you might see on a rafting trip are matter because they have mass and take up space. Air, even though you cannot see it, is also matter because it has mass and takes up space. Light from the Sun is not matter because it does not have mass and does not take up space. Sounds, forces, and energy also are not matter.

Think about the properties of matter you would see on your white-water-rafting trip. The helmet you would wear would be hard and shiny. The rubber raft would be soft and flexible. The water would be cool and clear. Matter has many different properties. In this lesson, you will learn about some physical properties and chemical properties of matter. You will also read about how these properties help to identify many types of matter.

Review Vocabulary

matter anything that has mass and takes up space

List

1. a. List two examples of matter that you can see in your classroom.

_____

_____

   b. List two examples of matter you cannot see.

_____

_____

   c. List two examples of things that are not matter.

_____

_____

States of Matter

One property that is useful when you are describing different materials is the state of matter. Three familiar states of matter are solids, liquids, and gases. You can determine a material's state of matter by answering the following questions:

- Does it have a definite shape?
- Does it have a definite volume?

Volume *is the amount of space a sample of matter occupies.* As shown in **Table 1** a material's state of matter determines whether its shape and its volume change when it is moved from one container to another.

Solids, Liquids, and Gases

Notice in **Table 1** that a **solid** *is a state of matter with a definite shape and volume.* The shape and volume of a solid do not change, regardless of whether it is inside or outside a container. A **liquid** *is a state of matter with a definite volume but not a definite shape.* A liquid changes shape if it is moved to another container, but its volume does not change. *A state of matter without a definite shape or a definite volume is a* **gas**. A gas changes both shape and volume depending on the size and shape of its container.

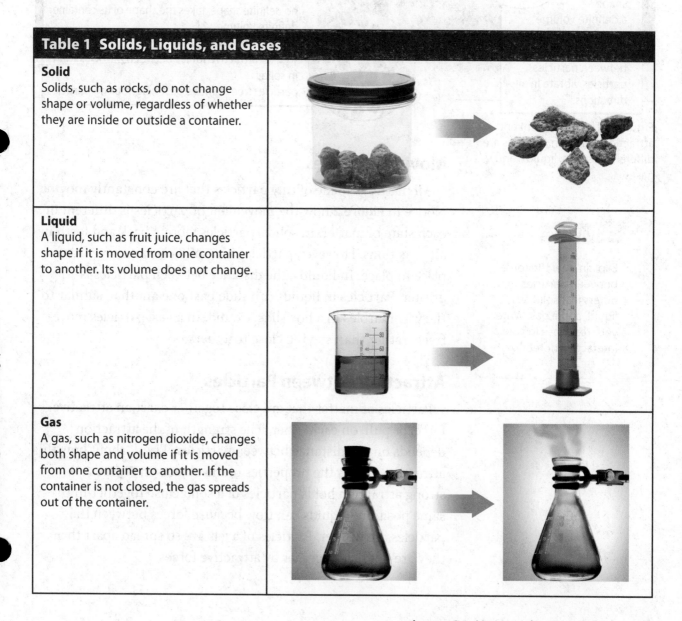

Table 1 Solids, Liquids, and Gases	
Solid Solids, such as rocks, do not change shape or volume, regardless of whether they are inside or outside a container.	
Liquid A liquid, such as fruit juice, changes shape if it is moved from one container to another. Its volume does not change.	
Gas A gas, such as nitrogen dioxide, changes both shape and volume if it is moved from one container to another. If the container is not closed, the gas spreads out of the container.	

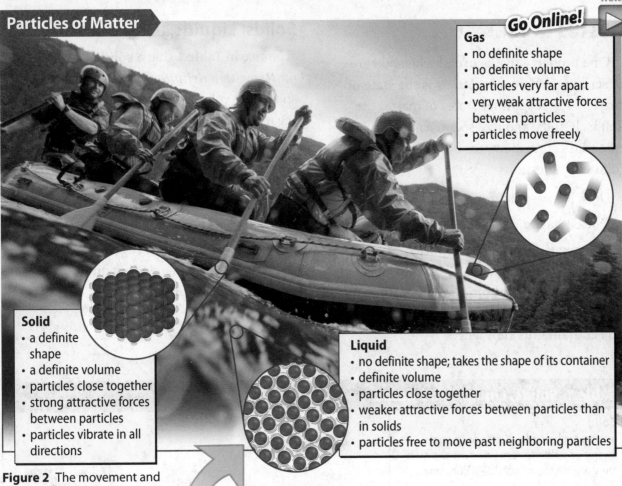

Gas
- no definite shape
- no definite volume
- particles very far apart
- very weak attractive forces between particles
- particles move freely

Watch
Go Online!

Solid
- a definite shape
- a definite volume
- particles close together
- strong attractive forces between particles
- particles vibrate in all directions

Liquid
- no definite shape; takes the shape of its container
- definite volume
- particles close together
- weaker attractive forces between particles than in solids
- particles free to move past neighboring particles

Figure 2 The movement and attraction between particles are different in solids, liquids, and gases.

 Compare

2. Explain how the force between particles differs in a solid, a liquid, and a gas. Write your response in your interactive notebook.

Moving Particles

All matter is made of tiny particles that are constantly moving. Notice in **Figure 2** how the movement of particles is different in each state of matter. In solids, particles vibrate back and forth in all directions. However, particles in a solid cannot move from place to place. In liquids, the distance between particles is greater. Particles in liquids can slide past one another, similar to the way marbles in a box slide around. In a gas, particles move freely rather than staying close together.

Attraction Between Particles

Particles of matter that are close together exert an attractive force, or pull, on each other. The strength of the attraction depends on the distance between particles. Think about how this attraction affects the properties of the objects in **Figure 2**. A strong attraction holds particles of a solid close together in the same position. Liquids can flow because forces between the particles are weaker. Particles of a gas are so spread apart that they are not held together by attractive forces.

Classify information about the three familiar states of matter.

	Solid	Liquid	Gas
Shape			
Volume			
Space between particles			
Strength of attraction between particles			
How particles move			

Connect it! Imagine that you can see the particles of ice, liquid water, and water vapor. **Model** and **describe** how these three states of matter of water differ. Write your response in your interactive notebook.

Organize it!

What are physical properties?   TEKS 6.6(B)

Think again about the properties of matter you might observe on a rafting trip. The water feels cold. The raft is heavy. The helmets are hard. The properties of all materials, or types of matter, depend on the substances that make them up. Recall that a substance is a type of matter with a composition that is always the same. *Any characteristic of matter that you can observe without changing the identity of the substances that make it up is a* **physical property**. State of matter, temperature, and the size of an object are all examples of physical properties.

Mass and Weight

Some physical properties of matter, such as mass and weight, depend on the size of the sample. **Mass** *is the amount of matter in an object.* Weight is the gravitational pull on the mass of an object. To measure the mass of a rock, you can use a balance, as shown in **Figure 3**. If more particles were added to the rock, its mass would increase, and the reading on the balance would increase. The weight of the rock would also increase.

Weight depends on the location of an object, but its mass does not. For example, the mass of an object is the same on Earth as it is on the Moon. The object's weight, however, is greater on Earth because the gravitational pull on the object is greater on Earth than on the Moon.

Figure 3 You can calculate a material's mass and volume and then calculate its density.

Differentiate

3. Highlight text evidence that supports the following statement: Your weight is different on Earth than it is on the Moon.

Mass, Volume, and Density

Go Online!   Tutor

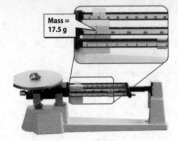

Mass
A balance measures an object's mass by comparing it to the known mass of the slides on the balance. Common units for measuring mass are the kilogram (kg) and the gram (g).

Volume
If a solid has a rectangular shape, you can find its volume by multiplying its length, its width, and its height together. A common unit of volume for a solid is the cubic centimeter (cm^3).

Copyright © McGraw-Hill Education   Hutchings Photography/Digital Light Source

Volume

Another physical property of matter that depends on the amount or size of the sample is volume. You can measure the volume of a liquid by pouring it into a graduated cylinder or a measuring cup and reading the volume mark. Two ways to measure the volume of a solid are shown in **Figure 3**. If a solid has a regular geometric shape, you can calculate its volume by using the correct formula. If a solid has an irregular shape, you can use the displacement method to measure its volume.

Density

Density is a physical property of matter that does not depend on the size or amount of the sample. **Density** *is the mass per unit volume of a substance.* Density is useful when identifying unknown substances because it is constant for a given substance, regardless of the size of the sample. For example, imagine hiking in the mountains and finding a shiny yellow rock. Is it gold? Suppose you calculate that the density of the rock is 5.0 g/cm³. This rock cannot be gold because the density of gold is 19.3 g/cm³. A sample of pure gold, regardless of the size, will always have a density of 19.3 g/cm³.

Copyright © McGraw-Hill Education   Hutchings Photography/Digital Light Source

Solve a One-Step Equation

A statement that two expressions are equal is an equation. For example, examine the density equation:

$$D = \frac{m}{V}$$

This equation shows that density, **D**, is equal to mass, **m**, divided by volume, **V**. To solve a one-step equation, place the variables you know into the equation. Then solve for the unknown variable. For example, if an object has a mass of **52 g** and a volume of **4 cm³**, calculate the density as follows:

$$D = \frac{52\ g}{4\ cm^3} = 13\ g/cm^3$$

Practice

A cube of metal measures 3 cm on each side. It has a mass of 216 g. What is the density of the metal?

Go Online!   Check   Tutor

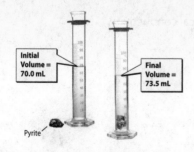

Pyrite

Volume of an Irregular-Shaped Solid

The volume of an irregular-shaped object can be measured by displacement. The volume of the object is the difference between the water level before and after the object is placed in water. The common unit for liquid volume is the milliliter (mL).

Initial Volume = 70.0 mL

Final Volume = 73.5 mL

Density Equation

$$\text{Density (in g/mL)} = \frac{\text{mass (in g)}}{\text{volume (in mL)}}$$

$$D = \frac{m}{V}$$

To find the density of the rock, first determine the mass and the volume of the rock:

mass: **m = 17.5 g**

volume: **V** = 73.5 mL - 70.0 mL = **3.5 mL**

Then divide the mass by the volume:

$$D = \frac{17.5\ g}{3.5\ mL} = 5.0\ g/mL$$

Density

Density can be calculated using the density equation. The common units of density are grams per milliliter (g/mL) or grams per cubic centimeter (g/cm³). 1 mL = 1 cm³

| Drink Mix | Sand |

Figure 4 The drink mix is soluble in water. The sand is not soluble in water.

STEMonline

Determine how much cargo can be loaded on a ship without sinking. Visit ConnectEd for the **STEM** activity **Cargo Ship Challenge.**

Resources

Go Online!

Solubility

You can observe another physical property of matter if you stir a powdered drink mix into water. The powder dissolves, or mixes evenly, in the water. **Solubility** *is the ability of one material to dissolve in another.* You cannot see the drink-mix powder in the left glass in **Figure 4** because the powder is soluble in water. The liquid is red because of the food coloring in the powder. The sand settles in the glass because it is not soluble in water.

Melting and Boiling Points

Melting point and boiling point also are physical properties. The melting point is the temperature at which a solid changes to a liquid. Ice cream, for example, melts when it warms enough to reach its melting point. The boiling point is the temperature at which a liquid changes to a gas. If you heat a pan of water, the water will boil, or change to a gas, at its boiling point. Different materials have different melting and boiling points. These temperatures do not depend on the size or amount of the material.

Recall

4. Highlight how a substance changes at its melting point.
   Underline how a substance changes at its boiling point.

Additional Physical Properties

Several other physical properties—magnetism, malleability, and electrical conductivity—are shown in **Figure 5**. Notice how the physical properties of each material make it useful. Can you think of other examples of materials chosen for certain uses because of their physical properties?

Physical Properties

Figure 5 Physical properties include magnetism, malleability, and electrical conductivity.

Magnetism is a physical property that allows some metals to attract certain other metals.

A malleable metal, such as aluminum foil, is useful because it can be hammered or rolled into thin sheets.

Some metals, such as copper, are used in electrical wire because of their high electrical conductivity.

Figure 6 Flammability and the ability to rust are examples of chemical properties.

Flammability
In 1937 the airship *Hindenburg* caught fire and crashed. It was filled with hydrogen, a highly flammable gas.

Ability to rust
The metal parts of an old car soon rust because the metal contains iron. The ability to rust is a chemical property of iron.

What are chemical properties?

Have you ever seen an apple turn brown? When you bite into or cut open apples or other fruits, substances that make up the fruit react with oxygen in the air. When substances react with each other, their particles combine to form a new, different substance. The ability of substances in fruit to react with oxygen is a chemical property of the substances. A chemical property is the ability or inability of a substance to combine with or change into one or more new substances. *A **chemical property** is a characteristic of matter that you observe as it reacts with or changes into a different substance.* For example, copper on the roof of a building turns green as it reacts with oxygen in the air. The ability to react with oxygen is a chemical property of copper. Two other chemical properties—flammability and the ability to rust—are shown in **Figure 6.**

Flammability

Flammability is the ability of a type of matter to burn easily. Suppose you are on a camping trip and want to light a campfire. You see rocks, sand, and wood. Which would you choose for your fire? Wood is a good choice because it is flammable. Rocks and sand are not flammable.

Materials are often chosen for certain uses based on flammability. For example, gasoline is used in cars because it burns easily in engines. Materials that are used for cooking pans must not be flammable. The tragedy shown in **Figure 6** resulted when hydrogen, a highly flammable gas, was used in the airship *Hindenburg.* Today, airships are filled with helium, a nonflammable gas.

Ability to Rust

You have probably seen old cars that have begun to rust like the one in **Figure 6.** You might also have seen rust on bicycles or tools left outside. Rust is a substance that forms when iron reacts with water and oxygen in the air. The ability to rust is a chemical property of iron or metals that contain iron.

Table 2 Identifying an Unknown Material by its Physical Properties

Substance	Color	Mass (g)	Melting Point (°C)	Density (g/cm³)
Table salt	white	14.5	801	2.17
Sugar	white	11.5	148	1.53
Baking soda	white	16.0	50	2.16
Unknown	white	16.0	801	2.17

Identifying Matter Using Physical Properties TEKS 6.6(B)

Physical properties are useful for describing types of matter, and they are also useful for identifying unknown substances. Look at the substances in **Table 2**. Notice how their physical properties are alike and how they are different. How can you use these properties to identify the unknown substance?

You cannot identify the unknown substance by its color. All of the substances are white. You also cannot identify the unknown substance by its mass or volume. Mass and volume are properties of matter that change with the amount of the sample present. However, recall that melting point and density are properties of matter that do not depend on the size or the amount of the sample.

Therefore, melting point and density are physical properties that are more reliable for identifying an unknown substance. Notice that both the melting point and the density of the unknown substance match those of table salt. The unknown substance must be table salt.

When you identify matter using physical properties, consider how the properties are alike and how they are different from known types of matter. It is important that the physical properties you use to identify an unknown type of matter are properties that do not change for any sample size. A cup of salt and a spoonful of salt will have the same melting point and density even though the mass and volume for each will be different.

Evaluate

5. In the table below, indicate whether the property can be useful in identifying an unknown substance.

Physical Property	Useful in identifying a substance (Y/N)	Why or why not?
boiling point		
volume		
density		
color		

Sorting Materials Using Properties

Both physical properties and chemical properties are useful for sorting materials. The beads in **Figure 7** are sorted by color and shape—two physical properties. When you bring groceries home from the store, you might put crackers in a cupboard, but you probably put milk and yogurt in the refrigerator to keep them from spoiling. The tendency to spoil is a chemical property of the milk and yogurt. You probably often sort other types of matter by physical or chemical properties without realizing it.

Separating Mixtures Using Physical Properties

Physical properties are useful for separating different types of matter that are mixed. For example, suppose you have a frozen juice pop on a stick. How could you separate the frozen juice from the stick? If you set the freezer pop on a counter, the frozen juice will melt and separate from the stick. Melting point is a physical property you can use to separate mixtures. Other ways that you can use physical properties to separate mixtures are shown in **Figure 8**.

Figure 7 These beads are sorted by color and shape.

Figure 8 Physical properties, such as state of matter, boiling point, and magnetism, can be used to separate mixtures.

Water can flow through the strainer because it is a liquid. The noodles cannot flow through because they are solid and too large.

If you boil a salt-water mixture, the liquid water turns to gas when it reaches its boiling point. The salt is left behind.

Iron filings, which are magnetic, can be separated from the sand using a magnet. The magnet attracts the iron filings but not the sand.

Describe

6. How could you separate a mixture of salt, sand, and iron filings?

Testing Physical Properties of Minerals

TEKS 6.6(C)

Scientists test materials using physical properties every day. Mineralogists, scientists who study minerals and their properties and uses, use simple tests to help identify and classify unknown minerals based on their physical properties.

Color

Similar to identifying matter using physical properties, color alone cannot be used to identify a mineral. Different minerals can have the same color. For example, the minerals olivine and pyroxene both are green. Also, one type of mineral can be found in different colors. Quartz can be clear, white, gray, purple, orange, or pink. The watermelon tourmaline, shown in **Figure 9**, is pink and green, but it can also be yellow and blue. Variations in color reflect the presence of chemical impurities, such as iron, chromium, or manganese.

Luster

What do you first notice when you see a bright object, such as a chrome wheel on a new car? Is it the shine? The way a mineral reflects or absorbs light at its surface is called luster. Metals such as gold and silver reflect light with a shiny luster called metallic luster. Nonmetallic minerals have luster types that might be shiny, but not as reflective as a metal. For example, polished diamond has brilliant luster. Minerals that are not shiny are often called earthy or dull. Other descriptions of luster include waxy, silky, pearly, and vitreous (glassy). A mineral's luster is directly related to its chemical composition. **Figure 10** shows the luster of two different minerals, one with metallic luster and one with nonmetallic luster.

Figure 9 Minerals are found in a variety of colors.

Figure 10 The luster of a mineral is caused by the way light interacts with its surface.

Hematite

Talc

Hardness

In 1812, the German mineralogist Friedrich Mohs developed a scale to compare the hardness of different minerals. Hardness is the resistance of a mineral to being scratched. Mohs' hardness scale ranges from 1 to 10, as shown in **Table 3**. A hardness of 1 is assigned to the softest mineral on the scale, talc. Diamond is the hardest mineral on the scale, with a hardness value of 10.

The mineral quartz has a hardness of 7. If a piece of quartz is rubbed across the surface of a mineral that is softer than quartz (with a hardness less than 7), the quartz will scratch the mineral. Quartz will scratch feldspar, calcite, and talc because each has a hardness less than 7. Quartz will not scratch topaz, corundum, or diamond because each has a hardness greater than 7.

Mineralogists compare the hardness of an unknown mineral to ordinary objects, as shown in **Table 3**. The hardness of a steel file, a piece of glass, a penny, and your fingernail are used as standards. Mineralogists have added these values to Mohs' hardness scale. For example, a mineral that scratches a penny but not quartz has a hardness between 3 and 7. A mineral that can be scratched by your fingernail has a hardness less than 2.5. As displayed in **Figure 11**, objects of known hardness can help you estimate the hardness of an unknown mineral sample.

Figure 11 A piece of glass can be used in the field or in the lab to test a mineral for hardness.

Table 3	Mohs' Hardness Scale	
Hardness	**Mineral or Ordinary Object**	
10	Diamond	
9	Corundum	
8	Topaz	
7	Quartz	
6.5	Steel file	
6	Feldspar	
5.5	Glass	
5	Apatite	
4.5	Iron nail	
4	Fluorite	
3.5	Penny	
3	Calcite	
2.5	Fingernail	
2	Gypsum	
1	Talc	

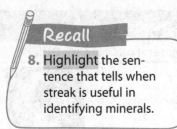

Recall

8. Highlight the sentence that tells when streak is useful in identifying minerals.

LAB Manager

LAB: *Identifying Unknown Minerals*

TEKS 6.1(A); 6.2(A), (C), (E); 6.4(A), (B); 6.6(B), (C)

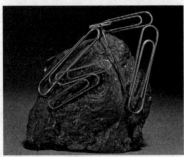

Figure 13 Calcite (top) is fluorescent when exposed to ultraviolet light. Magnetite (bottom) is magnetic due to the presence of iron in its chemical formula.

Streak

Some minerals produce a powdery residue, called streak, when rubbed across an unglazed porcelain streak plate. Streak is the color of a mineral in powdered form. Streak is useful in identifying only minerals that are softer than porcelain.

Nonmetallic minerals generally produce a white streak. Many metallic minerals, however, produce characteristic streak colors. Even if two samples of a given mineral are different colors, they will have the same streak color. As shown in **Figure 12**, both samples of hematite (Fe_2O_3) produce a reddish-brown streak, even though one of the samples is silver-colored with a metallic luster while the other sample is dull and red or gray.

Figure 12 These two samples of hematite are different colors, but they both produce the same reddish-brown streak color when scratched on a porcelain plate.

Special Properties

Some minerals have special properties that help you identify them. A mineral's texture, or how it feels, might be greasy or smooth to the touch. Graphite is greasy. Talc is smooth. Some minerals react. Calcite fizzes and produces a gas when it comes in contact with hydrochloric acid. Some minerals have distinctive odors. Sulfur smells like a match, and kaolinite smells like clay. Fluorescence, shown in **Figure 13**, is a mineral's ability to glow when exposed to ultraviolet light. Calcite and fluorite are two common minerals that fluoresce. Some minerals, such as magnetite shown in **Figure 13**, are magnetic.

3.1 Review

Summarize it!

Describe the physical properties of matter using the graphic organizer below.

Mass and Weight	Volume	Density
Mass: Weight:		

Physical Properties

Solubility	Melting and Boiling Points	Conductivity

Connect It! **Summarize** why it is necessary to consider multiple physical properties when trying to identify minerals. **TEKS** 6.6(C)

_____

_____

_____

_____

Matter and Its Properties

Apply the Essential Questions

1. **Distinguish** between physical and chemical properties. **TEKS** 6.6(C)

   _____

   _____

   _____

2. **Explain** which physical property is the best for identifying an unknown substance: color, volume, mass, or density. **TEKS** 6.6(B) *supporting*

   _____

   _____

   _____

   _____

3. **Identify** which physical properties are used to identify minerals. **TEKS** 6.6(C)

   _____

   _____

   _____

H.O.T. Questions (Higher Order Thinking)

4. **Design** an investigation you could use to calculate the density of a penny. **TEKS** 6.6(B) *supporting*

   _____

   _____

   _____

   _____

5. **Explain** There are several simple objects that can help you estimate the hardness of an unknown mineral. What are they? Why do you think these objects are good standards to use? **TEKS** 6.6(C)

   _____

   _____

   _____

Math Skills	**TEKS** 6.6(B) *supporting*;
	Math **TEKS** 6.1(A), (B); 6.3(E)

Solve a One-Step Equation

6. Use what you have learned about density to complete the table below. Then determine the identities of the two unknown metals.

Metal	Mass (g)	Volume (cm³)	Density (g/cm³)
Iron	42.5	5.40	
Lead	28.8	2.55	
Tungsten	69.5	3.60	
Zinc	46.4	6.50	
	61.0	5.40	
	46.4	2.40	

Check   Tutor

Go Online!

My Notes

INQUIRY

Where does it strike? Lightning strikes the top of the Empire State Building approximately 100 times a year. Why does lightning hit the top of this building instead of the city streets or buildings below?

Write your response in your interactive notebook.

LAB Manager

Go to your Lab Manual or visit connectED.mcgraw-hill.com to perform the labs for this lesson.

MiniLAB: *How well do materials conduct thermal energy?*

TEKS 6.1(A); 6.2(A), (C), (E); 6.4(A), (B); 6.6(A)

Explore Activity

TEKS 6.1(A); 6.2(A); 6.4(B); 6.6(A)

What properties make metals useful?

The properties of metals determine their uses. Copper conducts thermal energy, which makes it useful for cookware. Aluminum has low density, so it is used in aircraft bodies. What other properties make metals useful?

Procedure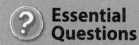

1. Read and complete a lab safety form.

2. With your group, observe the **metal objects** in your **container**. For each object, discuss the properties that allow the metal to be used in that way. Record your observations in your Lab Manual or interactive notebook.

3. Observe the **photographs of gold and silver jewelry**. What properties make these two metals useful in jewelry? Record your observations.

4. Examine **other objects around the room** that you think are made of metal. Do they share the same properties as the objects in your container? Do they have other properties that make them useful? Record your observations.

Think About This

1. Compare the properties that all the metals share. Contrast the properties that are different.

_____

_____

_____

_____

2. List at least four physical properties of metals that determine their uses.

_____

_____

_____

TEKS in this Lesson

6.6(A) Compare metals, nonmetals, and metalloids using physical properties such as luster, conductivity, or malleability

Also covers Process Standards:
6.1(A); 6.2(A), (C), (E); 6.4(A), (B)

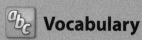 **Essential Questions**

- What elements are metals?
- What are the physical properties of metals?

Vocabulary

metal
luster
ductility
malleability
alkali metal
alkaline earth metal
transition element

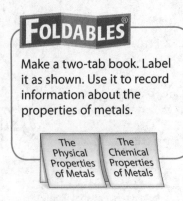

FOLDABLES®

Make a two-tab book. Label it as shown. Use it to record information about the properties of metals.

| The Physical Properties of Metals | The Chemical Properties of Metals |

The Periodic Table

Imagine trying to find a book in a library if all the books were unorganized. Books are organized in a library to help you easily find the information you need. The periodic table is like a library of information about all chemical elements.

A copy of the periodic table is in the back of your book. You can learn about some properties of an element from its position on the periodic table. Elements are organized in periods (rows) and groups (columns). The periodic table lists elements in order of atomic number. The atomic number increases from left to right as you move across a period. Elements in each group have similar chemical properties and react with other elements in similar ways. In this lesson, you will read more about how an element's position on the periodic table can be used to predict its properties.

Metals, Nonmetals, and Metalloids

The three main regions of elements on the periodic table are shown in **Figure 1**. Excluding hydrogen, elements on the left side of the table are metals. Nonmetals are on the right side of the table. Metalloids form the narrow stair-step region between metals and nonmetals.

Figure 1 Elements on the periodic table are classified as metals, nonmetals, or metalloids.

Watch

Go Online!

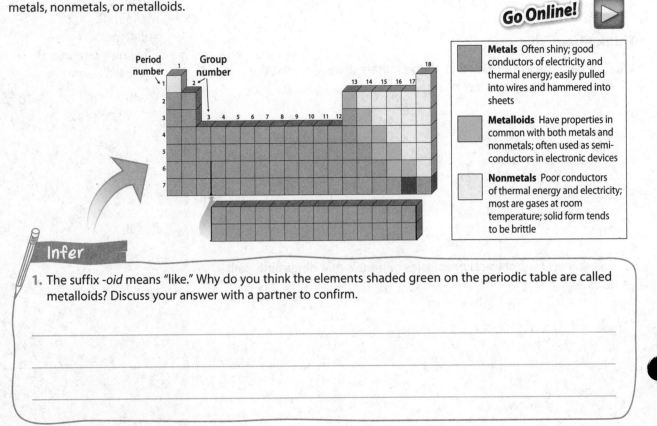

Metals Often shiny; good conductors of electricity and thermal energy; easily pulled into wires and hammered into sheets

Metalloids Have properties in common with both metals and nonmetals; often used as semi-conductors in electronic devices

Nonmetals Poor conductors of thermal energy and electricity; most are gases at room temperature; solid form tends to be brittle

Infer

1. The suffix -*oid* means "like." Why do you think the elements shaded green on the periodic table are called metalloids? Discuss your answer with a partner to confirm.

_____

_____

_____

Characterize

2. Use the text and **Figure 1** to describe characteristics of the periodic table.

Characteristic	Description
Period	
Group	
Metals	
Metalloids	
Nonmetals	

What is a metal? TEKS 6.6(A)

What do stainless-steel knives, copper wire, aluminum foil, and gold jewelry have in common? They are made from metals.

Most of the elements on the periodic table are metals. In fact, of all the known elements, more than three-quarters are metals. With the exception of hydrogen, all of the elements in groups 1–12 on the periodic table are metals. In addition, some of the elements in groups 13–15 are metals. To be a metal, an element must have certain properties.

Physical Properties of Metals

Recall that physical properties are characteristics used to describe or identify something without changing its makeup. All metals share certain physical properties.

A **metal** *is an element that is generally shiny and is easily pulled into wires or hammered into thin sheets.* A metal is a good conductor of electricity and thermal energy. Gold exhibits the common properties of metals.

Copyright © McGraw-Hill Education

Copyright © McGraw-Hill Education

Lesson 3.2 Metals **103**

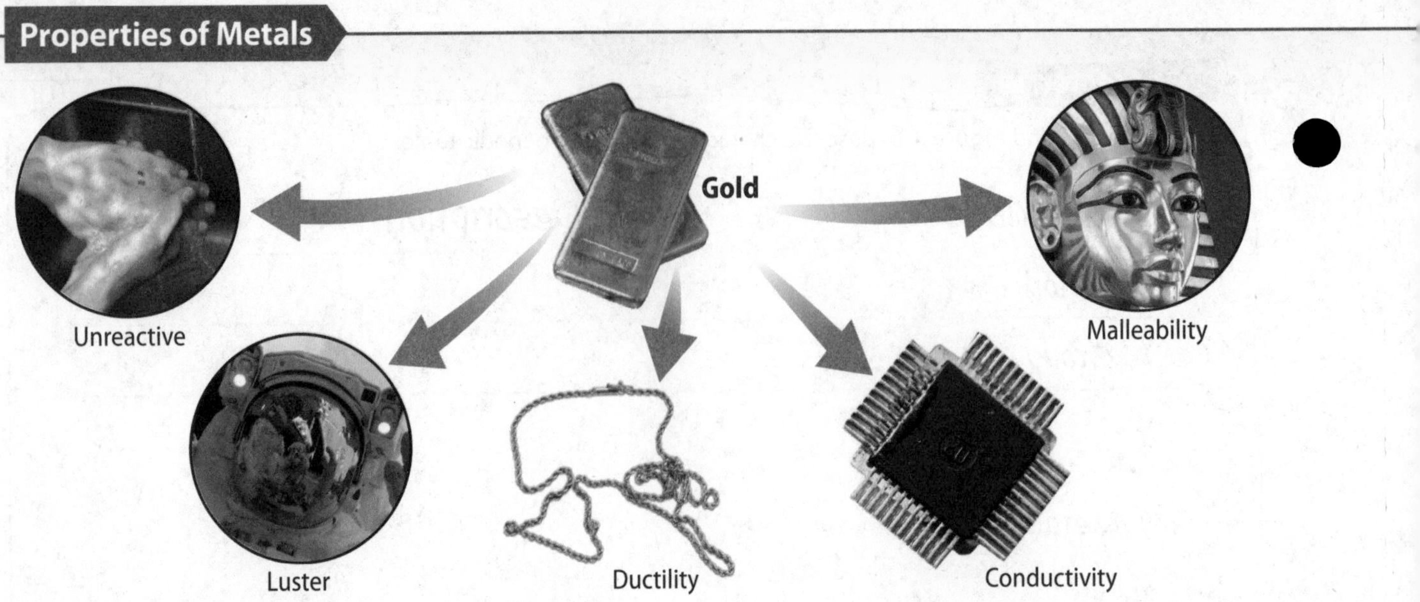

Gold

Unreactive

Luster

Ductility

Malleability

Conductivity

Figure 2 Gold has many uses based on its properties.

Copyright © McGraw-Hill Education (tl)McGraw-Hill Education, (tc)Paul Katz/Photodisc/Getty Images, (tr)Egyptian National Museum, Cairo, Egypt, Photo © Boltin Picture Library/The Bridgeman Art Library International, (bc)Hutchings Photography/Digital Light Source, (br)Charles Stirling/Alamy

Word Origin

ductility from Latin *ductilis*, means "may be led or drawn"

Infer

3. How does the density of most metals compare to most nonmetals?

Luster and Conductivity People use gold for jewelry because of its beautiful color and metallic luster. **Luster** *describes the ability of a metal to reflect light.* Gold is also a good conductor of thermal energy and electricity. However, gold is too expensive to use in normal electrical wires or metal cookware. Copper is often used instead.

Ductility and Malleability Gold is the most ductile metal. **Ductility** (duk TIH luh tee) *is the ability of a substance to be pulled into thin wires.* A piece of gold with the mass of a paper clip can be pulled into a wire that is more than 3 km long.

Malleability (mal yuh BIH luh tee) *is the ability of a substance to be hammered or rolled into sheets.* Gold is so malleable that it can be hammered into thin sheets. A pile of a million thin sheets would be only as high as a coffee mug.

Other Physical Properties of Metals In general, the density, strength, boiling point, and melting point of a metal are greater than those of other elements. Except for mercury, all metals are solid at room temperature. Many uses of a metal are determined by the metal's physical properties, as shown in **Figure 2**.

Chemical Properties of Metals

Recall that a chemical property is the ability or inability of a substance to change into one or more new substances. The chemical properties of metals can differ greatly. However, metals in the same group usually have similar chemical properties. For example, gold and other elements in group 11 do not easily react with other substances.

Group 1: Alkali Metals TEKS 6.6(A)

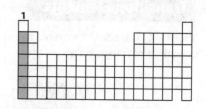

The elements in group 1 are called **alkali** (AL kuh li) **metals.** The alkali metals include lithium, sodium, potassium, rubidium, cesium, and francium.

Because they are in the same group, alkali metals have similar chemical properties. Alkali metals react quickly with other elements, such as oxygen. Therefore, in nature, they occur only in compounds. Pure alkali metals must be stored so that they do not come in contact with oxygen and water vapor in the air. **Figure 3** shows potassium and sodium reacting with water.

Alkali metals also have similar physical properties. Pure alkali metals have a silvery appearance. As shown in **Figure 3**, they are soft enough to cut with a knife. The alkali metals also have the lowest densities of all metals. A block of pure sodium metal could float on water because of its very low density.

Figure 3 Alkali metals react violently with water. They are also soft enough to be cut with a knife.

Watch
Go Online!

Potassium   **Sodium**   **Lithium**

Group 2: Alkaline Earth Metals TEKS 6.6(A)

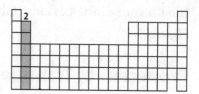

The elements in group 2 on the periodic table are called **alkaline** (AL kuh lihn) **earth metals.** These metals are beryllium, magnesium, calcium, strontium, barium, and radium.

Alkaline earth metals also react quickly with other elements. However, they do not react as quickly as the alkali metals do. Like the alkali metals, pure alkaline earth metals do not occur naturally. Instead, they combine with other elements and form compounds. The physical properties of the alkaline earth metals are also similar to those of the alkali metals. Alkaline earth metals are soft and silvery. They also have low density, but they have greater density than alkali metals.

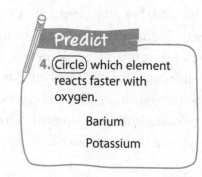

Predict

4. (Circle) which element reacts faster with oxygen.

   Barium

   Potassium

Figure 4 Transition elements are in blocks at the center of the periodic table. Many colorful materials contain small amounts of transition elements.

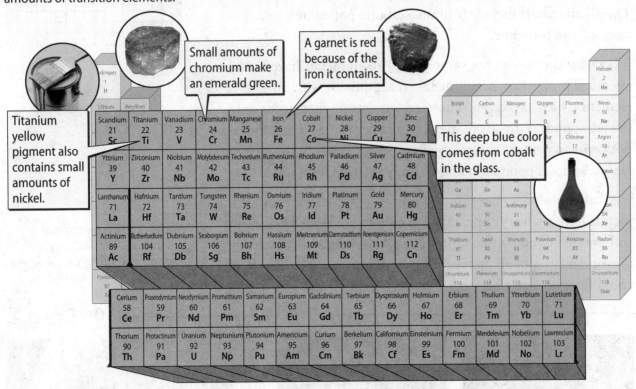

Titanium yellow pigment also contains small amounts of nickel.

Small amounts of chromium make an emerald green.

A garnet is red because of the iron it contains.

This deep blue color comes from cobalt in the glass.

Groups 3–12: Transition Elements TEKS 6.6(A)

The elements in groups 3–12 are called **transition elements.** The transition elements are in two blocks on the periodic table. The main block is in the center of the periodic table. The other block includes the two rows at the bottom of the periodic table, as shown in **Figure 4.**

Properties of Transition Elements

All transition elements are metals. They have higher melting points, greater strength, and higher densities than the alkali metals and the alkaline earth metals. Transition elements also react less quickly with oxygen. Some transition elements can exist in nature as free elements. An element is a free element when it occurs in pure form, not in a compound.

Uses of Transition Elements

Transition elements in the main block of the periodic table have many important uses. Because of their high densities, strength, and resistance to corrosion, transition elements such as iron make good building materials. Copper, silver, nickel, and gold are used to make coins. These metals are also used for jewelry, electrical wires, and many industrial applications.

Main-block transition elements can react with other elements and form many compounds. Many of these compounds are colorful. Artists use transition-element compounds in paints and pigments. The color of many gems, such as garnets and emeralds, comes from the presence of small amounts of transition elements, as illustrated in **Figure 4.**

Lanthanide and Actinide Series

Look at the periodic table in the back of your book. Two rows of transition elements are at the bottom of the periodic table. These elements were removed from the main part of the table so that periods 6 and 7 were not longer than the other periods. If these elements were included in the main part of the table, the first row, called the lanthanide series, would stretch between lanthanum and halfnium. The second row, called the actinide series, would stretch between actinium and rutherfordium.

Some lanthanide and actinide series elements have valuable properties. For example, lanthanide series elements are used to make strong magnets. Plutonium, one of the actinide series elements, is used as a fuel in some nuclear reactors.

Patterns in Properties of Metals  6.6(A)

Recall that the properties of elements follow repeating patterns across the periods of the periodic table. In general, elements increase in metallic properties such as luster, malleability, and electrical conductivity from right to left across a period, as shown in **Figure 5**. The elements on the far right of a period have no metallic properties at all. Potassium (K), the element on the far left in period 4, has the highest luster, is the most malleable, and conducts electricity better than all the elements in this period.

There are also patterns within groups. Metallic properties tend to increase as you move down a group, also shown in **Figure 5**. You could predict that the malleability of gold is greater than the malleability of either silver or copper because it is below these two elements in group 11.

LAB Manager

MiniLAB: *How well do materials conduct thermal energy?*

TEKS 6.1(A); 6.2(A), (C), (E); 6.4(A), (B); 6.6(A)

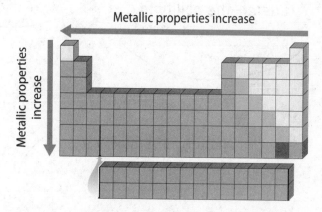

Metallic properties increase

Metallic properties increase

Figure 5 Metallic properties of elements increase as you move to the left and down on the periodic table.

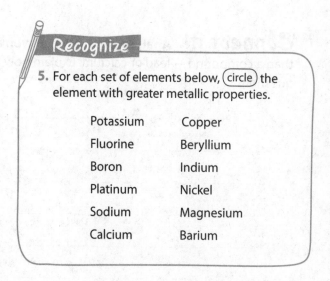

Recognize

5. For each set of elements below, circle the element with greater metallic properties.

Potassium	Copper
Fluorine	Beryllium
Boron	Indium
Platinum	Nickel
Sodium	Magnesium
Calcium	Barium

3.2 Review

Describe the physical properties of metals. *TEKS* 6.6(A)

Physical Properties of Metals

Luster—the ability to _____

Conductivity—the ability to conduct _____ and _____

Ductility—the ability to _____ _____

Malleability—the ability to _____ _____

Connect it!

Analyze which element you are more likely to find as a free element rather than a compound —lead or calcium. Explain how using the periodic table can help answer this question.

_____

_____

_____

_____

_____

Use Vocabulary

1. Elements that have the lowest densities of all the metals are called

_____ . **TEKS** 6.6(A) supporting

Apply the Essential Questions

2. **Describe** the physical properties that most metals have in common.
TEKS 6.6(A) supporting

_____

_____

_____

_____

3. **Describe** where most metals are found on the periodic table. **TEKS** 6.6(A) supporting

_____

_____

_____

_____

H.O.T. Questions (Higher Order Thinking)

4. **Evaluate** the physical properties of potassium, magnesium, and copper. Select the best choice to use for a building project. Explain why this metal is the best building material to use. **TEKS** 6.6(A) supporting

_____

_____

_____

_____

_____

5. **Apply** Why is mercury the only metal to have been used in thermometers?
TEKS 6.6(A) supporting

_____

_____

_____

_____

6. **Evaluate** the following types of metals as a choice to make a Sun reflector: alkali metals, alkaline earth metals, or transition metals. The metal cannot react with water or oxygen and must be shiny and strong.
TEKS 6.6(A) supporting

_____

_____

_____

_____

7. **Interpret Graphics** Examine this section of the periodic table. What metal will have properties most similar to those of chromium (Cr)? Why? **TEKS** 6.6(A) supporting

Vanadium 23 **V**	Chromium 24 **Cr**	Manganese 25 **Mn**
Niobium 41 **Nb**	Molybdenum 42 **Mo**	Technetium 43 **Tc**

_____

_____

_____

Fireworks

Metals add a variety of colors to fireworks.

About 1,000 years ago, Chinese people discovered the chemical formula for gunpowder. Using this formula, they invented the first fireworks. One of the primary ingredients in gunpowder is saltpeter, or potassium nitrate. Find potassium on the periodic table. Notice that potassium is a metal. How does the chemical behavior of a metal contribute to a colorful fireworks show?

Purple: mix of strontium and copper compounds

Blue: copper compounds

Yellow: sodium compounds

Gold: iron burned with carbon

White-hot: barium-oxygen compounds or aluminum or magnesium burn

Metal compounds contribute to the variety of colors you see at a fireworks show. Recall that metals have special chemical and physical properties. Compounds that contain metals also have special properties. For example, each metal turns a characteristic color when burned. Lithium, an alkali metal, forms compounds that burn red. Copper compounds burn blue. Aluminum and magnesium burn white.

Orange: calcium compounds

Green: barium compounds

Red: strontium and lithium compounds

It's Your Turn!

FORM AN OPINION Fireworks contain metal compounds. Are they bad for the environment or for your health? In groups, research the effects of metals on human health and on the environment. Decide if fireworks are safe to use in holiday celebrations.

INQUIRY

Why don't they melt?

What do you expect to happen to something when a flame is placed against it? As you can see, the flower in the photograph is protected from the heat. What properties does the solid substance need to have to protect the flower?

 Write your response in your interactive notebook.

 LAB Manager

Go to your Lab Manual or visit connectED.mcgraw-hill.com to perform the labs for this lesson.

MiniLAB: *Which insulates better?*

TEKS 6.1(A); 6.2(A), (C), (E); 6.4(A); 6.6(A)

Explore Activity

TEKS 6.1(A); 6.2(A), (C),(E); 6.4(A), (B); 6.6(A)

What are some properties of nonmetals?

You now know the properties of metals. What properties do nonmetals have?

Procedure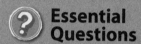

1. Read and complete a lab safety form.

2. Examine pieces of **copper**, **carbon**, **aluminum**, and **sulfur**. Describe the appearance of these elements in your Lab Manual or interactive notebook.

3. Use a **conductivity tester** to check how well these elements conduct electricity. Record your observations in your Lab Manual or interactive notebook.

4. Wrap each element sample in a **paper towel**. Carefully hit the sample with a **hammer**. Unwrap the towel and observe the sample. Record your observations in your Lab Manual or interactive notebook.

Think About This

1. Locate copper, carbon, aluminum, and sulfur on the periodic table. Based on their locations, which elements are metals? Which elements are nonmetals?

   _____

   _____

2. Using your results, compare the properties of metals and nonmetals.

   _____

   _____

   _____

3. What property of a nonmetal makes it useful for insulating electrical wires?

   _____

   _____

TEKS in this Lesson

6.6(A) Compare metals, nonmetals, and metalloids using physical properties such as luster, conductivity, or malleability

Also covers Process Standards: 6.1(A); 6.2(A), (C), (E); 6.4(A), (B)

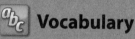 **Essential Questions**

- Where are nonmetals and metalloids on the periodic table?
- What are the physical properties of nonmetals and metalloids?

Vocabulary

nonmetal
halogen
noble gas
metalloid
semiconductor

The Elements of Life TEKS 6.6(A)

Do you know that more than 96 percent of the mass of your body comes from just four elements? As shown in **Figure 1,** all four of these elements—oxygen, carbon, hydrogen, and nitrogen—are nonmetals. **Nonmetals** *are elements that have no metallic properties.*

Of the remaining elements in your body, the two most common elements—phosphorus and sulfur—also are nonmetals. These six elements form the compounds in proteins, fats, nucleic acids, and other large molecules in your body and in all other living things.

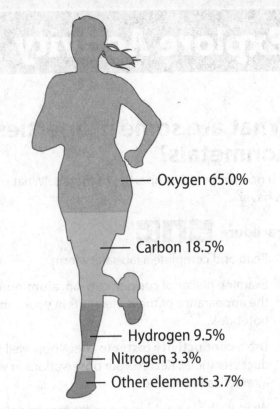

Oxygen 65.0%

Carbon 18.5%

Hydrogen 9.5%
Nitrogen 3.3%
Other elements 3.7%

Figure 1 Like other living things, this woman's mass comes mostly from nonmetals.

Identify

1. Highlight the six most common elements in the human body.

FOLDABLES

Cut out the Lesson 3.3 Foldable in the back of the book. Use it to organize information about nonmetals and metalloids.

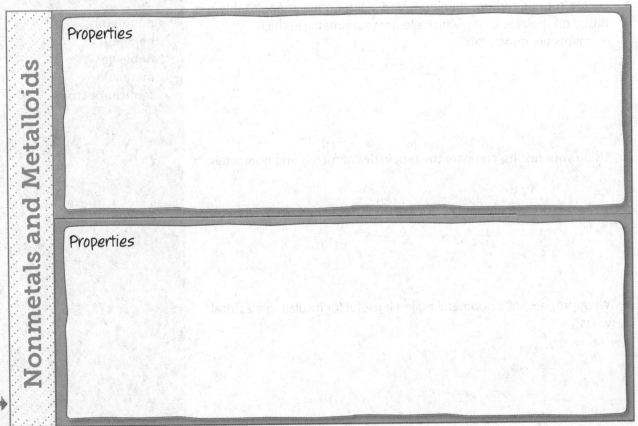

Nonmetals and Metalloids

Properties

Properties

Tape here

Metal

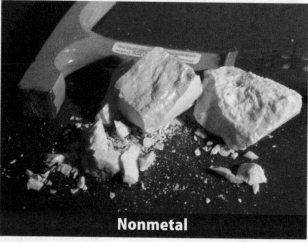

Nonmetal

Figure 2 Solid metals, such as copper, are malleable. Solid nonmetals, such as sulfur, are brittle.

How are nonmetals different from metals? TEKS 6.6(A)

Recall that metals have luster. They are ductile, malleable, and good conductors of electricity and thermal energy. All metals except mercury are solids at room temperature.

The properties of nonmetals are different from those of metals. Many nonmetals are gases at room temperature. Those that are solid at room temperature have a dull surface, which means they have no luster. Because nonmetals are poor conductors of electricity and thermal energy, they are good insulators. For example, nose cones on space shuttles are insulated from the intense thermal energy of reentry by a material made from carbon, a nonmetal. **Figure 2** and **Figure 3** show several properties of nonmetals.

Figure 3 Nonmetals have properties that are different from those of metals.

Properties of Nonmetals

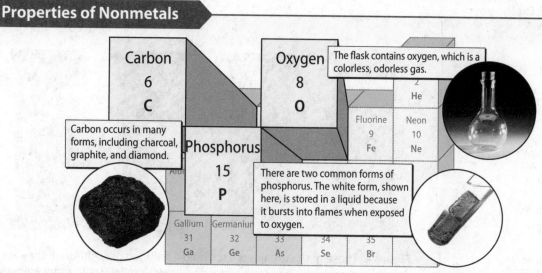

Carbon
6
C

Carbon occurs in many forms, including charcoal, graphite, and diamond.

Phosphorus
15
P

There are two common forms of phosphorus. The white form, shown here, is stored in a liquid because it bursts into flames when exposed to oxygen.

Oxygen
8
O

The flask contains oxygen, which is a colorless, odorless gas.

| | 2 He |
| Fluorine 9 Fe | Neon 10 Ne |

Gallium 31 Ga | Germaniun 32 Ge | 33 As | 34 Se | 35 Br

Nonmetals in Groups 14–16

Look at the periodic table in the back of your book. Notice that groups 14–16 contain metals, nonmetals, and metalloids. The chemical properties of the elements in each group are similar. However, the physical properties of the elements can be quite different.

Carbon is the only nonmetal in group 14. It is a solid that has different forms. Carbon is in most of the compounds that make up living things. Nitrogen, a gas, and phosphorus, a solid, are the only nonmetals in group 15. These two elements form many different compounds with other elements, such as oxygen. Group 16 contains three nonmetals. Oxygen is a gas that is essential for many organisms. Sulfur and selenium are solids that have the physical properties of other solid nonmetals.

Group 17: The Halogens

An element in group 17 of the periodic table is called a **halogen** (HA luh jun). **Figure 4** shows the halogens fluorine, chlorine, bromine, and iodine. The term *halogen* refers to an element that can react with a metal and form a salt. For example, chlorine gas reacts with solid sodium and forms sodium chloride, or table salt. Calcium chloride is another salt often used on icy roads.

Halogens react readily with other elements and form compounds. They react so readily that halogens can occur naturally only in compounds. They do not exist as free elements. They form compounds even with other nonmetals, such as carbon. In general, the halogens are less reactive as you move down the group.

Word Origin

halogen from Greek *hals*, means "salt"; and *-gen*, means "to produce"

Predict

2. Will bromine react with sodium? Explain your answer.

Figure 4 These glass containers each hold a halogen gas. Although they are different colors in their gaseous states, they react similarly with other elements.

Group 18: The Noble Gases

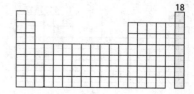

The elements in group 18 are known as the **noble gases**. The elements helium, neon, argon, krypton, xenon, and radon are the noble gases. Unlike the halogens, the only way elements in this group react with other elements is under special conditions in a laboratory. These elements were not yet discovered when Mendeleev constructed his periodic table because they do not form compounds naturally. Once they were discovered, they fit into a group at the far right side of the table.

Hydrogen

Figure 5 shows the element key for hydrogen. Of all the elements, hydrogen has the smallest atomic mass. It is also the most common element in the universe.

Is hydrogen a metal or a nonmetal? Hydrogen is most often classified as a nonmetal because it has many properties like those of nonmetals. For example, like some nonmetals, hydrogen is a gas at room temperature. However, hydrogen also has some properties similar to those of the group 1 alkali metals. In its liquid form, hydrogen conducts electricity just like a metal does. In some chemical reactions, hydrogen reacts as if it were an alkali metal. However, under conditions on Earth, hydrogen usually behaves like a nonmetal.

Copyright © McGraw-Hill Education   NASA/ESA/JPL/Arizona State Univ.

Explain

3. How does hydrogen show properties of both metals and nonmetals?

Hydrogen is a colorless, odorless gas. It is the most common element in the universe.

Hydrogen
1
H

Figure 5 More than 90 percent of all the atoms in the universe are hydrogen atoms. Hydrogen is the main fuel for the nuclear reactions that occur in stars.

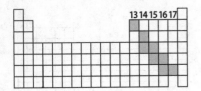

Metalloids TEKS 6.6(A)

Between the metals and the nonmetals on the periodic table are elements known as metalloids. A **metalloid** (ME tul oyd) *is an element that has physical and chemical properties of both metals and nonmetals.* The elements boron, silicon, germanium, arsenic, antimony, tellurium, polonium, and astatine are metalloids. Silicon is the most abundant metalloid in the universe. Most sand is made of a compound containing silicon. Silicon is also used in many different products, some of which are shown in **Figure 6**.

Semiconductors

Recall that metals are good conductors of thermal energy and electricity. Nonmetals are poor conductors of thermal energy and electricity but are good insulators. A property of metalloids is the ability to act as a semiconductor. A **semiconductor** *conducts electricity at high temperatures, but not at low temperatures.* At high temperatures, metalloids act like metals and conduct electricity. However, at lower temperatures, metalloids act like nonmetals and stop electricity from flowing. This property is useful in electronic devices such as computers, televisions, and solar cells.

Word Origin

semiconductor from Latin *semi-*, means "half"; and *conducere*, means "to bring together"

Uses of Silicon

Figure 6 The properties of silicon make it useful for many different products.

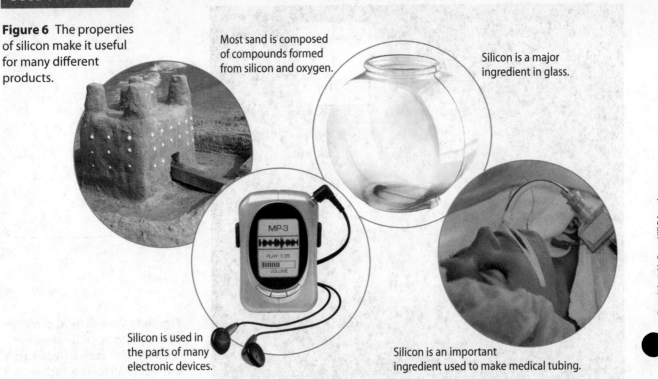

Most sand is composed of compounds formed from silicon and oxygen.

Silicon is a major ingredient in glass.

Silicon is used in the parts of many electronic devices.

Silicon is an important ingredient used to make medical tubing.

Properties and Uses of Metalloids

Pure silicon is used in making semiconductor devices for computers and other electronic products. Germanium is also used as a semiconductor. However, metalloids have other uses, as shown in **Figure 7.** Pure silicon and germanium are used in semiconductors. Boron is used in water softeners and laundry products. Boron also glows bright green in fireworks. Silicon is one of the most abundant elements on Earth. Sand, clay, and many rocks and minerals are made of silicon compounds.

Figure 7 This microchip conducts electricity at high temperatures using a semiconductor.

 Tutor

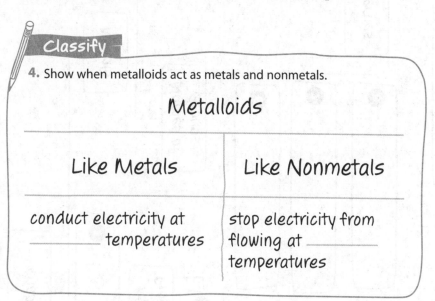

Classify

4. Show when metalloids act as metals and nonmetals.

Metalloids

Like Metals	Like Nonmetals
conduct electricity at _____ temperatures	stop electricity from flowing at _____ temperatures

Metals, Nonmetals, and Metalloids   TEKS 6.6(A)

You have read that all metallic elements have common characteristics, such as malleability, conductivity, and ductility. However, each metal has unique properties that make it different from other metals. The same is true for nonmetals and metalloids. How can knowing the properties of an element help you evaluate its uses?

Look again at the periodic table. An element's position on the periodic table tells you a lot about the element. By knowing that sulfur is a nonmetal, for example, you know that it breaks easily and does not conduct electricity. You would not choose sulfur to make a wire. You would not try to use oxygen as a semiconductor or sodium as a building material. You know that transition elements are strong, malleable, and do not react easily with oxygen or water. Because of these characteristics, these metals make good building materials. Understanding the properties of elements can help you decide which element to use in a given situation.

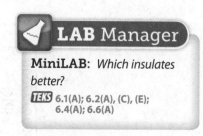

LAB Manager

MiniLAB: *Which insulates better?*
TEKS 6.1(A); 6.2(A), (C), (E); 6.4(A); 6.6(A)

Copyright © McGraw-Hill Education   PhotoLink/Getty Images

Go Online! Check Virtual

Summarize it!

Summarize the physical properties of metals, nonmetals, and metalloids. **TEKS** 6.6(A)

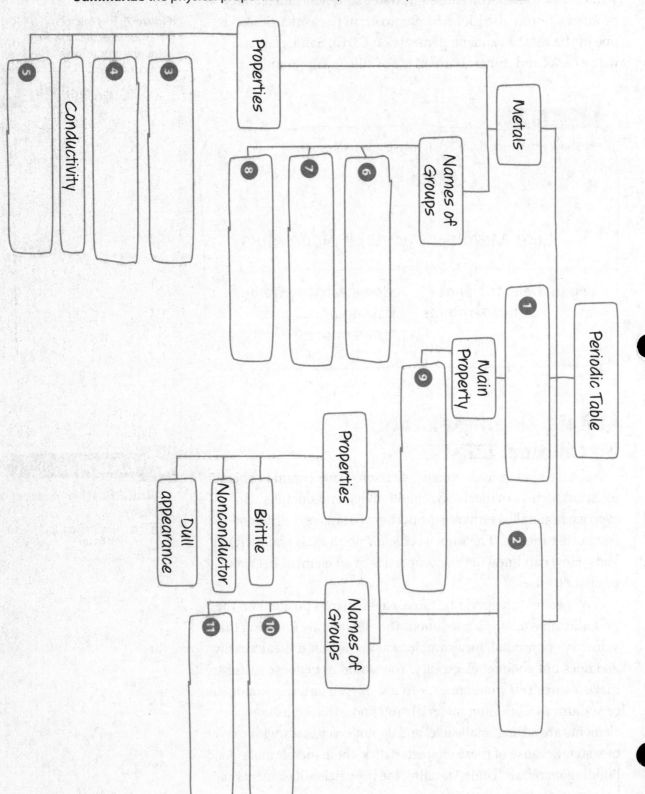

Summarize it!

Nonmetals and Metalloids

Apply the Essential Questions

1. **Classify** each of the following elements as a metal, a nonmetal, or a metalloid:
   TEKS 6.6(A) *supporting*

   boron: _____

   carbon: _____

   aluminum: _____

   silicon: _____

2. **Determine** the physical properties of iodine. **TEKS** 6.6(A) *supporting*

   _____

   _____

   _____

3. **Explain** why metalloids are most often used in electronics. **TEKS** 6.6(A) *supporting*

   _____

   _____

   _____

   _____

 H.O.T. Questions (Higher Order Thinking)

4. **Assess** how your classroom would be different if no metalloids were present.
   TEKS 6.6(A) *supporting*

   _____

   _____

   _____

   _____

5. **Recommend** an element to use to fill bottles that contain ancient paper. The element should be a gas at room temperature, should be denser than helium, and should not easily react with other elements. Explain your choice.
   TEKS 6.6(A) *supporting*

   _____

   _____

   _____

   _____

   _____

   _____

6. **Compare** metals, nonmetals, and metalloids based on their physical properties.
   TEKS 6.6(A) *supporting*

   _____

   _____

   _____

   _____

   _____

   _____

   _____

Writing in Science

7. **Create** a plan on a separate piece of paper that shows how a metal, a nonmetal, and a metalloid could be used when constructing a building. **TEKS** 6.6(A) *supporting*

The World's LARGEST Helium Well

Not Just for Balloons

What element can be used to fill both party balloons and rocket engines? It's helium! Helium is a noble gas and is the second lightest element. It has many characteristics that make it an extremely valuable resource. Helium is inert, which means that it is stable or not chemically reactive. It also has extremely low melting (-272.2°C) and boiling points (-268.9°C)!

Helium is produced in a couple ways. It can be formed by the fusion, or combining, of hydrogen atoms in stars and the fission, or splitting, of radioactive elements in Earth's crust, such as uranium. In order to use helium, it must first be isolated. Helium is separated from other gases during the extraction of natural gas from Earth's crust. Once it has been isolated, helium can be used for a variety of applications, but once it's released into the air, helium rises into the atmosphere and is lost into space.

Everyone knows that helium can make a balloon float, but it has many other important uses! Helium can be used as a pressurizing agent in liquid-filled rockets. Liquid helium is also used in superconducting magnets, which are required in tools such as MRI (magnetic resonance imaging) machines and in particle colliders.

Texas plays an important role in helium storage and distribution since it is home to the world's largest helium well. Nearly 30 percent of the world's helium supply is stored in the Federal Helium Reserve at Cliffside Storage Facility. The reserve is currently able to produce around 2 billion cubic feet of helium per year, but that rate is expected to decline soon. Because of its rate of formation, helium is a nonrenewable resource. Once the available helium is used, it cannot be replaced.

NASA uses helium to fly weather balloons that monitor and record weather related data.

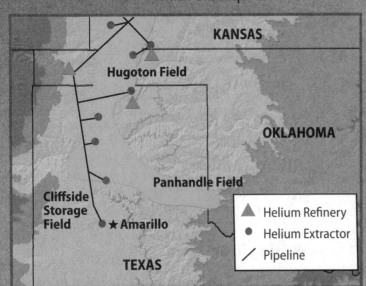

KANSAS

Hugoton Field

OKLAHOMA

Panhandle Field

Cliffside Storage Field

★ Amarillo

TEXAS

▲ Helium Refinery
● Helium Extractor
╱ Pipeline

Federal Helium Reserve outside of Amarillo, Texas

It's Your Turn!

PREDICT Why is it important to conserve helium? Explain. Predict some possible consequences of wasting this resource.

Test-Taking Strategy

Analyze a Table Tables are often used to organize data. The top row of the table is the header row. It identifies the categories of information in each column. A row usually contains different types of information (identified by the column headers) about a single object or event.

Example

Use the table to answer question 7.

Substance	Density (g/cm³)
Iron	7.9
Lead	11.3
Steel	7.8
Tungsten	19.3

① Carefully read the question and determine what it is asking. Then look at the information that is given in the table and ask yourself how it can be used to answer the question. This question asks you to identify a substance and the table gives the density of different substances.

7 Students examine a sample of an unknown substance. They determine that its mass is 15.8 g. When placed in a graduated cylinder full of water, the water level rises from 10 mL to 12 mL. What is the substance?

② TEKS 6.6(B) *supporting;* 6.2(E)

② Use the information given in the problem to calculate the density of the unknown substance. Since density equals mass divided by volume, calculate
$15.8 \text{ g} / (12 - 10 \text{ mL}) = 7.9 \text{ g/cm}^3$.

③ Find 7.9 g/cm^3 in the table. Follow the row to identify the substance. The substance is iron, choice A.

A iron

B lead

C steel

D tungsten

TIP: As you work through each question and work through problems, make notes on scrap paper or on your test booklet.

Multiple Choice

1

> Metals and nonmetals have different physical properties. One physical property of metals is that they conduct thermal energy and electricity. Metals are also malleable. This means they can be hammered into different shapes. Nonmetals are brittle, so nonmetals usually shatter when struck with a hammer. They also do not conduct thermal energy and electricity. There is an exception to this. The nonmetal carbon has one form, called graphite, which is an electrical conductor.

Based upon the physical properties of metals and nonmetals, which statement is correct?
TEKS 6.6(A) *supporting*

A Being malleable means that a material is a conductor of electricity.

B Carbon is an excellent conductor of electricity.

C Metals will break if you bend them because they are brittle.

D Copper is a good choice to make electric wires.

2

> Jamal found an interesting rock on his way home from school. As he examined it, he thought it might actually be a mineral. It was a shade of dark green. Jamal noticed that when the sunlight hit the rock, it looked shiny. Its shape was oval. It was about 10 cm long and 5 cm wide. The rock seemed cool when Jamal touched it.

Jamal has observed some of the properties of his mineral. What other properties could he test to help him identify his mineral? **TEKS** 6.6(C)

A Color

B Hardness

C Luster

D Mass

3 The table below shows a comparison of two elements. From the data, identify each element as a metal or a nonmetal. Which statement is TRUE? **TEKS** 6.6(A) *supporting;* 6.2(E)

Comparison of Two Unknown Elements	
Element 1	**Element 2**
Dull in appearance	Looks shiny
Brittle	Ductile
Shatters when struck with hammer	Malleable
Good insulator	Good conductor
Used to manufacture rubber	Used to make tableware
Density 3.1 g/mL	Density 10.5 g/mL
Melting point 11.3°C	Melting point 96.2°C

A Element 1 is a metal, like silver and Element 2 is a nonmetal, like sulfur.

B Element 1 is a nonmetal, like sulfur and Element 2 is a metal, like silver.

C Element 2 is a metal, like silver and Element 1 is a metal like iron.

D Element 2 is a nonmetal, like oxygen and Element 1 is a nonmetal, like sulfur.

---

4 Nika is measuring density in order to identify an unknown gas. In a series of experiments to measure the density of this gas, she collected the data shown in the chart below.

TEKS 6.6(B) *supporting;* 6.2(D)

Trial #	Mass	Volume
1	44.1 g	22 L
2	87.9 g	44 L
3	132.2 g	66 L
4	175.8 g	88 L
5	275 g	110 L

Which trial does not result in the same density value as the other four trials? Record and bubble in your answer on the answer grid below.

5 Yuri conducted an experiment on three metal samples. She created the table below from the data she collected. **TEKS** 6.6(B) *supporting*; 6.2(E)

Sample #	Mass	Volume
1	33.8 g	4.30 cm³
2	1.93 g	1.11 cm³
3	6.10 g	2.26 cm³

Using the density table below, identify each sample.

Metal	Density (g/cm³)
Aluminum	2.70
Copper	8.96
Lead	11.35
Iron	7.87
Magnesium	1.74
Zinc	7.13

A Sample #1 is copper; sample #2 is magnesium; sample #3 is lead.

B Sample #1 is iron; sample #2 is magnesium; sample #3 is aluminum.

C Sample #1 is iron; sample #2 is aluminum; sample #3 is copper.

D Sample #1 is zinc; sample #2 is lead; sample #3 is aluminum.

6 You have an unknown mineral you would like to identify. Which set of properties should you test to help you identify your mineral? **TEKS** 6.6(C)

A boiling point, color, conductivity, and malleability

B color, brittleness, luster, and streak

C color, hardness, luster, and streak

D hardness, luster, malleability, and streak

4

Earth's Energy Resources

💡 The **BIG** Idea

Some of Earth's energy resources are available on a nearly continual basis, some can be renewed over a short period of time, and others cannot be renewed.

LESSON

4.1 Energy Resouces

Many of Earth's resources are nonrenewable and are used faster than they can be replaced by natural processes.

TEKS 6.7(A),(B); Also covers 6.1(A); 6.2(A), (D), (E); 6.3(B), (D); 6.4(A), (B)

LESSON

4.2 Renewable Energy Resources

Renewable resources are resources that can be replaced in a relatively short amount of time. Some resources used on Earth have nearly endless supplies.

TEKS 6.7(A), (B); Also covers 6.1(A); 6.2(A), (B), (C), (D), (E); 6.3(A), (B); 6.4(A), (B)

562

Natural Resources

Four friends argued about natural resources and their impact on the environment. This is what they said:

Kate: It is better to use natural resources because they don't harm our environment like human-made resources.

Clint: It is better to use human-made resources because they don't harm our environment like natural resources.

Abby: It doesn't matter—both natural and human-made resources can harm the environment.

Troy: Neither human-made nor natural resources are harmful. They are both good for the environment.

Which friend do you agree with most? _____ Explain why you agree.

INQUIRY

What's in the pipeline?

The Trans-Alaska Pipeline System carries oil more than 1,200 km from beneath Prudhoe Bay, Alaska, to the port city of Valdez, Alaska. How might the pipeline's construction and operation affect the habitats and organisms living along it? How do getting and using fossil fuels impact the environment?

 Write your responses in your interactive notebook.

562

 LAB Manager

Go to your Lab Manual or visit connectED.mcgraw-hill.com to perform the labs for this lesson.

MiniLAB: *What is your reaction?*

TEKS 6.1(A); 6.2(A), (E); 6.3(B); 6.4(B); 6.7(A)

How do you use energy resources?

In the United States today, the energy used for most daily activities is easily available at the flip of a switch or the push of a button. How do you use energy in your daily activities?

Procedure

1. Design a three-column data chart in your Lab Manual or your interactive notebook. Title the columns *Activity, Type of Energy Used,* and *Amount of Time.*

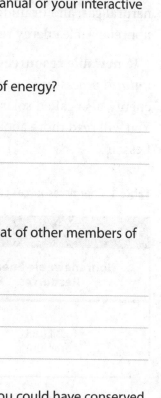

2. Record every instance that you use energy during a 24-hour period.

3. Total your usage of the different forms of energy and record them in your Lab Manual or your interactive notebook.

Think About This

1. How many times did you use each type of energy?

_____

_____

_____

2. Compare and contrast your usage with that of other members of your class.

_____

_____

_____

3. Are there instances of energy use when you could have conserved energy? Design a plan to explain how you would do it.

_____

_____

_____

_____

TEKS in this Lesson

6.7(A) Research and debate the advantages and disadvantages of using coal, oil, natural gas, nuclear power, biomass, wind, hydropower, geothermal, and solar resources.

6.7(B) Design a logical plan to manage energy resources in the home, school, or community.

Also covers Process Standards: 6.1(A); 6.2(A), (D), (E); 6.3(B), (D); 6.4(A), (B)

? Essential Questions

- What are the main sources of nonrenewable energy?
- What are the advantages and disadvantages of using nonrenewable energy resources?
- How can individuals help manage nonrenewable resources wisely?

abc Vocabulary

nonrenewable resource
renewable resource
nuclear energy
reclamation

Sources of Energy

Figure 1 The energy contained in food, gasoline, and wood originally came from the Sun.

Think about all the times you use energy in one day. Are you surprised by how much you depend on energy? You use it for electricity, transportation, recreation, and other needs. That is one reason it is important to know where energy comes from and how much is available for humans to use.

Almost all the energy you use can be traced to the Sun, as shown in **Figure 1**. For example, the chemical energy in the food you eat originally came from the Sun. The energy in fuels, such as gasoline, coal, and wood, also came from the Sun. In addition, a small amount of energy that reaches Earth's surface comes from inside Earth.

Table 1 lists different energy sources. Most energy in the United States comes from nonrenewable resources. **Nonrenewable resources** *are resources that are used faster than they can be replaced by natural processes.* Fossil fuels, such as coal, oil, and natural gas, and uranium, which is used in nuclear reactions, are nonrenewable energy resources.

Renewable resources *are resources that can be replaced by natural processes in a relatively short amount of time.* The Sun's energy, also called solar energy, is a renewable energy resource. You will read more about renewable energy resources in Lesson 2.

Table 1 Energy resources can be nonrenewable or renewable.

Table 1 Energy Sources	
Nonrenewable Energy Resources	**Renewable Energy Resources**
fossil fuels uranium	solar wind water geothermal

Identify

1. What are the main nonrenewable energy resources? Of those listed, which one is most commonly found in Texas?

_____

_____

Nonrenewable Energy Resources TEKS 6.7(A)

You might turn on a lamp to read, turn on a heater to stay warm, or ride the bus to school. In the United States, the energy to power lamps, heat houses, and run vehicles probably comes from nonrenewable energy resources, such as fossil fuels.

Fossil Fuels

Coal, oil (also called petroleum), and natural gas are fossil fuels. They are nonrenewable because they form over millions of years. The fossil fuels used today formed from the remains of prehistoric organisms. The decayed remains of these organisms were buried by layers of sediment and changed chemically by extreme temperatures and pressure. The type of fossil fuel that formed depended on three factors:

- the type of organic matter
- the temperature and pressure
- the length of time that the organic matter was buried

Coal Earth was very different 300 million years ago, when the coal used today began forming. Plants, such as ferns and trees, grew in prehistoric swamps. As shown in **Figure 2**, the first step of coal formation occurred when those plants died.

Bacteria, extreme temperatures, and pressure acted on the plant remains over time. Eventually a brownish material, called peat, formed. Peat can be used as a fuel. However, peat contains moisture and produces a lot of smoke when it burns. As shown in **Figure 2**, peat eventually can change into harder and harder types of coal. The hardest coal, anthracite, contains the most carbon per unit of volume and burns most efficiently.

Explain

2. Why are fossil fuels considered a nonrenewable resource?

Go Online! Watch

Figure 2 Much of the coal used today began forming more than 300 million years ago from the remains of prehistoric plants.

Prehistoric Swamp

When plants in prehistoric swamps died, their remains built up. Over time, sediment covered the plant remains. Inland seas formed where the swamps once were.

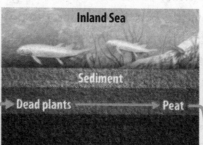

Inland Sea

Sediment

Dead plants ⟶ Peat

Bacteria broke down the organic remains, leaving behind mostly carbon. Extreme temperatures and pressure compressed the material and squeezed out gas and moisture. A brownish material, called peat, formed.

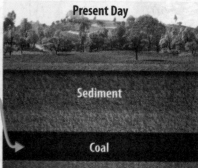

Present Day

Sediment

Coal

As additional layers of sediment covered and compacted the peat, over time it changed into successively harder types of coal.

Copyright © McGraw-Hill Education

Figure 3 Reservoirs of oil and natural gas often are under layers of impermeable rock.

Water between spaces in rock

Impermeable rock

Natural gas

Oil

Impermeable rock

Copyright © McGraw-Hill Education

Order

3. Order the steps of oil and natural gas formation.

Plankton die and fall to the ocean floor.

Bacteria decompose the material; pressure and high temperature form _____ .

Greater temperature and pressure form

_____ .

Oil and Natural Gas Like coal, the oil and natural gas used today formed millions of years ago. The process that formed oil and natural gas is similar to the process that formed coal. However, oil and natural gas formation involves different types of organisms. Scientists theorize that oil and natural gas formed from the remains of microscopic marine organisms called plankton. The plankton died and fell to the ocean floor. There, layers of sediment buried their remains. Bacteria decomposed the organic matter, and then pressure and extreme temperatures acted on the sediments. During this process, thick, liquid oil formed first. If the temperature and pressure were great enough, natural gas formed.

Most of the oil and natural gas used today formed where forces within Earth folded and tilted thick rock layers. Often hundreds of meters of sediments and rock layers covered oil and natural gas. However, oil and natural gas were less dense than the surrounding sediments and rock. As a result, oil and natural gas began to rise to the surface by passing through the pores, or small holes, in rocks. As shown in **Figure 3**, oil and natural gas eventually reached impermeable rock layers—layers of rock through which they could not pass. Deposits of oil and natural gas formed under these impermeable rocks. The less-dense natural gas settled on top of the denser oil.

Advantages of Fossil Fuels

Do you know that fossil fuels store chemical energy? Burning fossil fuels transforms this energy. The steps involved in changing chemical energy in fossil fuels into electric energy are fairly easy and direct. This process is one advantage of using these nonrenewable resources. Also, fossil fuels are relatively inexpensive and easy to transport. Coal is often transported by trains, and oil is transported by pipelines or large ships called tankers.

Because fossil fuels are inexpensive and easy to transport, they are used in a variety of ways. Coal, for example, is used to heat buildings and to produce steel and concrete. Gasoline, fuel oil, diesel, and kerosene are made from petroleum. Petroleum is also used as a raw material for making plastics. Half of the homes in the United States are heated by natural gas. Burning natural gas produces less pollution than burning other fossil fuels.

Disadvantages of Fossil Fuels

Although fossil fuels provide energy, there are disadvantages to using them.

Limited Supply One disadvantage of fossil fuels is that they are nonrenewable. No one knows for sure when supplies will be gone. Scientists estimate that, at current rates of consumption, known reserves of oil will last only another 50 years.

Habitat Disruption In addition to being nonrenewable, the process of obtaining fossil fuels disturbs environments. Coal comes from underground mines or strip mines, such as the one shown in **Figure 4**. Oil and natural gas come from wells drilled into Earth. Mines in particular disturb habitats. Forests might be fragmented, or broken into areas of trees that are no longer connected. Fragmentation can negatively affect birds and other organisms that live in forests.

Identify

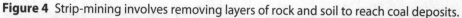

4. <u>Underline</u> how much longer scientists estimate known oil reserves are predicted to last.

Figure 4 Strip-mining involves removing layers of rock and soil to reach coal deposits.

Pollution Another disadvantage of fossil fuels as an energy resource is pollution. For example, runoff from coal mines can pollute soil and water. Oil spills from tankers can harm living things, such as the bird shown in **Figure 5**.

Pollution also occurs when fossil fuels are used. Burning fossil fuels releases chemicals into the atmosphere. These chemicals react in the presence of sunlight and produce a brownish haze. This haze can cause respiratory problems, particularly in young children. The chemicals also can react with water in the atmosphere and make rain and snow more acidic. The acidic precipitation can change the chemistry of soil and water and harm living things.

Fossil Fuels and Climate Change The burning of fossil fuels releases carbon dioxide gas into Earth's atmosphere. Carbon dioxide is one of the gases that helps keep Earth's surface warm. However, over the past 100 years, Earth's surface has warmed by about 0.7°C. Some of this warming is due to the increasing amount of carbon dioxide produced by burning fossil fuels.

Figure 5 One disadvantage of fossil fuels is pollution, which can harm living things. This bird was covered with oil after an oil spill.

Organize

5. Identify information about fossil fuels.

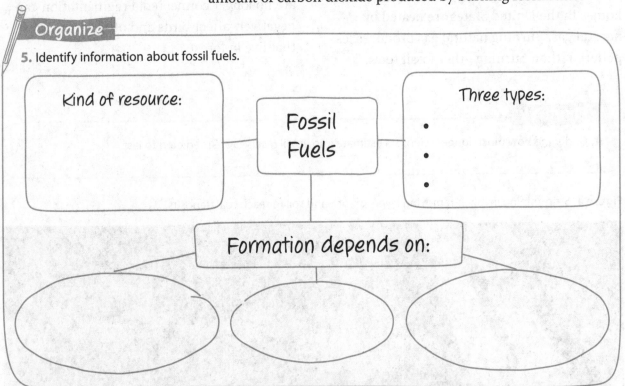

Kind of resource:

Fossil Fuels

Three types:
-
-
-

Formation depends on:

Nuclear Energy

Atoms are too small to be seen with the unaided eye. Although they are small, atoms can release large amounts of energy. *Energy released from atomic reactions is called* **nuclear energy.** Stars release nuclear energy by fusing atoms. The type of nuclear energy used on Earth involves a different process.

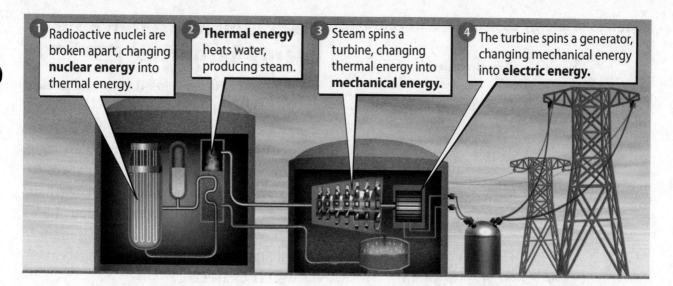

① Radioactive nuclei are broken apart, changing **nuclear energy** into thermal energy.

② **Thermal energy** heats water, producing steam.

③ Steam spins a turbine, changing thermal energy into **mechanical energy.**

④ The turbine spins a generator, changing mechanical energy into **electric energy.**

Nuclear Fission Nuclear power plants, such as the one shown in **Figure 6**, produce electricity using nuclear fission. This process splits atoms. Uranium atoms are placed into fuel rods. Neutrons are aimed at the rods and hit the uranium atoms. Each atom splits and releases two to three neutrons and thermal energy. The released neutrons hit other atoms, causing a chain reaction of splitting atoms. Countless atoms split and release large amounts of thermal energy. This energy heats water and changes it to steam. The steam turns a turbine connected to a generator, which produces electricity.

Figure 6 In a nuclear power plant, thermal energy released from splitting uranium atoms is transformed into electrical energy.

Go Online!

Advantages and Disadvantages of Nuclear Energy

One advantage of using nuclear energy is that a relatively small amount of uranium produces a large amount of energy. In addition, a well-run nuclear power plant does not pollute the air, the soil, or the water.

However, using nuclear energy has disadvantages. Nuclear power plants use a nonrenewable resource—uranium—for fuel. In addition, the chain reaction in the nuclear reactor must be carefully monitored. If it gets out of control, it can lead to a release of harmful radioactive substances into the environment.

The waste materials from nuclear power plants are highly radioactive and dangerous to living things. The waste materials remain dangerous for thousands of years. Storing them safely is important for the environment and public health.

LAB Manager

MiniLAB: *What is your reaction?*

TEKS 6.1(A); 6.2(A), (E); 6.3(B); 6.4(B); 6.7(A)

Classify

6. Highlight why it is important to control a chain reaction.

Sources of Energy Used in the U.S. in 2010

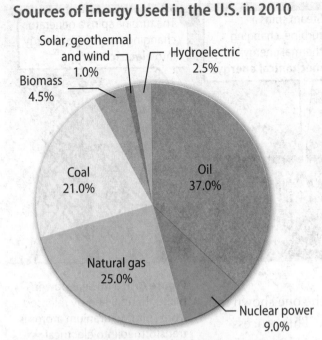

Solar, geothermal and wind 1.0%

Hydroelectric 2.5%

Biomass 4.5%

Coal 21.0%

Oil 37.0%

Natural gas 25.0%

Nuclear power 9.0%

Figure 7 About 92 percent of the energy used in the United States comes from nonrenewable resources.

FOLDABLES

Cut out the Lesson 4.1 Foldable in the back of your book. Use it to compare and contrast the use of fossil fuels and nuclear energy.

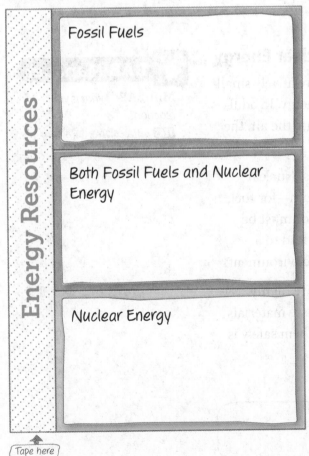

Energy Resources

Fossil Fuels

Both Fossil Fuels and Nuclear Energy

Nuclear Energy

Tape here

Managing Nonrenewable Energy Resources TEKS 6.7(B)

As shown in **Figure 7**, fossil fuels and nuclear energy provide about 92 percent of U.S. energy. Because these sources eventually will be gone, we must understand how to manage and conserve them. This is important because energy use in the United States is higher than in other countries. Although only about 4.5 percent of the world's population lives in the United States, it uses more than 22 percent of the world's total energy.

Management Solutions

Mined land must be reclaimed. **Reclamation** *is a process in which mined land must be recovered with soil and replanted with vegetation.* Laws also help ensure that mining and drilling take place in an environmentally safe manner. In the United States, the Clean Air Act limits the amount of pollutants that can be released into the air. In addition, the U.S. Atomic Energy Act and the Energy Policy Act include regulations that protect people from nuclear emissions.

What You Can Do

Have you ever heard of vampire energy? Vampire energy is the energy used by appliances and other electronic equipment, such as microwave ovens, washing machines, televisions, and computers that are plugged in 24 hours per day. Even when turned off, they still consume energy. These appliances consume about 5 percent of the energy used each year. You can conserve energy by unplugging DVD players, printers, and other appliances when they are not in use.

You also can walk or ride your bike to help conserve energy. And, you can use renewable energy resources, which you will learn about in the next lesson.

4.1 Review

Research the advantages and disadvantages of fossil fuels and nuclear energy.
Use the information you find to fill in the table below. **TEKS** 6.7(A)

	Advantages	Disadvantages
Fossil Fuels		
Nuclear Energy		

 Connect it! If you were choosing to move to a new town based on energy management, which kind of power plant would you look for to produce your electricity? Why? Write your response in your interactive notebook. Discuss your responses with a partner.

Summarize it!

Energy Resources

Use Vocabulary

1. **Define** fossil fuels in your own words.
   TEKS 6.7(A)

_____

_____

Apply the Essential Questions

2. **Identify** the source of most energy in the United States. Why is it used over other types of energy? **TEKS** 6.7(A)

_____

_____

_____

3. **Summarize** the advantages and disadvantages of using nonrenewable energy resources. **TEKS** 6.7(A)

_____

_____

_____

_____

4. **Draw** a comic strip on a separate piece of paper showing one example of conserving energy. **TEKS** 6.7(B)

🔥 **H.O.T. Questions** (Higher Order Thinking)

5. **Analyze** Do the advantages of using fossil fuels outweigh the disadvantages? Explain your answer. **TEKS** 6.7(A)

_____

_____

6. **Evaluate** Suppose the house below is heated by electricity produced from burning coal. Which areas of the house have the greatest loss of thermal energy? Why is it important for the residents to reduce thermal energy loss? **TEKS** 6.7(A)

_____

_____

_____

_____

7. **Research** Suppose that a nuclear power plant will be built near your town. Would you support the plan? Why or why not? **TEKS** 6.7(A)

_____

_____

_____

Writing in Science

8. **Design** a plan on a separate sheet of paper that manages the usage of energy resources in your home. **TEKS** 6.7(B)

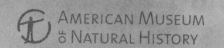

Fossil Fuels and Rising CO₂ Levels

Investigate the link between energy use and carbon dioxide in the atmosphere.

You use energy every day—when you ride in a car or on a bus, turn on a television, and even when you send an e-mail.

Much of the energy that produces electric current, heats and cools buildings, and powers engines comes from burning fossil fuels— coal, oil, and natural gas. When fossil fuels burn, the carbon in them combines with oxygen in the atmosphere and forms carbon dioxide gas (CO_2). Carbon dioxide is one of the greenhouse gases. In the atmosphere, greenhouse gases absorb energy. This causes the atmosphere and Earth's surface to become warmer. Greenhouse gases make Earth warm enough to support life. Without greenhouse gases, Earth's surface would be frozen.

However, over the past 150 years, the amount of CO_2 in the atmosphere has increased faster than at any time in the past 800,000 years. Most of this increase is the result of burning fossil fuels. This additional carbon dioxide will cause average global temperatures to increase. As temperatures increase, weather patterns worldwide could change. More storms and heavier rainfall could occur in some areas, and other regions could become drier. Increased temperatures also will cause more of the polar ice sheets to melt, causing sea levels to rise. Higher sea levels will cause more flooding in coastal areas.

Developing other energy sources, such as geothermal, solar, nuclear, wind, and hydroelectric power, would reduce the use of fossil fuels and slow the increase in atmospheric CO_2.

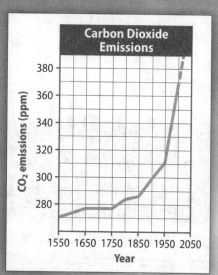

Carbon Dioxide Emissions

CO_2 emissions (ppm) vs. Year (1550, 1650, 1750, 1850, 1950, 2050)

300 Years OF CARBON DIOXIDE

1712
A new invention, the steam engine, is powered by burning coal that heats water to produce steam.

Early 1800s
Coal-fired steam engines, able to pull heavy trains and power steamboats, transform transportation.

1882
Companies make and sell electric energy from coal for everyday use. Electricity was used to power the first lightbulbs, which give off 20 times the light of a candle.

1908
The first mass-produced automobiles are made available. By 1915, Ford is selling 500,000 cars per year. Oil becomes the fuel of choice for car engines.

Late 1900s
Electric appliances transform the way we live, work, and communicate. Most electricity is generated by coal-burning power plants.

2007
There are more than 800 million cars and light trucks on the world's roads.

It's Your Turn!

MAKE A LIST How can CO_2 emissions be reduced? Work with a partner. List five ways people in your home, school, or community could reduce their energy consumption. Combine your and your classmates' lists to make a master list.

4.2 Renewable Energy Resources

INQUIRY

What do these panels do? These solar panels convert energy from the Sun into electrical energy. These panels at Webberville Solar Farm in Manor, Texas, produce enough electricity to power 5,000 homes. What are some of the advantages of using energy from the Sun? What are some of the disadvantages?

Write your responses in your interactive notebook.

LAB Manager

Go to your Lab Manual or visit connectED.mcgraw-hill.com to perform the labs for this lesson.

MiniLAB: *How are renewable energy resources used at your school?*
TEKS 6.2(A), (E); 6.4(A); 6.7(B)

Skill Practice: *How can you analyze energy use data for information to help conserve energy?*
TEKS 6.2(A), (E); 6.7(B)

Skill Practice: *What color is best for solar panels?*
TEKS 6.1(A); 6.2(B), (C), (D), (E); 6.3(A); 6.4(A), (B); 6.7(A)

LAB: *Pinwheel Power*
TEKS 6.1(A); 6.2(A), (C), (D), (E); 6.3(B); 6.4(A), (B); 6.7(A)

How are energy resources different?

Is there an infinite supply of usable energy, or could we someday run out of energy resources? In this activity, the red beans represent an energy resource that is available in limited amounts. The white beans represent an energy resource that is available in unlimited amounts.

Procedure

1. Read and complete a lab safety form.

2. Place **40 red beans** and **40 white beans** in a **paper bag.** Mix the contents of the bag.

3. Each team should remove 20 beans from the bag without looking at the beans. Record the numbers of red and white beans.

4. Put the red beans aside. They are "used up." Return all the white beans to the bag. Mix the beans in the bag. Repeat steps 3 and 4 three more times.

Think About This

1. What would eventually happen to the red beans in the bag?

_____

_____

2. How would changing the number of beans drawn in each round make the red beans last longer? Explain your answer.

_____

_____

_____

3. What do you think are the advantages of using energy resources available in unlimited amounts over resources available in limited amounts?

_____

_____

_____

_____

TEKS in this Lesson

6.7(A) Research and debate the advantages and disadvantages of using coal, oil, natural gas, nuclear power, biomass, wind, hydropower, geothermal, and solar resources

6.7(B) Design a logical plan to manage energy resources in the home, school, or community.

Also covers Process Standards: 6.1(A); 6.2(A), (B), (C), (D), (E); 6.3(A), (B); 6.4(A), (B)

? Essential Questions

- What are the main sources of renewable energy?

- What are the advantages and disadvantages of using renewable energy resources?

- What can individuals do to encourage the use of renewable energy resources?

abc Vocabulary

solar energy
wind farm
hydroelectric power
geothermal energy
biomass energy

Renewable Energy Resources

TEKS 6.7(A)

Could you stop the Sun from shining or the wind from blowing? These might seem like silly questions, but they help make an important point about renewable resources. Renewable resources come from natural processes that have been happening for billions of years and will continue to happen.

Solar Energy

Solar energy *is energy from the Sun.* Because the Sun will produce energy for billions of years, solar energy is considered an inexhaustible energy resource. An inexhaustible energy resource is an energy resource that is available on a nearly continuous basis.

Solar cells, such as those in watches and calculators, capture light energy and transform it to electrical energy. Solar power plants can generate electricity for large areas. They transform radiant energy, energy in sunlight, into electrical energy, which then turns turbines connected to generators.

Some people use solar energy in their homes, as shown in **Figure 1**. Active solar energy uses technology such as solar panels, which gather and store solar energy that heats water and homes. Passive solar energy uses design elements that capture energy in sunlight. For example, windows on the south side of a house can let in sunlight that helps heat a room.

Figure 1 People can use solar energy to provide electricity for their homes.

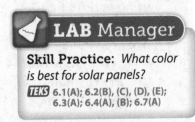

LAB Manager

Skill Practice: *What color is best for solar panels?*

TEKS 6.1(A); 6.2(B), (C), (D), (E); 6.3(A); 6.4(A), (B); 6.7(A)

Identify

1. Why is solar energy considered to be an inexhaustible energy resource?

_____

_____

_____

_____

Wind Energy

Have you ever dropped your school papers outside and had them scattered by the wind? If so, then you experienced wind energy. Wind energy is another inexhaustible energy resource. This renewable resource has been used since ancient times to sail boats and to turn windmills. Today, wind turbines such as the ones shown in **Figure 2** can produce electricity on a large scale. The wind turbines convert the kinetic energy in wind into electric energy. Wind spins a propeller that is connected to an electric generator. *A group of wind turbines that produce electricity is called a* **wind farm.**

Water Energy

A widely used renewable energy resource is flowing water. Water energy produces electricity using different methods, such as hydroelectric power and tidal power.

Hydroelectric Power *Electricity produced by flowing water is called* **hydroelectric power.** To produce hydroelectric power, humans build a dam across a powerful river. **Figure 3** shows how flowing water is used to produce electricity.

Tidal Power Coastal areas that have great differences between high and low tides can be a source of tidal power. Water flows across turbines as the tide comes in during high tides and as it goes out during low tides. The flowing water turns turbines connected to generators that produce electricity.

Figure 2 Offshore wind farms are called wind parks. This wind park is in Denmark.

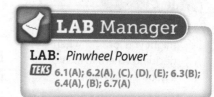

LAB Manager

LAB: *Pinwheel Power*
TEKS 6.1(A); 6.2(A), (C), (D), (E); 6.3(B); 6.4(A), (B); 6.7(A)

Figure 3 In a hydroelectric power plant, energy from flowing water produces electricity.

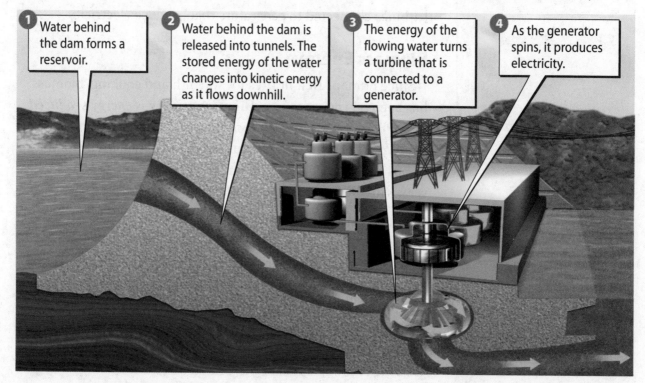

1 Water behind the dam forms a reservoir.

2 Water behind the dam is released into tunnels. The stored energy of the water changes into kinetic energy as it flows downhill.

3 The energy of the flowing water turns a turbine that is connected to a generator.

4 As the generator spins, it produces electricity.

Figure 4 Geothermal power plants use thermal energy from Earth's interior to produce electricity.

Go Online!
Watch

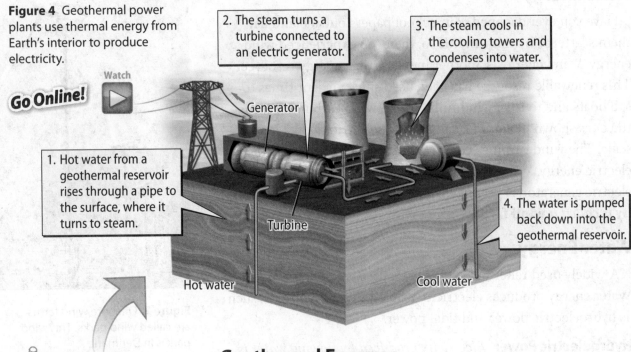

2. The steam turns a turbine connected to an electric generator.

3. The steam cools in the cooling towers and condenses into water.

Generator

1. Hot water from a geothermal reservoir rises through a pipe to the surface, where it turns to steam.

Turbine

4. The water is pumped back down into the geothermal reservoir.

Hot water

Cool water

2. Which land features might you look for when deciding where to locate a geothermal plant?

_____

_____

_____

_____

_____

Geothermal Energy

Earth's core is nearly as hot as the Sun's surface. This thermal energy flows outward to Earth's surface. *Thermal energy from Earth's interior is called* **geothermal energy.** This energy comes from the decay of radioactive nuclei deep inside Earth. It can be used to heat homes and generate electricity in power plants such as the one shown in **Figure 4**. People drill wells to reach hot, dry rocks or bodies of magma. The thermal energy from the hot rocks or magma heats water that makes steam. The steam turns turbines connected to generators that produce electricity.

Biomass Energy

Since humans first lit fires for warmth and cooking, biomass has been an energy source. **Biomass energy** *is energy produced by burning organic matter, such as wood, food scraps, and alcohol.* Wood is the most widely used biomass. Industrial wood scraps and organic materials such as grass clippings and food scraps are burned to generate electricity on a large scale.

Biomass also can be converted into fuels for vehicles. Ethanol is made from sugars in plants such as corn. Ethanol often is blended with gasoline. This reduces the amount of oil used to make the gasoline. Adding ethanol to gasoline also reduces the amount of carbon monoxide and other pollutants released by vehicles. Another renewable fuel, biodiesel, is made from vegetable oils and fats. It emits few pollutants and is the fastest-growing renewable fuel in the United States.

FOLDABLES

Make a vertical five-tab Foldable. Label the tabs as illustrated. Identify the advantages and disadvantages of alternative energy sources.

Solar

Wind

Water

Geothermal

Biomass

Describe how people make use of renewable energy.

Type	Description of Its Use
Solar energy	
Wind energy (Wind farms)	
Hydroelectric power	
Tidal power	
Geothermal energy	
Biomass energy	

Connect it! **Research** whether renewable energy resources are being used in Texas. If they are, which ones are being used? Are there any near your hometown? **TEKS** 6.7(A)

Advantages and Disadvantages of Renewable Resources TEKS 6.7(A)

A big advantage of using renewable energy resources is that they are renewable. They will be available for millions of years to come. In addition, renewable energy resources produce less pollution than fossil fuels.

There are disadvantages associated with using renewable resources, however. Some are costly or limited to certain areas. For example, large-scale geothermal plants are limited to areas with tectonic activity. Recall that tectonic activity involves the movement of Earth's plates. **Table 1** lists the advantages and disadvantages of using renewable energy resources.

Table 1 Most renewable energy resources produce little or no pollution.

Watch
Go Online!

Table 1	Renewable Resources—Advantages and Disadvantages	
Renewable Resource	**Advantages**	**Disadvantages**
Solar energy	• nonpolluting • available in the United States	• less energy produced on cloudy days • no energy produced at night • high cost of solar cells • requires a large surface area to collect and produce energy on a large scale
Wind energy	• nonpolluting • relatively inexpensive • available in the United States	• large-scale use limited to areas with strong, steady winds • best sites for wind farms are far from urban areas and transmission lines • potential impact on bird populations
Water energy	• nonpolluting • available in the United States	• large-scale use limited to areas with fast-flowing rivers or great tidal differences • negative impact on aquatic ecosystems • production of electricity affected by long periods of little or no rainfall
Geothermal energy	• produces little pollution • available in the United States	• large-scale use limited to tectonically active areas • habitat disruption from drilling to build a power plant
Biomass energy	• reduces amount of organic material discarded in landfills • available in the United States	• air pollution results from burning some forms of biomass • less energy efficient than fossil fuels, costly to transport

Managing Renewable Energy Resources TEKS 6.7(B)

Renewable energy currently meets only 8 percent of U.S. energy needs. As shown in **Figure 5**, most renewable energy comes from biomass. Solar energy, wind energy, and geothermal energy meet only a small percentage of U.S. energy needs. However, some states are passing laws that require the state's power companies to produce a percentage of electricity using renewable resources. Management of renewable resources often focuses on encouraging their use.

Management Solutions

The U.S. government has begun programs to encourage use of renewable resources. In 2009, billions of dollars were granted to the U.S. Department of Energy's Office of Efficiency and Renewable Energy for renewable energy research and programs that reduce the use of fossil fuels.

What You Can Do

You might be too young to own a house or a car, but you can help educate others about renewable energy resources. You can talk with your family about ways to use renewable energy at home. You can participate in a renewable energy fair at school. As a consumer, you also can make a difference by buying products that are made using renewable energy resources.

Energy Resources in the United States

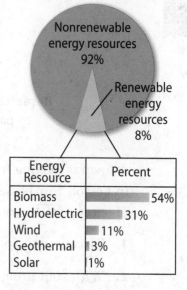

Energy Resource	Percent
Biomass	54%
Hydroelectric	31%
Wind	11%
Geothermal	3%
Solar	1%

Figure 5 The renewable energy resource used most in the United States is biomass energy.

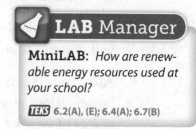

LAB Manager

MiniLAB: *How are renewable energy resources used at your school?*

TEKS 6.2(A), (E); 6.4(A); 6.7(B)

 TEKS 6.4(A); 6.7(B)

Manage Energy Resources in Your School

The energy that you use every day can come from nonrenewable energy resources or renewable resources. How are resources used in your school? How can you manage them wisely?

1. With a partner, research how energy is used in your school. For example, when are lights turned on and off? Is electronic equipment always on? You can interview a school administrator or facilities manager.

2. With your partner, design a plan to manage and reduce the usage of energy in your school. Be sure the solutions are realistic.

3. When your plan is finalized, create a computer slide show presentation to outline your plan to the class. Listen to the other presentations and take notes.

4. After the presentations, as a class, select the best solutions and present them to the principal, school administrator, or facilities manager.

4.2 Review

Research and debate nonrenewable and renewable resources by participating in a debate on Earth's energy resources.

A town is looking to receive its electricity from one of the resources discussed in Lesson 1 or Lesson 2. Your groups will argue for or against using the forms of energy. TEKS 6.3(A); 6.7(A)

1. Discuss with your teacher the procedures and rules for a debate.

2. With your group, research the advantages and disadvantages of using the energy resource assigned to you by your teacher. Your teacher will also instruct whether you will argue for the advantages or disadvantages of your assigned energy resource. Use Internet resources or resources from the library. Record your research in your interactive notebook.

3. Prepare a slide show presentation to support your stated opinions. Each team will present its arguments to the class.

4. After your team's presentation, listen carefully to the counterargument presentations given by the other teams. Take notes to record the different points of view for each energy resource. Follow the debate rules for counter-arguments as instructed by your teacher.

5. After each argument has been presented, conduct a class survey to determine which team won the debate.

Connect it! Analyze Suppose that you have two friends who want to use a renewable energy resource to heat their homes. One friend lives in Arizona, and the other lives in Michigan. What suggestions could you offer? Write your response in your interactive notebook.

Renewable Energy Resources

Apply the Essential Questions

1. **Analyze** Your family wants to use renewable energy to heat your home. Which renewable energy resource is best suited to your area? Explain your answer. **TEKS** 6.7(A)

_____

_____

_____

_____

2. **Evaluate** the advantages and disadvantages of using renewable energy resources. **TEKS** 6.7(A)

_____

_____

_____

_____

_____

3. **Design** a poster on a separate piece of paper that encourages individuals to use renewable energy resources. **TEKS** 6.7(B)

H.O.T. Questions (Higher Order Thinking)

4. **Compare and contrast** the advantages and disadvantages of solar energy and wind energy. **TEKS** 6.7(A)

_____

_____

_____

5. **Evaluate** Research how geothermal energy is used in homes. Is it similar to how geothermal power plants work? Is it different? What is an advantage and disadvantage to using it in your home? Explain. **TEKS** 6.7(A)

_____

_____

_____

_____

_____

6. **Explain** why biomass fuels are often used by developing countries. What are the disadvantages to biofuels? **TEKS** 6.7(A)

_____

_____

_____

_____

Writing in Science

7. **Critique** Climate change and depletion of fossil fuels might make you ask about solar energy. Research the size and cost of the solar panels necessary to power a typical home in the United States. Do the benefits outweigh the cost? Write an essay on a separate piece of paper to discuss your findings. **TEKS** 6.7(A)

8. **Research** a town in the United States that uses hydroelectric power. What advantages of hydroelectric power has the town experienced? What disadvantages? Discuss your findings on a separate piece of paper. **TEKS** 6.7(A)

Green SCIENCE

A Greener Greensburg

AMERICAN MUSEUM ᴼꜰ NATURAL HISTORY

A town struck by disaster makes the world a greener place.

In May 2007, a powerful tornado struck the small Kansas town of Greensburg. The tornado destroyed almost every home, school, and business. Six months later, the town's officials and residents decided to rebuild Greensburg as a model green community.

The town's residents pledged to use fewer natural resources; to produce clean, renewable energy; and to reuse and recycle waste. As part of this effort, every new home and building would be designed for energy efficiency. The homes also would be constructed of materials that are healthful for the people who live and work in them.

What is a model green town? Here are some ways Greensburg will help the environment, save money, and make life better for its residents.

Rain gardens help improve water quality by filtering pollutants from runoff.

USE RENEWABLE ENERGY

- **Produce clean energy** with renewable energy sources such as wind and sunlight. Wind turbines capture the abundant wind power of the Kansas plains.

- **Cut back on greenhouse gas emissions** with electric or hybrid city vehicles.

- **Make the most of natural daylight** for indoor lighting with many windows, which also can be opened for fresh air.
- **Use green materials** that are nontoxic and locally grown or made from recycled materials.

CONSERVE WATER

- **Capture runoff and rainwater** with landscape features such as rain gardens, bowl-shaped gardens designed to collect and absorb excess rainwater.
- **Use low-flow** faucets, showerheads, and toilets.

BUILD GREEN BUILDINGS

- **Design every home, school, and office** to use less energy and promote better health.

CREATE A HEALTHY ENVIRONMENT

- **Provide parks and green spaces** filled with native plants that need little water or care.
- **Create a "walkable community"** that encourages people to drive less and be more active and that has a town center connected to neighborhoods by sidewalks and trails.

It's Your Turn!

PROBLEM SOLVING With your group, design a logical plan to manage energy resources in the home, school, or community.

Test-Taking Strategy

Identify Signal Words Signal words are used to identify exactly what is being asked in a question. These words help to clarify what information you need to use in order to correctly answer the question.

Example

Use the chart below to answer question 3.

Sources of Energy Used in the U.S. in 2010

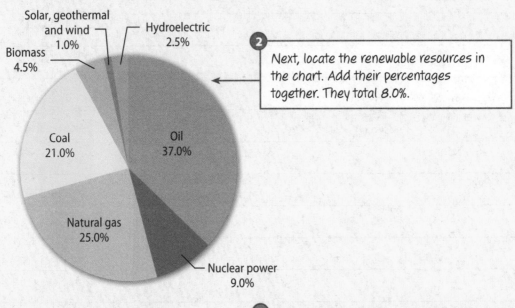

2 Next, locate the renewable resources in the chart. Add their percentages together. They total *8.0%*.

3 What combined percentage of energy used in the United States comes from renewable resources?
TEKS 6.7(A)

A 1.0%

B 2.5%

C 8.0%

D 9.0%

1 Carefully read the question and identify signal words to understand what the question is asking. The words *combined percentage* let us know that we are going to have to add percentages together. In this case, we are asked to combine the percentages of energy for all the *renewable resources*.

3 Find *8.0%* in the possible answers. The correct answer is choice *C*.

Tip: Each question will have important words that will tell you exactly what you information you need. Other important signal words include *not, no, never, now, always, only, best, except,* and *exactly*.

Multiple Choice

1 Maria and her classmates are designing a plan to help manage energy use at their school. They want to choose the best type of light bulbs so the school can save energy and lower costs. Maria finds this table with data comparing different types of light bulbs. Which is the most logical way for Maria and her classmates to use this data? **TEKS** 6.7(B); 6.1(B)

Bulb type	Lifespan in hours	Watts per bulb	Price per bulb	Bulbs needed for 50,000 hours use	Energy usage per 50,000 hours (KWh)
LED	50,000	10	$20.00	1	400
CFL	10,000	14	$2.00	5	700
Incandescent	1,200	60	$1.00	42	3000

A lifespan in hours, energy usage per 50,000 hours, and bulbs needed per 50,000 hours use

B the number of bulbs needed for 50,000 hours use, the energy usage per 50,000 hours, and the price per bulb

C the price per bulb, the bulbs needed for 50,000 hours use only, and ignore the rest of the data

D the price per bulb, the lifespan in hours only, and ignore the rest of the data

2

> Matthew and Sarah live in a town that gets electricity from a local power company. One very hot day in August, homes and businesses turned on their air conditioning. During the hottest part of the day, Matthew and Sarah noticed that the lights of various store signs were dimming. Matthew and Sarah decided to develop a plan for keeping their houses cooler on hot days without overusing their air conditioners.

What is the most logical plan that Matthew and Sarah should develop to conserve energy? **TEKS** 6.7(B); 6.1(B)

A Close the curtains on the shady side of the house only, open the doors to all rooms, and set the air conditioning to a slightly warmer temperature.

B Close the curtains on the sunny side of the house only, close the doors to unused rooms, and set the air conditioner to a slightly warmer temperature.

C Open the curtains on the shady side of the house only, close the doors to unused rooms, and set the air conditioning to the usual temperature.

D Open the curtains on the sunny side of the house only, open the doors to all rooms, and set the air conditioning to a slightly cooler temperature.

3 Javier wants to install solar panels at his house. He has a brochure that includes this graph. The brochure also claims that solar panels help save money on the cost of electricity. **TEKS** 6.7(A); 6.2(E)

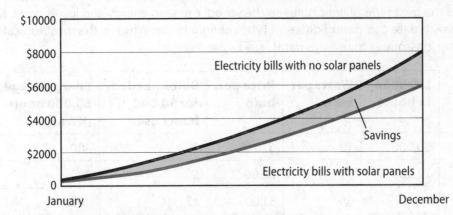

Based on the graph, how much money will Javier save over one year because of the solar panels? Record and bubble your answer in the answer document.

4

> Julia is preparing for a class debate on alternative fuels such as biodiesel. Biodiesel can be used as fuel in cars and trucks. She learns that many crop plants, such as soybeans, corn, and cotton, can be used to make biodiesel. Julia decides that this makes biodiesel the ideal fuel because you can make more just by growing more plants.

Which is one challenge to Julia's position that her debate opponents could use? Growing more plants for biodiesel fuel _____ . **TEKS** 6.7(A); 6.2(E)

A means that the crops for biodiesel need to be transported longer distances.

B takes land and water that could be used for growing food.

C will make us less dependent on oil.

D will only supply enough biodiesel for the months after harvest time.

5

A small city builds a reservoir for drinking water in a mountain valley. The mountain valley is located several hundred miles away. The water flows downhill to the city, so there is no need to use pumps to bring the water to the city. The city also uses the flowing water to turn turbines in a hydropower plant. This plant produces electricity for the city's light rail system.

Which is a disadvantage of using this type of power system? **TEKS** 6.7(A); 6.3(A)

A It is expensive to run water pumps.

B The building of the dam, reservoir, and power plant destroys habitats.

C The dam is too far from the city.

D The plant will burn fossil fuels that will pollute the air in the city.

---

6 The U.S. has a large percentage of the world's coal resources. These resources can provide enough coal to last at least 200 years. Coal is burned as fuel to generate electrical power. Almost 40% of electrical power in Texas comes from burning coal. Based on this information, which best summarizes the advantages and disadvantages of coal power? **TEKS** 6.7(A); 6.3(A)

	Advantages	Disadvantages
A	Coal is good for generating solar power.	Coal resources in the U.S. may run out in 200 years.
B	There is enough coal in the U.S. for the entire world.	Coal is expensive to mine and transport to power plants.
C	Coal resources are currently plentiful.	Coal releases pollutants when it is burned.
D	Coal can be imported from other countries.	Coal mining can damage plants and animals.

My Notes

TEKS Strand 3
Force, Motion, and Energy

![TEKS] **in this strand**

✓ **6.8** The student knows force and motion are related to potential and kinetic energy.

✓ **6.9** The student knows that the Law of Conservation of Energy states that energy can neither be created nor destroyed, it just changes form.

✓ Also includes the following Scientific Investigation and Reasoning strand TEKS: **6.1; 6.2; 6.3; 6.4**

Texas Fun Fact

Did You Know? The longest zipline in Texas is at Lake Travis, just outside Austin. Imagine the thrill of soaring more than 600 meters above the water and canyons suspended from a pulley on a stainless steel cable. So, whether you call it a zipline, flying fox, zip wire, aerial runway, aerial ropeslide, or canopy tour, gravity can propel you to the time of your life.

Force and Motion

The **BIG** Idea
The motion and energy of an object are changed by a pushing or pulling force which affects its potential and kinetic energies.

Beach Ball

When does gravitational force act on a beach ball? Check off all the descriptions that are examples of gravity acting on a beach ball.

- [ ] **A.** Beach ball tossed up into the air, moving upward

- [ ] **B.** Beach ball falling downward after it is tossed into the air

- [ ] **C.** Beach ball floating in a swimming pool

- [ ] **D.** Person holding a beach ball

- [ ] **E.** Beach ball resting on the ground, not moving

Explain your thinking in the space below. What rule or reasoning did you use to decide when gravity acts on a beach ball?

INQUIRY

How are they moving? As people move about a mall, the motion of each person changes. They speed up, slow down, and change direction. How would you describe the position of a person at any moment in time? What words could you use to describe the person's motion?

Write your response in your interactive notebook.

LAB Manager

Go to your Lab Manual or visit connectED.mcgraw-hill.com to perform the labs for this lesson.
MiniLAB: *How can you determine average speed?*
TEKS 6.1(A); 6.2(A), (C), (E); 6.4(A), (B); 6.8(C)

Skill Practice: *How can you test and describe an object's motion?*
TEKS 6.1(A); 6.2(A), (C), (D), (E); 6.4(A), (B); 6.8(C)

Explore Activity

Where are you right now?

Suppose you place a pencil next to a book. How could you describe the location of the pencil? You could say it is next to the book. A clearer description might be 5 cm to the right of the book. How can you write a clear description of where an object is located?

Procedure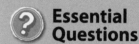

1. Choose an **object in your classroom,** such as a chair. Work with others in your group to describe the location of the object.

2. Discuss the description with your group. Does it clearly describe the object's location? If not, work together to change the description.

3. Get a **card** from your teacher that names a place, such as your school or your city. In your Lab Manual or interactive notebook, write a description of where you are within the place written on your card. Could someone find you using your description? Share and discuss your description with others in your group.

Think About This

1. Was there only one possible description in each case, or more than one? Why?

_____

_____

_____

_____

2. What three things do you think make up a good description of where an object or a person is located?

_____

_____

_____

_____

TEKS in this Lesson

6.8(C) Calculate average speed using distance and time measurements

Also covers Process Standards: 6.1(A); 6.2(A), (C), (D), (E); 6.4(A), (B)

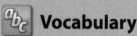 Essential Questions

- How do you describe an object's motion?
- How can you calculate average speed?

Vocabulary

reference point
position
displacement
motion
speed
velocity
acceleration

163

Word Origin

reference
from Latin *referre*, means
"to carry or direct back"

Interpret

1. How do you describe an object's position?

_____

_____

_____

_____

_____

_____

_____

Describing Position

Think about calling a friend on his or her cell phone. One of the first questions you might ask is, "Where are you?" Your friend might answer, "I am at the mall" or "I am two blocks north of school" or "I am 3 m away from you. Look down the hall."

What do all these answers have in common? Each one has a reference point that helps describe your friend's position. A **reference point** *is the starting point you choose to describe the location, or position, of an object.* In the example above, your friend describes his or her location by starting with a reference point, such as the mall, the school, or even you. Then your friend compares his or her position to that reference point.

Your friend also gives you other information to describe his or her location. Your friend might tell you a distance, such as 2 blocks or 3 m. Your friend might also mention a direction, such as north or down the hall. In doing so, your friend describes his or her position. **Position** *describes an object's distance and direction from a reference point.* Position always includes a distance, a direction, and a reference point.

Apply

2. Analyze the position in each description below. Note the distance, direction, and reference point. Then, in the space to the right, draw a diagram representing the description.

The park is 3 km west of the school.

A rock fell down from a 30 m-high cliff.

Using Reference Points

Suppose you are watching a soccer game. The position of a player depends on a reference point, as shown in **Figure 1.** If the reference point is the goal, or point A, the player's position is 10 m in front of the goal. If the reference point is center field, point B, the position of the player is 40 m toward the goal. Notice that the actual location of the player has not changed. Only the description of the position changed because the reference point changed.

Distance and Displacement

During one play in the soccer game shown in **Figure 1,** the player runs 41.2 m from position D to position C. Then she runs 10 m to position B. Her path is shown by the dotted blue lines. The total distance the player travels is 41.2 m + 10 m = 51.2 m.

The solid blue arrow in **Figure 1** shows the player's displacement. **Displacement** *is the difference between the initial, or starting, position and the final position.* The player starts at point D and finishes at point B. Her displacement is 40 m in front of her initial position. An object's displacement and the distance it travels are not always equal.

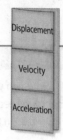
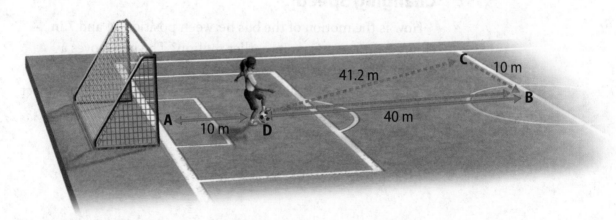

Figure 1 The position of the ball depends on the reference point. The distance traveled by the player and her displacement are not the same.

Describe

3. How would you describe the position of point B in **Figure 1** without using the words *center line*?

_____

_____

Copyright © McGraw-Hill Education

Motion

Suppose that with 5 s left on the clock during a soccer game, the ball is 50 m from the goal. When the game ends, the ball is in the goal. What happened to the ball during the last 5 s of the game? The ball was in motion. **Motion** *is the process of changing position.*

Speed TEKS 6.8(C)

How fast does the vehicle that takes you to a soccer game move? On a highway, it might move fast. In traffic, it probably moves more slowly. **Speed** *is the distance an object moves in a unit of time.* Any unit of time, such as 1 s, 1 min, 1 h, or 1 y, may be used to calculate average speed. For example, a bus might travel 15 km/h or 0.25 km/min.

Constant Speed

The bus in **Figure 2** moves from positions 1 to 2 to 3 to 4 at the same speed of 2 m/s. When an object moves the same distance over a given unit of time, it is said to have a constant speed. The bus has a constant speed from positions 1 to 4.

Changing Speed

How is the motion of the bus between positions 4 and 7 in **Figure 2** different from its earlier motion? The bus moves a greater distance each second. When the distance an object moves increases or decreases over a given unit of time, the object is said to be changing speed.

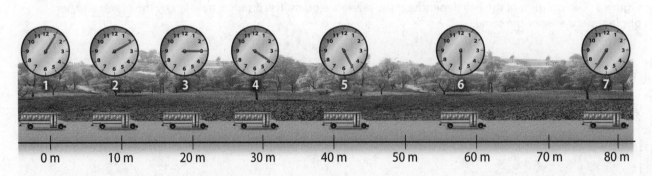

Figure 2 The bus moves at a constant speed from positions 1 to 4. After position 4, the bus's speed increases. It takes the bus 5 s to move from one position to the next.

Calculating Average Speed

The speed of most moving objects is not constant, which is why the speedometer in a car is always slightly changing. Therefore, when you describe your speed over an entire trip to someone, you are describing average speed. Average speed is equal to the total distance traveled divided by the total time.

$$\text{average speed} = \frac{\text{total distance}}{\text{total time}}$$

The bus in **Figure 2** travels 80 m from position 1 to position 7, during 30 s on the stopwatch. Therefore, the average speed of the bus is 80 m/30 s or approximately 2.7 m/s.

Distinguish

4. Relate the concepts below to speed.

Term	What it means
Speed	
Constant Speed	
Changing Speed	
Average Speed	

Math Skills TEKS 6.8(C); Math TEKS 6.1(A), (B); 6.3(E); 6.4(A)

Use a Formula

The formula for calculating average speed is

$$\text{average speed} = \frac{\text{total distance}}{\text{total time}}.$$

A bus carrying students to a soccer game traveled 10 km in 30 min. What was the average speed of the bus in km/h?

1. Change minutes to hours.

$$30 \text{ min} = 0.5 \text{ h}$$

2. Replace the terms in the formula with the given terms.

$$\text{average speed} = \frac{10 \text{ km}}{0.5 \text{ h}}$$

3. Divide to get the answer.

$$10 \text{ km}/0.5 \text{ h} = 20 \text{ km/h}$$

Practice

If, on a hike, you traveled 2,800 m in 2 h, what was your average speed in m/h?

Check   Tutor

Go Online!

Velocity

If you talked to your friends about how fast a bus was traveling as it took you to a game, you would probably describe the bus's speed. What else would you need to know to understand the motion of the bus? Which way was it going? **Velocity** *is the speed and the direction of a moving object.* For example, the speed of an object might be 5 m/s, while its velocity might be 5 m/s to the east. The words *speed* and *velocity* have different meanings, just as *distance* and *displacement* have different meanings.

In a drawing, you can use arrows to show the velocity of an object. The length of an arrow represents the speed of an object. The longer the arrow, the faster the object is moving. The head of an arrow points in the direction the object moves. In **Figure 3,** the boy skates east at a greater speed than the girl skateboards west.

LAB Manager

Skill Practice: *How can you test and describe an object's motion?*

TEKS 6.1(A); 6.2(A), (C), (D), (E); 6.4(A), (B); 6.8(C)

Figure 3 The lengths of the velocity arrows show speed. The arrows point in the direction of the motion.

Identify

5. After reading the text under **Changing Velocity**, write two ways to change an object's velocity.

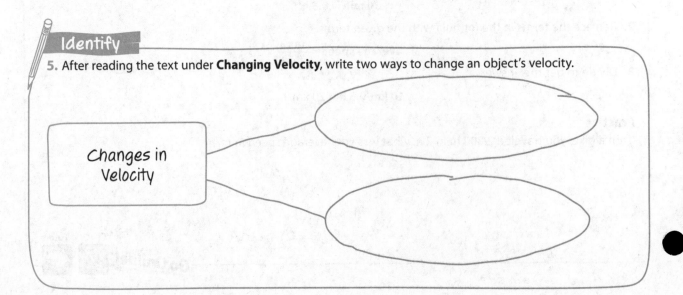

Changes in Velocity

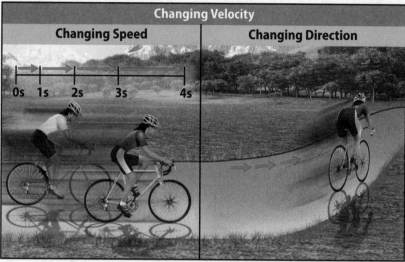

Constant Velocity	Changing Velocity	
	Changing Speed	Changing Direction

0s 1s 2s 3s 4s

0s 1s 2s 3s 4s

Figure 4 Velocity is constant if both speed and direction are constant.

Constant Velocity

Suppose a road biker rides along a flat straight road, as shown in the first panel of **Figure 4.** He or she moves with constant velocity. Constant velocity means that an object moves with constant speed and its direction does not change. If the biker's velocity is constant, then the arrows that represent the biker's velocity are all the same length and point in the same direction.

Changing Velocity

How is the motion of the bikers in the second and third panels of **Figure 4** different from the motion of the bikers in the first panel? In the second and third panels, the arrows that represent velocity are different from each other. In the second panel, the arrows have different lengths. In the third panel, the arrows point in different directions. Because the arrows are not identical, you know that the velocity is changing. Velocity changes when either an object's speed or direction of motion changes.

Change in Speed Imagine that the biker in the blue jersey in the second panel wants to pass the other biker. She goes faster. Each second, the rider moves a greater and greater distance. Her speed changes. Therefore, her velocity also changes.

Change in Direction The biker in the third panel of **Figure 4** rides along a turn in the road. Even though the biker's speed is constant, her direction changes, as shown by the different angles of the arrows. Because the rider's direction changes, her velocity changes.

Explain

6. How do you know that the bikers in the first panel in **Figure 4** are moving at a constant speed?

Acceleration

Imagine that you are on a roller coaster like the one in **Figure 5.** As your roller-coaster car goes down a hill, you move faster and faster. You feel as if you are being pushed back against the seat. Because the speed of the car increases, the velocity of the car increases. Next, your car climbs a hill. The car moves slower and slower as it climbs. Because the speed of the car decreases, the velocity of the car decreases. Suddenly, the roller-coaster cars enter a curve. The velocity changes again because the direction of the car's motion changes. When the velocity of an object changes, it accelerates. **Acceleration** *is a measure of how quickly the velocity of an object changes.*

Speeding Up

As the roller-coaster car at the left of **Figure 5** travels downhill, it covers a greater distance each second. The velocity increases. The roller-coaster car's acceleration is in the same direction as its motion. This is called positive acceleration. The green arrow shows the acceleration.

Slowing Down

As the roller-coaster car climbs the next hill, it moves a shorter and shorter distance each second. The velocity decreases. This means that the roller-coaster car's acceleration is in the opposite direction of its motion. This is shown by the green arrow on the uphill part of **Figure 5.** The action of slowing down is called negative acceleration, also known as deceleration.

Changing Direction of Motion

As the roller-coaster car travels through the loop, the direction of its motion constantly changes. If the car is changing direction, then its velocity is changing and the car is accelerating. Because the car is accelerating, there must be unbalanced forces acting on it. The track applies an unbalanced force on the roller-coaster car by pushing it toward the center of the loop. This creates the roller-coaster car's circular motion. The green arrows show that the roller-coaster car accelerates toward the center of the loop.

Identify

7. In **Figure 5,** place an "X" over each roller-coaster car that is accelerating.

Figure 5 A roller coaster can accelerate many times throughout the ride.

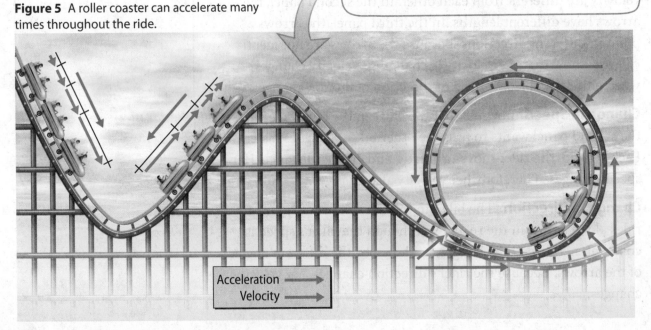

Acceleration
Velocity

Summarize it!

Differentiate between the distance and displacement for an object that started at point A and traveled as shown to point B.

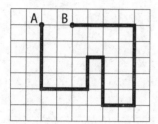

Distance: _____ units

Displacement: _____ units

Characterize motion using the graphic organizer below.

Motion

Definition:

Description depends on:

Connect it! Describe a situation in which an object's displacement and distance are the same.

_____

Describing Motion

Use Vocabulary

1. A _____ is the starting point from which you describe an object's position.

2. If a bird's velocity is 3 m/s south, its _____ is 3 m/s.

3. **Define** acceleration in your own words.

_____

_____

_____

Apply the Essential Questions

4. **Calculate** A jet airliner flies 4,100 km from New York City to San Francisco in 4.25 h. What is its average speed?

TEKS 6.8(C) *supporting*

_____

_____

_____

5. **Evaluate** A race car moves at a constant speed around an oval track. Is the car accelerating? Why or why not?

_____

_____

_____

_____

_____

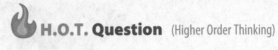

H.O.T. Question (Higher Order Thinking)

6. **Describe** A horse walks along a straight path. It travels 3 m in one second, 4 m in the next second, and 5 m in the third second. Describe the horse's motion in terms of its speed, velocity, and acceleration.

_____

_____

_____

_____

_____

Math Skills **TEKS** 6.8(C) *supporting;*
Math **TEKS** 6.1(A), (B); 6.3(E); 6.4(A)

Use a Formula

7. How long would it take a bus traveling at 50 km/h to travel 125 km? Show your work in the space below.

Check   Tutor

Go Online! ✓ 💬

Is it moving?

Fooling the Eye

You know that you describe an object's motion by explaining how its position changes. Did you know that you can use this concept to make a movie that shows nonmoving objects in motion? This process is called stop-motion photography. How does it work?

1 **First,** set an object in a scene and take a picture of it. Keep gradually changing the position of the object in the scene, taking a picture after each change.

2 **Now** use software to link all the pictures into a video. When you view the video, it will appear as if the object moved on its own. Of course, it is just an illusion. The illusion works because of the way your eye works. Motion is a change of position, and that is exactly what your eyes are seeing with stop-motion photography.

It's Your Turn!

EXPERIMENT Set up your own stop-motion photography studio. If you do not have a camera, make sketches of each change. When you are finished, make a flip book of your sketches or photographs.

INQUIRY

What is the turtle wearing? Some animals, such as this sea turtle, travel long distances out of the sight of humans. Biologists use tracking devices to help them better understand the lives of turtles. How might graphing the motion of turtles help save their lives?

Write your response in your interactive notebook.

LAB Manager

Go to your Lab Manual or visit connectED.mcgraw-hill.com to perform the labs for this lesson.

MiniLAB: *How can you make a speed-time graph?*
TEKS 6.2(E); 6.4(A); 6.8(D)

What does a graph show?

Measurements you make during an investigation can sometimes be difficult to understand. Graphing can help make the meaning of the data clearer. The data table here shows the distance an ant traveled each second. What does this look like on a graph?

Procedure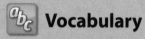

1. Use a **marker** to write the numbers 1 to 10 across the bottom of the long side of a piece of **construction paper.**

2. For each change in distance on the table, use **scissors** to cut a strip of **masking tape** that length. Place each strip vertically above the corresponding number of seconds.

Time (s)	Change in Distance (cm)
1	3
2	5
3	9
4	14
5	14
6	12
7	10
8	10
9	10
10	5

Think About This

1. What does the area represented by the strips of masking tape represent?

_____

_____

_____

2. What do you think happened to the speed of the ant during each second represented on the graph?

_____

_____

_____

_____

TEKS in this Lesson

6.8(D) Measure and graph changes in motion

Also covers Process Standards: 6.1(A); 6.2(E); 6.4(A)

? Essential Questions

- How can you graph an object's motion?
- How can a graph help you understand an object's motion?

ᵃᵇ𝒸 Vocabulary

distance-time graph
speed-time graph

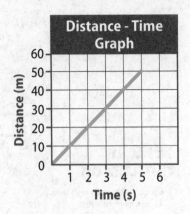

Distance - Time Graph

Distance (m): 60, 50, 40, 30, 20, 10, 0

Time (s): 1 2 3 4 5 6

Figure 1 The line on this distance-time graph represents an object traveling at a constant speed.

Describing Motion with Graphs TEKS 6.8(D)

How could you describe the motion of a sea turtle? You could measure the total distance the turtle traveled or the time it took the turtle to reach the ocean, but that would not give you a complete picture of its motion. When you study motion, you need to know how position changes as time passes. In this lesson, you will learn how to draw and interpret graphs of motion.

Distance-Time Graphs TEKS 6.8(D)

A graph that shows how distance and time are related is a **distance-time graph.** The *y*-axis shows the distance an object travels from a reference point. Time is on the *x*-axis. The line on a distance-time graph, such as the one in **Figure 1,** shows how an object's position changes during each time interval. With this information, you can determine an object's speed. For example, between 2 s and 3 s, the object traveled from 20 m to 30 m, a distance of 10 m. The speed of the object during that time interval was 10 m/s. If the slope of the line changes, you know that the speed changes. A distance-time graph does not show you the actual path the object took.

Compare

1. Organize information about distance-time graphs.

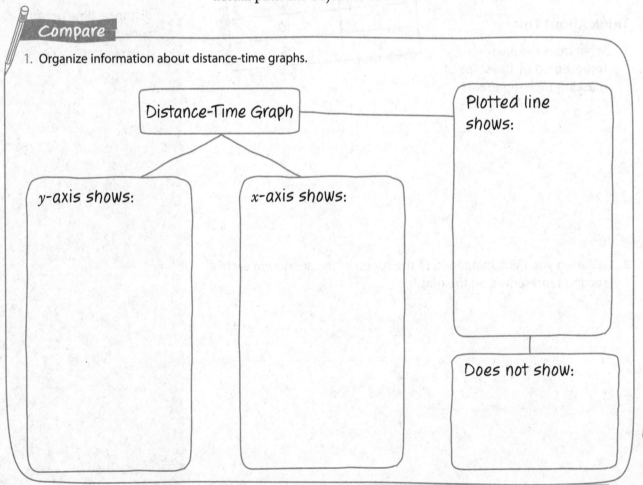

Distance-Time Graph

y-axis shows:

x-axis shows:

Plotted line shows:

Does not show:

Making a Distance-Time Graph

In order to better understand how sea turtles migrate through the oceans, marine biologists attach satellite tracking devices to turtles' shells. When turtles come to the ocean's surface for air, the devices send information to satellites orbiting Earth. The tracking devices record the turtles' positions and the times that they surface. Marine biologists can download and examine the data from the satellites. This helps them to understand turtle behavior and factors that can affect the health of the turtles.

Table 1 shows satellite tracking data that were gathered for a green sea turtle off the coast of Florida. The first column is the time since tracking began. The second column shows the distance the turtle swam from a reference point. **Figure 2** shows you how to use the data in **Table 1** to make a distance-time graph of the turtle's motion. As you read each step, study the part of the graph to which it refers. By following the same steps, you can make your own graph from similar data.

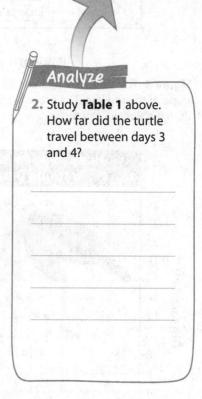

Table 1	Green Sea Turtle's Distance and Time Data
Time (days)	Distance (km)
0	0
1	16
2	32
3	48
4	64
5	80
6	96

Figure 2 The graph shows the steps in making a distance-time graph.

1. Draw x- and y-axes.

2. Label the x-axis for time measured in days. Label the y-axis for distance measured in kilometers.

3. Make tick marks on the axes and number them. Be sure the values you choose allow you to plot all the data.

4. Plot the data from each row of your data table. Move across the x-axis to the correct time and up the y-axis to the correct distance. Draw a small circle.

5. Connect data points with a line.

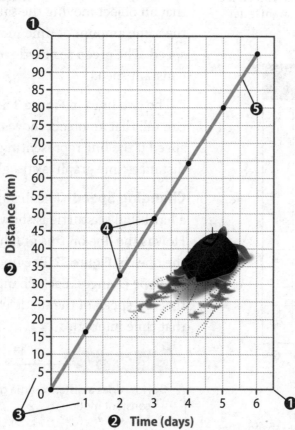

Analyze

2. Study **Table 1** above. How far did the turtle travel between days 3 and 4?

Go Online!

Watch   Tutor

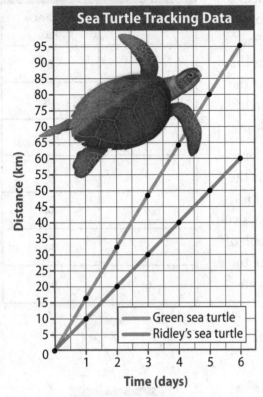

Sea Turtle Tracking Data

Distance (km): 95, 90, 85, 80, 75, 70, 65, 60, 55, 50, 45, 40, 35, 30, 25, 20, 15, 10, 5, 0

— Green sea turtle
— Ridley's sea turtle

Time (days): 1 2 3 4 5 6

Figure 3 The slope of the green line is greater than the slope of the red line. The green sea turtle swam faster than the Ridley's sea turtle.

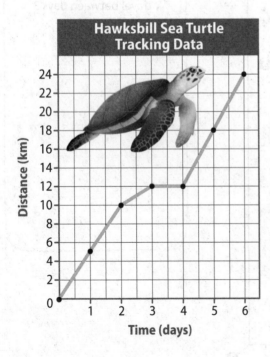

Hawksbill Sea Turtle Tracking Data

Distance (km): 24, 22, 20, 18, 16, 14, 12, 10, 8, 6, 4, 2, 0

Time (days): 1 2 3 4 5 6

Figure 4 The hawksbill sea turtle changed speed. The line is not straight.

Comparing Speed

You can use distance-time graphs to compare the motions of two objects. **Figure 3** is a distance-time graph that shows satellite tracking data for two sea turtles. The green line in **Figure 3** shows the motion of the green sea turtle. The red line shows the motion of a Ridley's sea turtle. After 6 days, the green sea turtle has traveled 96 km. The Ridley's sea turtle, on the other hand, has traveled 60 km.

Recall that average speed is total distance traveled divided by total time. The green sea turtle traveled a greater distance than the Ridley's sea turtle in the same amount of time. Therefore, the green sea turtle's average speed was greater. Notice that the green line is steeper than the red line. On distance-time graphs, lines with greater slope indicate a greater average speed.

Constant Speed Look again at **Figure 3.** Each day, the green sea turtle traveled 16 km. Recall that an object moving the same distance in the same amount of time moves at constant speed. The green sea turtle moved with constant speed.

The two lines in **Figure 3** are straight. You can tell that an object moves with constant speed if the line representing its motion on a distance-time graph is straight.

Changing Speed The distance-time graph of a hawksbill sea turtle is shown in **Figure 4.** How is the line on this graph different from the ones in **Figure 3?** The line is not straight. Its slope changes. Each change in slope means that the speed of the turtle changed during that time interval.

Infer

3. How does a distance-time graph show constant motion?

_____

Diagram Mark the floor of your classroom in 1-m segments along a track of your design. Roll a ball along the track. Have other students help you measure and record the time it takes the ball to roll each distance. Plot your distance-time data onto the graph below. **TEKS** 6.8(D)

Time	Distance
(_____)	(_____)

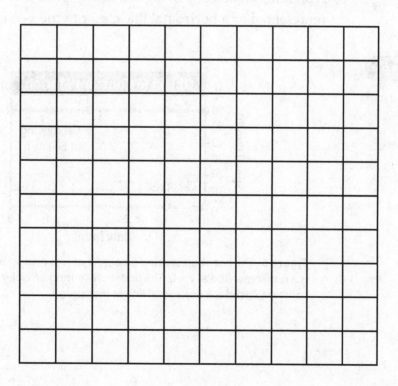

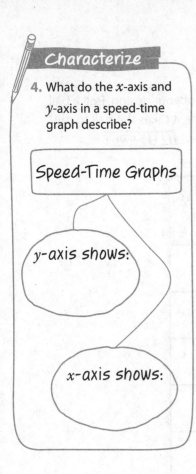

4. What do the *x*-axis and *y*-axis in a speed-time graph describe?

Speed-Time Graphs

y-axis shows:

x-axis shows:

Speed-Time Graphs TEKS 6.8(D)

You have read how distance-time graphs can help you describe an object's motion. Distance-time graphs show how the distance that the object travels changes during each unit of time. Another type of graph, called a speed-time graph, shows motion in a different way. A **speed-time graph** *shows the speed of an object on the y-axis and time on the x-axis*. A speed-time graph shows how the speed of the object changes during each interval of time.

Resting

Suppose you are in a parked car. What is your speed? Speed describes how much an object changes position in a unit of time. Because a parked car does not change position, your speed is zero. Your speed remains zero as long as the car remains at rest. The speed-time graph for an object at rest is a horizontal line at y = 0, shown as the orange line in **Figure 5.**

Constant Speed

Have you ever been in a car that had the cruise control turned on? The cruise control keeps the car moving at a constant speed, for example, 60 km/h. On a speed-time graph, an object moving with constant average speed is a horizontal line similar to the green line in **Figure 5.** A horizontal line farther from the *x*-axis represents an object moving at a faster speed than an object represented by a horizontal line closer to the *x*-axis.

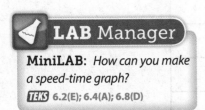

LAB Manager

MiniLAB: *How can you make a speed-time graph?*
TEKS 6.2(E); 6.4(A); 6.8(D)

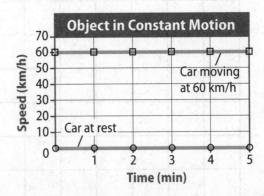

Figure 5 The line representing an object at rest on a speed-time graph is a horizontal line at y = 0. The line representing an object moving at constant speed is a horizontal line at that speed.

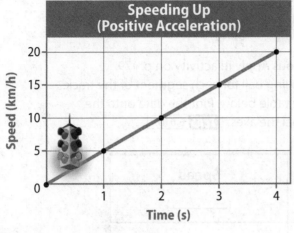

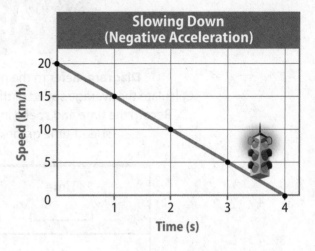

Changing Speed

Suppose you are in a car that is pulling away from a green traffic light. When the driver steps on the accelerator, the car's speed increases. Now the driver sees a red traffic light. The driver takes his or her foot off the accelerator, applies the brakes, and the car's speed decreases. What does the speed-time graph look like when the speed of an object changes?

Speeding Up As a car pulls away from the traffic light, its speed increases. The car covers a greater distance each second. As you can see on the left graph in **Figure 6,** a line on the graph that shows the motion of an object with increasing speed slopes upward from left to right. A line that slopes upward on a speed-time graph shows positive acceleration.

Slowing Down When a car slows down, its speed decreases and the car covers a smaller distance each second. The car's motion is a line that slopes downward from left to right, as shown on the graph on the right in **Figure 6.** This represents negative acceleration.

When the speed of an object changes, it accelerates. Therefore, if the line on a speed-time graph is not horizontal, you know that the object is accelerating. Objects also accelerate when their direction changes, but that is not shown on the speed-time graph. The line on the graph shows only a change in speed, not the direction the object is traveling.

Figure 6 The speed-time graph of an object that is speeding up slopes upward. The line slopes downward for an object that is slowing down.

FOLDABLES®

Use a sheet of grid paper to make a vertical three-tab book. Draw a Venn diagram on the front and label the tabs. Record what you have learned about distance-time graphs and speed-time graphs under the tabs. Draw examples of each on the front tabs. Under the middle tab, explain the graphs and describe what these two graphs have in common.

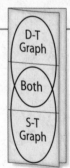

Explain

5. What is the difference between a sloping line on a speed-time graph and one on a distance-time graph?

_____

_____

_____

Diagram Refer to the previous Apply it! activity on p. 179. Calculate the average speed of the rolling ball for each segment of the track. Record the time and speed in the table below. Plot the data onto the speed-time graph. Label the axes. **TEKS** 6.8 (D)

Time (_____)	Speed (_____)

Connect it! In your interactive notebook, compare and contrast the graph from p. 179 with the graph on this page. What is the meaning of the slope of each graph?

Organize it!

5.2 Review

Jodi liked to run for exercise. To warm up, she walked at a constant speed for a distance of 100 m in 100 s. Then she increased her speed to 4 m/s. She ran at this speed for 5 min (300 s). At that point, she began going up a steep hill and her speed dropped back to 1 m/s. It took her 4 min (240 s) to reach the top of the hill. At that time, she stopped and rested for 3 min before continuing her run.

Illustrate Using the information in the above scenario, construct a distance-time graph and a speed-time graph. Label the axes. Then explain what is being shown as the slope of each graph changes. **TEKS** 6.8(D)

Distance (   )

Time (   )

Speed (   )

Time (   )

Summarize it!

Graphing Motion

Use Vocabulary

1. **Describe** a distance-time graph in your own words. **TEKS** 6.8(D) *supporting*

_____

_____

_____

2. **Distinguish** between a distance-time graph and a speed-time graph.
   TEKS 6.8(D) *supporting*

_____

_____

_____

H.O.T. Questions (Higher Order Thinking)

3. **Graph** Draw a speed-time graph of a cat that moved at a constant speed of 1 m/s for 10 s, slowed down, and then lay down for a nap. **TEKS** 6.8(D) *supporting*

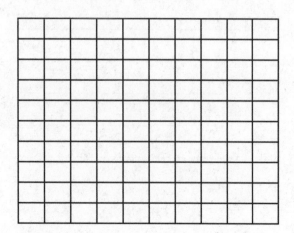

Interpret Graphics

4. **Analyze Data** The graph below shows the motion of an elevator. Explain its motion. **TEKS** 6.8(D) *supporting*

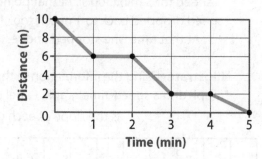

_____

_____

_____

_____

5. **Graph** Draw a distance-time graph and a speed-time graph using the data listed in the table. **TEKS** 6.8(D) *supporting*

Time (s)	Distance (m)	Time (s)	Distance (m)
0	0	3	30
1	10	4	40
2	20	5	50

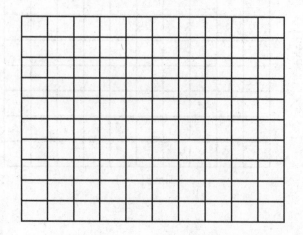

Using Satellites to Track Species

Using Technology to Help Wild Animals

Just as a GPS can provide information about the location of a car, satellite tracking technology can track wild animals. Data from the tracking provide scientists with information about animals' locations, migrations, and movement patterns. This information is useful in determining ways to help protect animals in the wild.

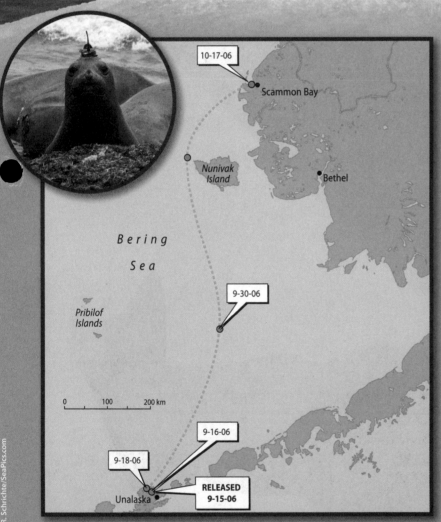

10-17-06
Scammon Bay

Nunivak Island
Bethel

Bering Sea

9-30-06

Pribilof Islands

0   100   200 km

9-16-06

9-18-06

RELEASED 9-15-06

Unalaska

Scientists pinpoint seal locations and convert the collected data to maps.

1 Collecting Data Researchers capture and attach satellite tags to animals and then release them back into their habitats. Animals are tagged with one of several devices that transmit signals to satellites. The satellites transmit location data back to a receiver. Satellite tags can be attached as collars or mini backpacks using glue or suction cups. Most tags are designed to fall off after a set period.

2 Studying Data Researchers combine location data with maps. Pinpointing exact latitude and longitude helps researchers plot an animal's movements or migration patterns.

3 Using Data Collected and analyzed data are useful tools in helping to protect some species. The data can assist in mapping an appropriately sized protected area. Data about animals' travels and habitats are useful in making informed decisions about how humans can better manage and protect these areas.

It's Your Turn!

PLOT DATA Refer to the satellite tracking map that shows the movements of a harbor seal during one month. Use the map key to determine the total distance the seal traveled. Then create a line graph showing kilometers traveled during each time period.

5.3 Forces

Does that hurt?

When a karate expert kicks a concrete block, the energy in his or her foot is transferred to the block. It hurts only if he or she does not break the block! What are other ways in which people change the motion of objects?

 Write your response in your interactive notebook.

 LAB Manager

Go to your Lab Manual or visit connectED.mcgraw-hill.com to perform the labs for this lesson.

MiniLAB: *Does a ramp make it easier to lift a load?*
TEKS 6.1(A); 6.2(A), (C), (E); 6.4(A), (B); 6.8(E)

MiniLAB: *Can you increase mechanical advantage?*
TEKS 6.1(A); 6.2(A), (C), (E); 6.8(E)

MiniLAB: *How do forces affect motion?*
TEKS 6.1(A); 6.2(A), (C), (E); 6.4(A), (B); 6.8(B)

LAB: *Comparing Two Simple Machines*
TEKS 6.1(A); 6.2(B), (C), (D), (E); 6.4(A); 6.8(E)

LAB: *Design a Safe Vehicle*
TEKS 6.1(A), (B); 6.2(B), (C), (E); 6.4(A), (B); 6.8(B)

Explore Activity

What affects the way objects fall?

If you drop a piece of paper and a book, will they fall in the same way?

Procedure

1. Read and complete a lab safety form.

2. Rest a **sheet of paper** on one hand and a **book** on the other hand with your palms up. Drop both hands at the same time. Observe how the objects fall. Record your observations in your Lab Manual or interactive notebook.

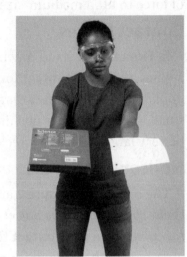

3. Wad an **identical sheet of paper** into a ball. Repeat step 2.

4. Place the flat sheet of paper on top of the book so that the edges are even. Drop them and observe how they fall. Record your observations.

Think About This

1. Describe the speeds of the objects as they fell.

_____

_____

_____

_____

_____

2. Why do you think the objects fell at the same or different speeds?

_____

_____

_____

_____

TEKS in this Lesson

6.8(B) Identify and describe the changes in position, direction, and speed of an object when acted upon by unbalanced forces

6.8(E) Investigate how inclined planes and pulleys can be used to change the amount of force to move an object

Also covers Process Standards: 6.1(A), (B); 6.2(A), (B), (C), (D), (E); 6.3(D); 6.4(A), (B)

? Essential Questions

- How are balanced and unbalanced forces related to motion?

- How do machines change the amount of force needed to move an object?

abc Vocabulary

force
contact force
noncontact force
gravity
friction
air resistance
Newton's first law of motion
Newton's second law of motion
Newton's third law of motion

Figure 1 The karate expert exerts a contact force on the boards.

What is force? [TEKS] 6.8 (B)

What have you pushed or pulled today? You might have pushed open a classroom door or pulled a zipper on your backpack. A **force** *is a push or a pull on an object.*

Force has both size and direction. Just as you used arrows to show the size and direction of velocity and acceleration, you can use arrows to show the size and direction of force, as shown in **Figure 1.** The unit for force is the newton (N). You use about 1 N of force to lift a medium-sized apple.

Contact Forces

In **Figure 1,** the hand touches the wood as the karate expert applies a force. A **contact force** *is a push or a pull one object applies to another object that is touching it.* Contact forces can be small, such as a finger pushing a button on a phone, or they can be very large, such as a wrecking ball crashing into a building.

Noncontact Forces

The balloons in **Figure 2** are pulling the girl's hair toward them. *A force that one object applies to another object without touching it is a* **noncontact force.** The force that attracts the girl's hair to the balloon is an electric force. The force acting between iron and a magnet is also a noncontact force.

FOLDABLES

Cut out the Lesson 5.3 Foldable in the back of the book. Use it to record under the tabs what you learn about forces.

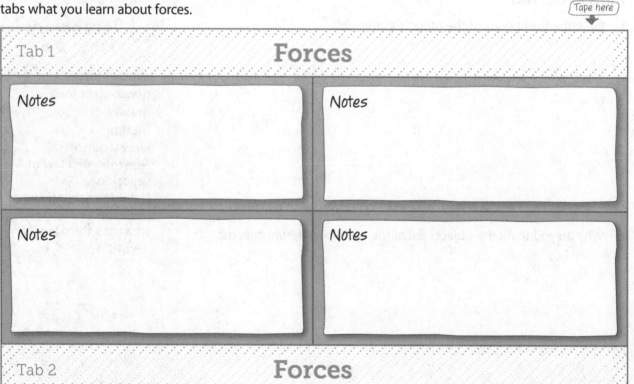

Tape here

Tab 1 | Forces

Notes

Notes

Notes

Notes

Tab 2 | Forces

Tape here

Gravity—A Noncontact Force *TEKS* 6.3 (D)

When you jump off a step, the force of Earth's gravity pulls you toward Earth. **Gravity** *is an attractive force that exists between all objects that have mass.* Mass is the amount of matter in an object. Both you and Earth have mass, so both you and Earth pull on each other.

The Law of Gravity

In the late 1600s, Sir Isaac Newton developed the law of universal gravitation, also known as the law of gravity. This law states that all objects are attracted to each other by a gravitational force. The strength of the force depends on the mass of each object and the distance between the objects.

Gravitational force depends on mass.

Figure 3 shows that if the mass of an object increases, the gravitational force between that object and another object increases. The gravitational force between you and Earth is strong because of Earth's large mass. The force holds you to Earth's surface. The gravitational force between you and your pencil is weak because you both have relatively small masses compared to Earth. You do not feel the attraction, even though it is present.

Gravitational force depends on distance.

As two objects move apart, the gravitational force between them decreases. **Figure 3** shows that the gravitational force between two objects 1 m apart is four times greater than the gravitational force between the same objects that are 2 m apart.

Figure 2 Noncontact forces attract the girl's hair.

Identify

1. Fill in the blanks in the boxes in **Figure 3** below to show the effects that distance and mass have on the force of gravity.

Go Online!

Tutor

Effects on Gravity

Figure 3
Gravitational force increases as mass increases and decreases as distance increases.

Effect of Mass on Force of Gravity

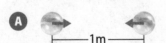

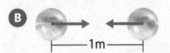

The force of attraction between the marbles in B is _____ than in A because the marbles in B have _____ mass.

Effect of Distance on Force of Gravity

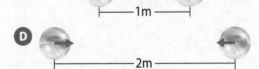

The force of attraction between the marbles in D is _____ than in C because the distance between the marbles is _____.

Model factors that affect the force of gravity. Draw circles to represent masses as described. The first one has been done for you.

Description	Drawing
A. A mass	⭕
B. A mass that produces larger gravitational force than A	
C. A mass that produces smaller gravitational force than A	
D. Two masses	
E. The same masses as D, but positioned to produce less gravitational force	
F. The same masses as D, but positioned to produce greater gravitational force	

Organize it!

Mass and weight are different.

Weight is a measure of the gravitational force acting on an object's mass. Therefore, weight depends on the masses of the objects and the distance between them. When comparing the weight of two objects at the same location on Earth, the object with more mass has a greater weight. The weights of the same objects on the Moon are less because the mass of the Moon is less, as shown in **Figure 4.**

Friction—A Contact Force TEKS 6.8 (B)

Rub your finger across your desk. Then rub it across a piece of your clothing. What did you feel? It is easy to run your finger over your desk because it is smooth. On your clothing, you probably felt a force called friction. **Friction** *is a contact force that resists the sliding motion of two surfaces that are touching.* Rough surfaces or materials tend to produce more friction.

Effects of Friction

Slide your book across the floor. The book slows down when you stop pushing it. The force of friction acts in the opposite direction of the book's motion. A heavier book is more affected by friction than a lighter one. In **Figure 5,** the force of friction between the sled and the ground acts in the direction opposite the force of the man pulling the sled.

Air Resistance

When you drop a piece of paper, it slowly drifts downward. Friction between the air and the paper's surface slows its motion. **Air resistance** *is the frictional force between air and objects moving through it.* When you crumple the paper into a ball, less surface area is in contact with the air. As air resistance decreases, the ball falls more quickly.

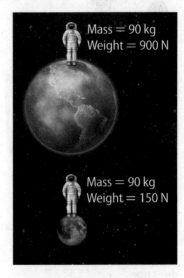

Figure 4 Because of its smaller mass, the Moon's gravity is only $\frac{1}{6}$ that of Earth's. An astronaut's weight on the Moon is $\frac{1}{6}$ his or her weight on Earth.

Differentiate

2. What is the difference between mass and weight?

_____

_____

_____

_____

_____

_____

_____

Figure 5 To move the sled, the pulling force must be greater than the friction force on the sled.

Copyright © McGraw-Hill Education   Zhang Jie/ChinaFotoPress/Getty Images

Figure 6 The net force acting on an object is the sum of the two forces and acts in the same direction.

Combining Forces TEKS 6.8(B)

Suppose you need to pull your desk away from the wall to get something that fell behind it. When you pull, the desk will not move, so you ask a friend to help you. With both of you pulling, you have enough force to overcome the force of friction, and the desk moves. When more than one force acts on an object, the forces combine and act as one force. The sum of all the forces acting on an object is called the net force. **Figure 6** shows how forces acting in the same direction form one net force.

When two forces act on the same object in opposite directions, as shown in **Figure 7,** you must include the direction of the forces when you add them. The positive direction is usually to the right. In the left photo of **Figure 7,** the girl's force on the dog's leash is +50 N. The dog's force on the leash is the same size as the girl's, but in the negative direction. The dog's force is –50 N. The net force on the leash is 50 N + (–50 N) = 0 N. The dog does not move.

Balanced Forces

If the net force on an object is 0 N, the forces acting on the object are called balanced forces. The net force on the leash in **Figure 7** is 0 N. The forces acting on the leash are balanced.

Unbalanced Forces

When the net force on an object is not 0, the forces acting on the object are unbalanced forces. The net force on the sled in the right photo of **Figure 7** is 100 N to the right. The forces acting on the sled are unbalanced, so it accelerates.

Calculating Net Force

Go Online! Tutor

Figure 7 To calculate the net force, add the forces acting on the object. Acceleration is in the direction of the larger force.

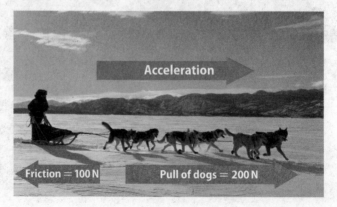

Organize it!

Explain combined forces on an object. **TEKS** 6.8 (B)

Factor	Explanation
Net force	
Balanced forces	
Unbalanced forces	
Net force = 0	
Net force ≠ 0	

In the box below, **draw and label** examples of balanced and unbalanced forces.

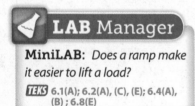

Figure 8 Two types of simple machines are shown here. An inclined plane and a pulley apply a force with one motion.

Force

Machines **TEKS** 6.8 (E)

Look again at the photograph of the boys pulling the desk in **Figure 6**. Suppose a force of 500 N is needed to overcome friction with the floor to start the desk moving. If the boys can pull with a combined force of only 250 N, how can they move the desk? They need a way to increase their applied force. They need a machine!

Simple Machines and Mechanical Advantage

In general, a machine is a mechanical device that is used to make work easier. Some machines, such as automobiles, are quite complicated and contain many parts. However, a simple machine has only one or two parts and is the simplest form of a device that can make work easier. A simple machine makes work easier by increasing or decreasing an applied force or by changing the direction of a force. Two types of simple machines are the inclined plane and the pulley, as shown in **Figure 8**.

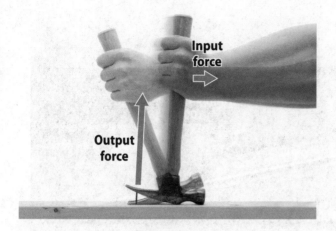

Input force

Output force

Figure 9 You exert an input force on the hammer. The hammer exerts an output force on the nail.

Input Force to Output Force

To use a machine, such as the hammer in **Figure 9,** you must apply a force to it. This force is the input force. The machine changes the input force into an output force. You apply an input force to a hammer when you pull on its handle. The hammer increases the input force to an output force great enough to pull a nail out of a board.

The mechanical advantage of a simple machine is the ratio of the output force to the input force, as shown below. In other words, a machine's mechanical advantage indicates how much the machine changes the force applied to it.

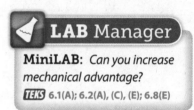

LAB Manager

MiniLAB: *Can you increase mechanical advantage?*

TEKS 6.1(A); 6.2(A), (C), (E); 6.8(E)

Mechanical Advantage

$$\text{mechanical advantage (no units)} = \frac{\text{output force (in newtons)}}{\text{input force (in newtons)}}$$

$$MA = \frac{F_{out}}{F_{in}}$$

Mechanical advantage can be less than 1, equal to 1, or greater than 1. A mechanical advantage greater than 1 means the output force is greater than the input force. A crowbar, for example, has a mechanical advantage greater than 1.

The ideal mechanical advantage, or IMA, is the mechanical advantage if no friction existed. Machines cannot operate at ideal mechanical advantage because friction always exists.

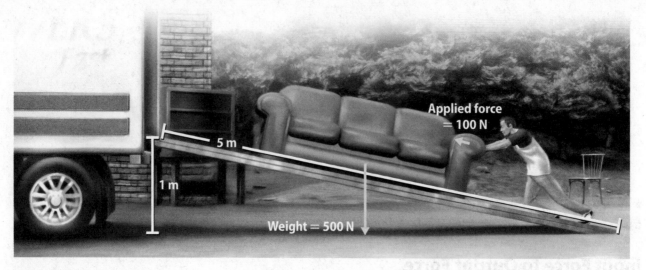

Applied force = 100 N

5 m

1 m

Weight = 500 N

Figure 10 Lifting is easier with a ramp. Here, using a ramp requires only a 100-N force to raise a 500-N sofa.

Inclined Plane

The ancient Egyptians built pyramids using huge stone blocks. Moving the blocks up the pyramid must have been difficult. To make the task easier, ramps were often used. A ramp, or an inclined plane, is a flat, sloped surface. It takes less force to raise an object along an inclined plane than it does to lift the object straight up. As shown in **Figure 10,** ramps are still useful for moving heavy loads. The mechanical advantage of an inclined plane equals its length divided by its height, as shown in the equation below.

Ideal Mechanical Advantage of an Inclined Plane

$$\text{Ideal mechanical advantage} = \frac{\text{length of inclined plane (in meters)}}{\text{height of inclined plane (in meters)}}$$

$$\text{IMA} = \frac{l}{h}$$

Note that increasing the length and decreasing the height of the inclined plane increases its mechanical advantage. The longer or less-sloped an inclined plane, the less force needed to move an object along its surface.

Illustrate

4. Using a ruler, make a scale drawing of an inclined plane which has a mechanical advantage of 4.

Fixed Pulley	Movable Pulley	Pulley System

100 N ↑   100 N ↓

100 N

100 N ↓

Mechanical advantage = 1

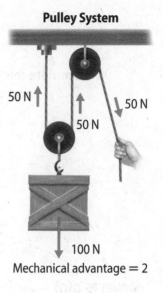

50 N ↑   50 N ↗

100 N ↓

Mechanical advantage = 2

Pulley System

50 N ↑   50 N ↑   50 N ↓

50 N

100 N ↓

Mechanical advantage = 2

Pulleys

You might have seen large cranes lifting heavy loads at construction sites. A crane uses a **pulley**—a simple machine that is a grooved wheel with a rope or a cable wrapped around it.

Fixed Pulleys Have you ever pulled down on a cord to raise a window blind? The cord passes through a fixed pulley mounted to the top of the window frame. A fixed pulley changes only the direction of the force, as shown **Figure 11**.

Movable Pulleys and Pulley Systems A pulley can also be attached to the object being lifted. This type of pulley, called a movable pulley, is shown in **Figure 11**. Movable pulleys decrease the force needed to lift an object. The distance over which the force acts increases.

A pulley system is a combination of fixed and movable pulleys that work together. An example of a pulley system is shown above in **Figure 11**.

Mechanical Advantage of Pulleys The mechanical advantage of a pulley or a pulley system is equal to the number of sections of rope pulling up on the object.

Figure 11 Pulleys can change force and direction.

Word Origin

pulley
from Greek *polos*, means "axis, pole"

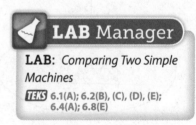

LAB Manager

LAB: *Comparing Two Simple Machines*

TEKS 6.1(A); 6.2(B), (C), (D), (E); 6.4(A); 6.8(E)

Explain

5. What is the simplest way to double the mechanical advantage of a fixed pulley?

_____

_____

Organize it!

Complete this graphic organizer by choosing terms from the word bank and writing them in the correct spaces. **TEKS** 6.8(E)

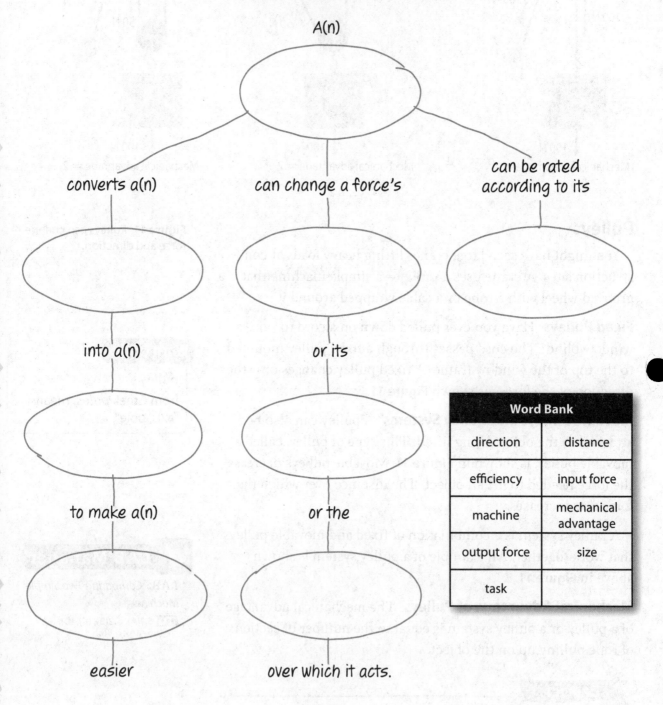

A(n) ⬭

converts a(n) ⬭

can change a force's ⬭

can be rated according to its ⬭

into a(n) ⬭

or its ⬭

to make a(n) ⬭

or the ⬭

easier

over which it acts.

Word Bank	
direction	distance
efficiency	input force
machine	mechanical advantage
output force	size
task	

Connect it! Automobile manufacturers use large tractor trailers to transport vehicles to be sold. How are the automobiles loaded on the trucks and why is this method used? Write your response in your interactive notebook.

Organize it!

Unbalanced Forces and Acceleration TEKS 6.8(B)

When unbalanced forces act on an object, the object's velocity changes. Unbalanced forces can change either the speed or the direction of motion, resulting in a change in position.

Change in Speed

The train in the top left image of **Figure 12** is pulling away from the station. The force of the engine is greater than the force of friction. The forces on the train are unbalanced, so it accelerates. The train speeds up.

Change in Direction

When the train goes around a curve, as shown in the bottom left image of **Figure 12,** the track exerts a sideways force on the train's wheels. These unbalanced forces change the train's motion by changing its direction and, therefore, its velocity. The train accelerates.

Balanced Forces and Constant Motion TEKS 6.8(B)

How do balanced forces affect an object's motion? The forces acting on the train sitting still on a track in **Figure 12** are balanced. The force of gravity pulls the train down toward Earth. The track pushes upward with an equal force. Thus, the position of the train remains the same.

The train in the bottom right image moves along a straight track. The force from the engine moves the train forward. The force of friction between the wheels and the track is equal in size to the engine's force, but in the opposite direction. The forces acting on the train are balanced. It does not accelerate; it moves at a constant velocity. When balanced forces act on an object, the motion is constant. The object is either at rest or moving at a constant velocity.

Figure 12 Acceleration is caused by unbalanced forces. Constant motion is caused by balanced forces.

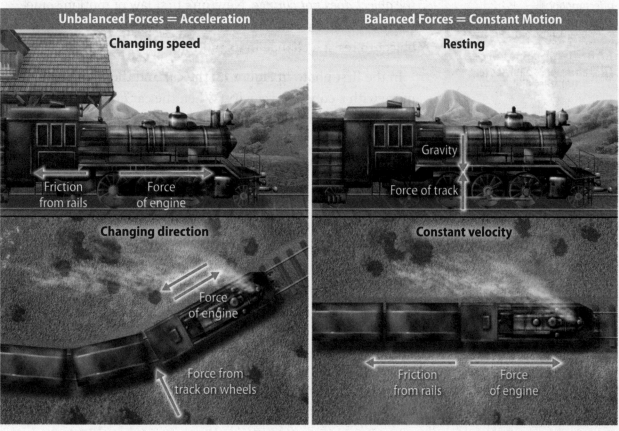

Figure 13 Because of inertia, the crash-test dummies without safety belts keep moving forward after the car stops at a barrier.

Forces and Newton's Laws of Motion

TEKS 6.3 (D); 6.8(B)

Isaac Newton was an English scientist and mathematician who lived in the late 1600s. He developed three important rules about motion called Newton's laws of motion.

Newton's First Law of Motion

As you just read, when balanced forces act on an object, the object's motion is constant. According to **Newton's first law of motion,** *if the net force acting on an object is zero, the motion of the object does not change.* Newton's first law of motion sometimes is called the law of inertia. Inertia is the tendency of an object to resist a change in its motion.

In the first photo in **Figure 13**, the car and the test dummies move with a constant velocity. When the car crashes into the wall, unbalanced forces act on the car, and it stops. However, the dummies, which are not attached to the car, continue to move with a constant velocity because of their inertia.

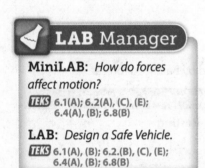

LAB Manager

MiniLAB: *How do forces affect motion?*

TEKS 6.1(A); 6.2(A), (C), (E); 6.4(A), (B); 6.8(B)

LAB: *Design a Safe Vehicle.*

TEKS 6.1(A), (B); 6.2.(B), (C), (E); 6.4(A), (B); 6.8(B)

Compare

6. Describe Newton's first law of motion, relating it to the meaning of inertia.

Newton's first law of motion:

Inertia:

Apply the Essential Questions

1. **Describe** how position, direction, and speed of an object changes when acted on by unbalanced forces. **TEKS** 6.8(B)

_____

_____

_____

_____

2. **Explain** how an inclined plane and a pulley are used to change the amount of force needed to move an object. **TEKS** 6.8(E)

_____

_____

_____

_____

_____

_____

 H.O.T. Questions (Higher Order Thinking)

3. **Describe** what might happen to the mass and/or distance between two objects to increase the gravitational force of attraction. **TEKS** 6.8(B)

_____

_____

_____

4. **Illustrate** a situation in which an object is acted upon by a net upward force of 20 N. **TEKS** 6.8(B)

5. **Describe** two ways to increase the mechanical advantage of an inclined plane. **TEKS** 6.8(E)

_____

_____

_____

_____

_____

Writing in Science

6. **Write** a short paragraph on a separate sheet of paper about using an inclined plane on the Moon. Remember, objects weigh less on the Moon than on Earth. Will this affect the mechanical advantage of the inclined plane or the way it is used? **TEKS** 6.8(E)

Copyright © McGraw-Hill Education Edward Kinsman/Photo Researchers

INQUIRY

Why is this cat glowing? A camera that detects temperature made this image. Dark colors represent cooler temperatures and light colors represent warmer temperatures. Temperatures are cooler where the cat's body emits less radiant energy and warmer where the cat's body emits more radiant energy. How might this type of photography be useful to you?

 Write your response in your interactive notebook.

 LAB Manager

Go to your Lab Manual or visit connectED.mcgraw-hill.com to perform the labs for this lesson.

MiniLAB: *Can a moving object do work?*

TEKS 6.1(A); 6.2(A), (C), (E); 6.4(A), (B)

Explore Activity

Can you make a change in matter?

You can observe many things changing. Birds change their positions when they fly. Bubbles form in boiling water. The filament in a light-bulb glows when you turn on a light. How can you cause a change in matter?

Procedure

1. Read and complete a lab safety form.

2. Half-fill a **foam cup** with **sand.** Place the bulb of a **thermometer** about halfway into the sand. *Do not stir.* Record the temperature in your Lab Manual or interactive notebook.

3. Remove the thermometer and place a **lid** on the cup. Hold down the lid and shake the cup vigorously for 10 min.

4. Remove the lid. Measure and record the temperature of the sand.

Think About This

1. What change did you observe in the sand?

_____

_____

_____

_____

2. Predict how you could change your results.

_____

_____

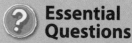

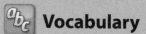

TEKS in this Lesson

6.8(A) Compare and contrast potential and kinetic energy

Also covers Process Standards: 6.1(A); 6.2(A), (C), (E); 6.3(D); 6.4(A), (B)

? Essential Questions

- What is energy?
- What are potential and kinetic energy?

abc Vocabulary

energy
kinetic energy
potential energy
work
mechanical energy
sound energy
thermal energy
electric energy
radiant energy
nuclear energy

What is energy?

It might be exciting to watch a fireworks display like the one shown in **Figure 1.** Over and over, you hear the crack of explosions and see bursts of colors in the night sky. Fireworks release energy when they explode. **Energy** *is the ability to cause change.* The energy in the fireworks causes the changes you see as bursting flashes of light and hear as loud booms.

Energy also causes other changes. The plant in **Figure 1** uses the energy from the Sun and makes food that it uses for growth and other processes. Energy can cause changes in the motions and positions of objects, such as the nail in **Figure 1.** Can you think of other ways energy might cause changes?

Interview

1. Ask another student in class to list his or her three favorite ways of using energy. Compare your findings with those of other students.

_____

_____

_____

_____

_____

_____

Figure 1 The explosion of the fireworks, the growth of the flower, and the motion of the hammer all involve energy.

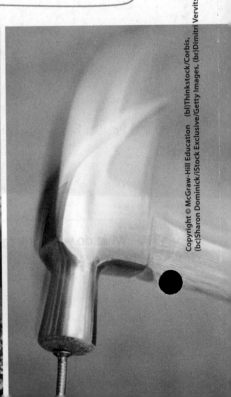

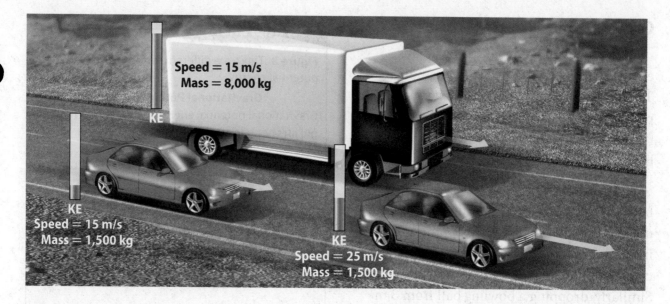

Speed = 15 m/s
Mass = 8,000 kg
KE

KE
Speed = 15 m/s
Mass = 1,500 kg

KE
Speed = 25 m/s
Mass = 1,500 kg

Kinetic Energy TEKS 6.8(A)

Have you ever been to a bowling alley? If so, when you rolled the ball and it hit the pins, a change occurred—the pins fell over. This change occurred because the ball had a form of energy called kinetic (kuh NEH tik) energy. **Kinetic energy** *is energy due to motion.* All moving objects have kinetic energy.

Kinetic Energy and Speed

An object's kinetic energy depends on its speed. The faster an object moves, the more kinetic energy it has. For example, the blue car has more kinetic energy than the green car in **Figure 2** because the blue car is moving faster.

Kinetic Energy and Mass

A moving object's kinetic energy also depends on its mass. If two objects move at the same speed, the object with more mass has more kinetic energy. For example, the truck and the green car in **Figure 2** are moving at the same speed, but the truck has more kinetic energy because it has more mass.

Potential Energy TEKS 6.8(A)

Energy can be present even if objects are not moving. If you
~~~~~~~~~~~ gravitational interaction ~~~~~~~~~
~~~ ball and Earth

energy called potential (pun ~~~~
is stored energy due to the interactions between objects or particles. Gravitational potential energy, elastic potential energy, and chemical potential energy are all forms of potential energy.

Figure 2 The kinetic energy of an object depends on its speed and its mass. The vertical bars show the kinetic energy of each vehicle.

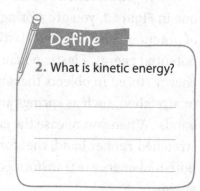

Define

2. What is kinetic energy?

FOLDABLES

Make a 3-in fold along the long edge of a sheet of paper and make a two-pocket book. Label it as shown. Organize information about the forms of energy on quarter sheets and put them ~~~~~~~~

Kinetic Energy | Potential Energy

Gravitational Potential Energy

Even when you are just holding a book, energy is stored between the book and Earth. This type of energy is called gravitational potential energy. The girl in **Figure 3** increases the gravitational potential energy between her backpack and Earth by lifting the backpack.

The gravitational potential energy stored between an object and Earth depends on the object's weight and height. Dropping a bowling ball from a height of 1 m causes a greater change than dropping a tennis ball from 1 m. Similarly, dropping a bowling ball from 3 m causes a greater change than dropping the same bowling ball from 1 m.

Elastic Potential Energy

When you stretch a rubber band, like the one in **Figure 3,** you are storing another form of potential energy called elastic (ih LAS tik) potential energy. Elastic potential energy is energy stored in objects that are compressed or stretched, such as springs and rubber bands. When you release the end of a stretched rubber band, the stored elastic potential energy is transformed into kinetic energy.

Chemical Potential Energy

Food, gasoline, and other substances are made of atoms joined together by chemical bonds. Chemical potential energy is energy stored in the chemical bonds between atoms, as shown in **Figure 3.** Chemical potential energy is released when chemical reactions occur. Your body uses the chemical potential energy in foods for all its activities. People also use the chemical potential energy in gasoline to drive cars and buses.

Figure 3 There are different forms of potential energy.

Gravitational Potential Energy
Gravitational potential energy increases when the girl lifts her backpack.

Elastic Potential Energy
The rubber band's elastic potential energy increases when you stretch the rubber band.

Chemical Potential Energy
Foods and other substances, including glucose, have chemical potential energy stored in the bonds between atoms.

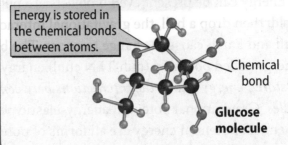

Energy is stored in the chemical bonds between atoms.

Chemical bond

Glucose molecule

Apply it!

Draw a picture of a yo-yo as it moves up and down a string. **Label** your drawing with the terms below. **TEKS** 6.8(A)

potential energy   kinetic energy

Connect it! Describe the yo-yo when it has no potential energy and no kinetic energy.

_____

_____

Figure 4 The girl does work on the box as she lifts it. The work she does transfers energy to the box. The colored bars show the work that the girl does (W) and the box's potential energy (PE).

Energy and Work

You can transfer energy by doing work. **Work** *is the transfer of energy that occurs when a force is applied over a distance.* For example, the girl does work on the box in **Figure 4.** As the girl lifts the box onto the shelf, she transfers energy from herself to the gravitational interaction between the box and Earth.

Work depends on both force and distance. You do work on an object only if that object moves. Imagine that the girl in **Figure 4** tries to lift the box but cannot actually lift it off the floor. Then she does no work on the box and transfers no energy.

An object that has energy also can do work. For example, when a bowling ball collides with a bowling pin, the bowling ball does work on the pin. Some of the ball's kinetic energy is transferred to the bowling pin. Because of this connection between energy and work, energy is sometimes described as the ability to do work.

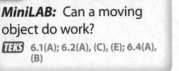

LAB Manager

MiniLAB: Can a moving object do work?
TEKS 6.1(A); 6.2(A), (C), (E); 6.4(A), (B)

Other Forms of Energy

Some other forms of energy are shown in **Table 1.** All energy can be measured in joules (J). A softball dropped from a height of about 0.5 m has about 1 J of kinetic energy just before it hits the floor.

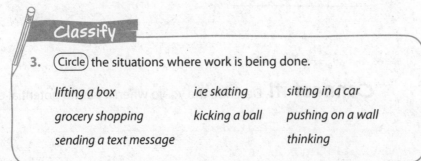

Classify

3. (Circle) the situations where work is being done.

lifting a box	ice skating	sitting in a car
grocery shopping	kicking a ball	pushing on a wall
sending a text message		thinking

Table 1   Forms of Energy

Mechanical Energy

The total energy of an object or group of objects due to large-scale motions and interactions is called **mechanical energy.** For example, the mechanical energy of a basketball increases when a player shoots the basketball. However, the mechanical energy of a pot of water does not increase when you heat the water.

Sound Energy

When you pluck a guitar string, the string vibrates and produces sound. *The energy that sound carries is* **sound energy.** Vibrating objects emit sound energy. However, sound energy cannot travel through a vacuum, such as the space between Earth and the Sun.

Thermal Energy

All objects and materials are made of particles that are always moving. Because these particles move, they have energy. **Thermal energy** *is energy due to the motion of particles that make up an object.* Thermal energy moves from warmer objects to cooler objects. When you heat objects, you transfer thermal energy to those objects from their surroundings.

Electric Energy

An electric fan uses another form of energy—electric energy. When you turn on a fan, there is an electric current through the fan's motor. **Electric energy** *is the energy that an electric current carries.* Electric appliances, such as fans and dishwashers, change electric energy into other forms of energy.

Radiant Energy—Light Energy

The Sun gives off energy that travels to Earth as electromagnetic waves. Unlike sound waves, electromagnetic waves can travel through a vacuum. Light waves, microwaves, and radio waves are all electromagnetic waves. *The energy that electromagnetic waves carry is* **radiant energy.** Sometimes radiant energy is called light energy.

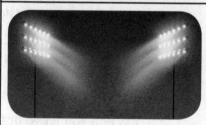

Nuclear Energy

At the center of every atom is a nucleus. **Nuclear energy** *is energy that is stored in the nucleus of an atom.* In the Sun, nuclear energy is released when nuclei join together. In a nuclear power plant, nuclear energy is released when the nuclei of uranium atoms are split apart.

5.4 Review

Compare and Contrast Fill in the blanks to summarize what you know about potential energy and kinetic energy. **TEKS** 6.8(A)

Forms of Energy

A. What is energy?

1. _____ is the ability to cause change.

2. Energy can cause an object to _____ the position of its motion.

B. Kinetic Energy—Energy of Motion

1. Energy due to motion is _____ .

2. The faster an object moves, the _____ kinetic energy it has.

3. The kinetic energy of an object depends on its _____ as well as its speed.

4. If two objects move at the same speed, the object with the _____ mass will have more kinetic energy.

C. Potential Energy—Stored Energy

1. _____ is stored energy.

2. When you are holding a book, energy is stored between the book and Earth; this type of energy is called _____ potential energy. This type of potential energy stored between an object and Earth depends on the _____ and _____ of the object.

3. Elastic potential energy is energy stored in objects that are compressed or _____ .

4. When you stretch a rubber band, you are storing _____ potential energy. When you let go of the rubber band, stored elastic potential energy is transformed into _____ energy.

5. Food has _____ potential energy, which is the energy stored in the bonds between atoms. This energy is released when _____ occurs.

Forms of Energy

Use Vocabulary

1. **Compare and contrast** kinetic energy and potential energy. **TEKS** 6.8(A) *supporting*

Apply the Essential Questions

2. **Define** energy.

3. **Explain** the factors that determine an object's kinetic energy. **TEKS** 6.8(A) *supporting*

4. The gravitational potential energy stored between an object and Earth depends on **TEKS** 6.8(A) *supporting*

   A. the object's height and weight.

   B. the object's mass and speed.

   C. the object's size and weight.

   D. the object's speed and height.

5. **Interpret Graphics** Fill in the graphic organizer to identify three types of potential energy.

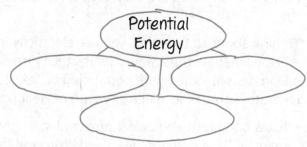

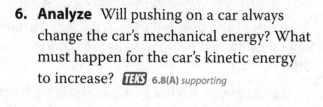 **H.O.T. Questions** (Higher Order Thinking)

6. **Analyze** Will pushing on a car always change the car's mechanical energy? What must happen for the car's kinetic energy to increase? **TEKS** 6.8(A) *supporting*

7. **Infer** Juanita lifts a round box and a square box to a shelf. The gravitational potential energy (GPE) for the round box increases by 50 J. The GPE for the square box increases by 100 J. On which box did Juanita do more work? Explain your reasoning. **TEKS** 6.8(A) *supporting*

Copyright © McGraw-Hill Education

NUCLEAR POWER IN TEXAS

This Pool is Not for Swimming!

Think about all the times you use electricity in one day. Now imagine the amount of electricity used by 25 million people – the entire population of Texas! Texas generates some of its electricity with nuclear power.

Texas operates two nuclear power plants – the Comanche Peak facilities, near Glen Rose, and the South Texas facilities, in Bay City. Together they produce more than 10 percent of Texas' electricity every year. To create this energy, the nonrenewable resource, uranium, is used as fuel.

However, the uranium used in nuclear reactions is still radioactive even after it is finished being used as fuel. Used nuclear fuel must be properly stored.

Spent nuclear fuel is temporarily held in storage pools, like the one at Comanche Power Plant, shown above.

Spent, or used, nuclear fuel is stored at each power plant in a used-fuel pool. A used-fuel pool is an above ground, steel-lined tank that stores nuclear waste for around five years. As the used-fuel pools near capacity, nuclear power plant operators move the spent fuel to dry cask storage systems.

A dry cask consists of a steel cylinder containing the spent fuel and an inert gas. These cylinders are encased in an additional layer of steel or concrete. The spent fuel can then be stored at a safe but still temporary location. Although this is a good, immediate storage solution, it won't last forever.

Humans need to find a long-term storage solution for spent nuclear fuel. The radioactive half-life of uranium is around 4.5 billion years. Scientists and power companies are working together with government agencies to find a way to permanently store the spent fuel. One day, researchers hope to be able to recycle and reuse the spent fuel.

It's Your Turn!

RESEARCH Scientists have proposed many ways to dispose of used nuclear fuel. Research one of the more recent proposals. Compare and contrast it with another proposal researched by another student in your class. Summarize why you think one proposal is better than the other.

Test-Taking Strategy

Eliminate Choices If you are unsure about a question, an easy way to increase your odds of getting the correct answer is to eliminate choices. If you know that one or two of the possible answers are not correct, you should eliminate them from your options. Then you can focus on determining which of the final two possible answers is correct.

Example

Use the graph to answer question 7.

Sea Turtle Tracking Data

Distance (km): 0, 5, 10, 15, 20, 25, 30, 35, 40, 45, 50, 55, 60, 65, 70, 75, 80, 85, 90, 95

Time (days): 1, 2, 3, 4, 5, 6

— Green sea turtle
— Ridley's sea turtle

2 From the graph, you know the green sea turtle traveled faster. So you can eliminate choices **C** and **D** from your options.

1 Carefully read the question and determine what it is asking. This question asks you to identify the turtle that moved at a faster average speed and calculate how much faster it moved than the slower turtle. In order to do this, you'll need to calculate the average speed for both turtles.

7 The distances two sea turtles swam over a period of six days were tracked and plotted on a line chart. Which turtle swam at a faster average speed? How much faster? **TEKS** 6.8(C) *supporting*

   A Green sea turtle; 16 km/day

   B Green sea turtle; 6 km/day

   C Ridley's sea turtle; 10 km/day

   D Ridley's sea turtle; 6 km/day

3 In order to calculate the average speed, you need to divide the distance traveled by the amount of time. The green sea turtle traveled 96 km in 6 days, or 16 km/day. The Ridley's sea turtle traveled 60 km in 6 days, or 10 km/day. The green sea turtle traveled 6 km/day faster than the Ridley's sea turtle. The correct answer is choice **B**.

Tip: When working with graphs and charts, track your pencil from the axis to the point to ensure you have the correct data value.

Multiple Choice

1   Four drivers took cars out for test drives on an open stretch of road. A graph
    of their distances and times is shown below. **TEKS** 6.8(C) *supporting;* 6.2(E)

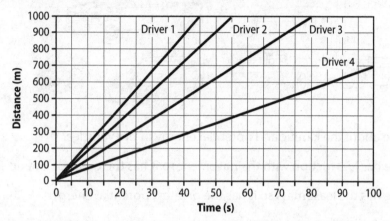

Use the graph to calculate the average speed of Driver 4. Round your answer to the nearest tenth of a
meter per second. Record and bubble in your answer on the answer document.

2

> A hotel has a balcony area above the lobby. The balcony is
> small and cannot be reached by elevator. The hotel manager
> wants a grand piano put up on the balcony. She hires movers
> to lift the piano up and over the railing. After investigating the
> problem, the movers develop a plan.

The piano movers decide to use a simple machine with one pulley called a moveable pulley system.
They will stand on the balcony and raise the piano. Determine how this machine will help them with
their task. **TEKS** 6.8(E)

A   It changes the direction of the force without changing the input force.

B   It increases the input force while changing the direction of the force.

C   It enables them to push the piano instead of lifting it to the balcony.

D   It reduces the input force, while keeping the direction of the force the same.

3 Imagine that the four different vehicles, shown below, are going in the same direction. The vehicles are traveling at the same speed. **TEKS** 6.8(A) *supporting*

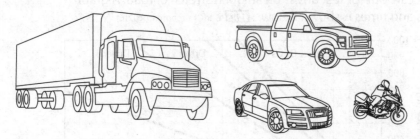

Which statement is true about the kinetic and potential energy of the vehicles?

A The motorcycle has less friction with the pavement so it has the greatest kinetic energy.

B The motorcycle has the least mass so it has the greatest potential energy.

C The moving van has the greatest kinetic energy because it has a greater mass.

D The pickup and the car have equal potential energy because they are moving at the same speed.

4

> Some students raced their radio-controlled cars. On different streets, different cars won the races. They noticed that Monica's car always won on Jorge's street. Jorge's car always won on Brian's street and Kuniko's street. Lily's car always won on Monica's street. They decided to investigate the forces involved so they could explain the results.

What might they include in their investigation plan to identify and describe why different cars were faster on different streets? **TEKS** 6.8(B); 6.2(B)

A a list of radio frequencies that radio-controlled cars use

B a table of traffic statistics for each street

C an analysis of the slope and surface of each street

D a record of the times of day each race was run

5 The drawing below shows a person playing pool. There are three balls on the table. **TEKS** 6.8(B)

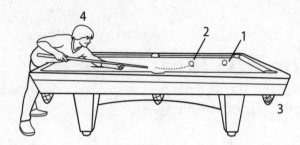

Identify the point in the diagram that shows an example of unbalanced forces.

A the ball at point 1

B the ball at point 2

C the table at point 3

D the student at point 4

6 A mechanical advantage is gained when using some simple machines. For example, an inclined plane can be used to raise an object that is too heavy to lift without a machine. Which inclined plane described in the chart would have the greatest mechanical advantage? **TEKS** 6.8(E)

	Length of inclined plane (m)	Height (m)
Inclined plane 1	60	15
Inclined plane 2	15	5
Inclined plane 3	25	10
Inclined plane 4	60	10

A Inclined plane 1

B Inclined plane 2

C Inclined plane 3

D Inclined plane 4

6

Energy and Energy Transformations

💡 ## The **BIG** Idea

Energy neither can be created nor destroyed; it changes form in predictable ways.

Soccer Ball

Five soccer players argued about when a soccer ball has energy. This is what they said:

☐ **Jorge:** The ball has to be moving to have energy.

☐ **Kurt:** The ball has energy only at the moment it is kicked.

☐ **Amos:** The ball has energy only when it is not moving.

☐ **Alan:** The ball has energy when it is moving and not moving.

☐ **Flavio:** The ball has no energy. There is no source of energy in the ball.

Who do you agree with the most? _____

Explain your thinking. What rule or reasoning did you use to decide when the soccer ball has energy?

INQUIRY

What's that sound?

Blocks of ice breaking off the front of this glacier can be bigger than a car. Imagine the loud rumble they make as they crash into the sea. But after the ice falls into the sea, it will gradually melt. All these processes involve energy transformations—energy changing from one form to another. What other energy transformations occur as the ice melts?

Write your response in your interactive notebook.

 LAB Manager

Go to your Lab Manual or visit connectED.mcgraw-hill.com to perform the labs for this lesson.

MiniLAB: *How does a flashlight work?*

TEKS 6.1(A); 6.2(A), (C), (E); 6.4(A), (B); 6.9(C)

MiniLAB: *How does energy change form?*

TEKS 6.1(A); 6.2(A), (C), (E); 6.4(A), (B); 6.9(C)

Skill Practice: *Can you identify energy transformations?*

TEKS 6.1(A); 6.2(A), (C), (D), (E); 6.4(A), (B); 6.9(C)

Explore Activity

TEKS 6.1(A); 6.2(A), (E); 6.4(B); 6.9(C)

Is energy lost when it changes form?

Energy can have different forms. What happens when energy changes from one form to another?

Procedure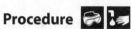

1. Read and complete the lab safety form.

2. Three students should sit in a circle. One student has 30 **buttons,** one has 30 **pennies,** and one has 30 **paper clips.**

3. Each student should exchange 10 items with the student to the right and 10 items with the student to the left.

4. Repeat step 3.

Think About This

1. If the buttons, pennies, and paper clips represented different forms of energy, what represented changes from one form of energy to another?

_____

_____

_____

_____

2. If each button, penny, and paper clip represented one unit of energy, did the total amount of energy increase, decrease, or stay the same? Explain your answer.

_____

_____

_____

_____

_____

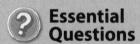

TEKS in this Lesson

6.8(A) Compare and contrast potential and kinetic energy

6.9(C) Demonstrate energy transformations such as energy in a flashlight battery changes from chemical energy to electrical energy to light energy

Also covers Process Standards: 6.1(A); 6.2(A), (C), (D), (E); 6.4(A), (B)

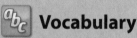

Essential Questions

- How are potential and kinetic energy the same? How are they different?
- How does energy change forms?

Vocabulary

law of conservation of energy

friction

223

Changes Between Forms of Energy *TEKS* 6.9(C)

It is the weekend, and you are ready to make some popcorn in the microwave and watch a movie. Energy changes form when you make popcorn and watch TV. As shown in **Figure 1**, a microwave changes electric energy into radiant energy. Radiant energy changes into thermal energy in the popcorn kernels.

The changes from electric energy to radiant energy to thermal energy are called energy transformations. As you watch the movie, energy transformations also occur in the television. A television transforms electric energy into sound energy and radiant energy.

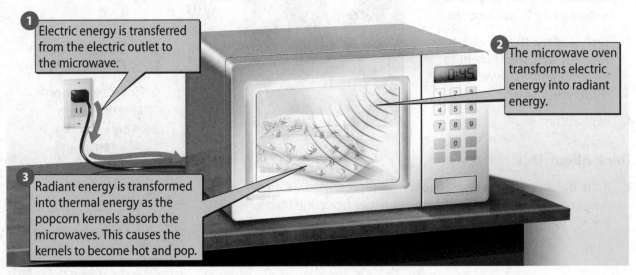

Electric energy is transferred from the electric outlet to the microwave.

The microwave oven transforms electric energy into radiant energy.

Radiant energy is transformed into thermal energy as the popcorn kernels absorb the microwaves. This causes the kernels to become hot and pop.

Figure 1 Energy changes from one form to another when you use a microwave oven to make popcorn.

Illustrate

1. In the graphic organizer below, draw your ideas of the energy transformations discussed in **Figure 1**. On the lines at the bottom, list any other energy transformations you can think of that occur when you use a microwave oven.

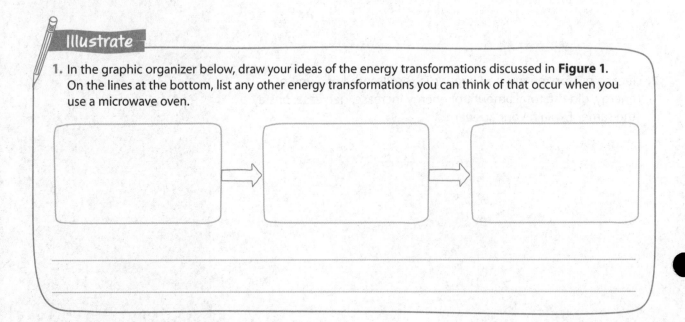

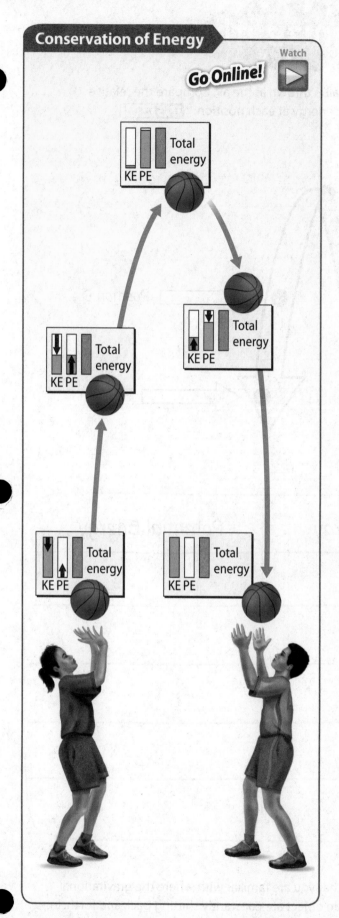

Go Online!   Watch ▶

Total energy
KE PE

Total energy
KE PE

Total energy
KE PE

Total energy
KE PE

Total energy
KE PE

Figure 2 The ball's kinetic energy (KE) and potential energy (PE) change as it moves.

Changes Between Kinetic Energy and Potential Energy TEKS 6.8(A)

Recall that kinetic energy and potential energy are forms of energy and that they have the ability to cause change. Because they are forms of energy, energy transformations can occur between them. When you toss a ball upward, as shown in **Figure 2**, the ball slows down as it moves upward, and then it gains speed as it moves downward. The ball's speed and height change as energy changes from one form to another.

Kinetic Energy to Potential Energy

The ball is moving fastest and has the most kinetic energy as it leaves your hand, as shown in **Figure 2**. As the ball moves upward, its speed and kinetic energy decrease. However, the potential energy is increasing because the ball's height is increasing. Kinetic energy is changing into potential energy. At the ball's highest point, the gravitational potential energy is greatest, and the ball's kinetic energy is the least.

Potential Energy to Kinetic Energy

As the ball moves downward, potential energy decreases. At the same time, the ball's speed increases. Therefore, the ball's kinetic energy increases. Potential energy is transformed into kinetic energy. When the ball reaches the player's hand again, its kinetic energy is at the maximum value once more.

✎ *Recognize*

2. In Figure 2, (circle) the basketball where it has the greatest gravitational potential energy.

Describe how energy changes as a ball is thrown in the air. Compare the relative amounts of potential and kinetic energy at each position. **TEKS** 6.8(A)

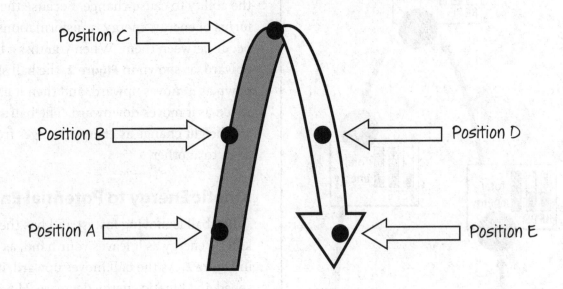

Position C

Position B

Position A

Position D

Position E

Position	Kinetic Energy	Potential Energy
A		
B		
C		
D		
E		

Connect it! Think of a situation that you are familiar with where the gravitational potential energy and kinetic energy of an object are constantly shifting back and forth. In your interactive notebook, write a description of the object and the energy transformations that occur.

Organize it! (left margin)

Copyright © McGraw-Hill Education (right margin)

226   Chapter 6

The Law of Conservation of Energy TEKS 6.9(C)

Think about turning on a flashlight. According to **the law of conservation of energy,** *energy can be transformed from one form into another or transferred from one region to another, but energy cannot be created or destroyed.* The total amount of energy in the universe does not change.

In the flashlight shown in **Figure 3**, chemical energy of the battery is transformed to electric energy (moving electrons) that moves through the contact strip to the bulb. The electric energy is transformed into radiant energy and thermal energy in the lightbulb. The law of conservation of energy indicates that the amount of radiant energy that shines out of the flashlight cannot be greater than the chemical energy stored in the battery.

The amount of radiant energy given off by the flashlight is less than the chemical energy in the battery. Where is the missing energy? As you read this lesson, you will learn that in every energy transformation some energy transfers to the environment.

Define

3. What is the law of conservation of energy?

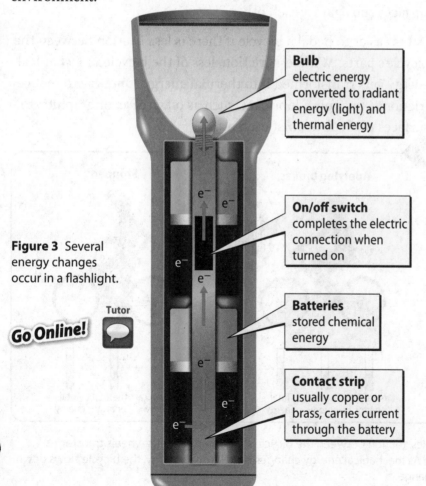

Bulb
electric energy converted to radiant energy (light) and thermal energy

On/off switch
completes the electric connection when turned on

Batteries
stored chemical energy

Contact strip
usually copper or brass, carries current through the battery

Figure 3 Several energy changes occur in a flashlight.

Go Online! Tutor

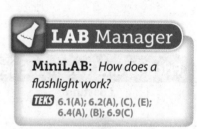

LAB Manager

MiniLAB: *How does a flashlight work?*
TEKS 6.1(A); 6.2(A), (C), (E); 6.4(A), (B); 6.9(C)

STEMonline

Become an electrical engineer and design and build an electrical security system. Visit ConnectED for the **STEM** activity **Keeping It Safe: An Electrical Security System.**

Resources

Go Online!

Copyright © McGraw-Hill Education

Friction and the Law of Conservation of Energy

Sometimes it may seem as though the law of conservation of energy is not accurate. Imagine riding a bicycle as in **Figure 4**. The moving bicycle has mechanical energy. What happens to this mechanical energy when you apply the brakes and the bicycle stops?

When you apply the brakes, the bicycle's mechanical energy is not destroyed. Instead the bicycle's mechanical energy is transformed into thermal energy, as shown in **Figure 4**. The total amount of energy never changes. The additional thermal energy causes the brakes, the wheels, and the air around the bicycle to become slightly warmer.

Friction *is a force that resists the sliding of two surfaces that are touching.* Friction between the bicycle's brake pads and the moving wheels transforms mechanical energy into thermal energy.

There is always some friction between any two surfaces that are rubbing against each other. As a result, some mechanical energy is always transformed into thermal energy when two surfaces rub against each other.

It is easier to pedal a bicycle if there is less friction between the bicycle's parts. With less friction, less of the bicycle's mechanical energy gets transformed into thermal energy. One way to reduce friction is to apply a lubricant, such as oil, grease, or graphite, to surfaces that rub against each other.

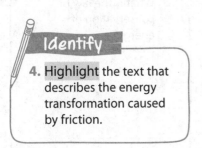

Identify

4. Highlight the text that describes the energy transformation caused by friction.

LAB Manager

Skill Practice: *Can you identify energy transformations?*

TEKS 6.1(A); 6.2(A), (C), (D), (E); 6.4(A), (B); 6.9(C)

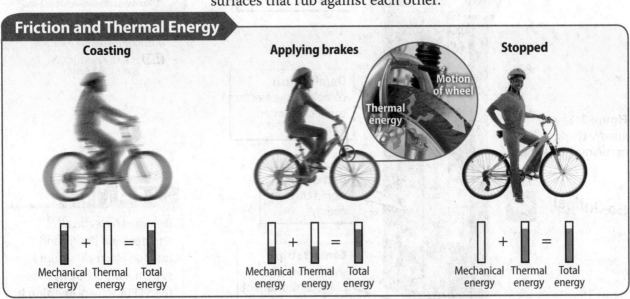

Friction and Thermal Energy

Coasting

Mechanical energy + Thermal energy = Total energy

Applying brakes

Motion of wheel

Thermal energy

Mechanical energy + Thermal energy = Total energy

Stopped

Mechanical energy + Thermal energy = Total energy

Figure 4 When the girl applies the brakes, friction between the bicycle's brake pads and its wheels transforms mechanical energy into thermal energy. As mechanical energy changes into thermal energy, the bicycle slows down. The total amount of energy does not change.

Copyright © McGraw-Hill Education   Hutchings Photography/Digital Light Source

Using Energy

Every day you use different forms of energy to do different things. You might use the radiant energy from a lamp to light a room, or you might use the chemical energy stored in your body to run a race. When you use energy, you usually change it from one form into another. For example, the lamp changes electric energy into radiant energy and thermal energy.

Using Thermal Energy

All forms of energy can be transformed into thermal energy. People often use thermal energy to cook food or provide warmth. A gas stove transforms the chemical energy stored in natural gas into the thermal energy that cooks food. An electric space heater transforms the electric energy from a power plant into the thermal energy that warms a room. In a jet engine, burning fuel releases thermal energy that the engine transforms into mechanical energy.

Using Chemical Energy

During photosynthesis, a plant transforms the Sun's radiant energy into chemical energy that it stores in chemical compounds. Some of these compounds become food for other living things. Your body transforms the chemical energy from your food into the kinetic energy necessary for movement. Your body also transforms chemical energy into the thermal energy necessary to keep you warm.

Using Radiant Energy

The cell phone in **Figure 5** sends and receives radiant energy using microwaves. When you are listening to someone on a cell phone, that cell phone is transforming radiant energy into electric energy and then into sound energy. When you are speaking into a cell phone, it is transforming sound energy into electric energy and then into radiant energy.

Figure 5 A cell phone changes sound energy into radiant energy when you speak.

Sound waves carry energy into the cell phone.

The cell phone converts the energy carried by sound waves into radiant energy that is carried away by microwaves.

Peter Cade/Photodisc/Getty Images

Give Examples

5. Describe one way you use thermal, chemical, or radiant energy. Do not use an example from the text.

_____

_____

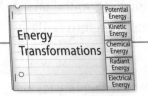
FOLDABLES®

Cut three sheets of paper in half. Use the six half sheets to make a side-tab book with five tabs and a cover. Use your book to organize your notes on energy transformations.

> Energy Transformations
>
> Potential Energy
> Kinetic Energy
> Chemical Energy
> Radiant Energy
> Electrical Energy

Using Electric Energy

Many of the devices you might use every day, such as handheld video games, mp3 players, and hair dryers, use electric energy. Some devices, such as hair dryers, use electric energy from electrical power plants. Other appliances, such as handheld video games, transform the chemical energy stored in batteries into electric energy.

Waste Energy

When energy changes form, some thermal energy is always released. For example, a lightbulb converts some electric energy into radiant energy. However, the lightbulb also transforms some electric energy into thermal energy. This is what makes the lightbulb hot. Some of this thermal energy moves into the air and cannot be used.

Scientists often refer to thermal energy that cannot be used as waste energy. Whenever energy is used, some energy is transformed into useful energy and some is transformed into waste energy. For example, we use the chemical energy in gasoline to make the cars in **Figure 6** move. However, most of that chemical energy ends up as waste energy—thermal energy that moves into the air.

Identify

6. Underline in the text the description of the type of energy most often released as waste energy by automobiles.

Figure 6 Cars transform most of the energy in gasoline into waste energy.

Summarize it!

Summarize the change in energy as the boy who was in-line skating slowed down. **TEKS** 6.9(C)

1. When the boy was skating, kinetic energy was _____ and thermal energy was _____ .

2. As the boy applied his brake pad, kinetic energy was _____ and thermal energy was _____ .

3. When the boy stopped, kinetic energy was _____ and thermal energy was _____ .

4. At all times, *total energy* = _____ *energy* + _____ *energy*.

Identify how energy changed form so it could be used in each example. **TEKS** 6.9(C)

A space heater warms a room.	→	
You eat dinner.	→	
A radio plays.	→	

Connect it! Classify the phrases in the box as examples of potential or kinetic energy. Place each phrase number under the correct heading. Some numbers may be placed in both categories. **TEKS** 6.8(A)

1. standing at the top of a slide	5. roll down a grassy hill	9. frog leaping into the water
2. wind up for the pitch	6. an unburned lump of coal	10. book falls from a high shelf
3. juice in an orange	7. throw a curve ball	11. a parked car
4. move downhill in a roller coaster	8. a battery	12. frog sitting on a lily pad

Potential Energy	Kinetic Energy

Summarize it!

Apply the Essential Questions

1. **Demonstrate** the law of conservation of energy in terms of energy transformations in a toaster. **TEKS** 6.9(C) *supporting*

_____

_____

_____

_____

_____

_____

_____

2. **Explain** how potential energy and kinetic energy are the same. How are they different? **TEKS** 6.8(A) *supporting*

_____

_____

_____

3. **Propose** Describe in your own words a situation where chemical energy is transformed to potential energy. **TEKS** 6.9(C) *supporting*

_____

_____

_____

 H.O.T. Questions (Higher Order Thinking)

4. **Identify** Choose two electrical devices. For each device, identify the forms of energy that electric energy is transformed into. **TEKS** 6.9(C) *supporting*

_____

_____

_____

_____

5. **Explain** the energy transformation that takes place as a skateboard coasting on a flat surface slows down and comes to a stop. **TEKS** 6.9(C) *supporting*

_____

_____

_____

6. **Critique** Harold stretches a rubber band and lets it go. The rubber band flies across the room. He says this demonstrates the transformation of kinetic to elastic potential energy. Is Harold correct? Explain. **TEKS** 6.8(A) *supporting*

_____

_____

_____

_____

Energy Transformations... and YOU!

You just learned about energy transformations. So what? What does this mean to you? How does this affect your life? Why should you care about how energy changes form?

Well, actually, nothing you do, nothing anybody does, nothing that happens in the entire universe could occur without energy changing forms. Stars would not shine. Your mp3 player would not play, and you would not even get up in the morning.

It all starts with the Sun. Radiant energy from the Sun reaches Earth. This solar energy is changed through photosynthesis to chemical energy stored in the carbohydrate molecules in plant cells. When you eat a plant, or eat an animal that ate a plant, the energy stored in the plant is moved to the cells of your body.

When you sit up in bed each morning, energy stored as sugar molecules in your body's cells is transformed to thermal energy that powers your muscles. Your muscles then transform that thermal energy into the kinetic energy of your moving body. And, of course, the same thing needs to happen just so you can open your eyes!

Eyes are special energy transformers. Your eyes change radiant energy, such as sunlight, to electric energy that travels through nerves to the brain. The brain processes the electric signals and gives the sense of sight.

How about when you play or work hard? Your body might begin to sweat. Believe it or not, sweat is an important energy transformer, too. When your body begins to overheat, sweat comes to the rescue. Some of your body's thermal energy transforms to the increased kinetic energy of the vibrating water molecules of your sweat. As the sweat evaporates, the water molecules carry the excess energy away from your body, keeping you cool.

And these are only a few of the millions of energy transformations that affect your life every day.

Our bodies transform chemical energy into fuel for motion.

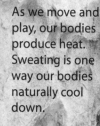
As we move and play, our bodies produce heat. Sweating is one way our bodies naturally cool down.

So **WHAT?!**

Energy transformations do have an impact on you. They are happening all the time, all around you. Your life depends on them!

THAT'S what!!

INQUIRY

Catchin' Some Waves? This Texas horned lizard regulates its body temperature by absorbing thermal energy from its environment. Some lizards raise their body temperature well above the air temperature by absorbing radiant energy transferred by waves from the Sun. How do you sometimes absorb energy like the Texas horned lizard?

Write your response in your interactive notebook.

LAB Manager

Go to your Lab Manual or visit connectED.mcgraw-hill.com to perform the labs for this lesson.

MiniLAB: *How does thermal energy move?*
TEKS 6.1(A); 6.2(A), (C), (E); 6.4(A), (B); 6.9(B)

MiniLAB: *How do the particles in a liquid move when heated?*
TEKS 6.1(A); 6.2(A), (C), (E); 6.4(A), (B); 6.9(A)

MiniLAB: *What affects the transfer of thermal energy?*
TEKS 6.1(A); 6.2(A), (C), (E); 6.3(A); 6.4(A), (B); 6.9(A)

LAB: *Design an Insulated Container*
TEKS 6.1(A); 6.2(B), (C), (E); 6.3(A); 6.4(A), (B); 6.9(A)

Explore Activity

TEKS 6.1(A); 6.2(A), (C), (E); 6.4(A), (B); 6.9(A)

Where is it the hottest?

Would your hands get just as warm if you held them at the sides of a campfire instead of directly over a campfire?

Procedure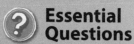

⚠ *Tie back hair and roll up sleeves.*

1. Read and complete a lab safety form.

2. Use **modeling clay** to hold a **birthday candle** upright. Use a **ring stand and clamp** to mount a **thermometer** horizontally above the candle flame. The thermometer bulb should be 10 cm above the top of the candle. Record the temperature on the thermometer in your table. Use a **match** to light the candle. Record the temperature every 30 seconds until the temperature reaches 70°C. Add more time columns to the table if needed. Blow out the candle.

⚠ *Do not put the thermometer within 10 cm of the flame.*

3. Repeat step 2 with a new candle. This time mount the thermometer 10 cm to the side of the candle flame.

Thermometer Above Flame								
Time (sec)	0	30	60	90	120	150	180	210
Temp (°C)								

Thermometer to the Side of Flame								
Time (sec)	0	30	60	90	120	150	180	210
Temp (°C)								

Think About This

1. How do you think the energy from the flame traveled to the thermometer in each trial? Explain.

_____

_____

_____

_____

TEKS in this Lesson

6.9(A) Investigate methods of thermal energy transfer, including conduction, convection, and radiation

6.9(B) Verify through investigations that thermal energy moves in a predictable pattern from warmer to cooler until all the substances attain the same temperature such as an ice cube melting

Also covers Process Standards: 6.1(A); 6.2(A), (B), (C), (E); 6.3(A); 6.4(A), (B)

? Essential Questions

- In which three ways is thermal energy transferred?
- Does thermal energy move in predictable patterns?

abc Vocabulary

temperature
heat
conduction
radiation
convection
vaporization
thermal conductor
thermal insulator

Kinetic Molecular Theory TEKS 6.9(A), (B)

In every energy transformation, some of the energy is transformed into thermal energy. Some of this thermal energy transfers to other materials. The transfer of thermal energy between materials depends on the movement of particles in the materials. The kinetic molecular theory explains how particles move. It has three major points:

- All matter is made of particles.

- Particles are in constant, random motion.

- Particles constantly collide with each other and with the walls of their container.

The kinetic molecular theory explains that the carbonated beverage in **Figure 1** is made of particles. The particles move in different directions and at different speeds. They collide with each other and with the particles that make up the ice and the glass.

Temperature

When you pick up a glass of ice cold soda, the glass feels cold. Could you estimate its temperature? The temperature of something depends on how much kinetic energy the particles that make up the material have. *The measure of the average kinetic energy of the particles in a material is* **temperature**. If most of the drink particles have little kinetic energy, then the drink has a low temperature and the glass feels cold. The SI unit for temperature is the kelvin (K). However, scientists often use the Celsius temperature scale (°C) to measure temperature.

STEMonline

Become an extreme-conditions engineer designing a safe and structurally sound research building to be used in the harsh conditions of Antarctica. Visit ConnectED for the **STEM** activity **Thermal Energy: An Antarctic Challenge.**

Resources

Go Online!

Recall

1. Highlight in the text the three points of the kinetic molecular theory.

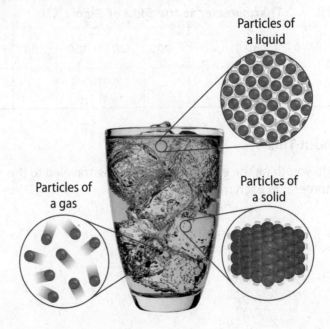

Particles of a liquid

Particles of a gas

Particles of a solid

Figure 1 Particles that make up all matter, including carbonated beverages, are in constant motion. On average, solid particles move slowest, liquid particles move faster, and gas particles move the fastest.

Watch

Go Online!

Thermal Expansion

Suppose your teacher told everyone in your classroom to run around. There probably would not be enough space in your classroom for everyone to run as fast as they could. But, if you were in a large gymnasium, then everyone could run very quickly. When the particles that make up a material move slowly, they occupy less volume than they do at a higher temperature. As the temperature of a material increases, particles begin to move faster. They collide with each other more often and push each other farther apart. Thermal expansion is the increase in volume of a material due to a temperature increase, as shown in **Figure 2**. When the temperature of a material decreases, its volume decreases. This is thermal contraction.

Most materials contract as their temperature decreases, but water is an exception. When water is cooled to near its freezing point, interactions between water molecules push the molecules apart. Water expands as it freezes because of these molecular interactions, as shown in **Figure 3**.

Figure 2 The balloon on the top was cooled to −198°C using liquid nitrogen. As the balloon warms to room temperature, the molecules move faster and expand. The balloon undergoes thermal expansion.

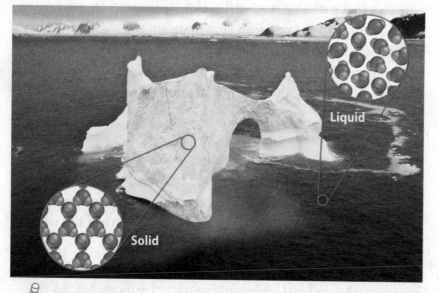

Liquid

Solid

Figure 3 Because of the structure of a water molecule, as water freezes, the molecules attract in a way that creates empty spaces between them. This makes ice less dense than water. Because ice is less dense than water, ice floats on water.

Show

2. Relate temperature to thermal expansion.

When temperature increases, the _____ of particles _____ .

Thermal expansion occurs when particles _____ and _____ .

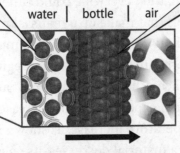

Particles in the water hit particles in the bottle and cause the bottle particles to vibrate faster—average kinetic energy (temperature) of the bottle increases.

When the cool air particles hit the warm bottle particles, the air particles move faster after the collision. The average kinetic energy (temperature) of the air increases.

water | bottle | air

Thermal energy moves from the warm water to the cool air by the collision of particles.

Thermal energy moves from warm to cooler materials.

Figure 4 Thermal energy is transferred by collisions of particles.

MiniLAB: *How does thermal energy move?*
TEKS 6.1(A); 6.2(A), (C), (E); 6.4(A), (B); 6.9(B)

Transferring Thermal Energy

Suppose you put a warm bottle of water in the refrigerator. As shown in **Figure 4**, moving water molecules collide with the particles that make up the bottle. These collisions transfer kinetic energy to the particles that make up the bottle, and they vibrate faster. As the particles move faster, their average kinetic energy, or temperature, increases. The particles that make up the bottle then collide with particles that make up the air in the refrigerator.

The average kinetic energy of the particles that make up the air in the refrigerator increases. In other words, the temperature of the air in the refrigerator increases. The average kinetic energy of the particles of water decreases as thermal energy moves from the water to the bottle. Therefore, the temperature of the water decreases.

As the kinetic energy of the particles that make up a material increases, the thermal energy of the particles increases. As the kinetic energy of the particles that make up a material decreases, the thermal energy of the particles decreases. So, when particles transfer kinetic energy, they transfer thermal energy.

Infer

3. What happens to the kinetic energy of a cup of warm water when it is placed in a refrigerator?

_____

_____

Thermal Energy and Heat

Thermal energy moves from warmer materials, such as the warm water in the bottle, to cooler materials, such as the cool air in the refrigerator. *The movement of thermal energy from a region of higher temperature to a region of lower temperature is called* **heat**. Because your hand is warmer than the water bottle, thermal energy moves from your hand to the bottle. When you place the warm bottle in the refrigerator, thermal energy moves from the warm bottle to the cool air in the refrigerator.

Thermal Equilibrium

What happens if you leave the water in the refrigerator for several hours? The temperature of the water, the bottle, and the air in the refrigerator become the same. When the temperatures of materials that are in contact are the same, the materials are said to be in thermal equilibrium. After the materials reach thermal equilibrium, the particles that make up the water, the bottle, and the air continue to collide with each other. The particles transfer kinetic energy back and forth, but the average kinetic energy of all the particles remains the same.

Word Origin

equilibrium from Latin *aequus*, means "equal"; and *libra*, means "a balance or scale"

FOLDABLES

Cut out the Lesson 6.2 Foldable in the back of the book. Use it to explain the different ways in which thermal energy is transferred.

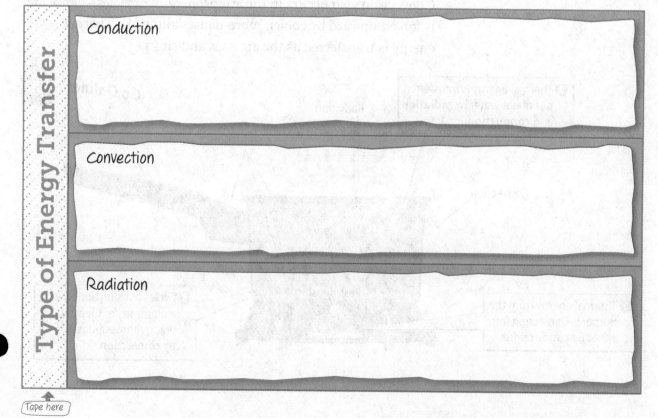

Type of Energy Transfer

Conduction

Convection

Radiation

Tape here

Heat Transfer TEKS 6.9(A)

Suppose you want to heat water to cook pasta, as shown in **Figure 5**. You put a pan of water on the stove and turn the stove on. How is thermal energy transferred to the water?

❶ Conduction Fast-moving particles of the gases in the flame collide with the particles that make up the pan. This transfers thermal energy to the pan. Then, the particles that make up the pan collide with particles of water, transferring thermal energy to the water. **Conduction** *is the transfer of thermal energy by collisions between particles in matter.*

❷ Radiation If you put your hands near the side of the pan, you feel warmth. *The thermal energy you feel is from* **radiation**—*the transfer of thermal energy by electromagnetic waves.* All objects emit radiation, but warmer materials, such as hot water, emit more radiation than cooler ones.

❸ Convection The flame, or hot gases, heats water at the bottom of the pan. The water at the bottom of the pan undergoes thermal expansion and is now less dense than the water above it. The denser water sinks and forces the less dense, warmer water upward. The water continues this cycle of warming, rising, cooling, and sinking, as thermal energy moves throughout the water. *The transfer of thermal energy by the movement of the particles from one part of a material to another is* **convection.** Convection also occurs in the atmosphere. Warm, less-dense air is forced upward by cooler, more-dense falling air. Thermal energy is transferred as the air rises and sinks.

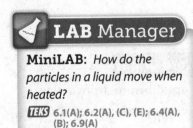

LAB Manager

MiniLAB: *How do the particles in a liquid move when heated?*

TEKS 6.1(A); 6.2(A), (C), (E); 6.4(A), (B); 6.9(A)

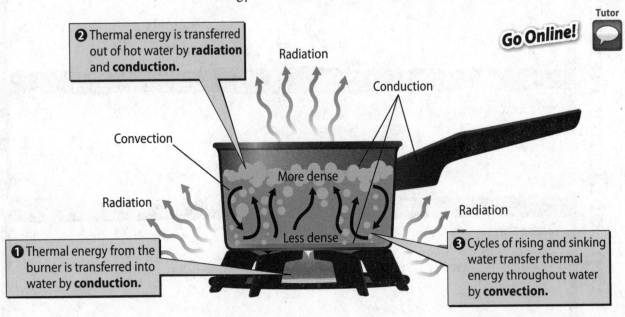

❷ Thermal energy is transferred out of hot water by **radiation** and **conduction.**

Radiation

Conduction

Go Online! Tutor

Convection

More dense

Less dense

Radiation

❶ Thermal energy from the burner is transferred into water by **conduction.**

Radiation

❸ Cycles of rising and sinking water transfer thermal energy throughout water by **convection.**

Figure 5 Conduction, radiation, and convection are ways in which thermal energy is transferred.

Complete the graphic organizer below. **TEKS** 6.9(A)

Characterize convection.

occurs in fluids

transfer of: _____

by: _____

Characterize radiation.

can happen through

- solids
- liquids
- gases
- vacuum

transfer of: _____

by: _____

Characterize conduction.

can happen in

- solids
- liquids
- gases

transfer of: _____

by: _____

Figure 6 If enough thermal energy is added to a material, it will change state.

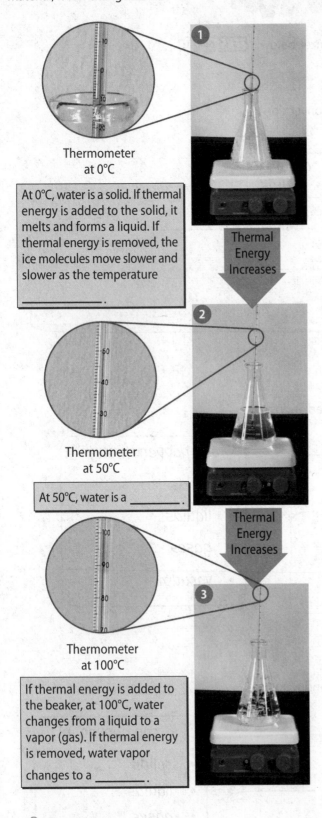

Thermometer at 0°C

At 0°C, water is a solid. If thermal energy is added to the solid, it melts and forms a liquid. If thermal energy is removed, the ice molecules move slower and slower as the temperature _____.

Thermal Energy Increases

Thermometer at 50°C

At 50°C, water is a _____.

Thermal Energy Increases

Thermometer at 100°C

If thermal energy is added to the beaker, at 100°C, water changes from a liquid to a vapor (gas). If thermal energy is removed, water vapor changes to a _____.

Infer

4. In **Figure 6** above, fill in the blanks to help explain changes in state.

Heat and Changes of State

When thermal energy is added or removed from a substance, sometimes only the temperature changes. At other times, a more dramatic change occurs—a change of state.

Changes Between Solids and Liquids

What happens if you place a flask of ice on a hot plate, as shown in **Figure 6?** Thermal energy moves from the hot plate through the flask to the ice. The temperature of the ice increases. When the temperature of the ice reaches the melting point of ice, 0°C, the ice begins to melt. Melting is the change of state from a solid to a liquid. Other materials have different melting points. For example, silver melts at 962°C, and diamonds melt at a temperature greater than 3,550°C.

As thermal energy transfers to the melting ice, the temperature of the ice does not change. However, the potential energy of the ice increases. As the water molecules move farther apart, the potential energy between the molecules increases.

The reverse process occurs as thermal energy is removed from water. When water is placed in a freezer, thermal energy moves from the water to the colder air in the freezer. The average kinetic energy of the water decreases. When the temperature of the water reaches 0°C, the water begins to freeze. Freezing is the change of state from a liquid to a solid. The freezing point of water is the same as the melting point of ice. Freezing is the opposite of melting.

While water is freezing, the temperature remains at 0°C until all the water is frozen. After all the water freezes, the temperature of the ice begins to decrease. As the temperature decreases, the water molecules vibrate in place at a slower and slower rate.

Changes Between Liquids and Gases

What happens when ice melts? As thermal energy transfers to the ice, the particles move faster and faster. The average kinetic energy of the water particles that make up ice increases, and the ice melts. The temperature of the water continues to increase until it reaches 100°C. At 100°C, the water begins to vaporize. **Vaporization** *is the change of state from a liquid to a gas.* While the water is changing state—from a liquid to a gas—the kinetic energy of the particles remains constant.

Liquids vaporize in two ways—boiling and evaporation. Vaporization that occurs within a liquid is called boiling. Vaporization that occurs at the surface of a liquid is called evaporation. Have you heard the term water vapor? The gaseous state of a substance that is normally a liquid or a solid at room temperature is called vapor. Because water is a liquid at room temperature, its gaseous state is referred to as water vapor.

The reverse process also can occur. Removing thermal energy from a gas changes it to a liquid. The change of state from a gas to a liquid is condensation. The condensation of water vapor that forms on grass overnight is called dew.

Changes Between Solids and Gases

Usually, water transforms from a solid to a liquid and then to a gas as it absorbs thermal energy. However, this is not always the case. On cold winter days, ice often changes directly to water vapor without passing through the liquid state. Sublimation is the change of state that occurs when a solid changes to a gas without passing through the liquid state. Dry ice, or solid carbon dioxide, sublimes as shown in **Figure 7**. Dry ice is used to keep foods frozen when they are shipped.

When thermal energy is removed from some materials, they undergo deposition. Deposition is the change of state from a gas directly to a solid without passing through the liquid state. Water vapor undergoes deposition when it freezes and forms frost, as shown in **Figure 7**.

Copyright © McGraw-Hill Education   (l)Charles D. Winters/Photo Researchers, (r)Thomas Sbampato/Alaskastock/photolibrary.com

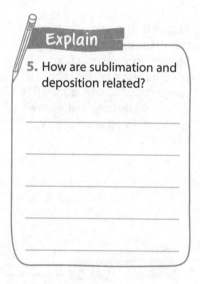

Science Use v. Common Use

sublime

Science Use to change from a solid state to a gas state without passing through the liquid state

Common Use Inspiring awe; supreme, outstanding, or lofty in thought or language

Explain

5. How are sublimation and deposition related?

_____

_____

_____

_____

_____

Figure 7 Not all materials go through all three states of matter when they change state. Some materials undergo sublimation (left), and other materials undergo deposition (right).

Conductors and Insulators TEKS 6.9(A)

When you put a metal pan on a burner, the pan gets very hot. If the pan has a handle made of wood or plastic, such as the one in **Figure 8**, the handle stays cool. Why doesn't the handle get hot like the pan as a result of thermal conduction?

The metal that makes up the pan is a **thermal conductor**, *a material in which thermal energy moves quickly*. The atoms that make up thermal conductors have electrons that are free to move, transferring thermal energy easily. The material that makes up the pan's handles is a **thermal insulator**, *a material in which thermal energy moves slowly*. The electrons in thermal insulators are held tightly in place and do not transfer thermal energy easily.

Figure 8 The color variations of this thermogram show the temperature variations in the pan and stove burner. The temperature scale is from white (warmest) through red, yellow, green, cyan, blue, and black (coolest).

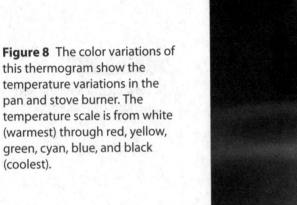 Illustrate

6. Draw cartoon characters of two electrons in the space below. One of the electrons should be in a material that is a good thermal insulator, and the other electron should be in a material that is a good thermal conductor. Show how they are alike and how they are different. Include a caption under your cartoon.

6.2 Review

Go Online! Check

Draw an open view of your home in the space below. Show as many different rooms as you can. Then, throughout the rooms, illustrate where thermal energy is transferred by convection, conduction, and radiation.

TEKS 6.9(A)

Summarize it!

Particles in Motion

Use Vocabulary

1. **Define** *radiation* in your own words. Give an example of radiation.
   TEKS 6.9(A)

Apply the Essential Questions

2. **Explain** the methods of thermal energy transfer in conduction, convection, and radiation. **TEKS** 6.9(A)

3. **Explain** how you could decrease the thermal energy of a can of soup you just took out of your pantry. **TEKS** 6.9(B)

4. **Describe** how thermal conductors and insulators are different. **TEKS** 6.9(A)

🔥 H.O.T. Questions (Higher Order Thinking)

5. **Summarize** why conduction occurs in all materials but convection only occurs in liquids and gases. **TEKS** 6.9(A)

6. **Write** an explanation of why people do not come to thermal equilibrium with the air on cold days. **TEKS** 6.9(B)

7. **Compare** You hold a 65°C cup of cocoa. Your hand is 37°C and the outside air is 6°C. Describe the flow of thermal energy. **TEKS** 6.9(B)

Biomass

Fresh Ideas About Not-So-Fresh Sources of Fuel

Grass clippings can be broken down to produce methane gas. The device used to convert grass clippings to methane gas is called a digester. The methane gas produced can be used in place of natural gas in appliances. It also can be used to power turbines that produce electricity.

Many people consider grass clippings, dog waste, and used cooking oil garbage. But instead of seeing these materials as garbage, some innovative thinkers see them as sources of biomass energy.

For centuries, humans have used biomass, such as wood, for energy. New technology is expanding the ways biomass can be used. Now biomass can be converted into fuel that can be used to power automobiles, heat homes, and generate electricity.

The use of these fuel sources has several benefits. First, any fuel produced using biomass decreases dependence on nonrenewable resources such as fossil fuels. Also, use of these materials for fuel decreases the amount of waste going to landfills. Technologies that generate fuel from biomass continue to be developed and improved. Who knows what will be used for fuel in the future!

▲ Dog waste can be converted to fuel in a methane digester. Dog waste contains a lot of energy because of the healthy, energy-rich foods that are fed to most dogs in the United States.

▲ Used cooking oil is an expensive disposal problem for restaurants. Instead, it can be collected and used on its own or combined with diesel fuel to power specially equipped vehicles.

It's Your Turn!

RESEARCH Technology has been developed that uses waste from slaughterhouses to make oil. Find out more about this process. Prepare an oral presentation to share what you have learned with other students in your class.

Test-Taking Strategy

Calculations Some test questions require calculations. By carefully reading the question, you can determine what you are being asked to calculate.

Example

Use the chart below to answer question 1.

Phase Changes of Elements		
Element	**Melting Point**	**Boiling Point**
Helium	−272°C	−269°C
Lead	328°C	1740°C
Iron	1535°C	2750°C
Carbon	3500°C	4827°C

2 Next, calculate the difference between the melting and boiling points for each element. Subtract the melting point temperature from the boiling point temperature for each element.

1 Which element in the table has the largest range of liquid state temperature? **TEKS** 6.9(A)

A helium

B lead

C iron

D carbon

1 Carefully read the question and identify what the question is asking. In this case, you are asked to find which element has the largest range of liquid state temperature, or the temperature between melting point and boiling point.

3 Lead has the largest liquid range at 1412°C. The correct answer is choice **B**.

Tip: Calculation questions will have important words that will tell you exactly what information you need. Other important signal words include *most, least, difference, range, maximum, minimum, sum,* and *average.*

Multiple Choice

1

> Thermal energy is the energy a substance has because of its moving particles. This energy can be transferred between two systems. Systems with faster moving particles will transfer their energy to systems with slower moving particles.

Some students want to demonstrate thermal energy transfer. They devise the following method: A large black balloon is taken to a shady area and filled with cool air. The balloon is then taken to a bright sunny location. After a short time, the balloon begins to expand. This investigation verifies that _____. **TEKS** 6.9(A); 6.2(B)

   A a balloon filled with cool air will rise into the atmosphere

   B solar energy was transferred to the balloon by radiation

   C the air inside the balloon cooled by convection

   D the sunlight caused the air in the balloon to contract

2 Aisha wants to verify that thermal energy moves from warmer substances to cooler substances until all the substances attain the same temperature. She writes her experimental plan after forming her hypothesis about what will happen to the temperatures at different locations throughout the system. She develops a materials list and procedure for her investigation. **TEKS** 6.9(B); 6.4(B)

Materials	Procedure	Communication
hotplate 500 mL beaker thermometers timer piece of ice water	1. Place water and ice in the beaker. 2. Take the temperature of the water at the bottom of the beaker, the center of the beaker and the top of the beaker. 3. Start the stopwatch and record the temperature. 4. Place the beaker with water and ice on the hotplate. Turn the hot plate to medium heat. 5. Every 2 min, record the time and temperature until the water boils. 6. Continue heating and take two more temperature readings.	Create a graph with the data. Write a report that includes the hypothesis, whether the hypothesis is supported, and a conclusion statement about thermal energy movement.

Which lab equipment did Aisha omit from her materials list that will ensure her personal safety as she performs her experiment?

   A balance scale, candle, glass dish

   B goggles, apron, heat-resistant gloves

   C metal tongs, Bunsen burner, spark igniter

   D vent hood, fire safety handbook, eye-wash station

3

Conduction can take place between two objects that are in contact with each other. Heat flows from the warmer object to the cooler object. Conduction takes place when the faster moving molecules of warmer materials transfer some of their energy to slower moving molecules of cooler materials.

Sarah has four diagrams that show methods of heat transfer. Which image shows only conduction?

TEKS 6.9(A)

A

B

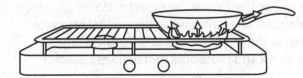

C

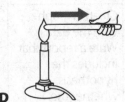

D

4 Jake and Sonya perform a laboratory investigation to verify thermal energy transfer. Jake measures the temperature of a beaker with hot water to be 50°C. He fills a small aluminum cup with the hot water and places it inside a foam cup of cold water, which he measures and records at 10°C. Sonya places a temperature probe into each cup of water. They attach the two probes to a graphing program of a computer. After a period of time, Jake prints a graph. Which picture shows a possible graph made by the computer? **TEKS** 6.9(B); 6.2(C)

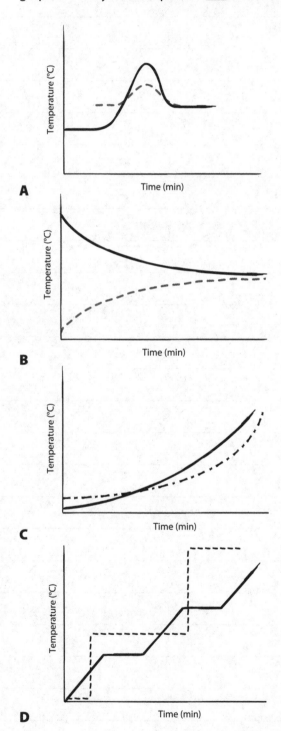

A

B

C

D

TEKS Strand 4
Earth and Space

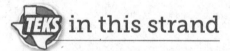 **in this strand**

✓ **6.10** The student understands the structure of Earth, the rock cycle, and plate tectonics.

✓ **6.11** The student understands the organization of our solar system and the relationships among the various bodies that comprise it.

✓ Also includes the following Scientific Investigation and Reasoning strand TEKS: **6.1; 6.2; 6.3; 6.4**

Texas FunFact

Did You Know? There are robots working in space! The Robonaut is a specially designed robot that was created by engineers and scientists at the Johnson Space Center in Houston, Texas. The engineers' challenge was to design a machine that can help humans work and explore space. The Robonaut is currently aboard the *International Space Station* and was the first humanoid robot in space. It is capable of working side by side with people and can also perform tasks that are too dangerous for human astronauts. Robotic technology, including the Robonaut, will play a big role in future space exploration missions. That is one giant step for robot-kind!

Earth's Structure

The **BIG** Idea

Earth's structure consists of several layers, including an outer layer of moving tectonic plates.

LESSON

7.1 Spherical Earth

Earth's major systems interact by exchanging matter and energy. A change in one of Earth's systems affects all of the other Earth systems.

TEKS 6.1(A); 6.2(A), (C), (E); 6.3(B); 6.4(A), (B)

LESSON

7.2 Earth's Interior

Earth is made up of several different layers. Each layer has a unique composition and set of properties.

TEKS 6.10(A); Also covers 6.1(A); 6.2(A), (C), (E); 6.3(B), (C), (D); 6.4(A), (B)

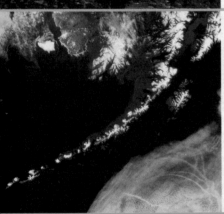

LESSON

7.3 The Theory of Plate Tectonics

Earth's crust is made of 14 tectonic plates that interact at their boundaries in various ways.

TEKS 6.10(C), (D); Also covers 6.1(A), (B); 6.2(A), (C), (E); 6.3(B); 6.4(A), (B)

Meteorite Impacts

A meteorite is a solid object that comes from space, passes through our atmosphere, and lands on Earth. If a large meteorite were to strike Earth today, where would it most likely fall? (Circle) your prediction.

land

ice

ocean

fresh water

Explain your thinking. What reasoning did you use to make your prediction?

Copyright © McGraw-Hill Education   ©Bloomimage/Corbis

INQUIRY

Why is Earth spherical? This image of Earth was taken from space. Notice Earth's shape and the wispy clouds that surround part of the planet. What else do you notice about Earth?

Write your response in your interactive notebook.

LAB Manager

Go to your Lab Manual or visit connectED.mcgraw-hill.com to perform the labs for this lesson.

MiniLAB: *Which materials will sink?*

TEKS 6.1(A); 6.2(A); 6.4(A), (B)

Explore Activity

How can you model Earth's spheres?

Earth has different spheres made of water, solid materials, air, and life. Each sphere has unique characteristics.

Procedure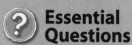

1. Read and complete a lab safety form.

2. Set a **clear plastic container** on your table, and add **gravel** to a depth of about 2 cm.

3. Pour equal volumes of **corn syrup** and **colored water** into the container.

4. Observe the container for 2 minutes. Record your observations in your Lab Manual or interactive notebook.

Think About This

1. What happened to the materials?

_____

_____

2. Which Earth sphere did each material represent?

_____

_____

_____

_____

_____

TEKS in this Lesson

This lesson provides background support for the following TEKS:

6.10(A) Build a model to illustrate the structural layers of Earth, including the inner core, outer core, mantle, crust, asthenosphere, and lithosphere.

Also covers Process Standards: 6.1(A); 6.2(A), (C), (E); 6.3(B); 6.4(A), (B)

? Essential Questions

- What are Earth's major systems and how do they interact?
- Why does Earth have a spherical shape?

abc Vocabulary

sphere
geosphere
gravity
density

1. Before you read this lesson, think about what you know about the structure of Earth. Record your thoughts in the first column. Pair with a partner and discuss his or her thoughts. Write those thoughts in the second column. Then record what you both would like to share with the class in the third column

Think	Pair	Share

Describing Earth

Imagine standing on a mountaintop. You can probably see that the land stretches out beneath you for miles. But you cannot see all of Earth—it is far too large. People have tried to determine the shape and size of Earth for centuries. They have done so by examining the parts they can see.

Many years ago, people believed that Earth was a flat disk with land in the center and water at the edges. Later they used clues to determine Earth's true shape, such as studying Earth's shadow on the Moon during an eclipse.

The Size and Shape of Earth

Now there are better ways to get a view of our planet. Using satellites and other technology, scientists know that Earth is a sphere. *A* **sphere** *is shaped like a ball, with all points on the surface at an equal distance from the center.* But Earth is not a perfect sphere. As illustrated in **Figure 1**, Earth is somewhat flattened at the poles with a slight bulge around the equator. Earth has a diameter of almost 13,000 km. It is the largest of the four rocky planets closest to the Sun.

Figure 1 Earth is shaped like a sphere that is somewhat flattened at the poles and is slightly bulging around the equator.

Earth Systems

Earth is large and complex. To simplify the task of studying Earth, scientists describe five Earth systems, as shown in **Figure 2**. All five of these systems interact by exchanging matter and energy. For example, water from the ocean evaporates and enters the atmosphere. Later, the water precipitates onto land and washes salts into the ocean.

The Atmosphere, the Hydrosphere, and the Cryosphere

The atmosphere is the layer of gases surrounding Earth. It is Earth's outermost system. This layer is about 100 km thick. It is a mixture of nitrogen, oxygen, carbon dioxide, and traces of other gases. The hydrosphere is water on Earth's surface, water underground, and liquid water in the atmosphere.

Most of the water in the hydrosphere is in salty oceans. Freshwater is in most rivers and lakes and underground. Frozen water, such as glaciers, is part of the hydrosphere and the cryosphere. Water continually moves between the atmosphere and the hydrosphere. This is one example of how Earth systems interact.

The Geosphere and the Biosphere

*The **geosphere** is Earth's entire solid body.* It contains a thin layer of soil and sediments covering a rocky center. It is the largest Earth system. The biosphere includes all living things on Earth. Organisms in the biosphere live within and interact with the atmosphere, hydrosphere, and even the geosphere.

Identify

2. Highlight Earth's major systems and what comprises them.

Figure 2 Earth's systems interact. A change in one Earth system affects all other Earth systems. They exchange energy and matter, making Earth suitable for life.

Atmosphere: layer of gases surrounding Earth

Hydrosphere: liquid water on Earth

Geosphere: Earth's entire solid body

Biosphere: all living organisms on Earth

Cryosphere: frozen water on Earth

How did Earth form?

Earth formed about 4.6 billion years ago (bya), along with the Sun and the rest of our solar system. Materials from a large cloud of gas and dust came together, forming the Sun and all the planets. In order to understand how this happened, you first need to know how gravity works.

The Influence of Gravity

Gravity *is the force that every object exerts on all other objects because of their masses.* The force of gravity between two objects depends on the objects' masses and the distance between them. The more mass either object has, or the closer together they are, the stronger the gravitational force, as shown in **Figure 3**.

Explain

3. Why does Earth exert a greater gravitational force on you than other objects do?

Force of Gravity

Figure 3 Mass and distance affect the strength of the gravitational force between objects.

The two objects in row A are the same distance apart as the two objects in row B. One of the objects in row B has more mass, creating a stronger gravitational force between the two objects in row B.

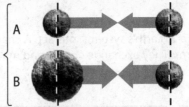

All four objects have the same mass. The two objects in row C are closer to each other than the two objects in row D and, therefore, have a stronger gravitational force between them.

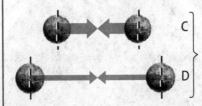

The force of gravity is strongest between the objects in row B. Even though the objects in row A are the same distance apart as those in row B, the force of gravity between them is weaker because they have less mass. The force of gravity is weakest between the objects in row D.

As illustrated in **Figure 4**, all objects on or near Earth are pulled toward Earth's center by gravity. Earth's gravity holds us on Earth's surface. Since Earth has more mass than any object near you, it exerts a greater gravitational force on you than other objects do. You don't notice the gravitational force between less massive objects.

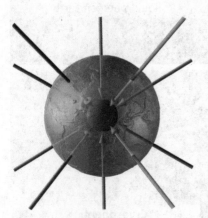

Figure 4 Earth's gravity pulls objects toward the center of Earth.

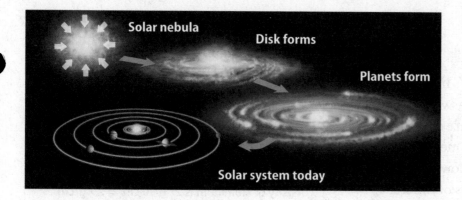

Figure 5 Gravity helped change a cloud of dust, gas, and ice, called a nebula, into our solar system. The Sun formed first, and the planets formed from the swirling disk of particles that remained.

Tutor

Go Online!

The Solar Nebula

The force of gravity played a major role in the formation of our solar system. As shown in **Figure 5**, the solar system formed from a cloud of gas, ice, and dust called a nebula. Gravity pulled the materials closer together. The nebula shrank and flattened into a disk. The disk began to rotate. The materials in the center of the disk became denser, forming a star—the Sun.

Next, the planets began to take shape from the remaining bits of material. Earth formed as gravity pulled these small particles together. As they collided, they stuck to each other and formed larger, unevenly shaped objects. These larger objects had more mass and attracted more particles. Eventually enough matter collected and formed Earth. But how did the unevenly shaped, young planet become spherical?

Early Earth

Eventually the newly formed Earth grew massive and generated thermal energy, commonly called heat, in its interior. The rocks of the planet softened and began to flow.

Gravity pulled in the irregular bumps on the surface of the newly formed planet. As a result, Earth developed a relatively even spherical surface.

FOLDABLES

Make a half book from a sheet of paper. Label it as shown. Use it to organize your notes about Earth's formation.

How Earth Formed   Why Earth Is a Sphere

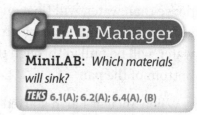

LAB Manager

MiniLAB: *Which materials will sink?*

TEKS 6.1(A); 6.2(A); 6.4(A), (B)

Describe

4. How did Earth develop its spherical shape?

_____

_____

_____

_____

The Formation of Earth's Layers

Thermal energy from Earth's interior affected Earth in other ways, as well. Before heating up, Earth was a mixture of solid particles. The thermal energy melted some of this material and it began to flow. As it flowed, Earth developed distinct layers of different materials.

The different materials formed layers according to their densities. **Density** *is the amount of mass in a material per unit volume.* Density can be described mathematically as

$$D = m/V$$

where D is the density of the material, m is the material's mass, and V is its volume. If two materials have the same volume, the denser material will have more mass.

There is a stronger gravitational force between Earth and a denser object than there is between Earth and a less dense object. You can see this if you put an iron block and a pinewood block with the same volumes in a pan of water. The wooden block, which is less dense than water, will float on the water's surface. The iron block, which is denser than water, will be pulled through the water to the bottom of the pan.

When ancient Earth started melting, something much like this happened. The densest materials sank and formed the innermost layer of Earth. The least dense materials stayed at the surface and formed a separate layer. The materials with intermediate densities formed layers in between the top layer and the bottom layer. Earth's three major layers are shown in **Figure 6**.

Math Skills   Math TEKS 6.1(A), (B); 6.3(E)

Solve One-Step Equations

Comparing the masses of substances is useful only if the same volume of each substance is used. To calculate density, divide the mass by the volume. The unit for density is a unit of mass, such as grams (g), divided by a unit of volume, such as cm³. For example, an aluminum cube has a mass of 27 g and a volume of 10 cm³. The density of aluminum is 27 g/10 cm³ = 2.7 g/cm³.

Practice

A chunk of gold with a volume of 5.00 cm³ has a mass of 96.5 g. What is the density of gold?

Check   Tutor

Go Online! ✓ 💬

Word Origin

density
from Latin *densus*, means "thick, crowded"

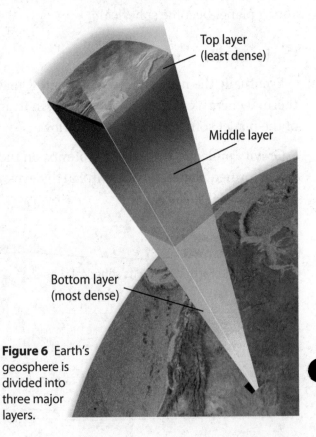

Top layer (least dense)

Middle layer

Bottom layer (most dense)

Figure 6 Earth's geosphere is divided into three major layers.

7.1 Review

Go Online! Check ✓

Summarize it!

Compare the formation of Earth and the formation of Earth's layers in the graphic organizer below.

Topic: _____

Concept 1: [_____]

Concept 2: [_____]

How are
they alike?

[_____]

How are
they different?

[_____] [_____]

Connect it! Apply the "How are they alike?" ideas to the formation of the Sun, or the Moon, or another planetary body. How do these same concepts apply? Write your response in your interactive notebook.

Summarize it!

Spherical Earth

Use Vocabulary

1. Identify The Earth system made mainly of surface water is called the

_____

Apply the Essential Questions

2. Name Earth's major systems.

_____

_____

_____

3. Describe how gravity affected Earth's shape during Earth's formation.

_____

_____

_____

_____

H.O.T. Questions (Higher Order Thinking)

4. Combine your understanding of how Earth became spherical and observations of the Moon. Then form a hypothesis about the formation of the Moon.

_____

_____

_____

_____

_____

5. Determine As Earth formed, did it become larger or become smaller? Explain your answer.

_____

_____

_____

_____

6. Infer how gravity would affect you differently on a planet with less mass than Earth, such as Mercury.

_____

_____

_____

_____

7. Relate how Earth's systems interact.

_____

_____

_____

_____

_____

Math Skills **Math** TEKS 6.1(A), (B); 6.3(E)

Solve One-Step Equations

8. At a given temperature, $3.00 \ m^3$ of carbon dioxide has a mass of 5.94 kg. What is the density of carbon dioxide at this temperature?

Check   Tutor

Go Online!

Earth's Interior

INQUIRY

What is inside Earth? Earth is thousands of kilometers thick. The deepest mines and wells in the world barely scratch Earth's surface. How do you think scientists learn about Earth's interior?

Write your response in your interactive notebook.

LAB Manager

Go to your Lab Manual or visit connectED.mcgraw-hill.com to perform the labs for this lesson.

MiniLAB: *Which liquid is densest?*
TEKS 6.1(A); 6.2(A), (E); 6.3(B), (C); 6.4(A), (B); 6.10(A)

LAB: *Modeling Earth and Its Layers*
TEKS 6.1(A); 6.2(A), (C), (E); 6.3(B), (C); 6.4(B); 6.10(A)

Explore Activity

TEKS 6.1(A); 6.2(A), (C), (E); 6.3(B), (C); 6.4(A), (B); 6.10(A)

How can you model Earth's layers?

Earth is made of three main layers: the thin outer crust, the thick mantle, and the central core. You can use different objects to model these layers.

Procedure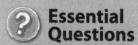

1. Read and complete a lab safety form.

2. Place a **hard-cooked egg** on a **paper towel**. Use a **magnifying lens** to closely examine the surface of the egg. Is its shell smooth or rough? Record your observations in your Lab Manual or interactive notebook.

3. Carefully peel away the shell from the egg.

4. Use the **plastic knife** to cut the egg in half. Observe the characteristics of the shell, the egg white, and the yolk.

5. Illustrate the egg's layers in your Lab Manual or interactive notebook. Which layers could represent layers of Earth? Label the layers as *crust, mantle,* or *core.*

Think About This

1. What other objects could be used to model Earth's layers?

_____

_____

_____

2. Explain why a hard-cooked egg is a good model for Earth's layers.

_____

_____

_____

_____

Copyright © McGraw-Hill Education Hutchings Photography/Digital Light Source

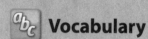

TEKS in this Lesson

6.10(A) Build a model to illustrate the structural layers of Earth, including the inner core, outer core, mantle, crust, asthenosphere, and lithosphere.

Also covers Process Standards: 6.1(A); 6.2(A), (C), (E); 6.3(B), (C), (D); 6.4(A), (B)

? Essential Questions

- What are the interior layers of Earth?
- What evidence indicates that Earth has a solid inner core and a liquid outer core?

abc Vocabulary

crust
mantle
lithosphere
asthenosphere
core
magnetosphere

1. Before reading this lesson on Earth's interior, write down what you know. In the first column, write down what you know already about Earth's interior. In the second column, write down what you want to learn. And after you have completed this lesson, you will write down what you learned in the third column.

What I Know	What I Want to Learn	What I Learned

Clues to Earth's Interior TEKS 6.3(D)

Were you ever given a gift and had to wait to open it? Maybe you tried to figure out what was inside by tapping on it or shaking it. Using methods such as these, you might have been able to determine the gift's contents. Scientists can't see what is inside Earth, either. But they can use indirect methods to discover what Earth's interior is like.

What's below Earth's surface?

Deep mines and wells give scientists hints about Earth's interior. The deepest mine ever constructed is a gold mine in South Africa. It is more than 3 km deep. People can go down the mine to explore the geosphere.

Drilled wells are even deeper. The deepest well is on the Kola Peninsula in Russia. It is more than 12 km deep. Drilling to such great depths is extremely difficult—it took more than 20 years to drill the Kola well. Even though people cannot go down in the well, they can send instruments down to make **observations** and bring samples to the surface. What have scientists learned about Earth's interior by studying mines and wells like the two mentioned above?

Review Vocabulary

observation an act of recognizing and noting a fact or an occurrence

Temperature and Pressure Increase with Depth

One thing that workers notice in deep mines or wells is that it is hot inside Earth. In the South African gold mines, 3.5 km below Earth's surface, the temperature is about 53°C (127°F). The temperature at the bottom of the Kola well is 190°C (374°F). That's hot enough to bake cookies! No one has ever recorded the temperature of Earth's center, but it is estimated to be about 6,000°C (10,832°F). As shown in **Figure 1,** temperature within Earth increases with increasing depth.

Not only does temperature increase, but pressure also increases as depth increases inside Earth. This is due to the weight of the overlying rocks. The high pressure squeezes the rocks and makes them much denser than surface rocks.

High temperatures and pressures make it difficult to drill deep wells. The depth of the Kola well is less than 1 percent of the distance to Earth's center. Therefore, only a small part of the geosphere has been sampled. How can scientists learn about what is below the deepest wells?

Using Earthquake Waves

As you read earlier, scientists use indirect methods to study Earth's interior. They get most of their evidence by analyzing earthquake waves. Earthquakes release energy in the form of three types of waves. As these waves move through Earth, they are affected by the different materials they travel through. Some waves cannot travel through certain materials. Other waves change direction when they reach certain materials. By studying how the waves move, scientists are able to infer the density and composition of materials within Earth.

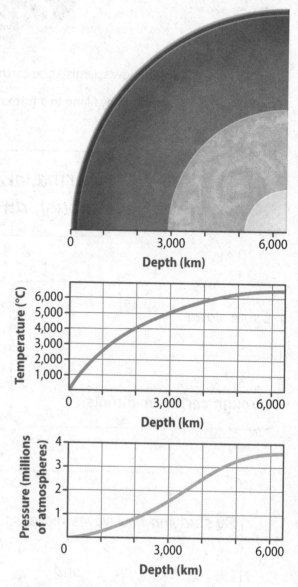

Figure 1 Temperature and pressure increase with depth in the geosphere.

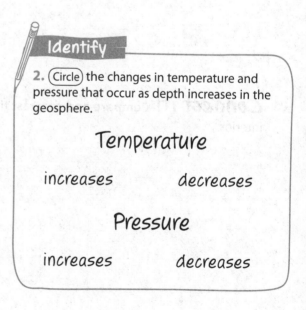

Identify

2. (Circle) the changes in temperature and pressure that occur as depth increases in the geosphere.

Temperature

increases   decreases

Pressure

increases   decreases

Organize it!

Explain how scientists use earthquake wave data to learn about Earth's interior structure by filling in information in the following organizer. **TEKS** 6.10 (A)

Earthquake waves travel differently through different kinds of materials.

Some waves _____ through certain materials.

Other waves _____ when they reach certain materials.

By studying how waves move, scientists are able to infer the _____ and _____ of materials inside Earth.

Connect it! **Compare and contrast** the different methods scientists use to study Earth's interior.

_____

_____

_____

_____

Organize it!

Earth's Layers TEKS 6.10(A)

Differences in density resulted in materials within Earth, forming layers. Each layer has a different composition, with the densest material in the center of Earth.

Crust

The brittle, rocky outer layer of Earth is called the **crust**. It is much thinner than the other layers, like the shell on a hard-cooked egg. It is the least dense layer of the geosphere. It is made mostly of elements of low mass, such as silicon and oxygen.

Crustal rocks are under oceans and on land. The crust under oceans is called oceanic crust. It is made of dense rocks that contain iron and magnesium. The crust on land is called continental crust. It is about four times thicker than oceanic crust. Continental crust is thickest under tall mountains. **Figure 2** shows a comparison of the two types of crust.

There is a distinct boundary between the crust and the layer beneath it. When earthquake waves cross this boundary, they speed up. This indicates that the lower layer is denser than the crust.

Name

3. What are the elements that make up the oceanic crust?

_____

_____

_____

LAB Manager

MiniLAB: *Which liquid is densest?*
TEKS 6.1(A); 6.2(A), (E); 6.3(B), (C); 6.4(A), (B); 6.10(A)

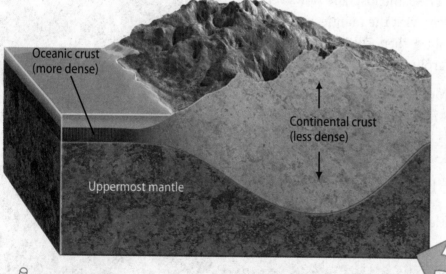

Oceanic crust (more dense)

Continental crust (less dense)

Uppermost mantle

Watch

Figure 2 This is a representation of oceanic crust and continental crust.

Compare

4. How does oceanic crust compare to continental crust?

_____

_____

Mantle

Earth's mantle is immediately below the crust. *The* **mantle** *is the thick middle layer in the solid part of Earth.* It contains more iron and magnesium than oceanic crust does. This makes it denser than either type of crust. Like the crust, the mantle is made of rock. The iron-rich rocks of this layer are peridotite and eclogite. Scientists group the mantle into four layers according to the way rocks react when forces push or pull on them. **Figure 3** shows the mantle and other layers.

Uppermost Mantle The rocks in the uppermost layer of the mantle are brittle and rigid, like the rocks in the crust. Because of this, *scientists group the crust and the uppermost mantle into a rigid layer called the* **lithosphere** (LIH thuh sfihr).

Asthenosphere Below the lithosphere, rocks are so hot that tiny bits melt. When this happens, the rocks are no longer brittle. They begin to flow. Scientists use the term plastic to describe rocks that flow in this way. *This plastic layer within the mantle is called the* **asthenosphere** (as THEN uh sfihr).

The asthenosphere does not resemble the plastics used to make everyday products. The word plastic refers to materials that are soft enough to flow. The asthenosphere flows very slowly. Even if it were possible to visit the mantle, you could never see this flow. Rocks in the asthenosphere move about as slowly as your fingernails grow.

Upper Mantle and Lower Mantle The rock below the asthenosphere is solid, but it is hotter than the rock in the asthenosphere. How can this be? The pressure at this depth is so great that no melting occurs. While increased temperature tends to melt rock, high pressure tends to prevent melting. High pressure squeezes the rock into a solid. This solid rock of the upper mantle and the lower mantle forms the largest layer of Earth.

asthenosphere from Greek *asthenes*, means "weak"; and *spharia*, means "sphere"

LAB Manager

LAB: *Modeling Earth and Its Layers*

TEKS 6.1(A); 6.2(A), (C), (E); 6.3(B), (C); 6.4(B); 6.10(A)

Figure 3 Earth's main layers include the crust, mantle, and core. The layers are subdivided according to chemical and physical characteristics.

Go Online! ▶ Watch

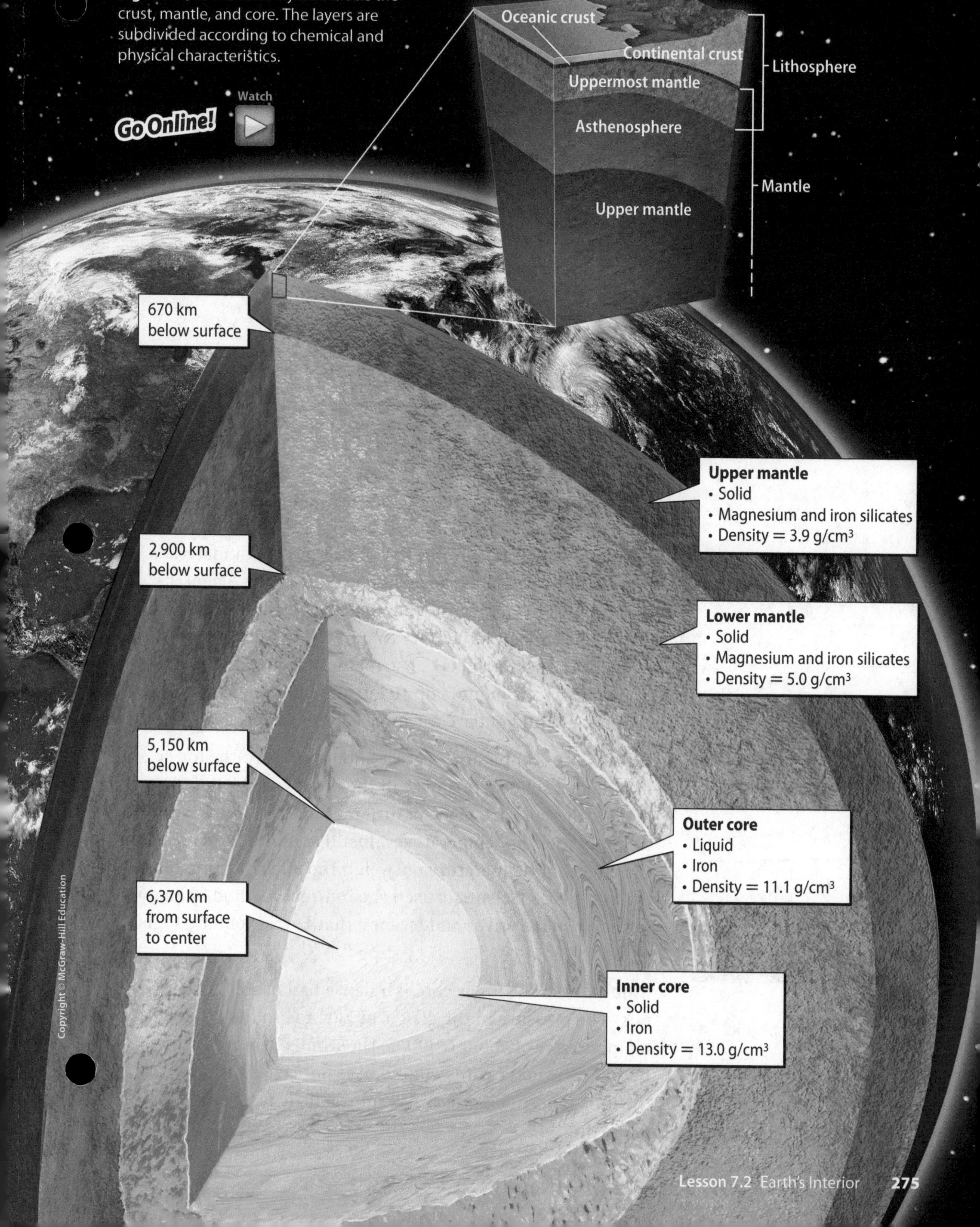

Oceanic crust

Continental crust

Lithosphere

Uppermost mantle

Asthenosphere

Mantle

Upper mantle

670 km below surface

2,900 km below surface

5,150 km below surface

6,370 km from surface to center

Upper mantle
- Solid
- Magnesium and iron silicates
- Density = 3.9 g/cm^3

Lower mantle
- Solid
- Magnesium and iron silicates
- Density = 5.0 g/cm^3

Outer core
- Liquid
- Iron
- Density = 11.1 g/cm^3

Inner core
- Solid
- Iron
- Density = 13.0 g/cm^3

Figure 4 Earth's core has a liquid outer layer surrounding a solid inner layer of iron. The inner core spins a little faster than the outer core.

Solid inner core

Liquid outer core

Science Use v. Common Use

nickel

Science Use a specific type of metal

Common Use a coin worth five cents

Core

The dense metallic center of Earth is the **core**, as shown in **Figure 4.** If you imagine Earth as a hard-cooked egg, the core is the yolk. Earth's crust and mantle are made of rock. Why is the core made of metal? Recall that in Earth's early history, the planet was much hotter than it is now. Earth materials flowed, like they do in the asthenosphere today. Scientists don't know how much of Earth melted. But they do know that it was soft enough for gravity to pull the densest material down to the center. This dense material is metal. It is mostly iron with small amounts of nickel and other elements. The core has a liquid outer core and a solid inner core.

Outer Core If pressure is great enough to keep the lower mantle in a solid state, how can the outer core be liquid? The mantle and core are made of different materials, and have different melting temperatures. Just like in the asthenosphere, the effects of temperature outweigh the effects of pressure in the outer core. Scientists used the indirect method of analyzing earthquake waves and learned that Earth's outer core is liquid.

Inner Core The inner core is a dense ball of solid iron crystals. The pressure in the center of Earth is so high that even at temperatures of about 6,000°C, the iron is in a solid state. Because the outer core is liquid, it is not rigidly attached to the inner core. The inner core spins a little faster than the rest of Earth.

Copyright © McGraw-Hill Education

Earth's Core and Geomagnetism

Why does a compass needle point north? The metallic compass needle lines up with the magnetic field surrounding Earth. Earth's spinning core creates the magnetic field.

Earth's Magnetic Field

Recall that Earth's inner core spins faster than the outer core. This produces streams of flowing, molten iron in the outer core. Earth's magnetic field is a region of magnetism produced in part by the flow of molten materials in the outer core. The magnetic field acts much like a giant bar magnet. It has opposite poles, as shown in **Figure 5.**

For centuries, people have used compasses and Earth's magnetic field to navigate. But, the magnetic field is not completely stable. Over geologic time, its strength and direction vary. At several times in Earth's history, the direction has even reversed.

Magnetosphere

Earth's magnetic field protects Earth from cosmic rays and charged particles coming from the Sun. It pushes away some charged particles and traps others. *The outer part of the magnetic field that interacts with these particles is called the* **magnetosphere**. Examine **Figure 6** to see how the shape of the magnetosphere is produced by the flow of these charged particles.

Figure 5 Earth's magnetic field is produced by the movement of molten materials in the outer core.

Word Origin

magnetosphere from Latin *magnes*, means "lodestone"; and *spharia*, means "sphere"

Figure 6 Trapped particles and Earth's magnetic field form a shield around Earth.

7.2 Review

FOLDABLES®

Cut out the Lesson 7.2 Foldable in the back of the book. Use the book to summarize information about Earth's crust, mantle, outer core, and inner core.

Earth's Layers

Tape here

Composition and Depth	Composition and Depth
Composition and Depth	Composition and Depth

Tab 1

Tab 2

Connect it! Explain why a peach is a good and a poor model of Earth's layers. **TEKS** 6.3(C); 6.10(A)

_____

_____

_____

_____

_____

_____

Summarize it!

Earth's Interior

Use Vocabulary

1. **Distinguish** between the crust and the lithosphere. TEKS 6.10(A)

_____
_____
_____

Apply the Essential Questions

2. **Explain** what scientists learned from earthquake waves. TEKS 6.3(D); 6.10(A)

_____
_____
_____
_____

3. **Name** Earth's layers. TEKS 6.10(A)

_____
_____
_____

4. **Classify** Earth's layers based on their physical properties. TEKS 6.10(A)

_____
_____
_____
_____
_____

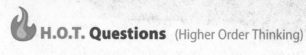

H.O.T. Questions (Higher Order Thinking)

5. **Build** a model to illustrate Earth's layers. List the materials needed to make your model. TEKS 6.10(A)

_____
_____
_____
_____
_____
_____

6. **Differentiate** the layers of the mantle. TEKS 6.10(A)

_____
_____
_____
_____
_____

7. **Draw** a model of Earth's magnetosphere below. Which layer of Earth is responsible for the production of the magnetosphere? TEKS 6.10(A)

Time Capsules

Going Up?

Diamond crystals form deep within the mantle under intense pressures and temperatures. They come to Earth's surface in molten rock, or magma. The magma pulls diamonds from rock deep underground and rapidly carries them to the surface. The magma erupts onto Earth's surface in small, explosive volcanoes. Diamonds and other crystals and rocks from the mantle are in deep, carrot-shaped cones called kimberlite pipes that are part of these rare volcanoes.

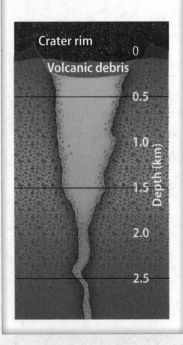

Crater rim — 0
Volcanic debris
— 0.5
— 1.0
— 1.5 Depth (km)
— 2.0
— 2.5

Formed billions of years ago in Earth's mantle, diamonds hold important clues about our planet's mysterious interior.

George Harlow is fascinated by diamonds. Not because of their dazzling shine or their value, but because of what they can reveal about Earth. He considers diamonds to be tiny time capsules that capture a picture of the ancient mantle, where they became crystals.

▲ George Harlow studies diamonds to learn more about Earth's interior.

Most diamonds we find today formed billions of years ago deep within Earth's mantle, over 161 km below Earth's surface. Tiny bits of mantle, called inclusions, were trapped inside these extremely hard crystals as they formed. Millions of years later, the inclusions' diamond cases still protect them.

Harlow collects these diamonds from places such as Australia, Africa, and Thailand. Back in the lab, Harlow and his colleagues remove inclusions from diamonds. First, they break open a diamond with a tool similar to a nutcracker. Then they use a microscope and a pinlike tool to sift through the diamond rubble. They look for an inclusion, which is about the size of a grain of sand. When they find one, they use an electron microprobe and a laser to analyze the inclusion's composition, or chemical makeup. The sample might be tiny, but it's enough for scientists to learn the temperature, pressure, and composition of the mantle in which the diamond formed.

Next time you see a diamond, you might wonder if it too has a tiny bit of ancient mantle from deep inside Earth.

It's Your Turn!

RESEARCH Diamonds are the world's most popular gemstone. What other uses do diamonds have? Research the properties of diamonds and how they are used in industry. Report your findings to your class.

The Theory of Plate Tectonics

INQUIRY

How did these islands form? The photograph shows a chain of active volcanoes. These volcanoes make up the Aleutian Islands of Alaska. Just south of these volcanic islands is a 6 km-deep ocean trench. Why did these volcanic mountains form in a line? Can you predict where volcanoes are? Are they related to plate tectonics?

Write your response in your interactive notebook.

LAB Manager

Go to your Lab Manual or visit connectED.mcgraw-hill.com to perform the labs for this lesson.

MiniLAB: *How can you model convection currents?*
TEKS 6.1(A); 6.2(A), (C), (E); 6.3(B); 6.4(A), (B)

LAB: *Movement of Plate Boundaries*
TEKS 6.1(A), (B); 6.2(A), (C), (E); 6.3(B); 6.4(B); 6.10(D)

Copyright © McGraw-Hill Education NASA

Explore Activity

Can you determine density by observing buoyancy?

Density is the measure of an object's mass relative to its volume. Buoyancy is the upward force a liquid places on objects that are immersed in it. If you immerse objects with equal densities into liquids that have different densities, the buoyant forces will be different. An object will sink or float depending on the density of the liquid compared to the object. Earth's layers differ in density. These layers float or sink depending on density and buoyant force.

Procedure

1. Read and complete a lab safety form.

2. Obtain four **test tubes**. Place them in a **test-tube rack**. Add **water** to one test tube until it is ¾ full.

3. Repeat with the other test tubes using **vegetable oil** and **glucose syrup**. One test tube should remain empty.

4. Drop **beads** of equal density into each test tube. Observe what the bead does when immersed in each liquid. Record your observations in your Lab Manual or interactive notebook.

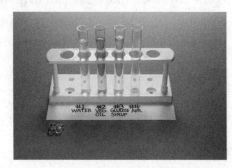

Think About This

1. How did you identify which liquid has the highest density?

_____

_____

_____

_____

2. Describe what happens when layers of rock with different densities collide. How might this cause geologic events to occur?

_____

_____

TEKS in this Lesson

6.10(C) Identify the major tectonic plates, including Eurasian, African, Indo-Australian, Pacific, North American, and South American.

6.10(D) Describe how plate tectonics causes major geological events such as ocean basins, earthquakes, volcanic eruptions, and mountain building.

Also covers Process Standards: 6.1(A), (B); 6.2(A), (C), (E); 6.3(B); 6.4(A), (B)

? Essential Questions

- What is the theory of plate tectonics?
- What are the three types of plate boundaries?
- What results from the interactions of tectonic plates?

abc Vocabulary

plate tectonics
divergent plate
  boundary
transform plate
  boundary
convergent plate
  boundary
subduction
convection
ridge push
slab pull

The Plate Tectonics Theory

When you blow into a balloon, the balloon expands and its surface area also increases. Similarly, if oceanic crust continues to form at mid-ocean ridges and is never destroyed, Earth's surface area should increase. However, this is not the case. The older crust must be destroyed somewhere—but where?

By the late 1960s a more complete theory, called plate tectonics, was proposed. The theory of **plate tectonics** states that *Earth's surface is made of rigid slabs of rock, or plates, that move with respect to each other.* This new theory suggested that Earth's surface is divided into large plates of rigid rock. Each plate moves over Earth's hot and semi-plastic mantle.

Geologists use the word *tectonic* to describe the forces that shape Earth's surface and the rock structures that form as a result. Plate tectonics provides an explanation for the occurrence of earthquakes, volcanic eruptions, and moutain ranges, like the one shown in **Figure 1**. When plates separate on the seafloor, earthquakes result and a mid-ocean ridge forms. When plates come together, one plate can dive under the other, causing earthquakes and creating a chain of volcanoes. When plates slide past each other, earthquakes can result.

Identify

1. Underline possible landforms created by tectonic plate interactions.

Define

2. What is plate tectonics?

_____

_____

_____

Figure 1 The Himalayas are a mountain chain that formed as a result of two tectonic plates colliding and pushing the crust upward.

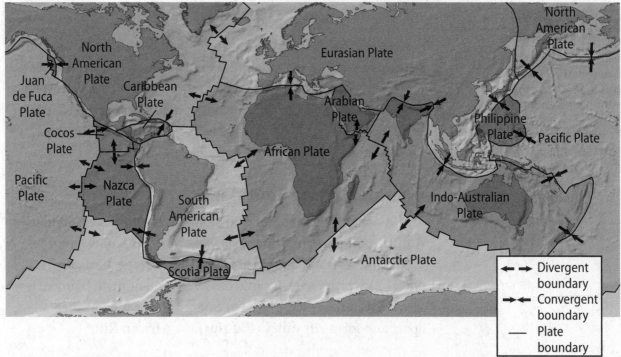

Figure 2 Earth's surface is broken into large plates that fit together like pieces of a giant jigsaw puzzle. The arrows show the general direction of movement of each plate.

Tectonic Plates

You read that the theory of plate tectonics states that Earth's surface is divided into rigid plates that move relative to one another. These plates are less dense than the mantle and "float" on top of the hot and semi-plastic mantle. The map in **Figure 2** illustrates Earth's major plates and the boundaries that define them. The Pacific Plate is the largest plate. The Juan de Fuca Plate is one of the smallest plates. It is between the North American and Pacific Plates. Notice the boundaries that run through the oceans. Many of these boundaries mark the positions of the mid-ocean ridges.

Earth's outermost layers are cold and rigid compared to the layers within Earth's interior. The cold and rigid outermost rock layer is called the lithosphere. It is made up of the crust and the solid, uppermost mantle. The lithosphere is thin below midocean ridges and thick below continents. Earth's tectonic plates are large pieces of lithosphere. These lithospheric plates fit together like the pieces of a giant jigsaw puzzle.

The layer of Earth below the lithosphere is called the asthenosphere (as THEN uh sfihr). This layer is so hot that it behaves like a **plastic** material. This enables Earth's plates to move because the hotter, plastic mantle material beneath them can flow. The interactions between lithosphere and asthenosphere help to explain plate tectonics.

Science Use v. Common Use

plastic

Science Use capable of being molded or changing shape without breaking

Common Use any of numerous organic, synthetic, or processed materials made into objects

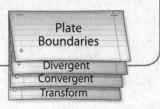
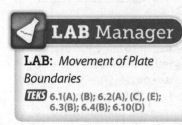

Plate Boundaries   TEKS 6.10(D)

Place two books side by side and imagine each book represents a tectonic plate. A plate boundary exists where the books meet. How many different ways can you move the books with respect to each other? You can pull the books apart, you can push the books together, and you can slide the books past one another. Earth's tectonic plates move in much the same way.

Divergent Plate Boundaries

Mid-ocean ridges are located along divergent plate boundaries. *A **divergent plate boundary** forms where two plates separate.* When the seafloor spreads at a mid-ocean ridge, lava erupts, cools, and forms new oceanic crust. Divergent plate boundaries also exist in the middle of a continent. They pull continents apart and form rift valleys like the East African Rift.

Transform Plate Boundaries

The famous San Andreas Fault in California is an example of a transform plate boundary. *A **transform plate boundary** forms where two plates slide past each other.* As they move past each other, the plates can get stuck and stop moving. Stress builds up where the plates are "stuck." Eventually, the stress is too great and the rocks break, suddenly moving apart. This results in a rapid release of energy as earthquakes.

Convergent Plate Boundaries

Convergent plate boundaries *form where two plates collide. The denser plate sinks below the other plate in a process called* **subduction.** The area where a denser plate descends into Earth along a convergent plate boundary is called a subduction zone.

When an oceanic plate and a continental plate collide, the denser oceanic plate subducts under the edge of the continent. This creates a deep ocean trench. A line of volcanoes forms above the subducting plate on the edge of the continent. This process can also occur when two oceanic plates collide. The older and denser oceanic plate will subduct beneath the younger oceanic plate. This creates a deep ocean trench and a line of volcanoes called an island arc.

When two continental plates collide, neither plate is subducted, and mountains form from uplifted rock. **Table 1** summarizes the interactions of Earth's tectonic plates.

Table 1 The direction of motion of Earth's plates creates a variety of features at the boundaries between the plates.

Table 1 Interactions of Earth's Tectonic Plates		Go Online!
Plate Boundary	**Relative Motion**	**Example**
Divergent plate boundary When two plates separate and create new oceanic crust, a divergent plate boundary forms. This process occurs where the seafloor spreads along a mid-ocean ridge, as shown to the right. This process can also occur in the middle of continents and is referred to as a continental rifting.	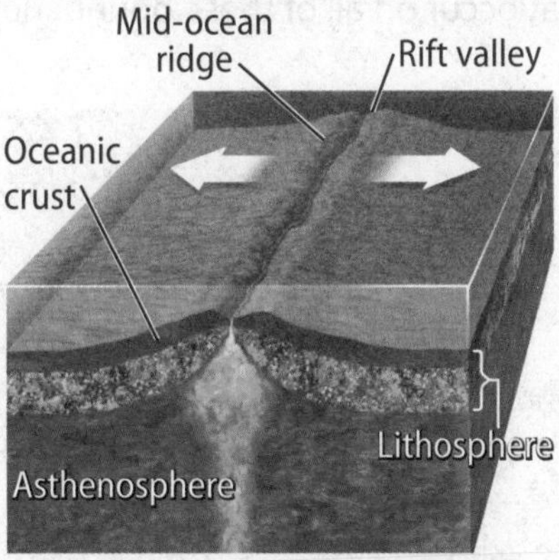	
Transform plate boundary Two plates slide horizontally past one another along a transform plate boundary. Earthquakes are common along this type of plate boundary. The San Andreas Fault, shown to the right, is part of the transform plate boundary that extends along the coast of California.	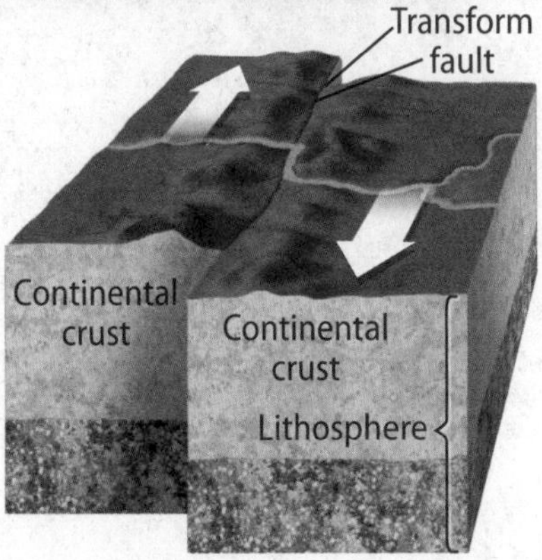	
Convergent plate boundary (ocean-to-continent) When an oceanic and a continental plate collide, they form a convergent plate boundary. The denser plate will subduct. A volcanic mountain, such as Mount Rainier in the Cascade Mountains, forms along the edge of the continent. This process can also occur where two oceanic plates collide, and the denser plate is subducted.	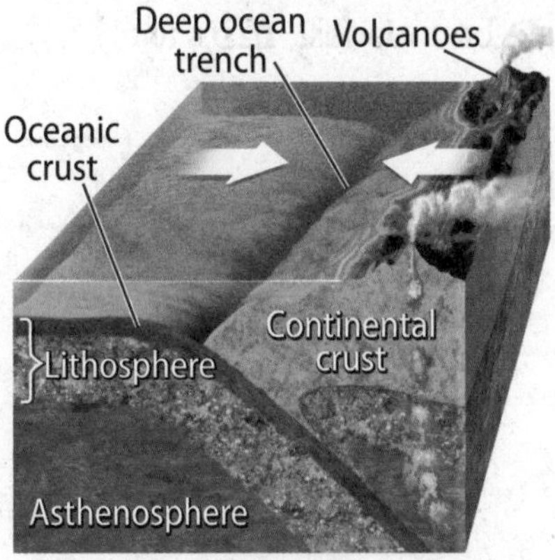	
Convergent plate boundary (continent-to-continent) Convergent plate boundaries can also occur where two continental plates collide. Because both plates are equally dense, neither plate will subduct. Both plates uplift and deform. This creates huge mountains like the Himalayas, shown to the right.	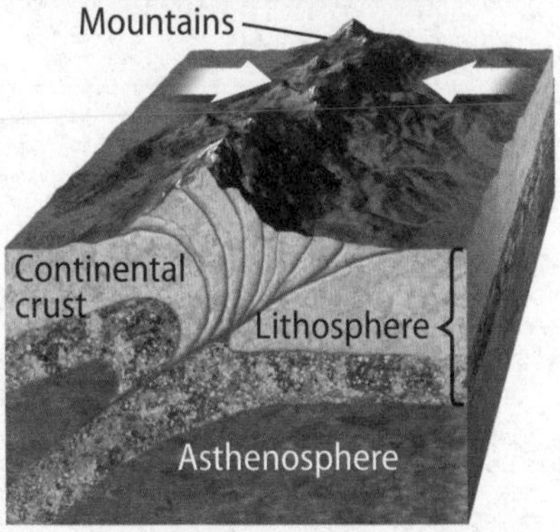	

Identify the major tectonic plates by labeling the figure below, including the Eurasian, African, Indo-Australian, Pacific, North American, and South American plates, and the types of plate boundaries and interactions that occur on all of these boundaries. **TEKS** 6.10(C)

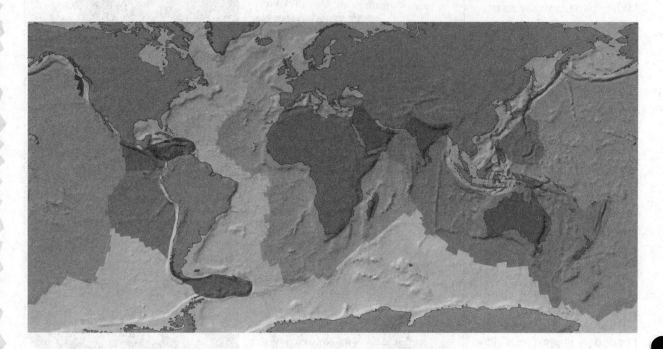

Connect it! Is it possible for one plate to have more than one type of plate boundary? What evidence is there for the plate boundaries? **TEKS** 6.10(D)

_____

_____

_____

_____

_____

_____

_____

_____

Apply it!

Evidence for Plate Tectonics **TEKS** 6.10(D)

Nearly 100 years ago, a man named Alfred Wegener proposed the continental drift hypothesis. This hypothesis stated that the continents slowly moved to their current locations. However, the technology used to measure how fast the continents move wasn't available during Wegener 's time. Recall that continents move apart or come together at speeds of a few centimeters per year.

Today, scientists can measure how fast continents move. A network of satellites orbiting Earth monitors plate motion. By keeping track of the distance between these satellites and Earth, it is possible to locate and determine how fast a tectonic plate moves. This network of satellites is called the Global Positioning System (GPS).

The theory of plate tectonics also provides an explanation for why earthquakes and volcanoes occur in certain places. Because plates are rigid, tectonic activity occurs where plates meet. When plates separate, collide, or slide past each other along a plate boundary, stress builds. A rapid release of energy can result in earthquakes. Volcanoes form where plates separate along a mid-ocean ridge or a continental rift or collide along a subduction zone. Mountains can form where two continents collide. **Figure 3** illustrates the relationship between plate boundaries and the occurrence of earthquakes and volcanoes. Refer back to the lesson opener photo. Find these islands on the map. Are they located near a plate boundary?

Connect

3. <u>Underline</u> how earthquakes and volcanoes are related to the theory of plate tectonics.

Figure 3 Notice that most earthquakes and volcanoes occur near plate boundaries.

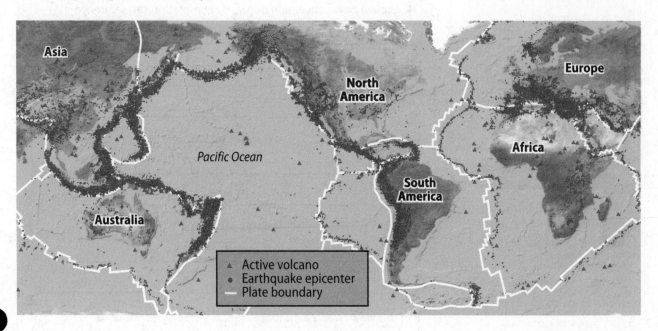

- ▲ Active volcano
- • Earthquake epicenter
- — Plate boundary

Copyright © McGraw-Hill Education

Figure 4 When water is heated, it expands. Less dense heated water rises because the colder water sinks, forming convection currents.

Tutor

Go Online!

Plate Motion TEKS 6.10(D)

The main objection to Wegener's continental drift hypothesis was that he could not explain why or how continents move. Scientists now understand that continents move because the asthenosphere moves underneath the lithosphere.

Convection Currents

You are probably already familiar with the process of **convection,** *the circulation of material caused by differences in temperature and density.* For example, the upstairs floors of homes and buildings are often warmer. This is because hot air rises while dense, cold air sinks. Look at **Figure 4** to see convection in action.

Plate tectonic activity is related to convection in the mantle, as shown in **Figure 5.** Radioactive elements, such as uranium, thorium, and potassium, heat Earth's interior. When materials such as solid rock are heated, they expand and become less dense. Hot mantle material rises upward and comes in contact with Earth's crust. Thermal energy is transferred from hot mantle material to the colder surface above. As the mantle cools, it becomes denser and then sinks, forming a convection current. These currents in the asthenosphere act like a conveyor belt moving the lithosphere above.

Illustrate

4. Explain how convection occurs by completing the sequence diagram below.

_____ elements heat the inside of Earth.

The _____ is transferred from the _____ to the _____. _____ currents form.

These currents in the asthenosphere move the _____ above it.

In this way, _____ move in response to _____.

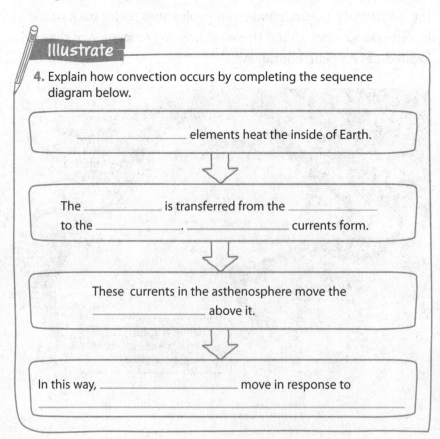

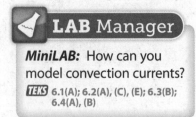

LAB Manager

MiniLAB: How can you model convection currents?
TEKS 6.1(A); 6.2(A), (C), (E); 6.3(B); 6.4(A), (B)

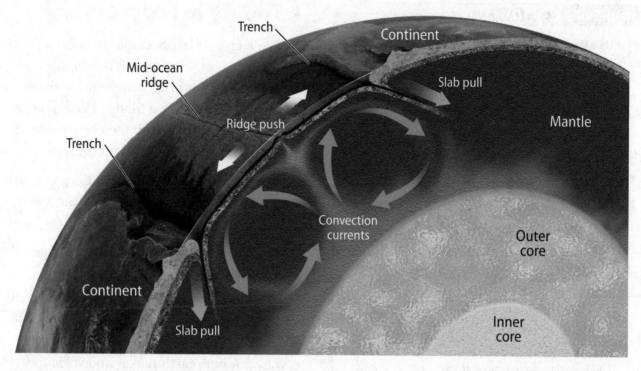

Trench

Continent

Mid-ocean ridge

Slab pull

Ridge push

Mantle

Trench

Convection currents

Outer core

Continent

Slab pull

Inner core

Forces Causing Plate Motion

How can something as massive as the Pacific Plate move? **Figure 5** shows the three forces that interact to cause plate motion and result in major geologic events. Scientists still debate over which of these forces has the greatest effect on plate motion.

Basal Drag Convection currents in the mantle produce a force that causes motion called basal drag. Notice in **Figure 5** how convection currents in the asthenosphere circulate and drag the lithosphere similar to the way a conveyor belt moves items along at a supermarket checkout.

Ridge Push Recall that mid-ocean ridges have greater elevation than the surrounding seafloor. Because mid-ocean ridges are higher, gravity pulls the surrounding rocks down and away from the ridge. *Rising mantle material at mid-ocean ridges creates the potential for plates to move away from the ridge with a force called* **ridge push.** Ridge push moves lithosphere in opposite directions away from the mid-ocean ridge.

Slab Pull As you read earlier in this lesson, when tectonic plates collide, the denser plate will sink into the mantle along a subduction zone. This plate is called a slab. Because the slab is old and cold, it is denser than the surrounding mantle and will sink. *As a slab sinks, it pulls on the rest of the plate with a force called* **slab pull.** Scientists are still uncertain about which force has the greatest influence on plate motion.

Figure 5 Convection occurs in the mantle underneath Earth's tectonic plates. Three forces act on plates to make them move: basal drag from convection currents, ridge push at mid-ocean ridges, and slab pull from subducting plates.

Describe

5. What is happening to a plate that is undergoing slab pull?

_____

_____

_____

_____

_____

_____

_____

_____

_____

_____

_____

Use Proportions

The plates along the Mid-Atlantic Ridge spread at an average rate of 2.5 cm/y. How long will it take the plates to spread 1 m? Use proportions to find the answer.

1. Convert the distance to the same unit.

$$1 \text{ m} = 100 \text{ cm}$$

2. Set up a proportion:

$$\frac{2.5 \text{ cm}}{1y} = \frac{100 \text{ cm}}{xy}$$

3. Cross multiply and solve for x as follows:

$$2.5 \text{ cm} \times xy = 100 \text{ cm} \times 1y$$

4. Divide both sides by 2.5 cm.

$$x = \frac{100 \text{ cm y}}{2.5 \text{ cm}}$$

$$x = 40y$$

Practice

The Eurasian plate travels the slowest, at about 0.7 cm/y. How long would it take the plate to travel 3 m?

$$(1 \text{ m} = 100 \text{ cm})$$

Go Online!   Check ✓   Tutor 💬

A Theory in Progress

Plate tectonics has become the unifying theory of geology. It explains the connection between continental drift and the formation and destruction of crust along plate boundaries. It also helps to explain the occurrence of earthquakes, volcanoes, and mountains.

The investigation that Wegener began nearly a century ago is still being revised. Several unanswered questions remain.

- Why is Earth the only planet in the solar system that has plate tectonic activity? Different hypotheses have been proposed to explain this. Extrasolar planets outside our solar system are also being studied.

- Why do some earthquakes and volcanoes occur far away from plate boundaries? Perhaps it is because the plates are not perfectly rigid. Different thicknesses and weaknesses exist within the plates. Also, the mantle is much more active than scientists originally understood.

- What forces dominate plate motion? Currently accepted models suggest that convection currents occur in the mantle. However, there is no way to measure or observe them.

- What will scientists investigate next? **Figure 6** shows an image produced by a technique called anisotropy that creates a 3-D image of seismic wave velocities in a subduction zone. This developing technology might help scientists better understand the processes that occur within the mantle and along plate boundaries.

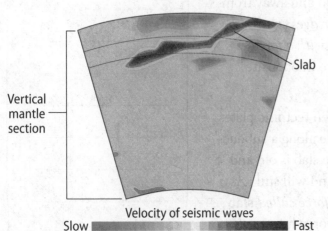

Vertical mantle section

Slab

Velocity of seismic waves

Slow ▬▬▬▬▬▬▬▬ Fast

Figure 6 Seismic waves were used to produce this tomography scan. These colors show a subducting plate. The blue colors represent rigid materials with faster seismic wave velocities.

Summarize it!

Describe the similarities and differences between two major plate boundaries. Include specific examples, naming the tectonic plates involved and the geologic events that result from the interaction. *TEKS* 6.10(C), (D)

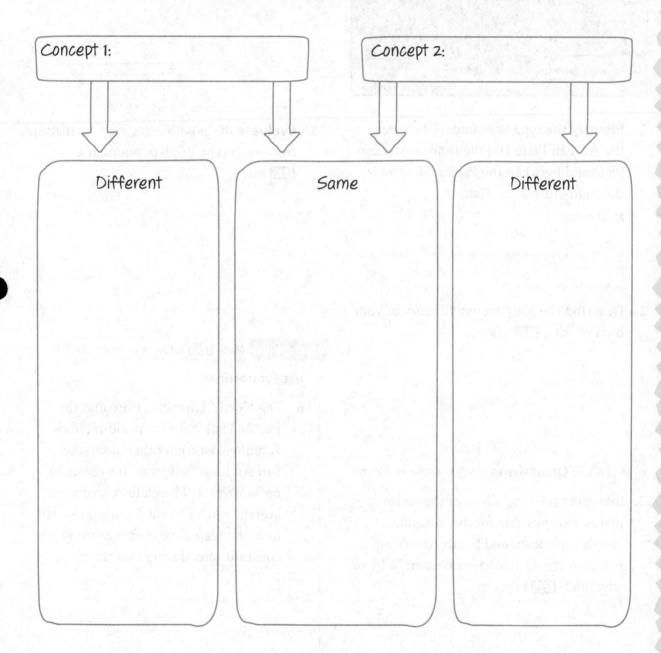

Concept 1:

Concept 2:

Different

Same

Different

 Connect it! Research a recent geologic event, such as an earthquake or a volcano, and identify the major tectonic plates involved. Write your findings in your interactive notebook. *TEKS* 6.10(C), (D)

The Theory of Plate Tectonics

Apply the Essential Questions

Use the image below to answer question 1.

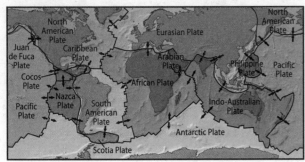

1. **Identify** the type of boundary between the African Plate and the Indo-Australian Plate and between the Pacific Plate and the Indo-Australian Plate.
   TEKS 6.10(C)

   _____

   _____

2. **Describe** the plate tectonic theory in your own words. **TEKS** 6.10(D)

   _____

   _____

   _____

H.O.T. Questions (Higher Order Thinking)

3. **Intrepret** the map above of the tectonic plates. Is it possible for the Eurasion, North American, and South American plates to create a deep sea trench? Why or why not? **TEKS** 6.10(C), (D)

   _____

   _____

   _____

4. **Examine** Why do earthquakes occur at greater depths along convergent plate boundaries? **TEKS** 6.10(D)

   _____

   _____

   _____

   _____

   _____

5. **Evaluate** the possible geologic formation from each type of plate boundary.
   TEKS 6.10(D)

   _____

   _____

   _____

   _____

Math Skills · Math **TEKS** 6.1(A), (B); 6.3(E); 6.4(H)

Use Proportions

6. The North American Plate and the Pacific Plate have been sliding horizontally past each other along the San Andreas fault zone for about 10 million years. The plates move at an average rate of about 5 cm/y. How far have the plates traveled, assuming a constant rate, during this time?

Check   Tutor

Test-Taking Strategy

Always, Not, Never Underline qualifier words such as *all, always, usually, only, never,* and *not* in multiple choice questions and answer choices. The use of these words can change the meaning of the question or answer choice, making it either correct or incorrect.

Example

Use the diagram below to answer question 2.

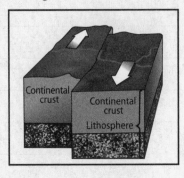

① After reading the question and studying the diagram, think about the answer before reading the choices.

2 Alaina is giving a presentation about the causes of earthquakes. She shows the diagram above. Which is the best description of the diagram?
TEKS 6.10(D)

② Read the answer choices. Underline the words *never, only, rarely,* and *usually.* Think about how these words change the meaning of the choices. Cross off any that do not agree with the answer you have already developed. Choices A and B can be eliminated.

A Earthquakes never occur along this type of plate boundary as plates slide past one another.

B Earthquakes only occur along this type of plate boundary as plates slide past one another.

③ The remaining choices contain the words *rarely* and *usually.* Decide which description best fits the diagram. Choice D is the best answer.

C Earthquakes rarely occur along this type of plate boundary as plates slide past one another.

D Earthquakes usually occur along this type of plate boundary as plates slide past one another.

TIP: When studying a diagram, look at all important words, arrows, and structures. Read all captions. Identify what parts of the diagram are important to answering the question.

Multiple Choice

1 Your teacher shows you a model of Earth's layers. **TEKS** 6.10(A); 6.3(B)

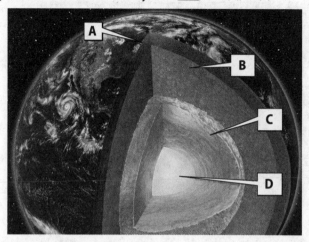

You have been asked to include the lithosphere in this model. Where would you place the lithosphere in the model?

A at point A because the lithosphere contains all water on Earth

B between points A and B because the lithosphere includes the crust and part of the upper mantle

C between points C and D because the lithosphere is the outer core and inner core combined

D at point D because the lithosphere, like the inner core, is made of metal

2

> Two continental tectonic plates began to collide about 70 million years ago. The density of these tectonic plates was roughly equal, so no subduction occurred. Instead, the collision of these plates resulted in the cracking and buckling of the two massive land masses. This collision continues to this day.

The above passage describes the collision of _____ **TEKS** 6.10(C)

A the African and Pacific plates forming a desert.

B the Indo-Australian and Eurasian plates forming the Himalayan Mountains.

C the North American and South American plates forming a canyon.

D the Pacific and Eurasian plates forming the Pacific Ocean.

3 The diagram below shows the type of boundary between the South American Plate and the African Plate. The Atlantic Ocean lies over this boundary. **TEKS** 6.10(D); 6.2(E)

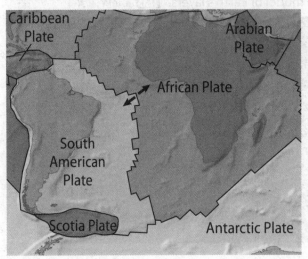

Describe what eventually will happen along this boundary.

   A The plates will collide to form tall mountains.

   B The Atlantic Ocean basin will narrow.

   C The Atlantic Ocean basin will widen.

   D The edges of the plates will break off due to violent earthquakes.

---

4 The breaking, tilting, and folding of Earth's crust results in mountain building. The illustration below shows the formation of a range of mountains. **TEKS** 6.10(D)

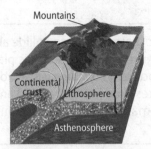

Which describes how the movement of Earth's crust causes the mountain building shown by the arrows in the illustration?

   A Blocks of rocks between two fault lines rise up from the asthenosphere.

   B Compression of the continental crust causes the rocks to move closer together.

   C Forces in Earth's crust cause the rocks to be pushed in opposite directions.

   D Tension in the layers of the lithosphere causes rock to move upward.

5 The illustration below identifies the major tectonic plates on Earth.
TEKS 6.10(C); 6.2(E)

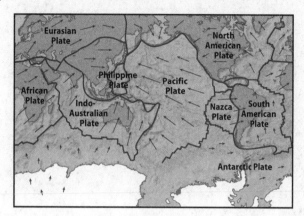

Which statement is correct about the movement of the tectonic plates?

A The African plate forms a subduction zone with the Eurasian plate.

B The Indo-Australian plate forms a convergent boundary with the African plate.

C The Philippine plate forms a divergent boundary with the Pacific plate.

D The Nazca plate forms a convergent boundary with the South American plate.

---

6 The diagram below shows a section of Earth's layers. **TEKS** 6.10(A); 6.3(C)

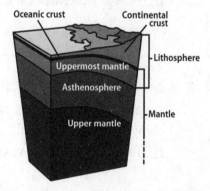

What is one way the model can be improved to show the structural layers of Earth?

A by illustrating the movement of Earth's plates

B by including the inner core and outer core

C by modeling the properties of the mantle's layers

D by showing the correct scale of Earth's layers

8 Rocks

The **BIG** Idea

Earth's rocks are classified by their formation processes.

8.1 Rocks and the Rock Cycle

LESSON

Scientists classify the three major types of rocks based on how the rocks form. In a series of processes called the rock cycle, rocks continually change into other types of rocks.

TEKS 6.10(B); Also covers 6.1(A); 6.2(A), (C), (E); 6.3(B); 6.4(A), (B)

8.2 Igneous Rocks

LESSON

Igneous rocks are formed from molten rock and are classified by the size of their crystals.

TEKS 6.10(B); Also covers 6.1(A); 6.2(A), (C), (E); 6.3(B); 6.4(A), (B)

8.3 Sedimentary Rocks

LESSON

Sedimentary rocks are formed from deposition and compaction of sediment.

TEKS 6.10(B); Also covers 6.1(A); 6.2(A), (C), (E); 6.4(A), (B)

8.4 Metamorphic Rocks

LESSON

Metamorphic rocks are formed from existing rocks that have undergone increases in temperature and pressure.

TEKS 6.10(B); Also covers 6.1(A), (B); 6.2(A), (C), (E); 6.3(B), (C); 6.4(A), (B)

What is a rock?

Three friends look at a rock. They each had different ideas about the rock.

1. Tanya: I think rocks are a type of mineral. All rocks are minerals.

2. Kylie: I think rocks are mixtures. They contain different materials.

3. George: I think rocks are large, solid objects. They are larger than stones.

Put a check by the friend you agree with the most. Explain why you agree by describing your ideas about rocks.

INQUIRY

What formed this feature? Over time, this stream has slowly carved a channel into layers of rock and ash from a volcanic eruption. Notice the sediment in the foreground. Where did all of this sediment come from? What will happen to this sediment over time?

Write your responses in your interactive notebook.

LAB Manager

Go to your Lab Manual or visit connectED.mcgraw-hill.com to perform the labs for this lesson.

MiniLAB: *Can you model the rock cycle?*

TEKS 6.1(A); 6.2(A), (C), (E); 6.3(B); 6.4(A), (B); 6.10(B)

What's in a rock?

You've probably seen different types of rock, either outside or in photographs. Rocks have different colors and textures, and they can contain a combination of minerals, shells, or grains. In this activity, you will observe differences among rock samples.

Procedure

1. Read and complete a lab safety form.

2. Obtain a few **rock samples** from your teacher.

3. Organize your rock samples into groups based on their similarities.

4. Examine each rock, both with and without a **magnifying lens**.

5. Describe each rock sample in detail. Record the color and texture, and describe the minerals or grains in the rock for each sample in your Lab Manual or interactive notebook.

Think About This

1. Write a brief description for each rock sample. Identify the ways in which your samples are similar and different.

_____

_____

_____

_____

2. Do you think all rocks go through the same process in their formation? Explain your reasoning.

_____

_____

_____

TEKS in this Lesson

6.10(B) Classify rocks as metamorphic, igneous, or sedimentary by the processes of their formation

Also covers Process Standards:
6.1(A); 6.2(A), (C), (E); 6.3(B); 6.4(A), (B)

 ## Essential Questions

- How are rocks classified?
- What is the rock cycle?

Vocabulary

rock
grain
texture
magma
lava
sediment
rock cycle

Figure 1 Rocks are everywhere on Earth. By studying rocks, geologists can gain a better understanding of the processes that create different rock types and the environments in which they form.

Rocks

Rocks are everywhere. Mountains, valleys, and the seafloor are made of rocks. Rock and mineral resources even make up parts of your home. Today it is common for floors, countertops, and even tabletops to be made of some type of rock.

A **rock** *is a natural, solid mixture of minerals or grains.* Individual **mineral** crystals, broken bits of minerals, or rock fragments make up these grains. Sometimes a rock contains the remains of an organism or volcanic glass. Processes on Earth's surface can cause rocks to break apart into many different-sized fragments, as shown in **Figure 1.** *Geologists call the fragments that make up a rock* **grains.** They use a grain's size, shape, and chemical composition to classify rocks.

Copyright © McGraw-Hill Education   ©Momatiuk - Eastcott/Corbis

Review Vocabulary

mineral a naturally occurring, inorganic solid with a definite chemical composition and an orderly arrangement of atoms

Organize

1. Organize information about rocks.

Rocks	Definition:	
	Grains identified according to:	
	Classified according to:	
	Particles made of:	
	Can also contain:	

Texture

Geologists also use two important observations to classify rocks: texture and composition. *The grain size and the way grains fit together in a rock are called* **texture.** When a geologist classifies a rock by its texture, he or she looks at the size of minerals or grains in the rock, the arrangement of these individual grains, and the overall feel of the rock.

Texture also can be used to determine the environment in which a rock formed. The granite shown in **Figure 2** has large mineral crystals. This colorful, crystalline texture helps a geologist classify this rock as an igneous rock. The conglomerate (kun GLAHM uh rut) shown in **Figure 2** has rounded rock fragments. Well-rounded rock fragments imply that strong forces, such as water or ice, carved the individual clasts and produced smooth surfaces. This is a sedimentary rock.

Composition

The minerals or grains present in a rock help geologists classify the rock's composition. This information can be used to determine where the rock formed, such as inside a volcano or alongside a river. Geologists conduct fieldwork using maps, a field journal, a compass, a rock hammer, and other tools to examine a rock's composition and texture, as shown in **Figure 3**. These tools also help geologists to interpret the specific conditions under which the rock formed. For example, the presence of certain minerals might suggest that the rock formed under extreme temperature and pressure. Other minerals indicate that the rock formed from molten material deep beneath Earth's surface.

Figure 2 Geologists use texture and composition to classify these rocks as granite (top) and conglomerate (bottom). You may have noticed differences in composition and texture with the rocks you observed in your Explore Activity.

Understand

2. <u>Underline</u> what important observations scientists use to classify rocks.

Figure 3 A geologist in the field uses tools such as a field journal, a rock hammer, and maps to interpret the conditions of rock formation.

Three Major Rock Types

TEKS 6.10(B)

Geologists classify rocks, or place them into groups, based on how they form. The three major groups of rocks are igneous, sedimentary, and metamorphic rocks. Geologists can interpret the environment where these rocks formed based on the physical and chemical characteristics of each rock type.

Igneous Rocks

You might remember that when **magma,** *molten or liquid rock underground,* cools, mineral crystals form. *Molten rock that erupts on Earth's surface is called* **lava.** When magma or lava cools and crystallizes, it creates igneous rock. As mineral crystals grow, they connect much like pieces of a jigsaw puzzle. These crystals become the grains in an igneous rock.

The texture and composition of these grains help geologists to classify the type of igneous rock and the environment where this rock may have formed. Igneous rocks form in a variety of environments including subduction zones, mid-ocean ridges, and hot spots where volcanoes are common.

Sedimentary Rocks

When rocks are exposed on Earth's surface, they can break down and be transported to new environments. Forces such as wind, running water, ice, and even gravity cause rocks on Earth's surface to break down. **Sediment** *is rock material that forms where rocks are broken down into smaller pieces or dissolved in water as rocks erode.* These materials, which include rock fragments, mineral crystals, or the remains of certain plants and animals, are the building blocks of sedimentary rocks.

Sedimentary rocks form where sediment is deposited. Sedimentary environments include rivers and streams, deserts, and valleys like the one shown in **Figure 4.** Even the loose sediment in the picture at the beginning of this lesson will someday turn into rock. Sedimentary rocks can be found in mountain valleys, along river banks, on the beach, or even in your backyard.

Recognize

3. Underline where igneous and sedimenatry rocks are commonly found.

Figure 4 Wind, water, ice, and the force of gravity can deposit sediments in environments like the mountain valley shown here.

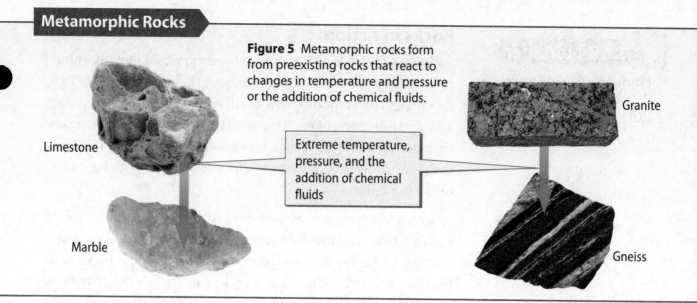

Figure 5 Metamorphic rocks form from preexisting rocks that react to changes in temperature and pressure or the addition of chemical fluids.

Limestone

Extreme temperature, pressure, and the addition of chemical fluids

Marble

Granite

Gneiss

Metamorphic Rocks

When rocks are exposed to extreme temperature and pressure, such as along plate boundaries, they can change to metamorphic rocks. The addition of chemical fluids can also cause rocks to become metamorphic rocks. The minerals that make up the rock's composition change, as well as the texture, or arrangement of the individual mineral grains. In many cases, the change is so intense that the arrangement of the grains appears as bent or twisted layers, as shown in the gneiss in **Figure 5.** Metamorphic rocks can form from any igneous or sedimentary rock or even another metamorphic rock. For example, the igneous rock granite metamorphoses into gneiss, and the sedimentary rock limestone metamorphoses into marble, as shown in **Figure 5.**

The Rock Cycle

When you look at a mountain of rock, it is hard to imagine it can ever change, but rocks are changing all the time. You usually do not see this change because it happens so slowly. *The series of processes that change one type of rock into another type of rock is called the* **rock cycle.** Forces on Earth's surface and deep within Earth drive this cycle. Because of these forces, the rock cycle never stops. This cycle describes how one rock type can change into another rock type through natural processes. Imagine an igneous rock that begins as lava. The lava cools and crystallizes. Over time, the igneous rock is exposed on Earth's surface. Water can erode this rock and form sediments that eventually cement together and become sedimentary rock. The rocks you see everyday might have been different types of rocks in the past.

FOLDABLES

Use a sheet of paper to make a horizontal half-book to illustrate and explain the rock cycle.

Rock Cycle

Connect

4. If rocks are changing all the time, then why is it difficult to see them change?

LAB Manager

MiniLAB: *Can you model the rock cycle?*

TEKS 6.1(A); 6.2(A), (C), (E); 6.3(B); 6.4(A), (B); 6.10(B)

Rocks in Action

Figure 6 shows how igneous, sedimentary, and metamorphic rocks originate and change throughout the rock cycle. The rectangles represent different Earth materials: magma, sediment, and the three rock types. The ovals represent natural processes that change one type of rock into another. The arrows indicate the many different pathways within the cycle both above and below the ground.

Some rock cycle processes occur only beneath Earth's surface, such as those that involve extreme temperature, pressure, and melting. Uplift is a tectonic process that forces these rocks onto Earth's surface. On the surface, rocks can change due to natural processes, such as weathering, erosion, deposition, compaction, and cementation.

Can you trace a complete pathway through the rock cycle using rock types and processes? Start anywhere on the cycle and see how many different pathways you can make.

Interpret

5. Use the diagram in **Figure 6** to identify some processes that can cause a rock to change.

_____

_____

_____

_____

_____

_____

_____

_____

_____

_____

_____

Figure 6 The rock cycle describes how Earth materials and processes continually form and change rocks.

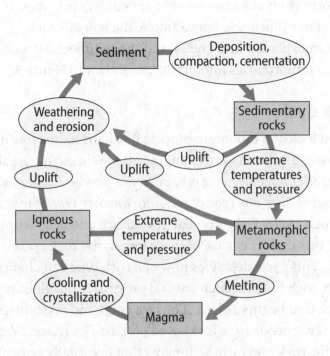

Summarize it!

Relate In the graphic organizer below, identify each type of rock. Then describe the process of how each forms. **TEKS** 6.10(B)

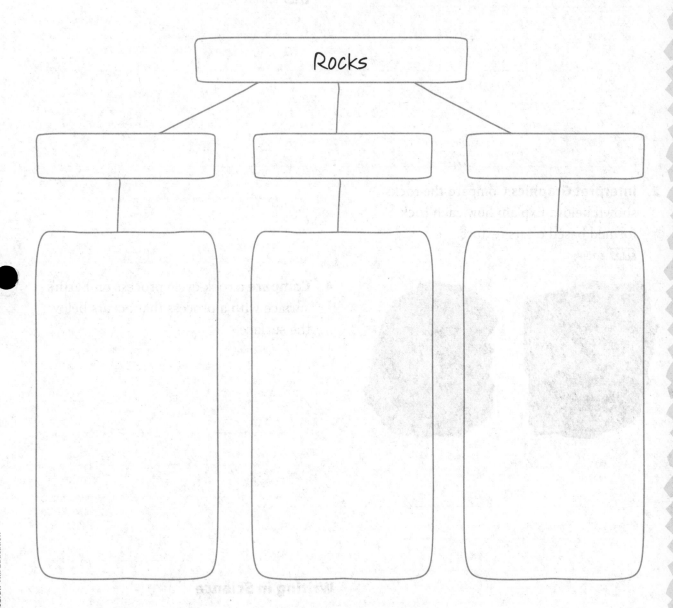

Rocks

 Connect it! **Defend** the following statement: *You find a sedimentary rock in your backyard. In the past, this rock could have been a different type of rock.* Support your reasoning with information from this section. Write your response in your interactive notebook. **TEKS** 6.10(B)

Rocks and the Rock Cycle

Apply the Essential Questions

1. **Explain** why there is no beginning or end to the rock cycle.

_____

_____

_____

_____

_____

2. **Interpret Graphics** Compare the rocks shown below. Explain how each rock formed based on its texture.
   TEKS 6.10(B)

_____

_____

_____

_____

_____

_____

H.O.T. Questions (Higher Order Thinking)

3. **Critique** the following statement: When igneous, sedimentary, or metamorphic rock is exposed to high temperatures and pressures, metamorphic rock forms.
   TEKS 6.10(B)

_____

_____

_____

_____

_____

_____

_____

_____

4. **Compare** a rock cycle process on Earth's surface with a process that occurs below the surface.

_____

_____

_____

_____

_____

_____

Writing in Science

5. **Analyze** Imagine if weathering and erosion had no impact on rocks. How might this affect the rock cycle? Write your response on a separate sheet of paper. **TEKS** 6.10(B)

Copyright © McGraw-Hill Education
(l)Colin Keates/Dorling Kindersley/Getty Images,
(r)Andreas Einsiedel/Dorling Kindersley

TEKS 6.10(B)

Earth's Oldest Rocks

Where did Earth's first rocks come from?

In 2008, scientists discovered rocks near Hudson Bay in Quebec, Canada, that formed 4.28 billion years ago. Then in 2010, scientists discovered isotopic evidence in rocks that reveals an even older geologic history. On Baffin Island, Canada, scientists discovered igneous rocks that they think came from Earth's early mantle, dating back 4.45 to 4.55 billion years—almost as old as the Earth itself! What evidence did scientists discover in these igneous rocks? Why are rocks with this type of geologic history so rare?

Earth formed 4.6 billion years ago. After its formation, the planet consisted entirely of molten material. As Earth cooled, this molten material cooled and crystallized, forming Earth's earliest crust, mantle, and core. Over time, geologic processes, such as seafloor spreading and subduction, have recycled much of Earth's densest crust—oceanic crust—back into the mantle. Continental crust is too buoyant to subduct, and therefore rocks in the center of a continent continue to age. It is unusual to discover rocks that date back to Earth's origin, because most of this material, even the center of a continent, has been affected by the rock cycle. Rocks exposed on Earth's surface are constantly subjected to erosional agents, such as water, wind, and ice.

Scientists have discovered that the igneous rocks on Baffin Island contain helium, lead, and neodymium isotope concentrations that match the composition of Earth's earliest mantle material. Helium is not produced in Earth's interior, but it is a primary ingredient in the universe. Scientists think that the igneous rocks on Baffin Island contain materials from the mantle before Earth differentiated into layers—that is, before heavier, denser materials sank in the mantle and less dense materials rose to the surface and formed the crust.

How do scientists know how old the rocks are? Scientists used radiometric dating techniques to determine the ages of zircon crystals and rare earth metals contained in the Hudson Bay rocks and helium, lead, and neodymium isotopes in the Baffin Island rocks. These dating techniques have led scientists to conclude that these igneous rocks formed during the Hadean eon, the first period of Earth's history.

It's Your Turn!

INVESTIGATE When did the rocks underneath Texas form? What kind of rocks lie beneath Texas? Investigate your city's geologic history and share your findings with your class.

8.2 Igneous Rocks

INQUIRY

Can rock be liquid? The composition and temperature of lava influence whether it will be thick and pasty or thin and fluid. How did this lava form? When it cools and crystallizes, what type of rock will it become? Where does this type of rock commonly form?

Write your responses in your interactive notebook.

LAB Manager

Go to your Lab Manual or visit connectED.mcgraw-hill.com to perform the labs for this lesson.

MiniLAB: *How are cooling rate and crystal size related?*
TEKS 6.1(A); 6.2(A), (C), (E); 6.3(B); 6.4(A), (B); 6.10(B)

Skill Practice: *How do you identify igneous rocks?*
TEKS 6.1(A); 6.2(A), (C), (E); 6.4(A); 6.10(B)

Explore Activity

TEKS 6.1(A); 6.2(A), (C), (E); 6.3(B); 6.4(A), (B); 6.10(B)

How does igneous rock form?

One way igneous rock forms is through the cooling and crystallization of lava. You might have seen video of molten lava flowing into the ocean. What do you think happens when the lava hits the cool ocean water?

Procedure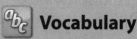

1. Read and complete a lab safety form.

2. Observe as your teacher drips **hot, melted sugar** slowly into a **beaker of cold water.** Record what happens in your Lab Manual or interactive notebook.

3. Observe as your teacher quickly pours hot, melted sugar into a beaker of cold water. Record what happens in your Lab Manual or interactive notebook.

4. Examine each of the "candy rocks" that formed in the cold water.

Think About This

1. What is the difference between the candy rocks that formed in step 2 and the candy rocks that formed in step 3?

_____

_____

_____

_____

2. Explain how this activity models the formation of igneous rocks.

_____

_____

_____

TEKS in this Lesson

6.10(B) Classify rocks as metamorphic, igneous, or sedimentary by the processes of their formation

Also covers Process Standards: 6.1(A); 6.2(A), (C), (E); 6.3(B); 6.4(A), (B)

? Essential Questions

- How do igneous rocks form?
- What are the common types of igneous rocks?

abc Vocabulary

extrusive rock
volcanic glass
intrusive rock

Igneous Rock Formation TEKS 6.10(B)

Figure 1 Stone Mountain in Georgia is made of igneous rocks that formed underground and are now exposed on Earth's surface.

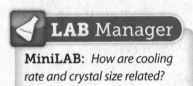

MiniLAB: *How are cooling rate and crystal size related?*
TEKS 6.1(A); 6.2(A), (C), (E); 6.3(B); 6.4(A), (B); 6.10(B)

Do you remember the difference between magma and lava? Magma is molten rock below Earth's surface, and lava is molten rock that has erupted onto Earth's surface. When you hear the word *lava*, you might picture a hot, gooey liquid that flows easily. When lava cools and crystallizes, it becomes igneous rock. The lava shown in the picture at the beginning of this lesson is already on its way to becoming solid igneous rock. It cools quickly after coming in contact with the cooler air around it. You can see where the lava has started to crystallize. It is the darker material on top of the red-hot, molten material below.

Not all molten rock makes it to Earth's surface. Large volumes of magma cool and crystallize beneath Earth's surface. Under these conditions, cooling and crystallization take a long time. The rock that results from magma cooling below the surface is different from the rock that results from lava cooling on Earth's surface. Over time, wind, rain, and other factors can wear away materials on Earth's surface. The rock that was once deep underground may now be exposed on Earth's surface. Stone Mountain, shown in **Figure 1,** is an example of igneous rock that formed from magma cooling slowly underground.

Compare

1. In the chart below, compare magma that forms inside Earth with lava that cools on Earth's surface.

	Magma Inside Earth	Lava on Earth's Surface
Rate of cooling		
Reason for rate of cooling		

Extrusive Rocks

When volcanic material erupts, cools, and crystallizes on Earth's surface, it forms a type of igneous rock called **extrusive rock.** Materials such as lava and ash solidify and form extrusive igneous rocks.

Lava can cool rapidly on Earth's surface. This means that there might not be enough time for any crystals to grow. Extrusive igneous rocks, therefore, have a fine-grained texture. **Volcanic glass** *is rock that forms when lava cools too quickly to form crystals,* such as the obsidian shown in **Figure 2.**

Magma stored underground can contain dissolved gases. As magma moves toward the surface, pressure decreases, and the gases separate from the molten mixture. This is similar to the carbon dioxide that escapes when you open a carbonated beverage. When gas-rich lava erupts from a volcano, gases escape. Among the most noticeable features of some extrusive igneous rocks, such as pumice (PUH mus), are holes that are left after gas escapes, as shown in **Figure 2.**

Obsidian

Pumice

Figure 2 Geologists study the texture and composition of extrusive igneous rocks to determine how they formed.

FOLDABLES

Cut out the Lesson 8.2 Foldable in the back of your book. Use it to review the two types of igneous rocks. Define the words *intrusive* and *extrusive*. Then relate the words *extrusive* and *intrusive* to the words *exterior* and *interior*.

Tape here

Types of Igneous Rocks

Relate to "exterior"

Relate to "interior"

Basalt

Exposed
granite

Granite

Intrusive

Continental
crust

Extrusive

Granite

Magma

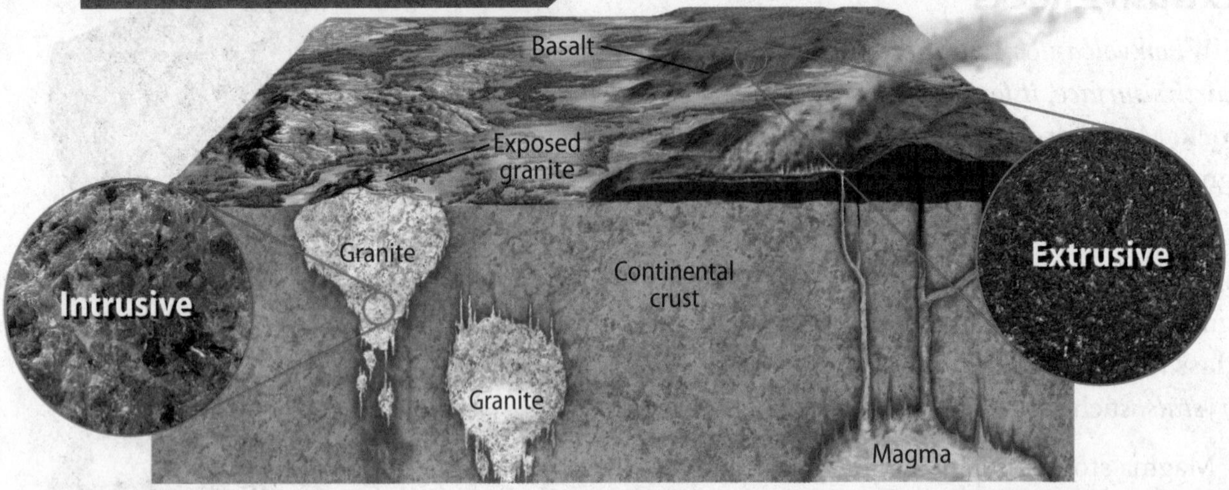

Figure 3 Magma that cools and crystallizes beneath Earth's surface forms intrusive igneous rock. Lava or ash that erupts and cools on Earth's surface forms extrusive igneous rock.

Intrusive Rocks

Igneous rocks that form as magma cools underground are called **intrusive rocks.** Because magma within Earth is insulated by solid rock, it cools more slowly than lava on Earth's surface. When magma cools slowly, large, well-defined crystals form.

Figure 3 shows a cross-section of Earth's crust where a magma chamber has solidified and formed intrusive rock. The arrangement of crystals in intrusive rocks is random. Crystals interlock like jigsaw-puzzle pieces. A random arrangement and large crystals are typical of intrusive igneous rocks.

Copyright © McGraw-Hill Education (l)McGraw-Hill Education, Ken Cavanagh, photographer, (r)©Photolibrary/age fotostock

Igneous Rock Identification TEKS 6.10(B)

Two characteristics can help geologists to identify all rocks: texture and composition. Geologists can identify an igneous rock using texture by using the arrangement and size of mineral crystals in the rock. Mineral composition can also be used for igneous rock identification.

Texture

Geologists determine whether an igneous rock is extrusive or intrusive by studying the rock's texture. Texture relates to how large or small the individual mineral grains are in the rock. If the crystals in the rock are small or impossible to see without a magnifying lens, the rock is extrusive. If all the crystals in the rock are large enough to see without a magnifying lens and have an interlocking texture, the rock is intrusive.

Word Origin

intrusive from Latin *intrudere,* means "to push in"

Determine

2. How do geologists determine whether an igneous rock is extrusive or intrusive? Write your response in your interactive notebook.

Composition

In addition to texture, geologists study the mineral composition of igneous rocks. Igneous rocks are classified, in part, based on their silica content. Light-colored minerals, such as quartz and feldspar, contain greater amounts of silica. Dark-colored minerals, such as olivine and pyroxene, contain less silica and greater amounts of elements like magnesium and iron. If minerals are difficult to identify, you can sometimes estimate the composition by observing how dark in color the rock is. Lighter-colored rocks are similar to granite in mineral composition. Darker-colored rocks are similar to basalt in composition.

Magma composition, the location where the lava or magma cools and crystallizes, and the cooling rate determine the type of igneous rock that forms. For example, granite is high in silica, and it cooled slowly beneath Earth's surface. Granite is an intrusive igneous rock. Basalt is an extrusive igneous rock that has low silica content. It formed as lava rapidly cooled on Earth's surface.

Table 1 organizes common igneous rocks according to their texture and mineral composition. Notice that an extrusive igneous rock can have the same mineral composition as an intrusive igneous rock, but their textures differ. Also notice that the minerals present in the rock affect the rock color.

Understand

3. Underline the difference between high and low silica content. Then circle how scientists determine the type of igneous rock that can form.

LAB Manager

Skill Practice: *How do you identify igneous rocks?*

TEKS 6.1(A); 6.2(A), (C), (E); 6.4(A); 6.10(B)

Table 1 Texture indicates whether an igneous rock is intrusive or extrusive. The color of the minerals gives clues to a rock's composition.

Watch

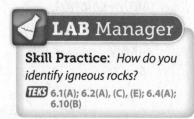

Table 1 Common Igneous Rocks		
Important Rock-Forming Minerals Present	**Intrusive Texture** *(all crystals visible with unaided eye)*	**Extrusive Texture** *(some or no crystals visible with unaided eye)*
Quartz, feldspar, mica, amphibole	granite	rhyolite
Pyroxene, feldspar, mica, amphibole, some quartz	diorite	andesite
Olivine, pyroxene, feldspar, mica, amphibole, little or no quartz	gabbro	basalt

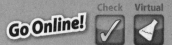

Organize information about how geologists classify igneous rocks. **TEKS** 6.10(B)

| If the rock is light-colored, **then** the rock is likely _____ in silica. | Determine _____ | If the rock is dark-colored, **then** the rock is likely _____ in silica. |

Classifying Igneous Rock

| If the crystals are visible with an unaided eye, **then** the rock is _____. | Look at _____ | If the crystals are not visible with an unaided eye, **then** the rock is _____. |

Connect it! **Create** an analogy that you could use to distinguish between the formation of intrusive igneous rocks and extrusive igneous rocks. **TEKS** 6.10(B)

_____

_____

_____

_____

_____

_____

Igneous Rocks

Use Vocabulary

1. **Explain** the formation of *volcanic glass*.
   TEKS 6.10(B)

   _____

   _____

   _____

Apply the Essential Questions

2. **Describe** the process of how a sedimentary rock can become an igneous rock. **TEKS** 6.10(B)

   _____

   _____

   _____

   _____

   _____

   _____

3. **Classify** the most common types of igneous rocks. Then give an example of each. **TEKS** 6.10(B)

   _____

   _____

   _____

   _____

   _____

   _____

   _____

H.O.T. Questions (Higher Order Thinking)

4. **Predict** the texture of an igneous rock formed from an explosive volcanic eruption. Explain your reasoning. **TEKS** 6.10(B)

   _____

   _____

   _____

   _____

   _____

   _____

   _____

   _____

5. **Relate** the presence of holes in pumice to its ability to float in water. How does this type of rock form? **TEKS** 6.10(B)

   _____

   _____

   _____

   _____

   _____

   _____

   _____

   _____

Careers in SCIENCE

AMERICAN MUSEUM OF NATURAL HISTORY

A supervolcano quietly simmers.

Volcanic rocks tell a story about a supervolcano's explosive past and provide clues about future eruptions.

Yellowstone National Park in Wyoming is home to thousands of natural wonders such as erupting geysers, simmering steam vents, gurgling mud pots, and colorful hot springs. The source of the thermal energy that drives these geologic marvels—superheated magma—is stored in a magma chamber a few kilometers below the park. Yellowstone is home to the largest active volcanic area in North America. Some of its past eruptions were so explosive that ash spread across the North American continent, earning Yellowstone the title of supervolcano.

How do supervolcanoes form? Sarah Fowler, a geologist with the American Museum of Natural History, is searching for clues. She studies magma chambers under supervolcanoes such as Yellowstone to determine the causes of explosive eruptions. Since she cannot sample the magma chamber directly, she analyzes rocks that formed from lava that erupted from the supervolcano in the past.

Pumice

What do the rocks tell her? Fowler studies pumice, a lightweight volcanic rock filled with tiny holes. These holes were left behind as gas escaped from molten material during cooling and crystallization. Lava and ash that contain trapped gas erupt explosively. Therefore, Fowler knows the presence of pumice indicates an explosive past. Fowler also studies a volcanic rock called tuff. During a gas-rich eruption, a volcano ejects ash into the atmosphere. The ash settles and eventually accumulates in layers, fusing together and forming tuff. Fowler examines the size of the ash to determine where the blast originated. Larger fragments fall closer to the source. Smaller ones are carried by wind and fall farther away. When Fowler finds rocks such as pumice and tuff, she records their location and studies their texture and composition. With these data, she can produce computer models that simulate past eruptions.

Tuff

It is unlikely that Yellowstone will erupt any time soon; however, geologists monitor earthquake activity and other indicators for signs of a future eruption.

It's Your Turn!

WRITE Imagine you are a geologist, and you discover an igneous rock, such as basalt or granite. Describe the rock in your interactive notebook. Conduct some research to explain where this rock formed and the processes that led to its formation.

How did these broken rock fragments form?

This river contributes to the formation of sedimentary rocks. The flowing water erodes rock and deposits broken fragments in the riverbed. Some of these rock fragments could have originated in the mountains above. What will happen to all this material?

Write your response in your interactive notebook.

LAB Manager

Go to your Lab Manual or visit connectED.mcgraw-hill.com to perform the labs for this lesson.

MiniLAB: *Where did these rocks form?*

TEKS 6.1(A); 6.2(A), (C), (E); 6.10(B)

Skill Practice: *How are sedimentary rocks classified?*

TEKS 6.1(A); 6.2(A), (C), (E); 6.4(A), (B); 6.10(B)

How do sedimentary rocks differ?

Sedimentary rocks are made from mixtures of mineral grains, rock fragments, and sometimes organic material. Can you compare grain sizes and determine types of sedimentary rock?

Procedure

1. Read and complete a lab safety form.

2. Obtain a set of **labeled samples** from your teacher.

3. Use a **hand lens** to closely examine the sediment that makes up Rock Sample A. Record your observations in your Lab Manual or your interactive notebook.

4. Repeat step 3 with the other samples in your set.

5. Review your notes and determine how many different types of sedimentary rocks you have. Check with your teacher to see if you are correct.

Think About This

1. What characteristics did you use to distinguish between the rock samples?

_____

_____

2. Why do you think sedimentary rocks are so common on Earth's surface?

_____

_____

_____

3. Do you think all sedimentary rocks form by the same processes? Explain your reasoning.

_____

_____

TEKS in this Lesson

6.10(B) Classify rocks as metamorphic, igneous, or sedimentary by the processes of their formation

Also covers Process Standards:
6.1(A); 6.2(A), (C), (E); 6.4(A), (B)

 Essential Questions

- How do sedimentary rocks form?
- What are the three types of sedimentary rocks?

 Vocabulary

compaction
cementation
clastic rock
clast
chemical rock
biochemical rock

Figure 1 After sediments are deposited, the processes of compaction and cementation begin.

Sedimentary Rock Formation TEKS 6.10(B)

Like igneous rocks, sedimentary rocks can form in different environments through a series of natural steps. Water and air can change the physical or chemical properties of rock. This change can cause rock to break apart, to dissolve, or to form new minerals. When water travels through rock, some of the elements in the rock can dissolve and be transported to new locations. Mineral and rock fragments can also be transported by water, glacial ice, gravity, or wind. The sediments eventually are deposited, or laid down, where they can then accumulate in layers.

Imagine sediment deposits becoming thicker over time. Younger sediment layers bury older sediment layers. Eventually, the old and young layers of sediment can be buried by even younger sediment deposits. *The weight from the layers of sediment forces out fluids and decreases the space between grains during a process called* **compaction.** Compaction can lead to a process called cementation. *When minerals dissolved in water crystallize between sediment grains, the process is called* **cementation.** Mineral cement holds the grains together, as shown in **Figure 1.** Common minerals that cement sediment together include quartz, calcite, and clay.

Contrast

1. What is the difference between compaction and cementation?

_____

_____

_____

_____

_____

Sedimentary Rock Identification TEKS 6.10(B)

Like igneous rocks, sedimentary rocks are classified according to how they form. Sedimentary rocks form when sediments, rock fragments, minerals, or organic materials are deposited, compacted, and then cemented together. They also form during evaporation when minerals crystallize from water or when organisms remove minerals from the water to grow their shells or skeletons.

Go Online! Tutor

324   Chapter 8

Clastic Sedimentary Rocks

Some rocks, such as sandstone, have a gritty texture that is similar to sugar. Sandstone is a common clastic sedimentary rock. *Sedimentary rocks that are made up of broken pieces of minerals and rock fragments are known as **clastic** (KLAH stik) **rocks.** The broken pieces and fragments are called **clasts.**

Geologists identify clastic rocks according to clast size and shape. The conglomerate in **Figure 2** is an example of a rock that was deposited in a river channel. The large sediment pieces were polished and rounded as they bounced along the bottom of the channel. However, the angular fragments in the breccia in **Figure 2** probably were not transported far, because their sharp edges were not worn away.

Recognize

2. What characteristics do scientists use to classify a clastic sedimentary rock?

_____

Sediment size alone cannot be used to determine the environment in which a clastic rock formed. For example, sediment deposited by a glacier can be as large as a car or as small as a grain of flour. The reason is that ice can move both large and small clasts. Geologists study the shape of clasts to help determine the environment in which a rock formed. For example, a fast-flowing river and ocean waves tend to move large sediment. Small, gritty sediment is typically deposited in calm environments such as the seafloor or the bottom of a lake.

Copyright © McGraw-Hill Education   (l)Andreas Einsiedel/Dorling Kindersley, (r)Joyce Photographics/Photo Researchers

Conglomerate

Breccia

Word Origin

clastic
from Greek *klastos,* means "broken"

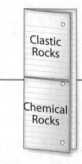

FOLDABLES®

Use a sheet of paper to make a vertical two-tab book. Collect information on clastic and chemical sedimentary rocks.

Clastic Rocks

Chemical Rocks

Figure 2 The clasts in the conglomerate on the left were rounded by a fast-flowing river. The forces that created the angular fragments of the breccia on the right might not have been as strong or as long-lived.

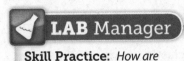
Chemical Sedimentary Rocks

Remember that as water flows through cracks or empty spaces in rock, it can dissolve minerals in the rock. Eventually, rivers carry these dissolved minerals to the oceans. Dissolved minerals entering the ocean contribute to the saltiness of seawater.

Water can become saturated with dissolved minerals. When this occurs, particles can crystallize out of the water and form minerals. **Chemical rocks** *form when minerals crystallize directly from water.* Rock salt, shown in **Figure 3,** rock gypsum, and limestone are examples of common chemical sedimentary rocks.

Restate

3. How do chemical rocks form?

_____

_____

_____

_____

Chemical sedimentary rocks often have an interlocking crystalline texture, similar to the textures of many igneous rocks. One difference between intrusive igneous rocks and chemical sedimentary rocks is that igneous rocks are composed of a variety of minerals and they appear multicolored. Chemical sedimentary rocks are generally composed of one dominant mineral and are uniform in color. For example, granite is made of quartz, feldspar, and mica, but rock salt is composed only of the mineral halite.

Figure 3 The water that once filled this lake bed was saturated, or filled, with dissolved halite. The water evaporated, and crystalline rock salt formed.

Table 1 Common Chemical and Biochemical Rocks

Go Online!

Rock Name	chemical limestone	rock gypsum	rock salt	fossiliferous limestone	chert	coal
Mineral Composition	calcite	gypsum	halite	aragonite or calcite	quartz	carbon**
Type	chemical	chemical	chemical	biochemical	biochemical*	biochemical
Example						

*Some chert is not biochemical. **Carbon in coal is not a mineral.

Table 1 Chemical and biochemical sedimentary rocks are common on Earth's surface.

Biochemical Sedimentary Rocks

Biochemical rock *is a sedimentary rock that was formed by organisms or contains the remains of organisms*. The most common biochemical sedimentary rock is limestone. Marine organisms make their shells from dissolved minerals in the ocean. When these organisms die, their shells settle onto the seafloor. This sediment is compacted and cemented and forms limestone. Sometimes the remains or traces of these organisms are preserved as fossils in sedimentary rock. Geologists call limestone that contains fossils fossiliferous (FAH suh LIH fuh rus) limestone, shown in **Table 1**. Limestone is classified as a type of carbonate rock because it contains the elements carbon and oxygen. Carbonate rocks will fizz when they come into contact with hydrochloric acid. Geologists use this chemical property to help identify different varieties of limestone.

Not all biochemical sedimentary rocks are carbonates. Some microscopic ocean organisms make their shells by removing silicon and oxygen from seawater. When these organisms die and settle on the ocean floor, compaction and cementation turn this sediment into the sedimentary rock chert.

Coal is another type of biochemical sedimentary rock. It is composed of the remains of plants and animals from prehistoric swamps. Over time, these organic remains were buried. Burial led to compression, which eventually changed the remains into sedimentary rock.

Distiguish

4. Create a graphic organizer that compares the formation of the biochemical sedimentary rocks fossiliferous limestone, chert, and coal. Write your response in your interactive notebook.

LAB Manager

MiniLAB: *Where did these rocks form?*
TEKS 6.1(A); 6.2(A), (C), (E); 6.10(B)

Summarize it!

Categorize the three types of sedimentary rocks and the processes by which they form. **TEKS** 6.10(B)

Sedimentary Rocks

[blank box connected to larger blank box]

[blank box connected to larger blank box]

[blank box connected to larger blank box]

Distinguish the two characteristics used to classify clastic rocks. Explain what each characteristic indicates. **TEKS** 6.10(B)

_____

_____

_____

_____

_____

Connect it! In a forested area you find a biochemical sedimentary rock which contains a seashell. **Describe** what this rock can tell us about how this forest might have looked in the past. Write your response in your interactive notebook.

Summarize it!

Use Vocabulary

1. **Distinguish** among clastic, chemical, and biochemcial sedimentary rock.
   TEKS 6.10(B)

   _____

   _____

   _____

   _____

   _____

Apply the Essential Questions

2. **Interpreting Graphics** Examine the rock above. What type of sedimentary rock is this? How did it form? Explain.
   TEKS 6.10(B)

   _____

   _____

   _____

   _____

   _____

3. **Identify** what can be determined by studying the shape of clastic grains.
   TEKS 6.10(B)

   _____

   _____

   _____

   _____

4. **Classify** the following sedimentary rocks as clastic, chemical, or biochemical: conglomerate, rock gypsum, fossiliferous limestone, and rock salt.
   TEKS 6.10(B)

   _____

   _____

   _____

   _____

   _____

   _____

   _____

 H.O.T. Questions (Higher Order Thinking)

5. Over time, limestone dissolves in the presence of acid precipitation on Earth's surface. **Critique** the use of limestone for the construction of buildings and monuments on a seperate sheet of paper.

Cave of Crystals

An Amazing Sight!

For any rock collector, a geode is a thrilling find. Splitting these hollow rocks in half reveals perfectly formed crystals inside. In 2000, two brothers found themselves inside something like a giant geode. They discovered the Cave of Crystals 300 m under the Chihuahuan Desert in Mexico. The limestone cave is filled with some of the largest crystals ever found—gigantic, shimmering beams the size of trees. Inside the cave, the temperature is about 43°C, and it is very humid. When researchers are in the cave, they wear special suits so they can work in the steaming hot conditions. Scientists are now working to identify and understand the natural conditions that allowed the crystals to become so large.

What are the crystals made of?

The crystals are made of the mineral selenite, a transparent and colorless form of gypsum. Gypsum has a hardness of 2 on Mohs' hardness scale. So even though some of the crystals have edges that are as sharp as blades, the crystals are soft enough to be scratched by your fingernail.

How did the crystals form?

Hundreds of thousands of years ago, a magma chamber below the caves heated groundwater in Earth's crust. The hot water became mineral-rich by dissolving minerals from the surrounding rock. It seeped through cracks in the limestone caves. As the water cooled over time, the dissolved minerals crystallized.

How did the crystals get so big?

The more time crystals have to grow, the bigger they become. The Cave of Crystals was left undisturbed for thousands of years, so the crystals grew very large. The crystals stopped growing only because local miners drained the groundwater, emptying the cave of the mineral-rich water.

These selenite crystals are the same shape as the giants in the Cave of Crystals. They are much smaller, though, because they did not have as much time to grow.

It's Your Turn!

CREATE Suppose you are in charge of tourism for the Cave of Crystals. Write a tourist brochure describing what visitors can expect to see and experience in the cave. Present your brochure to the class.

INQUIRY

How did this wrinkle?

Sediment is usually deposited in horizontal layers. Under the right conditions, those layers can be bent and twisted. What do you think caused this rock to bend and twist?

Write your response in your interactive notebook.

LAB Manager

Go to your Lab Manual or visit connectED.mcgraw-hill.com to perform the labs for this lesson.

MiniLAB: *Can you model metamorphism?*

TEKS 6.1(A); 6.2(A), (C); 6.3(B), (C); 6.4(B); 6.10(B)

LAB: *Identifying the Type of Rock*

TEKS 6.1(A); 6.2(A), (C), (E); 6.4(A), (B); 6.10(B)

Explore Activity

TEKS 6.1(A), (B); 6.2(A), (C), (E); 6.4(B); 6.10(B)

How does pressure affect rock formation?

How does pressure affect the minerals in a rock? The arrangement of minerals in a metamorphic rock can be used to help classify the rock.

Procedure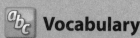

1. Read and complete a lab safety form.

2. Place some rice grains on a table.

3. Roll a **ball of clay** on top of the **rice**. Knead the ball until the rice is evenly mixed in the clay.

4. Use a **rolling pin** or a **round can** to roll the clay to a thickness of about 0.5 cm. Draw and label a picture of the sheet of clay. Record your observations in your Lab Manual or interactive notebook.

5. Fold the edge of the clay closest to you toward the edge away from you. Roll the clay in the direction you folded it. Repeat and flatten the clay to a thickness of 0.5 cm again. Draw and label a picture of the sheet of clay and the rice grains. Record your observations in your Lab Manual or interactive notebook.

6. Be sure to dispose of materials used in this lab appropriately.

Think About This

1. Describe the differences you observed in the orientation of rice grains between steps 4 and 5.

_____

_____

_____

2. Determine what force caused the orientation of rice grains in the clay to change. How might this process be similar to the formation of metamorphic rocks?

_____

_____

TEKS in this Lesson

6.10(B) Classify rocks as metamorphic, igneous, or sedimentary by the processes of their formation

Also covers Process Standards: 6.1(A), (B); 6.2(A), (C), (E); 6.3(B), (C); 6.4(A), (B)

? Essential Questions

- How do metamorphic rocks form?
- How do types of metamorphic rock differ?

abc Vocabulary

metamorphism
plastic deformation
foliated rock
nonfoliated rock
contact metamorphism
regional metamorphism

Metamorphic Rock Formation **TEKS** 6.10(B)

Imagine you left a cheese sandwich in your backpack on a hot day and then put your backpack in your locker. Would the sandwich look the same after school? Changes in temperature during the day would likely cause the cheese to soften. Pressure from the weight of your backpack would flatten the sandwich. Like the sandwich, rocks are also affected by changes in temperature and pressure. These rocks are called metamorphic rocks. **Metamorphism** *is any process that affects the structure or composition of a rock in a solid state as a result of changes in temperature or pressure, or the addition of chemical fluids.*

Most metamorphic rocks form deep within Earth's crust. Like igneous rocks, metamorphic rocks form under high temperature and pressure conditions. However, unlike igneous rocks, metamorphic rocks do not crystallize from magma. Unlike sedimentary rocks, metamorphic rocks do not result from erosion and deposition. The metamorphic rocks shown at the beginning of this lesson have changed shape. **Exposed** to extreme temperatures and pressure, the rocks were bent and twisted into wrinkly layers and are classified as metamorphic rocks.

Academic Vocabulary

expose *(verb)* to uncover or subject

Figure 1 The layers visible in this metamorphic outcrop show where this rock was changed by extreme heat and pressure deep below Earth's surface.

✏️ **Recall**

1. Underline where and under what conditions metamorphic rocks form.

Temperature and Pressure

Refer back to the rock in the lesson opener. What did you think caused the rock to bend and twist? When rocks experience an increase in temperature and pressure, they behave like a bendable plastic. Without melting, the rocks bend or fold. *This permanent change in shape by bending and folding is called* **plastic deformation.** This is one way the texture of a rock changes during metamorphism. Plastic deformation occurs during uplift events when tectonic plates collide and form mountains, such as the Himalayas in Asia. Changes in composition and structure are clues that a rock has been metamorphosed.

The rock that changes during metamorphism is called the parent rock. The temperatures required to metamorphose rock depend on the parent rock's composition. The lower limit of the temperature range for metamorphic rock formation is between 150°C and 200°C. In addition to temperature, pressure also increases with depth in Earth's crust and mantle, as shown in **Figure 2**. Pressure is measured in kilobars (kb).

Figure 2 Pressure increases with depth in Earth.

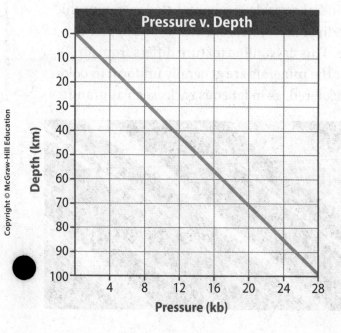

Pressure v. Depth

2. In the space below, draw a representation of plastic deformation in metamorphic rock. Then explain how temperature and pressure affect metamorphic rocks.

Use Graphs

The line graph in **Figure 2** represents pressure below Earth's surface. What is the pressure at a depth of 50 km?

a. Read the title of the graph to determine what data are represented.

b. Read the labels on the x- and y-axis to determine the units.

c. Move horizontally from 50 km to the orange line. Move vertically from the orange line to the x-axis. The pressure is 14 kb.

Practice

At what depth is the pressure 20 kb?

Word Origin

foliate
from Latin *foliatus*, means "consisting of thin, leaf-like layers"

Metamorphic Rock Identification **TEKS** 6.10 (B)

Changes in temperature or pressure, or the addition of chemical fluids can result in the rearrangement of minerals or the formation of new minerals in a metamorphic rock. Geologists study the texture and composition of minerals to identify metamorphic rocks.

Metamorphic rocks are classified into two groups based on texture. In many cases, changes in pressure cause minerals to align and form layers in metamorphic rocks. This layering can appear similar to the layers associated with clastic sedimentary rocks. However, the crystalline minerals present in a metamorphic rock distinguish it from a clastic sedimentary rock. In other cases, the rock can have blocky, interlocking crystals that appear uniform in color.

Foliated Rocks

The metamorphic rock gneiss, shown in **Figure 3**, is an example of a foliated rock. **Foliated rocks** *contain parallel layers of flat and elongated minerals.* Look closely at the layers of dark and light minerals in the gneiss. This layering results from an uneven distribution of pressure during metamorphism. Foliation is a common feature in metamorphic rocks.

Nonfoliated Rocks

Metamorphic rocks that have mineral grains with a random, interlocking texture are **nonfoliated rocks.** There is no obvious alignment of the mineral crystals in a nonfoliated metamorphic rock. Instead, the individual crystals are blocky and approximately equal in size. This crystalline texture differs from an igneous rock in that the minerals are generally uniform in color as opposed to multicolored, as in igneous rocks such as granite.

Figure 3 Elongated or flat minerals in foliated rocks line up in response to pressure.

Contact and Regional Metamorphism

One way a nonfoliated metamorphic rock can form is when magma intrudes rock. *During* **contact metamorphism**, *magma comes in contact with existing rock, and its thermal energy and gases interact with the surrounding rock, forming new metamorphic rock.* Contact metamorphism can increase crystal size or form new minerals and change rock. A common example of a nonfoliated rock, marble, is shown in **Figure 4.** Notice the uniform color and crystal size in this specimen. **Table 1** illustrates other examples of nonfoliated and foliated metamorphic rocks.

Regional metamorphism *is the formation of metamorphic rock bodies that are hundreds of square kilometers in size.* This process can create an entire mountain range of metamorphic rock. Changes in temperature and pressure and the presence of chemical fluids act on large volumes of rock and produce metamorphic textures. These textures can help unravel the mysteries of a mountain-building event. The Himalayas in Asia and the Appalachian Mountains of the eastern United States exhibit structures associated with regional metamorphism.

Figure 4 Nonfoliated rocks do not show obvious orientation of minerals.

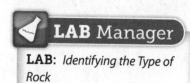

LAB Manager

LAB: *Identifying the Type of Rock*

TEKS 6.1(A); 6.2(A), (C), (E); 6.4(A), (B); 6.10(B)

Table 1 Metamorphic Rocks				
Texture		**Composition**	**Rock Name**	**Example**
Foliated	layered	quartz, mica, clay minerals	slate	
	layered	quartz, mica, clay minerals	phylite	
	color bands	quartz, feldspar, amphibole, mica	schist	
	color bands	quartz, feldspar, amphibole, pyroxene	gneiss	
Non-foliated	blocky crystals	quartz	quartzite	
	blocky crystals	calcite	marble	

Table 1 Metamorphic rocks are classified into two groups based on texture.

FOLDABLES®

Make a vertical two-tab book. Use it to organize your notes on contact and regional metamorphism.

Contact Metamorphism

Regional Metamorphism

Organize information about metamorphic rocks. **TEKS** 6.10(B)

┌─────────────────────────┐   ┌─────────────────────────┐
│ Formed at high: │   │ Formed within: │
│   │   │   │
│   │   │   │
└─────────────────────────┘   └─────────────────────────┘

┌──────────────────────┐
│   Metamorphic Rock   │
└──────────────────────┘

┌─────────────────────────┐   ┌─────────────────────────┐
│ Contrast with igneous   │   │ Contrast with sedimentary rock: │
│ rock: │   │   │
│   │   │   │
│   │   │   │
└─────────────────────────┘   └─────────────────────────┘

Summarize the two types of metamorphism. **TEKS** 6.10(B)

_____

_____

_____

_____

_____

_____

_____

 Connect it! **Discuss** what type of rock you think can tell us the most about Earth's past. Write your response in your interactive notebook. **TEKS** 6.10(B)

Summarize it!

Apply the Essential Questions

1. **Identify** the conditions needed for a metamorphic rock to form.
   TEKS 6.10(B)

   _____

   _____

2. **Classify** the following rocks as either foliated or nonfoliated: quartzite and schist. Explain your reasoning.

   _____

   _____

   _____

   _____

   _____

H.O.T. Question (Higher Order Thinking)

3. **Explain** Could the process of metamorphism occur if Earth's interior was cool?

   _____

   _____

   _____

   _____

   _____

   _____

   _____

Writing in Science

4. **Assess** the rock cycle processes that form metamorphic rocks and igneous rocks deep beneath Earth's surface. Write your response on a separate sheet of paper.
   TEKS 6.10(B)

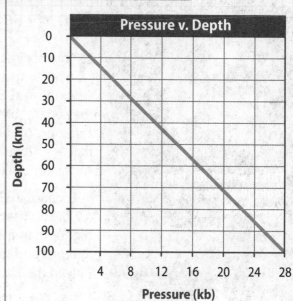

Math Skills   Math **TEKS** 6.1(B); 6.2

Pressure v. Depth

Use Graphs

5. Based on the graph above, what is the pressure at a depth of 40 km?

6. At what depth would the pressure be 30 kb?

7. Use the trend on the graph to predict the appropriate pressure at a depth of 200 km.

Check   Tutor

Go Online!

Enchanted Rock, near Fredericksburg, Texas, is a dome of pink granite.

The Llano Uplift

This is what blue topaz looks like when it is just mined.

This is what blue topaz looks like after cutting and polishing.

Can we see ancient rocks on Earth's surface?

Tourists visit Texas for countless reasons. Music, scenery, sporting events, or recreation are just a few of the reasons. Geologists also come to Texas for a number of reasons. They may come to collect rocks, to observe landforms and structures, or to study Earth's history. Although there are many places in Texas where geologists can do some of these things, the Llano Uplift is a location where they can do them all.

Located in Central Texas, the Llano Uplift is between 1.0 to 1.2 billion years old. Uplift occurs when older rocks are lifted higher than the surrounding younger rocks. These ancient igneous and metamorphic rocks underlie all of Texas, but it is only in the Llano Uplift that they appear at the surface.

The Llano Uplift's igneous and metamorphic rocks were formed by the same forces that caused the uplift. These rocks contain an abundance of minerals, including large crystals of quartz, feldspar, mica, hornblende, garnet, and staurolite. Less common, but still found in the Llano Uplift, are tourmaline, gold, and blue topaz, the Texas state mineral.

Enchanted Rock is one of the most striking features in the Llano Uplift. The granite dome was once a magma chamber that cooled deep below the surface. Erosion eventually exposed the dome which is now a destination for tourists and geologists.

It's Your Turn!

RESEARCH How close is your school to metamorphic rocks? Are the rocks closer by map distance or depth below the surface? Research the type and age of the rocks. Present your findings to your class.

TEKS Review

Test-Taking Strategy

Analyze a Graph Graphs are often used to display data. Each axis represents a different variable. You can plot points on a graph to show the relationship between the two variables at that point. The points can be connected to help show trends in data.

Example

Use the graph to answer question 1.

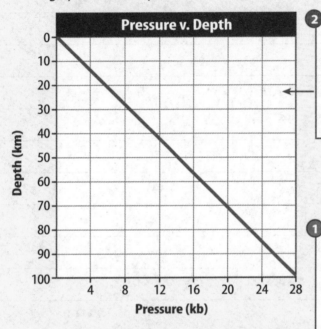

② Analyze the data in the graph. At a depth of 0 km, the pressure is 0 kb. As the depth increases to 100 km, the pressure reaches 28 kb. As depth increases in numeric value, the pressure also increases in numeric value.

① Carefully read the question and determine what it is asking. Then look at the information that is given in the graph and ask yourself how it can be used to answer the question. This question asks you to identify the relationship between depth and pressure.

1 Based on the graph, which of the following statements is true? **TEKS** 6.10(B)

③ The correct answer is choice **A**.

   A As depth increases, pressure increases.

   B As depth increases, pressure decreases.

   C As depth increases, pressure remains constant.

   D Depth and pressure are not related.

TIP: Graphs provide information that you can use to answer questions. Analyze ALL information provided before answering the question.

Multiple Choice

1 In which type of rock are you most likely to find fossils and why? **TEKS** 6.10(B)

A in extrusive rocks because the pressure of the water on top of a dead organism causes fossils to form

B in intrusive rocks because an organism's body gets trapped and preserved in hot lava

C in metamorphic rocks because the bones are changed to rock as they are fossilized

D in sedimentary rocks because the bones are covered with sediment that turns to rock

2

> Some students are working together to classify a set of rocks as igneous, metamorphic, or sedimentary. They develop a procedure to help them determine the characteristics of each rock. First, they will feel the rocks and observe the rocks with a magnifying lens, noting each rock's physical appearance. Next, they will place each rock in water and observe whether it sinks or floats. They will scratch the rocks with various instruments to see if the rocks are hard or soft and crumbly. Finally, they will perform an acid test on each rock to see whether a reaction occurs. They will carefully record their observations and then start their classifications.

Before the students begin, they realize they may not have enough time to do all of their tests. Which test could the students eliminate from their procedure and still be able to reasonably classify the rocks? **TEKS** 6.10(B); 6.2(A)

A Eliminate observing the rocks with a magnifying glass, because the appearance of a rock has little to do with how it is classified.

B Eliminate placing each rock in water, because nearly all rocks sink and the few that float can be identified by their appearance or other properties.

C Eliminate scratching the rocks to determine their hardness, because hardness is only a characteristic of minerals.

D Eliminate the acid test, because all rocks will erode when they come in contact with an acid.

3   While exploring a beach near a volcano, Louis discovers many rocks along the coast like the one shown below. He classifies the rocks as extrusive igneous rocks. **TEKS** 6.10(B); 6.3(A)

Which best justifies Louis' classification?

A The rocks were formed when lava is ejected from a volcano and cools quickly.

B The rocks were formed beneath the ocean under great pressure.

C The rocks were formed near the ocean and changed when heated by the volcano.

D The rocks were formed from magma that cooled slowly beneath Earth's surface.

4

A team of scientists who are studying volcanoes took core samples to find out how long ago the volcanoes erupted. A core sample shows rock layers that relate to different environmental conditions and geological events over time. Core sampling is a technique that allows scientists to see layers of rock beneath the surface of the ground. This helps them understand what happened a long time ago. In one core sample, the scientists discovered a light-colored igneous rock at a depth of 60 m below the surface. They found a thick layer of sedimentary rock directly above this that stretched from a depth of 34 m to 54 m below the surface.

What could best explain these observations? **TEKS** 6.10(B); 6.2(E)

A A long period with no volcanic activity allowed the slow buildup of sand and debris which then changed form as a result of heat and pressure.

B A long period with no volcanic activity was followed by eruption.

C An eruption occurred and was then followed by a period with no volcanic activity.

D An eruption occurred and the rock that formed then changed due to heat and pressure beneath Earth's surface.

5 Betty Jean has a collection of rocks. She organizes her observations about each rock in a table. **TEKS** 6.10(B); 6.2(E)

	Color	Grain/Crystal Size	Additional Observations
Rock 1	Pale color	Coarse-grained	Grains are tightly held together, but are not arranged in layers
Rock 2	Light gray	Fine-grained	Has many small pores that look like bubbles
Rock 3	Light gray	Fine-grained	Has the imprint of a shell
Rock 4	White, pink, and black	Coarse-grained	Has wavy, ribbon-like layers

Which rock should Betty Jean classify as a metamorphic rock?

A Rock 1 because it is coarse-grained and does not show layering.

B Rock 2 because it is fine-grained and light in color.

C Rock 3 because it contains fossils.

D Rock 4 because it has wavy, ribbon-like layers.

6 Lola finds a rock at a stream she is visiting. She is keeping a log of the rocks she finds, so she draws a sketch of the rock in her journal. **TEKS** 6.10(B)

How should Lola classify the rock she found?

A as a metamorphic rock because it was found near a stream and eroded by water

B as a sedimentary rock because it is formed from compacted products of erosion

C as an extrusive igneous rock because it clearly contains fossils of extinct organisms

D as an intrusive igneous rock because it is coarse-grained in texture and banded

The Solar System

The **BIG** Idea

Gravity is the force that organizes the objects in our solar system and controls their motions.

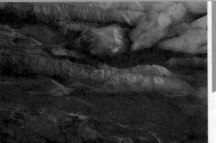

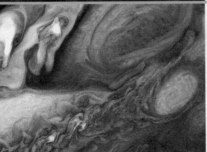

Go Online!
connectED.mcgraw-hill.com

Watch   Resources   Vocab   Tutor   IWB   Check   Lab

Objects in Our Solar System

A system consists of parts that make up a whole. What are the different parts that make up our solar system? Put an X next to each of the objects you think are part of our solar system.

☐ planets ☐ the Sun ☐ nearby stars other than the Sun

☐ distant stars ☐ constellations ☐ asteroids

☐ comets ☐ moons ☐ human-made satellites

☐ galaxies ☐ black holes ☐ universe

Explain your thinking. Describe what determines whether an object is part of our solar system.

9.1 The Structure of the Solar System

Are these stars? Did you know that shooting stars are not actually stars? The bright streaks are small, rocky particles burning up as they enter Earth's atmosphere. Why is the term *shooting star* misleading? These particles are part of the solar system and are often associated with comets. What types of objects do you think make up the solar system?

Write your response in your interactive notebook.

LAB Manager

Go to your Lab Manual or visit connectED.mcgraw-hill.com to perform the labs for this lesson.

MiniLAB: *Sunspots*
TEKS 6.11(A)

MiniLAB: *How can you model an elliptical orbit?*
TEKS 6.1(A); 6.2(A), (C); 6.11(A)

Explore Activity

TEKS 6.1(A); 6.2(A), (C), (E); 6.3(A); 6.4(A), (B); 6.11(A)

How do you know which distance unit to use?

You can use different units to measure distance. For example, millimeters might be used to measure the length of a bolt, and kilometers might be used to measure the distance between cities. In this lab, you will investigate why some units are easier to use than others for certain measurements.

Procedure

1. Read and complete a lab safety form.

2. Use a **centimeter ruler** to measure the length of a **pencil** and the thickness of a book. Record the distances in your Lab Manual or interactive notebook.

3. Use the centimeter ruler to measure the width of your classroom. Then measure the width of the room using a **meterstick**. Record the distances.

Think About This

1. Why are meters easier to use than centimeters for measuring the classroom?

_____

_____

_____

2. Describe why astronomers need a unit larger than a kilometer to measure locations of planets and distances in the solar system.

_____

_____

_____

_____

_____

TEKS in this Lesson

6.11(A) Describe the physical properties, locations, and movements of the Sun, planets, Galilean moons, meteors, asteroids, and comets.

6.11(B) Understand that gravity is the force that governs the motion of our solar system.

Also covers Process Standards: 6.1(A); 6.2(A), (C), (E); 6.3(A), (D); 6.4(A), (B)

? Essential Questions

- How are the inner planets different from the outer planets?
- What role does gravity play in the motion of objects in the solar system?
- What is the shape of a planet's orbit?

🔤 Vocabulary

asteroid
comet
astronomical unit
period of revolution
period of rotation

Figure 1 When looking at the night sky, you will likely see stars and planets. In the photo, the planet Venus is the bright object seen to the left above the Moon.

What is the solar system? **TEKS** 6.11(A)

Have you ever made a wish on a star? If so, you might have wished on a planet instead of a star. Sometimes, as shown in **Figure 1**, the first starlike object you see at night is not a star at all. It's Venus, the planet closest to Earth.

It's hard to tell the difference between planets and stars in the night sky because they all appear as tiny lights. Thousands of years ago, observers noticed that a few of these tiny lights moved, but others did not. The ancient Greeks called these objects planets, which means "wanderers." Astronomers now know that the planets do not wander about the sky; the planets move around the Sun. The Sun and the group of objects that move around it make up the solar system.

When you look at the night sky, a few of the tiny lights you can see are part of our solar system. Almost all the other specks of light are stars. They are much farther away than any objects in our solar system. Astronomers have discovered that some of those stars also have planets moving around them.

Recall

1. What object(s) do the planets in the solar system move around?

_____

_____

Objects in the Solar System TEKS 6.11(A), (B)

Ancient observers looking at the night sky saw many **stars** but only five planets—Mercury, Venus, Mars, Jupiter, and Saturn. The invention of the telescope in the 1600s led to the discovery of additional planets and many other space objects.

The Sun

The largest object in the solar system is the Sun, a star. Its diameter is about 1.4 million km—ten times the diameter of the largest planet, Jupiter. The Sun is made mostly of hydrogen gas. Its mass is about 99 percent of the entire solar system's mass.

The Sun, located at the center of the solar system, rotates on its own axis while it revolves around the galactic center of the Milky Way galaxy. Because the Sun is made up entirely of gases, the gases at the equator of the Sun rotate faster than the gases at the poles. The gases at the equator rotate every 25 days while the gases at the pole rotate every 36 days. Just as Earth and the other planets in the solar system revolve around the Sun, the Sun revolves around the center of the Milky Way. It takes about 200 million years for the Sun to revolve once.

Inside the Sun, a process called nuclear fusion produces an enormous amount of energy. The Sun emits some of this energy as light. The light from the Sun shines on all the planets every day. The Sun also applies gravitational forces to objects in the solar system. Gravitational forces cause the planets and other objects to move around, or **orbit,** the Sun.

Compile

2. Organize facts about the Sun in the following chart.

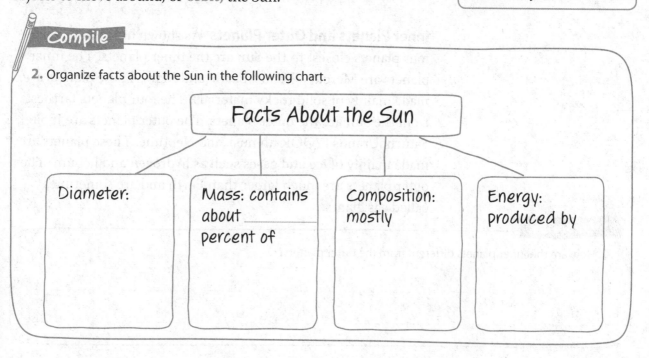

Facts About the Sun

Diameter:

Mass: contains about _____ percent of

Composition: mostly

Energy: produced by

Copyright © McGraw-Hill Education

Objects That Orbit the Sun

Different types of objects orbit the Sun. These objects include planets, dwarf planets, asteroids, and comets. Unlike the Sun, these objects don't emit light but only reflect the Sun's light.

Planets Astronomers classify some objects that orbit the Sun as planets, as shown in **Figure 2**. An object is a planet only if it orbits the Sun and has a nearly spherical shape. Also, the mass of a planet must be much larger than the total mass of all other objects whose orbits are close by. The solar system has eight objects classified as planets.

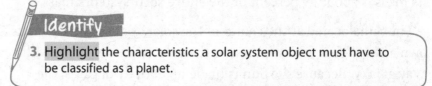

Identify

3. Highlight the characteristics a solar system object must have to be classified as a planet.

Figure 2 The orbits of the inner and outer planets are shown to scale. The Sun and the planets are not to scale. The outer planets are much larger than the inner planets.

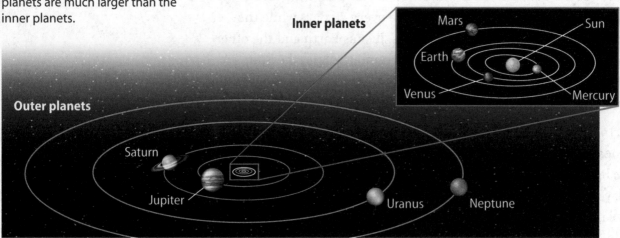

Inner Planets and Outer Planets As shown in **Figure 2**, the four planets closest to the Sun are the inner planets. The inner planets are Mercury, Venus, Earth, and Mars. These planets are made mainly of solid rocky materials. The four planets farthest from the Sun are the outer planets. The outer planets are Jupiter, Saturn, Uranus (YOOR uh nus), and Neptune. These planets are made mainly of ice and gases such as hydrogen and helium. The outer planets are much larger than Earth and are sometimes called gas giants.

Describe

4. How are the inner planets different from the outer planets?

_____

_____

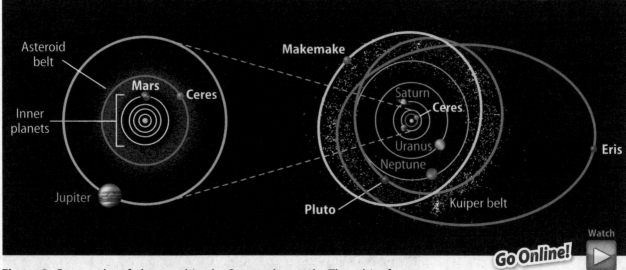

Asteroid belt
Inner planets
Mars
Ceres
Jupiter
Makemake
Saturn
Ceres
Uranus
Neptune
Pluto
Kuiper belt
Eris

Watch
Go Online!

Figure 3 Ceres, a dwarf planet, orbits the Sun as planets do. The orbit of Ceres is in the asteroid belt between Mars and Jupiter.

Dwarf Planets Scientists classify some objects in the solar system as dwarf planets. A dwarf planet is a spherical object that orbits the Sun. It is not a moon of another planet and is in a region of the solar system where there are many objects orbiting near it. But, unlike a planet, a dwarf planet does not have more mass than objects in nearby orbits. **Figure 3** shows the locations of the dwarf planets Ceres (SIHR eez), Eris (IHR is), Pluto, and Makemake (MAH kay MAH kay). Dwarf planets are made of rock and ice and are much smaller than Earth.

Asteroids *Millions of small, rocky objects called* **asteroids** *orbit the Sun in the asteroid belt between the orbits of Mars and Jupiter.* The asteroid belt is shown in **Figure 3**. Asteroids range in size from less than 1 meter to several hundred kilometers in length. Unlike planets and dwarf planets, *asteroids,* such as the one shown in **Figure 4,** usually are not spherical.

Comets You might have seen a picture of a comet with a long, glowing tail. *A* **comet** *is made of gas, dust, and ice and moves around the Sun in an oval-shaped orbit.* Comets come from the outer parts of the solar system. There might be 1 trillion comets orbiting the Sun.

Meteors A night of stargazing can lead to witnessing "shooting stars." A shooting star is not actually a star—it is a small piece of material that burns up as it enters Earth's atmosphere. This is called a meteor. A meteor can consist of iron, nickel, or rock. When a meteor impacts the surface of a planet or a moon, it is called a meteorite and creates an impact crater. These can be found on Earth and the Moon.

Locate

5. Which dwarf planet is farthest from the Sun?

Word Origin

asteroid from Greek *asteroeides,* means "resembling a star"

Figure 4 The asteroid Gaspra orbits the Sun in the asteroid belt. Its odd shape is about 19 km long and 11 km wide.

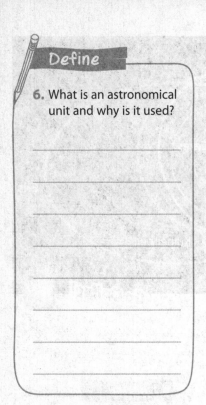

Define

6. What is an astronomical unit and why is it used?

_____

_____

_____

_____

_____

_____

_____

The Astronomical Unit

Recall what you learned in the Explore Activity about using different units of measurement. On Earth, distances are often measured in meters (m) or kilometers (km). Objects in the solar system, however, are so far apart that astronomers use a larger distance unit. *An **astronomical unit** (AU) is the average distance from Earth to the Sun—about 150 million km.* **Table 1** lists each planet's average distance from the Sun in km and AU.

Table 1	Average Distance of the Planets from the Sun	Go Online!
Planet	**Average Distance (km)**	**Average Distance (AU)**
Mercury	57,910,000	0.39
Venus	108,210,000	0.72
Earth	149,600,000	1.00
Mars	227,920,000	1.52
Jupiter	778,570,000	5.20
Saturn	1,433,530,000	9.58
Uranus	2,872,460,000	19.20
Neptune	4,495,060,000	30.05

FOLDABLES®

Make a tri-fold book from a sheet of paper and label it as shown. Use it to summarize information about the types of objects that make up the solar system.

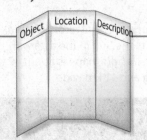

Object | Location | Description

The Motion of the Planets TEKS 6.11(A); 6.11(B)

Have you ever swung a ball on the end of a string in a circle over your head? In some ways, the motion of a planet around the Sun is like the motion of that ball. As shown in **Figure 5,** the Sun's gravitational force pulls each planet toward the Sun. This force is similar to the pull of the string that keeps the ball moving in a circle. The Sun's gravitational force pulls on each planet and keeps it moving along a curved path around the Sun.

Revolution and Rotation

Objects in the solar system move in two ways. They orbit, or revolve, around the Sun. *The time it takes an object to travel once around the Sun is its **period of revolution.*** Earth's period of revolution is one year. The objects also spin, or rotate, as they orbit the Sun. *The time it takes an object to complete one rotation is its **period of rotation.*** Earth has a period of rotation of one day.

7. Fill in information about the motion of the planets.

Motion of the Planets

Rotation	Revolution
The time that a planet takes to _____ _____ _____	The time that a planet takes to _____ _____ _____
Also called: _____	Also called: _____ Shape: _____

Planetary Orbits and Speeds

Unlike a ball swinging on the end of a string, planets do not move in circles. Instead, a planet's orbit is an ellipse—a stretched-out circle. Inside an ellipse are two special points, each called a focus. These focus points, or foci, determine the shape of the ellipse. The foci are equal distances from the center of the ellipse. As shown in **Figure 5,** the Sun is at one of the foci; the other foci is empty space. As a result, the distance between the planet and the Sun changes as the planet moves.

A planet's speed also changes as it orbits the Sun. The closer the planet is to the Sun, the faster it moves. This also means that planets farther from the Sun have longer periods of revolution. For example, Jupiter is more than five times farther from the Sun than Earth. Not surprisingly, Jupiter takes 12 times longer than Earth to revolve around the Sun.

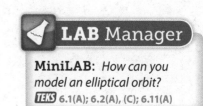

LAB Manager

MiniLAB: *How can you model an elliptical orbit?*
TEKS 6.1(A); 6.2(A), (C); 6.11(A)

Figure 5 Planets and other objects in the solar system revolve around the Sun because of its gravitational pull on them.

Go Online! Tutor

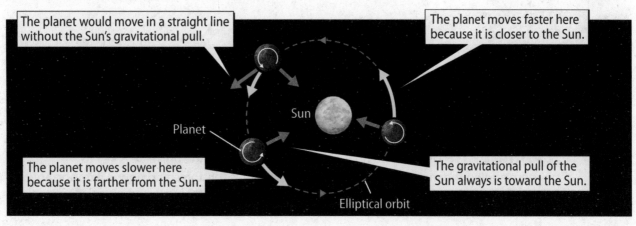

The planet would move in a straight line without the Sun's gravitational pull.

The planet moves faster here because it is closer to the Sun.

Sun

Planet

The planet moves slower here because it is farther from the Sun.

The gravitational pull of the Sun always is toward the Sun.

Elliptical orbit

Copyright © McGraw-Hill Education

Create a graphic organizer of your choice in the space below to assemble all of the information you have learned so far about the solar system. Be sure to include the following items: the Sun, inner planets, outer planets, dwarf planets, asteroids, comets, and meteors. *TEKS* 6.11(A)

Connect it! Understanding the one unifying force in the universe is key to understanding the motions of all space objects. What is this force and how is it important on Earth? Write your response in your interactive notebook. *TEKS* 6.11(B) *supporting*

The Structure of the Solar System

Apply the Essential Questions

1. **Apply** your understanding of how and why planets orbit the Sun and how and why a planet's speed changes in orbit.
   TEKS 6.11(B) *supporting*

   _____

   _____

   _____

   _____

2. **Compare** a dwarf planet to a planet.
   TEKS 6.11(A)

   _____

   _____

   _____

H.O.T. Questions (Higher Order Thinking)

3. **Evaluate** How would the speed of a planet be different if its orbit were a circle instead of an ellipse? **TEKS** 6.11(A)

   _____

   _____

   _____

4. **Summarize** the physical properties and location of the Sun, including its movements, both in the solar system and in the galaxy. **TEKS** 6.11(A)

   _____

   _____

5. **Relate** changes in speed during a planet's orbit to the shape of the orbit and the gravitational pull of the Sun.
   TEKS 6.11(B) *supporting*

   _____

   _____

   _____

   _____

   _____

6. **Interpret Graphics** Explain what each arrow in the diagram represents.
   TEKS 6.11(B) *supporting*

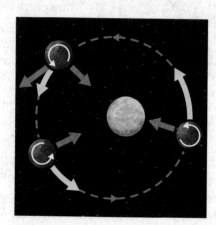

   _____

   _____

   _____

   _____

   _____

History from Space

AMERICAN MUSEUM
ᴼꜰ NATURAL HISTORY

Meteorites give a peek back in time.

About 4.6 billion years ago, Earth and the other planets did not exist. In fact, there was no solar system. Instead, a large disk of gas and dust, known as the solar nebula, swirled around a forming Sun, as shown in the top picture to the right. How did the planets and other objects in the solar system form?

Denton Ebel is looking for the answer. He is a geologist at the American Museum of Natural History in New York City. Ebel explores the hypothesis that over millions of years, tiny particles in the solar nebula clumped together and formed the asteroids, comets, and planets that make up our solar system.

Denton Ebel holds a meteorite that broke off the Vesta asteroid.

The solar nebula contained tiny particles called chondrules (KON drewls). They formed when the hot gas of the nebula condensed and solidified. Chondrules and other tiny particles collided and then accreted (uh KREET ed) or clumped together. This process eventually formed asteroids, comets, and planets. Some of the asteroids and comets have not changed much in over 4 billion years. Chondrite meteorites are pieces of asteroids that fell to Earth. The chondrules within the meteorites are the oldest solid material in our solar system.

For Ebel, chondrite meteorites contain information about the formation of the solar system. Did the materials in the meteorite form throughout the solar system and then accrete? Or did asteroids and comets form and accrete near the Sun, drift outward to where they are today, and then grow larger by accreting ice and dust? Ebel's research is helping to solve the mystery of how our solar system formed.

Accretion Hypothesis

According to the accretion hypothesis, the solar system formed in stages. First there was a solar nebula. The Sun formed when gravity caused the nebula to collapse.

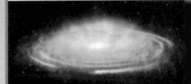

The rocky inner planets formed from accreted particles.

The gaseous outer planets formed as gas, ice, and dust condensed and accreted.

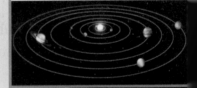

It's Your Turn!

TIME LINE Work in groups to learn more about the history of Earth from its formation until life began to appear. Create a time line showing major events. Present your time line to the class.

Copyright © McGraw-Hill Education ESA/DLR/FU Berlin (G. Neukum)

INQUIRY

Where is this? This spectacular landscape is the surface of Mars, one of the inner planets. Other inner planets have similar rocky surfaces. It might surprise you to learn that there are planets in the solar system that have no solid surface on which to stand. What can scientists learn by analyzing the appearance of a planet's surface?

Write your response in your interactive notebook.

🧪 LAB Manager

Go to your Lab Manual or visit connectED.mcgraw-hill.com *to perform the labs for this lesson.*

MiniLAB: *How can you model the inner planets?*
TEKS 6.2(A), (C); 6.3(B); 6.4(A), 6.11(A)

Skill Practice: *What can we learn about planets by graphing their characteristics?*
TEKS 6.2(A), (E); 6.11(A)

Explore Activity

TEKS 6.1(A); 6.2(A), (C), (E); 6.4(A), (B); 6.11(A)

What affects the temperature on the inner planets?

Mercury and Venus are closer to the Sun than Earth. What determines the temperature on these planets? Let's find out.

Procedure

1. Read and complete a lab safety form.

2. Insert a **thermometer** into a clear **2-L plastic bottle.** Wrap **modeling clay** around the lid to hold the thermometer in the center of the bottle. Form an airtight seal with the clay.

3. Rest the bottle against the side of a **shoe box** in direct sunlight. Lay a second **thermometer** on top of the box next to the bottle so the bulbs are at about the same height. The thermometer bulb should not touch the box. Secure the thermometer in place using **tape.**

4. Read the thermometers and record the initial temperatures in your Lab Manual or interactive notebook.

5. Wait 15 minutes and then read and record the temperatures again.

Think About This

1. How did the temperature of the two thermometers compare?

_____

_____

2. What do you think caused the difference in temperature?

_____

_____

_____

_____

3. Describe how this idea might apply on Mercury and Venus.

_____

_____

_____

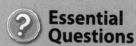

TEKS in this Lesson

6.11(A) Describe the physical properties, locations, and movements of the Sun, planets, Galilean moons, meteors, asteroids, and comets.

Also covers Process Standards: 6.1(A); 6.2(A), (C), (E); 6.3(B), (D); 6.4(A), (B)

? Essential Questions

- How are the inner planets similar?
- Why is Venus hotter than Mercury?
- What kind of atmospheres do the inner planets have?

abc Vocabulary

terrestrial planet
greenhouse effect

Figure 1 The inner planets are roughly similar in size. Earth is about two and half times larger than Mercury. All inner planets have a solid outer layer.

Mercury   Venus   Earth   Mars

Copyright © McGraw-Hill Education   (l)NASA/Johns Hopkins University Applied Physics Laboratory/Carnegie Institution of Washington, (cl)NASA, (cr)NASA Goddard Space Flight Center, (r)NASA/JPL/Malin Space Science Systems

Planets Made of Rock TEKS 6.11(A)

Imagine that you are walking outside. How would you describe the ground? You might say it is dusty or grassy. If you live near a lake or an ocean, you might say sandy or wet. But beneath the ground or lake or ocean is a layer of solid rock.

The inner planets—Mercury, Venus, Earth, and Mars—are called terrestrial planets. **Terrestrial planets** *are the planets closest to the Sun, are made of rock and metal, and have solid outer layers.* As shown in **Figure 1,** the inner planets have different sizes, atmospheres, and surfaces.

Ask

1. Compose three questions that you have about the inner planets. Come back and answer them as you read.

   A. _____

   _____

   _____

   B. _____

   _____

   _____

   C. _____

   _____

   _____

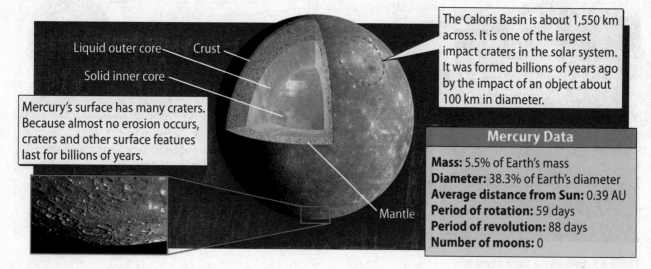

The Caloris Basin is about 1,550 km across. It is one of the largest impact craters in the solar system. It was formed billions of years ago by the impact of an object about 100 km in diameter.

Liquid outer core — Crust
Solid inner core

Mercury's surface has many craters. Because almost no erosion occurs, craters and other surface features last for billions of years.

Mantle

Mercury Data

Mass: 5.5% of Earth's mass
Diameter: 38.3% of Earth's diameter
Average distance from Sun: 0.39 AU
Period of rotation: 59 days
Period of revolution: 88 days
Number of moons: 0

Mercury TEKS 6.11(A)

The smallest planet and the planet closest to the Sun is Mercury, shown in **Figure 2.** Mercury has no atmosphere. A planet has an atmosphere when its gravity is strong enough to hold gases close to its surface. The strength of a planet's gravity depends on the planet's mass. Because Mercury's mass is so small, its gravity is not strong enough to hold onto an atmosphere. Without an atmosphere there is no wind that moves energy from place to place across the planet's surface. This results in temperatures as high as 450°C on the side of Mercury facing the Sun and as cold as −170°C on the side facing away from the Sun.

Mercury's Surface

Impact craters, depressions formed by collisions with objects from space, cover the surface of Mercury. There are smooth plains of solidified lava from long-ago eruptions. There are also high cliffs that might have formed when the planet cooled quickly, causing the surface to wrinkle and crack. Without an atmosphere, almost no erosion occurs on Mercury's surface. As a result, features that formed billions of years ago have changed very little.

Mercury's Structure

The structures of the inner planets are similar. Like all inner planets, Mercury has a core made of iron and nickel. Surrounding the core is a layer called the mantle. The mantle is mainly made of silicon and oxygen. The crust is a thin, rocky layer above the mantle. Mercury's large core might have been formed by a collision with a large object during Mercury's formation.

Figure 2 The Messenger space probe flew by Mercury in 2008 and photographed the planet's cratered surface.

FOLDABLES®

Make a four-door book. Label each door with the name of an inner planet. Use this Foldable to organize your notes on the inner planets.

Mercury   Earth
Venus   Mars

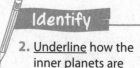

Identify

2. Underline how the inner planets are similar.

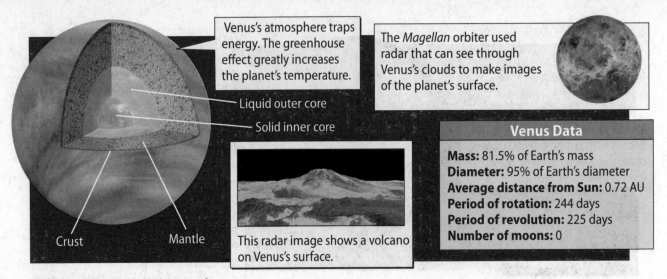

Venus's atmosphere traps energy. The greenhouse effect greatly increases the planet's temperature.

Liquid outer core

Solid inner core

The *Magellan* orbiter used radar that can see through Venus's clouds to make images of the planet's surface.

Crust

Mantle

This radar image shows a volcano on Venus's surface.

Venus Data

Mass: 81.5% of Earth's mass
Diameter: 95% of Earth's diameter
Average distance from Sun: 0.72 AU
Period of rotation: 244 days
Period of revolution: 225 days
Number of moons: 0

Figure 3 Because a thick layer of clouds covers Venus, its surface has not been seen. Between 1990 and 1994, the Magellan space probe mapped the surface using radar.

Venus *TEKS* 6.11(A)

The second planet from the Sun is Venus, as shown in **Figure 3.** Venus is about the same size as Earth. It rotates so slowly that its period of rotation is longer than its period of revolution. This means that a day on Venus is longer than a year. Unlike most planets, Venus rotates from east to west. Several space probes have flown by or landed on Venus.

Venus's Atmosphere

The atmosphere of Venus is about 97 percent carbon dioxide. It is so dense that the atmospheric pressure on Venus is about 90 times greater than on Earth. Even though Venus has almost no water in its atmosphere or on its surface, a thick layer of clouds made of acid covers the planet.

The Greenhouse Effect on Venus

With an average temperature of about 460°C, Venus is the hottest planet in the solar system. The high temperatures are caused by the greenhouse effect. *The* **greenhouse effect** *occurs when a planet's atmosphere traps solar energy and causes the surface temperature to increase.* Carbon dioxide in Venus's atmosphere traps some of the solar energy that is absorbed and then emitted by the planet. This heats up the planet. Without the greenhouse effect, Venus would be almost 450°C cooler.

Venus's Structure and Surface

Venus's internal structure is similar to Earth's. Radar images show that more than 80 percent of Venus's surface is covered by solidified lava. The lava might have been produced by volcanic eruptions that occurred about half a billion years ago.

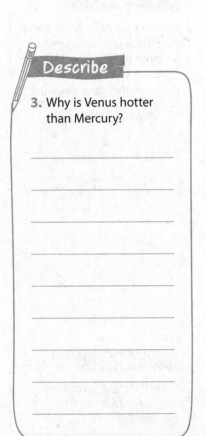

Describe

3. Why is Venus hotter than Mercury?

_____

_____

_____

_____

_____

_____

_____

_____

Copyright © McGraw-Hill Education
(tr)NASA Jet Propulsion Laboratory (NASA-JPL), (c)NASA/JPL

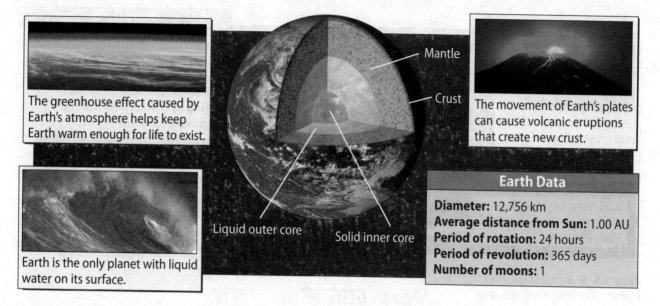

The greenhouse effect caused by Earth's atmosphere helps keep Earth warm enough for life to exist.

Earth is the only planet with liquid water on its surface.

Mantle

Crust

Liquid outer core   Solid inner core

The movement of Earth's plates can cause volcanic eruptions that create new crust.

Earth Data
Diameter: 12,756 km
Average distance from Sun: 1.00 AU
Period of rotation: 24 hours
Period of revolution: 365 days
Number of moons: 1

Figure 4 Earth has more water in its atmosphere and on its surface than the other inner planets. Earth's surface is younger than the surfaces of the other inner planets because new crust is constantly forming.

Earth TEKS 6.11(A)

Earth, shown in **Figure 4,** is the third planet from the Sun. Unlike Mercury and Venus, Earth has a moon.

Earth's Atmosphere

A mixture of gases and a small amount of water vapor make up most of Earth's atmosphere. They produce a greenhouse effect that increases Earth's average surface temperature. This effect and Earth's distance from the Sun warm Earth enough for large bodies of liquid water to exist. Earth's atmosphere also absorbs much of the Sun's radiation and protects the surface below. Earth's protective atmosphere, the presence of liquid water, and the planet's moderate temperature range support a variety of life.

Locate

4. Underline the reason Earth has liquid water on its surface.

Earth's Structure

As shown in **Figure 4**, Earth has a solid inner core surrounded by a liquid outer core. The mantle surrounds the liquid outer core. Above the mantle is Earth's crust. It is broken into large pieces, called plates, that constantly slide past, away from, or into each other. The crust is made mostly of oxygen and silicon and is constantly created and destroyed.

Identify

5. What conditions allow life to survive on Earth?

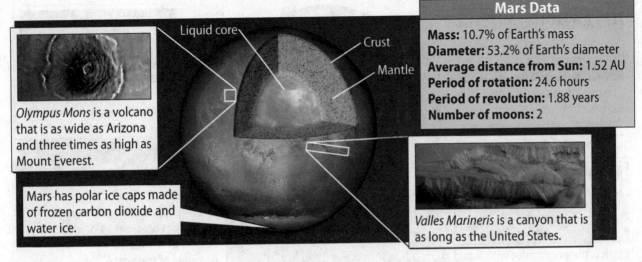

Liquid core

Crust

Mantle

Olympus Mons is a volcano that is as wide as Arizona and three times as high as Mount Everest.

Mars has polar ice caps made of frozen carbon dioxide and water ice.

Mars Data

Mass: 10.7% of Earth's mass
Diameter: 53.2% of Earth's diameter
Average distance from Sun: 1.52 AU
Period of rotation: 24.6 hours
Period of revolution: 1.88 years
Number of moons: 2

Valles Marineris is a canyon that is as long as the United States.

Figure 5 Mars is a small, rocky planet with deep canyons and tall mountains.

Mars TEKS 6.11(A)

The fourth planet from the Sun is Mars, shown in **Figure 5.** Mars is about half the size of Earth. It has two very small and irregularly shaped moons. These moons might be asteroids that were captured by Mars's gravity.

Many space probes have visited Mars. Most of them have searched for signs of water that might indicate the presence of living organisms. Images of Mars show features that might have been made by water, such as the gullies in **Figure 6.** Current research is focused on analyzing rock samples that may hold clues to past water activity on Mars.

Mars's Atmosphere

The atmosphere of Mars is about 95 percent carbon dioxide. It is thin and much less dense than Earth's atmosphere. Temperatures range from about −125°C at the poles to about 20°C at the equator during a martian summer. Winds on Mars sometimes produce great dust storms that last for months.

Mars's Surface

The reddish color of Mars is because its soil contains iron oxide, a compound in rust. Some of Mars's major surface features are shown in **Figure 5.** The enormous canyon Valles Marineris is about 4,000 km long. The Martian volcano Olympus Mons is the largest known mountain in the solar system. Mars also has polar ice caps made of frozen carbon dioxide and ice.

The southern hemisphere of Mars is covered with craters. The northern hemisphere is smoother and appears to be covered by lava flows. Scientists have proposed that the lava flows were caused by the impact of an object about 2,000 km in diameter.

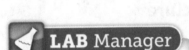

LAB Manager

MiniLAB: *How can you model the inner planets?*
TEKS 6.2(A), (C); 6.3(B); 6.4(A); 6.11(A)

Skill Practice: *What can we learn about planets by graphing their characteristics?*
TEKS 6.2(A), (E); 6.11(A)

Figure 6 Gullies such as these might have been formed by the flow of liquid water.

9.2 Review

Summarize it!

Summarize information about the inner planets. Place a check mark in each box that applies to each planet. **TEKS** 6.11(A)

	Mercury	Venus	Earth	Mars
Atmosphere				
Inner and outer core				
Liquid outer core				
Liquid core only				
Solid inner core				
Atmosphere 90% CO_2				
Cratered surface				
Liquid water on surface				
Ice on surface				
A moon or moons				
Mantle and crust				
Signs of volcanic action				

 Connect it! **Analyze** the information above. What are some characteristics that are only found, or not found, on one planet? Write your response in your interactive notebook.

Summarize it!

The Inner Planets

Apply the Essential Questions

1. **Explain** why Venus is hotter than Mercury, even though Mercury is closer to the Sun. **TEKS** 6.11(A)

_____

_____

_____

_____

_____

2. **Describe** the relationship between an inner planet's distance from the Sun and its period of revolution. **TEKS** 6.11(A)

_____

_____

_____

_____

_____

3. **Infer** which planet, Mercury, Venus, or Mars, is most likely able to support life now or was able to in the past. Explain your answer. **TEKS** 6.11(A)

_____

_____

_____

_____

_____

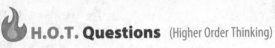 **H.O.T. Questions** (Higher Order Thinking)

4. **Imagine** how Mercury might be different if it had the same mass as Earth. Explain. **TEKS** 6.11(A)

_____

_____

_____

_____

5. **Apply** Like Venus, Earth's atmosphere contains carbon dioxide. What might happen on Earth if the amount of carbon dioxide in the atmosphere increases? **TEKS** 6.11(A)

_____

_____

_____

_____

6. **Infer** whether a planet with active volcanoes would have more or fewer craters than a planet without active volcanoes. **TEKS** 6.11(A)

_____

_____

_____

_____

Terraforming Mars *Life on Another Planet*

Terraforming is the process of transforming an environment that cannot support life into one that can. Making Mars like Earth would take more than just growing plants and adding water. You would need to consider how every abiotic factor needed to support life would be included in the new environment.

First, consider Mars's temperature. Although Mars gets plenty of sunlight, it is farther from the Sun than Earth is. Air temperatures go no higher than 0°C on a midsummer Martian day. Don't even think about trying to survive a winter night on Mars, as temperatures fall below −89°C.

How could you change the temperature on Mars? Releasing greenhouse gases such as chlorofluorocarbons (CFCs) into the atmosphere can cause the planet to get warmer. Raising the average temperature by only 4°C would melt the polar ice caps, releasing frozen CO_2, another greenhouse gas. This also would cause bodies of water to form. As temperatures rise, liquid water trapped in the soil would turn into a gas, providing the planet with water vapor, an important abiotic factor.

With water and warmer temperatures, plant life could be introduced. While turning light energy into food, plants would introduce another abiotic factor—oxygen. With all the needed abiotic factors accounted for, NASA scientists think that in a few centuries Mars could support life similar to that on Earth.

Mars is cold and dry, with no sign of life on its dusty, red surface.

Life as it is on Earth does not exist on Mars. However, when you compare all the planets in our solar system, Mars is the most like Earth.

It's Your Turn!

DEBATE Why would people want to move to Mars? Would this be the right choice? Research these questions and then debate the issues.

What's below? Clouds often prevent airplane pilots from seeing the ground below. Similarly, clouds block the view of Jupiter's surface. What do you think is below Jupiter's colorful cloud layer? The answer might surprise you—Jupiter is not at all like Earth.

Write your response in your interactive notebook.

LAB Manager

Go to your Lab Manual or visit connectED.mcgraw-hill.com to perform the labs for this lesson.

MiniLAB: *How do Saturn's moons affect its rings?*

TEKS 6.1(A); 6.2(A), (C), (E); 6.3(B); 6.4(A), (B)

Explore Activity

TEKS 6.1(A); 6.2(A), (C), (E); 6.4(A), (B); 6.11(A)

How do we see distant objects in the solar system?

Some of the outer planets were discovered hundreds of years ago. Why weren't all planets discovered?

Procedure

1. Read and complete a lab safety form.

2. Use a **meterstick, masking tape,** and the **data table** to mark and label the position of each object on the tape on the floor along a straight line.

3. Shine a **flashlight** from "the Sun" horizontally along the tape.

4. Have a partner hold a printed copy of **Figure 1** in the flashlight beam at each planet location. Record your observations in your Lab Manual or interactive notebook.

Object	Distance from the Sun (cm)
Sun	0
Jupiter	39
Saturn	71
Uranus	143
Neptune	295

Think About This

1. What happens to the image on the page as you move away from the flashlight?

_____

_____

_____

2. Why do you think it is more difficult to observe the outer planets than the inner planets?

_____

_____

_____

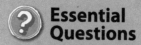

TEKS in this Lesson

6.11(A) Describe the physical properties, locations, and movements of the Sun, planets, Galilean moons, meteors, asteroids, and comets.

Also covers Process Standards: 6.1(A); 6.2(A), (C), (E); 6.3(B); 6.4(A), (B)

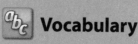

Essential Questions

- How are the outer planets similar?
- What are the outer planets made of?

Vocabulary

Galilean moons

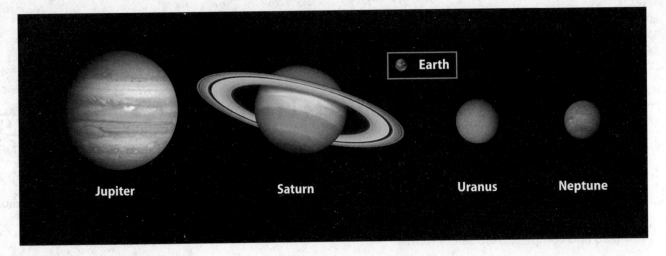

Figure 1 The outer planets are primarily made of gases and liquids.

The Gas Giants TEKS 6.11(A)

Have you ever seen water drops on the outside of a glass of ice? They form because water vapor in the air changes to a liquid on the cold glass. Gases also change to liquids at high pressures. These properties of gases affect the outer planets.

The outer planets, shown in **Figure 1**, are called the gas giants because they are primarily made of hydrogen and helium. These elements are usually gases on Earth.

The outer planets have strong gravitational forces due to their large masses. The strong gravity creates tremendous atmospheric pressure that changes gases to liquids. Thus, the outer planets mainly have liquid interiors. In general, the outer planets have a thick gas and liquid layer covering a small, solid core.

Describe

1. Hydrogen, helium, and methane are gases on Earth. Why are these substances liquids on the gas giants?

Copyright © McGraw-Hill Education   (l)NASA/JPL/USGS, (c)NASA and The Hubble Heritage Team (STScI/AURA)/Acknowledgment: R.G. French (Wellesley College), J. Cuzzi (NASA/Ames), L. Dones (SwRI), and J. Lissauer (NASA/Ames), (c)NASA Goddard Space Flight Center, (cr r)NASA/JPL

Jupiter **TEKS** 6.11(A)

Figure 2 describes Jupiter, the largest planet in the solar system. Jupiter's diameter is more than 11 times larger than the diameter of Earth. Its mass is more than twice the mass of all the other planets combined. One way to understand just how big Jupiter is is to realize that more than 1,000 Earths would fit within this gaseous planet's volume.

Jupiter takes almost 12 Earth years to complete one orbit. Yet, it rotates faster than any other planet. Its period of rotation is less than 10 hours. Jupiter and all the outer planets have a ring system.

Jupiter's Atmosphere

The atmosphere on Jupiter is about 90 percent hydrogen and 10 percent helium and is about 1,000 km thick. Within the atmosphere are layers of dense, colorful clouds. Because Jupiter rotates so quickly, these clouds stretch into colorful, swirling bands. The Great Red Spot on the planet's surface is a storm of swirling gases.

Jupiter's Structure

Overall, Jupiter is about 80 percent hydrogen and 20 percent helium with small amounts of other materials. The planet is a ball of gas swirling around a thick liquid layer that conceals a solid core. About 1,000 km below the outer edge of the cloud layer, the pressure is so great that the hydrogen gas changes to liquid. This thick layer of liquid hydrogen surrounds Jupiter's core. Scientists do not know for sure what makes up the core. They suspect that the core is made of rock and iron. The core might be as large as Earth and could be 10 times more massive.

Figure 2 Jupiter is mainly hydrogen and helium. Throughout most of the planet, the pressure is high enough to change the hydrogen gas into a liquid.

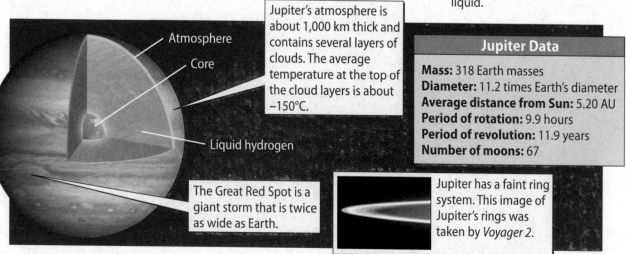

Jupiter's atmosphere is about 1,000 km thick and contains several layers of clouds. The average temperature at the top of the cloud layers is about −150°C.

Atmosphere
Core
Liquid hydrogen

The Great Red Spot is a giant storm that is twice as wide as Earth.

Jupiter Data

Mass: 318 Earth masses
Diameter: 11.2 times Earth's diameter
Average distance from Sun: 5.20 AU
Period of rotation: 9.9 hours
Period of revolution: 11.9 years
Number of moons: 67

Jupiter has a faint ring system. This image of Jupiter's rings was taken by *Voyager 2*.

Organize it!

Describe Jupiter by completing the spider map. **TEKS** 6.11(A)

core: solid and made of _____ and _____

overall composition: 80% _____ and 20% _____

mass: _____ _____ or more than 2 x mass of all other planets combined

Facts About Jupiter

atmosphere: _____ km thick

size _____ times the diameter of Earth

period of revolution: _____ _____

period of rotation: _____ _____

Organize it!

The Moons of Jupiter

Jupiter has at least 67 confirmed moons. In 1610 the astronomer Galileo Galilei was the first person to see Jupiter's four largest moons. *The four largest moons of Jupiter—Io, Europa, Ganymede, and Callisto—are known as the* **Galilean moons**. The Galilean moons, described in **Table 1**, orbit around Jupiter while keeping the same face towards the giant gas planet, just like the Moon orbits with the same face towards Earth.

Io is the closest large moon to Jupiter and fifth moon from the planet. Jupiter's tremendous gravitational force and the gravity of Europa, another Galilean moon, pull on Io. This force heats Io, causing it to be the most volcanically active object in the solar system. Some of its volcanoes reach 300 km above Io's surface.

Europa is slightly smaller than Earth's moon and the sixth moon from Jupiter. Europa's surface is an icy crust covering an ocean of salty water. Tidal heating of Europa provides for the possibility of life in its salty ocean.

In the seventh position from Jupiter is the moon Ganymede, the largest moon in our solar system—larger even than the planet Mercury! Ganymede has a metallic iron core that produces a magnetic field. The surface of Ganymede is an icy crust.

The eighth moon from Jupiter is Callisto. The last of Jupiter's large moons, it is composed of a small, rocky core and a thick, icy mantle. Callisto's surface is the darkest of the Galilean moons, but it twice as bright as the Earth's moon. Callisto is the most heavily cratered celestial body in the solar system. Studying Jupiter's moons adds to knowledge about the origin of Earth and the rest of the solar system.

Match

3. Highlight the names of the Galilean moons and their location from Jupiter.

Copyright © McGraw-Hill Education

Ratios

A ratio is a quotient—it is one quantity divided by another. Ratios can be used to compare distances. For example, Jupiter is 5.20 AU from the Sun, and Neptune is 30.05 from the Sun. Divide the larger distance by the smaller distance:

$$\frac{30.05 \text{ AU}}{5.20 \text{ AU}} = 5.78$$

Neptune is 5.78 times farther from the Sun than Jupiter.

Practice

How many times farther from the Sun is Uranus (distance = 19.20 AU) than Saturn (distance = 9.58 AU)?

Check   Tutor

Go Online!

Table 1 Galilean Moons	
Io	The most volcanically active object in the solar system; lava on Io is a mixture of sulfur and silica, which give the distinctive reddish and orange colors; the atmosphere is primarily sulfur dioxide
Europa	Revolution period of 3.5 days; an iron core; a rocky mantle; an ocean of salt water with an icy crust
Ganymede	the only moon in the solar system that generates its own magnetic field; thin oxygen atmosphere; larger than Mercury and Pluto
Callisto	almost the size of Mercury; geologic age of the surface is thought to be 4 billion years old; geologically inactive; heavily cratered

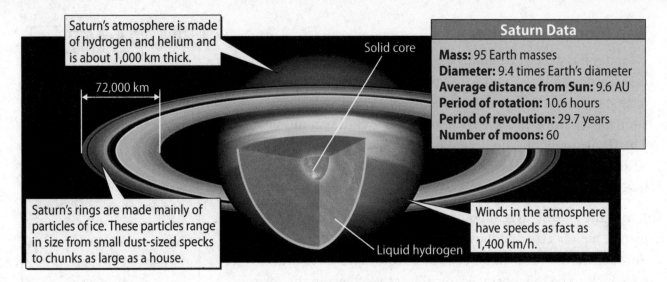

Saturn's atmosphere is made of hydrogen and helium and is about 1,000 km thick.

Solid core

72,000 km

Saturn Data

Mass: 95 Earth masses
Diameter: 9.4 times Earth's diameter
Average distance from Sun: 9.6 AU
Period of rotation: 10.6 hours
Period of revolution: 29.7 years
Number of moons: 60

Saturn's rings are made mainly of particles of ice. These particles range in size from small dust-sized specks to chunks as large as a house.

Winds in the atmosphere have speeds as fast as 1,400 km/h.

Liquid hydrogen

Figure 3 Like Jupiter, Saturn is mainly hydrogen and helium. Saturn's rings are one of the most noticeable features of the solar system.

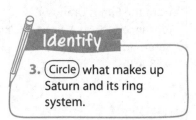

Identify

3. (Circle) what makes up Saturn and its ring system.

Word Origin

probe from Medieval Latin *proba*, means "examination"

Saturn TEKS 6.11(A)

Saturn is the sixth planet from the Sun. Like Jupiter, Saturn rotates rapidly and has horizontal bands of clouds. Saturn is about 90 percent hydrogen and 10 percent helium. It is the least dense planet. Its density is less than that of water.

Saturn's Structure

Saturn is made mostly of hydrogen and helium with small amounts of other materials. As shown in **Figure 3**, Saturn's structure is similar to Jupiter's structure—an outer gas layer, a thick layer of liquid hydrogen, and a solid core.

The ring system around Saturn is the largest and most complex in the solar system. Saturn has seven bands of rings, each containing thousands of narrower ringlets. The main ring system is over 70,000 km wide, but it is likely less than 1 km thick. The ice particles in the rings are possibly from a moon that was shattered in a collision with another icy object.

Figure 4 The five largest moons of Saturn are shown below. Titan is Saturn's largest moon.

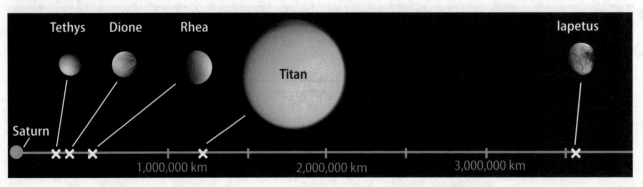

Tethys Dione Rhea Titan Iapetus

Saturn

1,000,000 km 2,000,000 km 3,000,000 km

Copyright © McGraw-Hill Education   (t)NASA and The Hubble Heritage Team (STScI/AURA)Acknowledgment: R.G. French (Wellesley College), J. Cuzzi (NASA/Ames), L. Dones (SwRI), and J. Lissauer (NASA/Ames), (others)NASA/JPL/Space Science Institute

Saturn's Moons

Saturn has at least 53 moons. The five largest moons, Titan, Rhea, Dione, Iapetus, and Tethys, are shown in **Figure 4**. Most of Saturn's moons are chunks of ice less than 10 km in diameter. However, Titan is larger than the planet Mercury. Titan is the only moon in the solar system with a dense atmosphere. In 2005 the Cassini orbiter released the Huygens (HOY guns) probe that landed on Titan's surface.

Uranus TEKS 6.11(A)

Uranus, shown in **Figure 5**, is the seventh planet from the Sun. It has a system of narrow, dark rings and a diameter about four times that of Earth. *Voyager 2* is the only space probe to explore Uranus. The probe flew by the planet in 1986.

Uranus has a deep atmosphere composed mostly of hydrogen and helium. The atmosphere also contains a small amount of methane. Beneath the atmosphere is a thick, slushy layer of water, ammonia, and other materials. Uranus might also have a solid, rocky core.

Uranus's Axis and Moons

Figure 5 shows that Uranus has a tilted axis of rotation. In fact, it is so tilted that the planet moves around the Sun like a rolling ball. This sideways tilt might have been caused by a collision with an Earth-sized object.

Uranus has at least 27 moons. The two largest moons, Titania and Oberon, are considerably smaller than Earth's moon. Titania has an icy cracked surface that once might have been covered by an ocean.

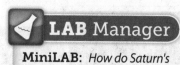

LAB Manager

MiniLAB: *How do Saturn's moons affect its rings?*
TEKS 6.1(A); 6.2(A), (C), (E); 6.3(B); 6.4(A), (B)

Describe

4. Provide three ways in which the outer planets are similar.

_____
_____
_____
_____
_____
_____
_____
_____
_____
_____
_____
_____
_____
_____
_____
_____
_____
_____
_____

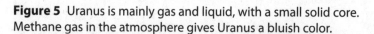

Figure 5 Uranus is mainly gas and liquid, with a small solid core. Methane gas in the atmosphere gives Uranus a bluish color.

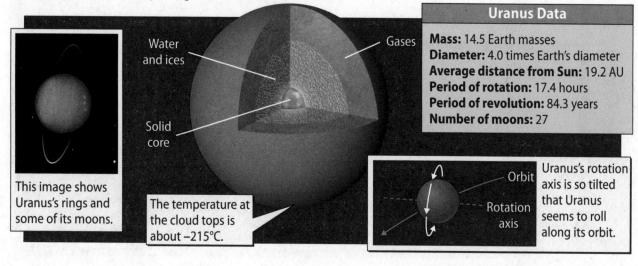

Water and ices

Gases

Solid core

This image shows Uranus's rings and some of its moons.

The temperature at the cloud tops is about −215°C.

Uranus Data

Mass: 14.5 Earth masses
Diameter: 4.0 times Earth's diameter
Average distance from Sun: 19.2 AU
Period of rotation: 17.4 hours
Period of revolution: 84.3 years
Number of moons: 27

Orbit

Rotation axis

Uranus's rotation axis is so tilted that Uranus seems to roll along its orbit.

Copyright © McGraw-Hill Education   (l)NASA/ESA and Erich Karkoschka, University of Arizona, (r)NASA/JPL

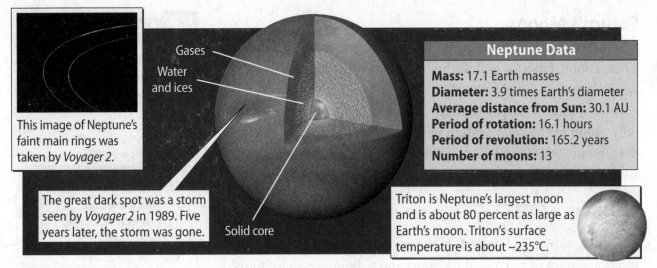

Gases

Water and ices

This image of Neptune's faint main rings was taken by *Voyager 2*.

The great dark spot was a storm seen by *Voyager 2* in 1989. Five years later, the storm was gone.

Solid core

Neptune Data

Mass: 17.1 Earth masses
Diameter: 3.9 times Earth's diameter
Average distance from Sun: 30.1 AU
Period of rotation: 16.1 hours
Period of revolution: 165.2 years
Number of moons: 13

Triton is Neptune's largest moon and is about 80 percent as large as Earth's moon. Triton's surface temperature is about −235°C.

Figure 6 The atmosphere of Neptune is similar to that of Uranus—mainly hydrogen and helium with a trace of methane. The dark circular areas on Neptune are swirling storms. Winds on Neptune sometimes exceed 1,000 km/h.

Neptune TEKS 6.11(A)

Neptune, shown in **Figure 6,** was discovered in 1846. Like Uranus, Neptune's atmosphere is mostly hydrogen and helium, with a trace of methane. Its interior also is similar to the interior of Uranus. Neptune's interior is partially frozen water and ammonia with a rock and iron core. Neptune has at least 13 moons and a faint, dark ring system. Its largest moon, Triton, is made of rock with an icy outer layer. It has a surface of frozen nitrogen and geysers that erupt nitrogen gas.

FOLDABLES

Cut out the Lesson 9.3 Foldable in the back of the book. Use the book to organize your notes on the outer planets.

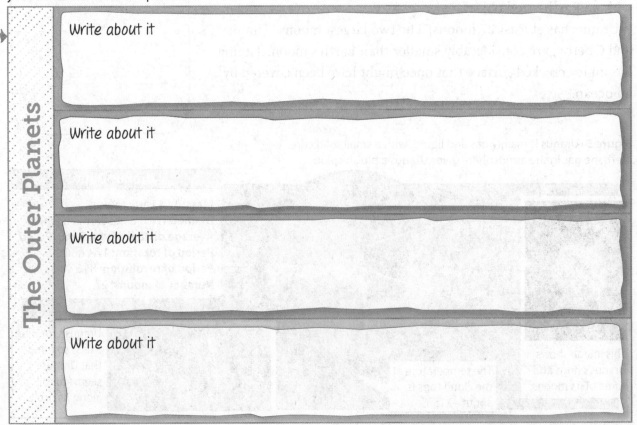

Tape here

The Outer Planets

Write about it

Write about it

Write about it

Write about it

Go Online!

Check ✓   Virtual

Summarize it!

Illustrate the outer planets and their orbits. Place the planets in their correct order from the Sun. Indicate where the Sun is in your drawing. **TEKS** 6.11(A)

✎ **Connect it!** **Attach** one specific identifying characteristic to each of the outer planets in your drawing above.

Summarize it!

The Outer Planets

Use Vocabulary

1. **Describe** the four Galilean moons of Jupiter, including their location around Jupiter. **TEKS** 6.11(A)

_____

_____

_____

Apply the Essential Questions

2. **Describe** how the rings of Saturn are different from the rings of Jupiter. **TEKS** 6.11(A)

_____

_____

_____

3. **List** the outer planets by increasing mass. **TEKS** 6.11(A)

_____

_____

_____

4. **Identify** which two gases make up most of the outer planets. **TEKS** 6.11(A)

   A. ammonia and helium

   B. ammonia and hydrogen

   C. hydrogen and helium

   D. methane and hydrogen

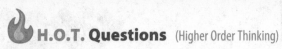 **H.O.T. Questions** (Higher Order Thinking)

5. **Predict** what would happen to Jupiter's atmosphere if its gravitational force suddenly decreased . **TEKS** 6.11(A)

_____

_____

_____

_____

_____

_____

6. **Relate** how the Galilean moons move similarly to Earth's moon. **TEKS** 6.11(A)

_____

_____

_____

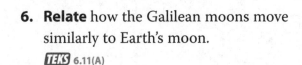 **Math Skills**   Math **TEKS** 6.1(A), 6.1(B), 6.3(E), 6.4(E)

Ratios

7. **Calculate** Mars is about 1.52 AU from the Sun, and Saturn is about 9.58 AU from the Sun. How many times farther from the Sun is Saturn than Mars?

Check   Tutor

9.4 Dwarf Planets and Other Objects

Will it return? You would probably remember a sight like this. This image of comet C/2006 P1 was taken in 2007. The comet is no longer visible from Earth. Why do you think comets appear then reappear hundreds to millions of years later?

Write your response in your interactive notebook.

LAB Manager

Go to your Lab Manual or visit connectED.mcgraw-hill.com to perform the labs for this lesson.

MiniLAB: *How do impact craters form?*

TEKS 6.2(A), (C); 6.3(B); 6.4(B); 6.11(A)

LAB: *Scaling down the Solar System*

TEKS 6.2(A), (C), (E); 6.3(B), (C); 6.4(A), (B); 6.11(A)

Explore Activity

How might asteroids and moons form?

In this activity, you will explore one way moons and asteroids might have formed.

Procedure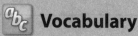

1. Read and complete a lab safety form.

2. Form a small ball from **modeling clay** and roll it in **sand**.

3. Press a thin layer of modeling clay around a **marble**.

4. Tie equal lengths of **string** to each ball. Hold the strings so the balls are above a **sheet of paper**.

5. Have someone pull back the marble so that its string is parallel to the tabletop and then release it. Record the results in your Lab Manual or interactive notebook.

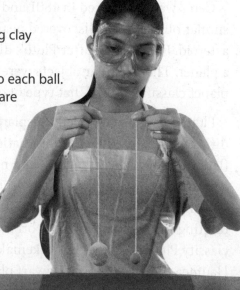

Think About This

1. Describe what would happen to the sand if the collision you modeled occurred in space?

_____

_____

2. Infer one way scientists propose moons and asteroids formed.

_____

_____

_____

TEKS in this Lesson

6.11(A) Describe the physical properties, locations, and movements of the Sun, planets, Galilean moons, meteors, asteroids, and comets.

Also covers Process Standards: 6.1(A); 6.2(A), (C), (E); 6.3(B), (C), (D); 6.4(A), (B)

? Essential Questions

- What is a dwarf planet?
- What are the characteristics of comets and asteroids?
- How does an impact crater form?

abc Vocabulary

meteoroid
meteor
meteorite
impact crater

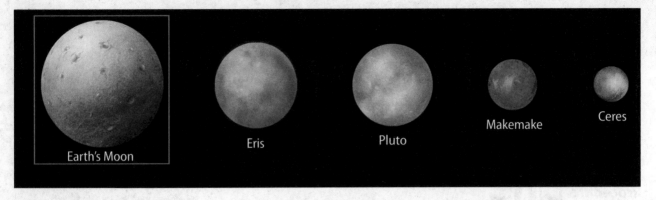

Figure 1 Four dwarf planets are shown to scale. All dwarf planets are smaller than the Moon.

Earth's Moon

Eris

Pluto

Makemake

Ceres

Dwarf Planets

Ceres was discovered in 1801 and was called a planet until similar objects were discovered near it. Then it was called an asteroid. For decades after Pluto's discovery in 1930, it was called a planet. Then, similar objects were discovered, and Pluto lost its planet classification. What type of object is Pluto?

Pluto once was classified as a planet, but it is now classified as a dwarf planet. In 2006, the International Astronomical Union (IAU) adopted "dwarf planet" as a new category. The IAU defines a dwarf planet as an object that orbits the Sun, has enough mass and gravity to form a sphere, and has objects similar in mass orbiting near it or crossing its orbital path. Astronomers classify Pluto, Ceres, Eris, Makemake (MAH kay MAH kay), and Haumea (how MAY uh) as dwarf planets. **Figure 1** shows four dwarf planets.

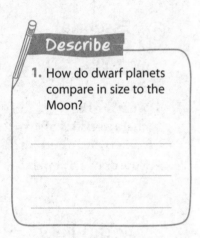

Describe

1. How do dwarf planets compare in size to the Moon?

_____

_____

_____

Distinguish

2. Show the similarities and differences between planets and dwarf planets.

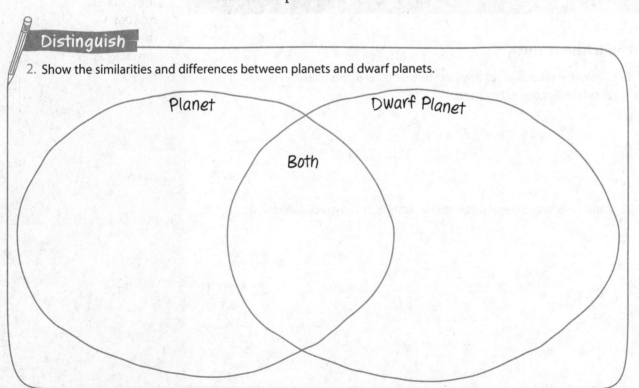

Planet

Dwarf Planet

Both

Copyright © McGraw-Hill Education

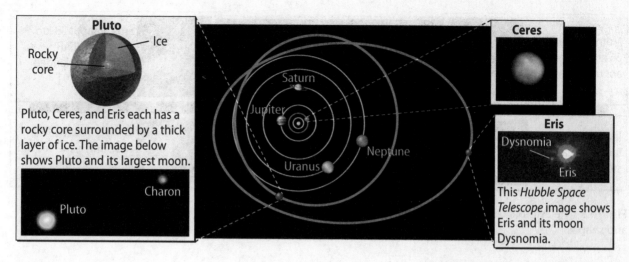

Pluto

Rocky core — Ice

Pluto, Ceres, and Eris each has a rocky core surrounded by a thick layer of ice. The image below shows Pluto and its largest moon.

Charon

Pluto

Ceres

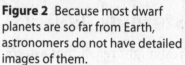

Eris

Dysnomia

Eris

This *Hubble Space Telescope* image shows Eris and its moon Dysnomia.

Figure 2 Because most dwarf planets are so far from Earth, astronomers do not have detailed images of them.

Ceres

Ceres, shown in **Figure 2,** orbits the Sun in the asteroid belt. With a diameter of about 950 km, Ceres is about one-fourth the size of the Moon. It is the smallest dwarf planet. Ceres might have a rocky core surrounded by a layer of water ice and a thin, dusty crust.

Pluto

Pluto is about two-thirds the size of the Moon. Pluto is so far from the Sun that its period of revolution is about 248 years. Like Ceres, Pluto has a rocky core surrounded by ice. With an average surface temperature of about –230°C, Pluto is so cold that it is covered with frozen nitrogen.

Pluto has three known moons. The largest moon, Charon, has a diameter that is about half the diameter of Pluto. Pluto also has two smaller moons, Hydra and Nix.

Eris

The largest dwarf planet, Eris, was discovered in 2003. Its orbit lasts about 557 years. Currently, Eris is three times farther from the Sun than Pluto is. The structure of Eris is probably similar to Pluto. Dysnomia (dis NOH mee uh) is the only known moon of Eris.

Makemake and Haumea

In 2008 the IAU designated two new objects as dwarf planets: Makemake and Haumea. Though smaller than Pluto, Makemake is one of the largest objects in a region of the solar system called the Kuiper (KI puhr) belt. The Kuiper belt extends from about the orbit of Neptune to about 50 AU from the Sun. Haumea is also in the Kuiper belt and is smaller than Pluto.

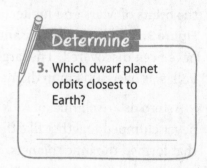

Determine

3. Which dwarf planet orbits closest to Earth?

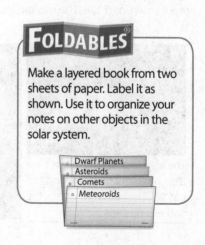

FOLDABLES

Make a layered book from two sheets of paper. Label it as shown. Use it to organize your notes on other objects in the solar system.

Dwarf Planets
Asteroids
Comets
Meteoroids

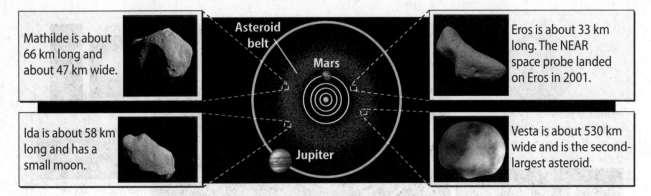

Mathilde is about 66 km long and about 47 km wide.

Ida is about 58 km long and has a small moon.

Asteroid belt

Mars

Jupiter

Eros is about 33 km long. The NEAR space probe landed on Eros in 2001.

Vesta is about 530 km wide and is the second-largest asteroid.

Figure 3 The asteroids that orbit the Sun in the asteroid belt are many sizes and shapes.

Asteroids TEKS 6.11(A)

You might recall that asteroids are pieces of rock and ice. Most asteroids orbit the Sun in the asteroid belt. The asteroid belt is between the orbits of Mars and Jupiter, as shown in **Figure 3.** Hundreds of thousands of asteroids have been discovered. The largest asteroid, Pallas, is over 500 km in diameter.

Asteroids are chunks of rock and ice that never clumped together like the rocks and ice that formed the inner planets. Some astronomers suggest that the strength of Jupiter's gravitational field might have caused the chunks to collide violently, and they broke apart instead of sticking together. This means that asteroids are objects left over from the formation of the solar system.

Comets TEKS 6.11(A)

Recall that comets are mixtures of rock, ice, and dust. The particles in a comet are loosely held together by the gravitational attractions among the particles. As shown in **Figure 4,** comets orbit the Sun in long elliptical orbits.

The Structure of Comets

The solid, inner part of a comet is its nucleus, as shown in **Figure 4.** As a comet moves closer to the Sun, it absorbs thermal energy and can develop a bright tail. Heating changes the ice in the comet into a gas. Energy from the Sun pushes some of the gas and dust away from the nucleus and makes it glow. This produces the comet's bright tail and glowing nucleus, called a coma.

Figure 4 When energy from the Sun strikes the gas and dust in the comet's nucleus, it can create a two-part tail. The gas tail always points away from the Sun.

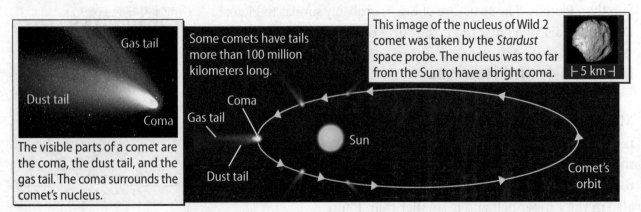

Gas tail

Dust tail

Coma

The visible parts of a comet are the coma, the dust tail, and the gas tail. The coma surrounds the comet's nucleus.

Some comets have tails more than 100 million kilometers long.

Coma

Gas tail

Dust tail

Sun

Comet's orbit

This image of the nucleus of Wild 2 comet was taken by the *Stardust* space probe. The nucleus was too far from the Sun to have a bright coma.

⊢ 5 km ⊣

Copyright © McGraw-Hill Education   (tl tr)NASA/JPL/JHUAPL, (cl)NASA/JPL/USGS, (cr)Ben Zellner (Georgia Southern University), Peter Thomas (Cornell University), NASA/ESA, (bl)Roger Ressmeyer/Photographer's Choice/Getty Images, (br)NASA/JPL–Caltech

Short-Period and Long-Period Comets

A short-period comet takes less than 200 Earth years to orbit the Sun. Most short-period comets come from the Kuiper belt. A long-period comet takes more than 200 Earth years to orbit the Sun. Long-period comets come from a area at the outer edge of the solar system, called the Oort cloud. It surrounds the solar system and extends about 100,000 AU from the Sun. Some longperiod comets take millions of years to orbit the Sun.

Meteoroids TEKS 6.11(A)

Every day, many millions of particles called meteoroids enter Earth's atmosphere. *A **meteoroid** is a small, rocky particle that moves through space.* Most meteoroids are only about as big as a grain of sand. As a meteoroid passes through Earth's atmosphere, friction makes the meteoroid and the air around it hot enough to glow. *A **meteor** is a streak of light in Earth's atmosphere made by a glowing meteoroid.* Most meteoroids burn up in the atmosphere. However, some meteoroids are large enough that they reach Earth's surface before they burn up completely. When this happens, it is called a meteorite. *A **meteorite** is a meteoroid that strikes a planet or a moon.*

When a large meteorite strikes a moon or a planet, it often forms a bowl-shaped depression such as the one shown in **Figure 5.** *An **impact crater** is a round depression formed on the surface of a planet, moon, or other space object by the impact of a meteorite.* There are more than 170 impact craters on Earth.

Figure 5 When a large meteorite strikes, it can form a giant impact crater like this 1.2-km wide crater in Arizona.

LAB Manager

MiniLAB: *How do impact craters form?*
TEKS 6.2(A), (C); 6.3(B); 6.4(B); 6.11(A)

LAB: *Scaling down the Solar System*
TEKS 6.2(A), (C), (E); 6.3(B), (C); 6.4(A), (B); 6.11(A)

Word Origin

meteor from Greek *meteoros*, means "high up"

Analyze

4. Which attribute is more important in classifying a solar system object: its size or composition? Explain.

_____
_____
_____
_____
_____
_____
_____
_____
_____

9.4 Review

Go Online!
Check ✓

Summarize it!

Complete the concept map below using this chapter's vocabulary terms. **TEKS** 6.11(A)

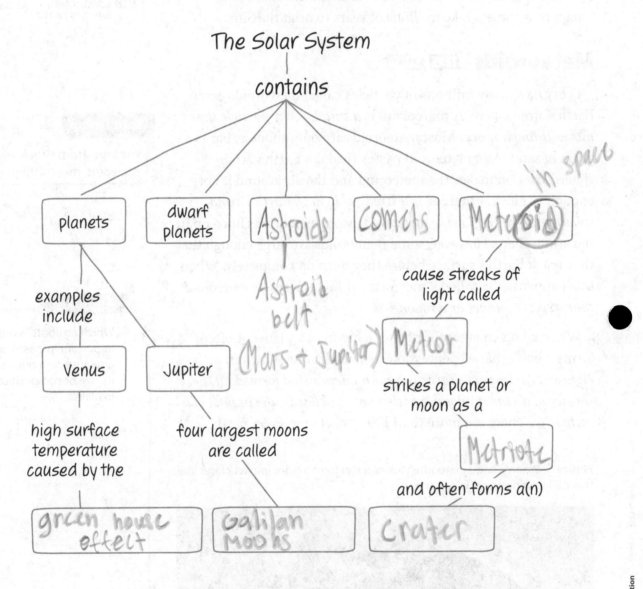

The Solar System

contains

| planets | dwarf planets | Astroids | Comets | Meteroid (in space) |

Astroid belt (Mars + Jupiter)

planets — examples include

cause streaks of light called

Meteor

strikes a planet or moon as a

Venus — high surface temperature caused by the

Jupiter — four largest moons are called

Meteorite

and often forms a(n)

green house effect

Galilan Moons

Crater

Connect it! Apply your knowledge of objects in the solar system to determine which planetary bodies will show the effects of impact craters longer. Explain your reasoning. Write your response in your interactive notebook.

Summarize it!

Dwarf Planets and Other Objects

Use Vocabulary

1. **Distinguish** between a meteorite and a meteoroid. **TEKS** 6.11(A)

   _____

   _____

   _____

Apply the Essential Questions

2. **Explain** where asteroids and comets are located. Then differentiate between asteroid and comet compositions and orbits. **TEKS** 6.11(A)

   _____

   _____

   _____

   _____

   _____

3. **Describe** the orbit of comets. Then explain why some comets have a two-part tail during portions of their orbit. **TEKS** 6.11(A)

   _____

   _____

4. **Identify** Which produces an impact crater? **TEKS** 6.11(A)

   A. comet   C. meteorite

   B. meteor   D. planet

 H.O.T. Questions (Higher Order Thinking)

5. **Evaluate** Do you agree with the decision to reclassify Pluto as a dwarf planet? Defend your answer. **TEKS** 6.11(A)

   _____

   _____

   _____

   _____

6. **Compare** what ways are planets and dwarf planets similar. **TEKS** 6.11(A)

   _____

   _____

   _____

7. **Reason** Are you more likely to see a meteor or a meteoroid? Explain. **TEKS** 6.11(A)

   _____

   _____

   _____

   _____

Writing in Science

8. **Create** a pamphlet that describes how the International Astronomical Union classifies planets, dwarf planets, and small solar system objects. **TEKS** 6.11(A)

Pluto

What in the world is it?

Since Pluto's discovery in 1930, students have learned that the solar system has nine planets. But in 2006, the number of planets was changed to eight. What happened?

Neil deGrasse Tyson is an astrophysicist at the American Museum of Natural History in New York City. He and his fellow Museum scientists were among the first to question Pluto's classification as a planet. One reason was that Pluto is smaller than six moons in our solar system, including Earth's moon. Another reason was that Pluto's orbit is more oval-shaped, or elliptical, than the orbits of other planets. Also, Pluto has the most tilted orbit of all planets—17 degrees out of the plane of the solar system. Finally, unlike other planets, Pluto is mostly ice.

Tyson also questioned the definition of a planet—an object that orbits the Sun. Then shouldn't comets be planets? In addition, he noted that when Ceres, an object orbiting the Sun between Jupiter and Mars, was discovered in 1801, it was classified as a planet. But, as astronomers discovered more objects like Ceres, it was reclassified as an asteroid. Then, during the 1990s, many space objects similar to Pluto were discovered. They orbit the Sun beyond Neptune's orbit in a region called the Kuiper belt.

These new discoveries led Tyson and others to conclude that Pluto should be reclassified. In 2006 the International Astronomical Union agreed. Pluto was reclassified as a dwarf planet—an object that is spherical in shape and orbits the Sun in a zone with other objects. Pluto lost its rank as smallest planet but became "king of the Kuiper belt."

This illustration shows what Pluto might look like if you were standing on one of its moons.

AMERICAN MUSEUM OF NATURAL HISTORY

Pluto
TIME LINE

1930
Astronomer Clyde Tombaugh discovers a ninth planet, Pluto.

1992
The first object is discovered in the Kuiper belt.

July 2005
Eris—a Pluto-sized object—is discovered in the Kuiper belt.

January 2006
NASA launches *New Horizons* spacecraft, expected to reach Pluto in 2015.

August 2006
Pluto is reclassified as a dwarf planet.

Neil deGrasse Tyson is director of the Hayden Planetarium at the American Museum of Natural History.

Copyright © McGraw-Hill Education   Frederick M. Brown/Getty Images

It's Your Turn!

RESEARCH With a group, identify the different types of objects in our solar system. Consider size, composition, location, and whether the objects have moons. Propose at least two different ways to group the objects.

Test-Taking Strategy

Reading Passage When presented with a reading passage, it is a good idea to first read the question and decide what type of information you are looking for. Then, as you read the passage you can underline the information as you find it.

Example

Use the reading passage to answer question 7.

Halley's Comet orbits the Sun and can be seen from Earth about every 76 years. However, before the work of Sir Isaac Newton and Edmond Halley, comets were thought to pass in a straight line through the solar system. In 1705, Edmond Halley used Newton's laws to determine the gravitational effects of Jupiter and Saturn on a comet that he observed in 1682. Using this information and historical records, he determined that comets seen in 1531 and 1607 were the same comet. Halley correctly calculated the orbit of the comet and predicted its return in 1758.

7 Newton's laws state that all objects exert gravitational force and that objects with more mass exert more force. Which objects have the greatest effect on the orbit of Halley's Comet? **TEKS** 6.11(A), 6.11(B) *supporting*

A Earth, the Sun, and the Moon

B the Sun, Jupiter, and Saturn

C asteroids, meteors, and dwarf planets

D Earth, the Sun, and Saturn

TIP: Always look back at the reading passage, rather than relying on memory, if you need help remembering key information.

2 Read the passage. Underline information that you can use to answer the question.

1 Read the question and decide what you are looking for in the passage. You need to look for the objects that have the greatest effect on the orbit of Halley's Comet.

3 Use what you know and the relevant information from the passage to find the correct answer. You know that comets orbit the Sun because of its gravity. The reading passage told you that Halley also used the effects of Jupiter and Saturn's gravity to correctly calculate the orbit. Choice B is correct.

Multiple Choice

1   Mrs. Ridley asked her class to draw a model of the solar system. She instructed them to be as accurate as possible. One student made this model of the solar system. **TEKS** 6.11(A); 6.3(B)

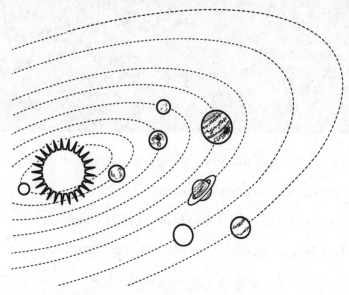

In using this model, which statement can the student use to describe the movements of the planets?

   A The length of a day on Mars is shorter than a day on Earth.

   B The length of a day on Jupiter is shorter than a day on Earth.

   C The length of a year on Mercury is longer than a year on Earth.

   D The length of a year on Jupiter is longer than a year on Earth.

2   The distance from the planets to the Sun is measured in astronomical units, which is abbreviated AU. One AU is equal to the average distance from Earth to the Sun, which is about 150 million km. Earth is 1 AU from the Sun. Based on this, calculate the distance in AU of Jupiter from the Sun, if Jupiter is about 778 million km from the Sun. Round your answer to the nearest hundredth. Record and bubble in your answer on the answer grid below. **TEKS** 6.11(A)

3 In the solar system planets orbit around the Sun. Other bodies such as comets, also orbit around the Sun in the solar system. The illustration shows the orbit of a comet in the solar system. **TEKS** 6.11(B) *supporting*

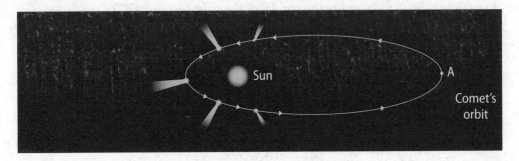

How does the orbit of the comet differ from the orbits of the objects found in the asteroid belt?

A Only a comet is held in its orbit by the Sun's gravitational pull.

B Only a comet's orbit can extend beyond the edge of the solar system.

C Only asteroids have long tails visible as they approach and orbit the Sun.

D Only the orbit of asteroids occurs between the largest two planets.

---

4 The chart below shows the surface temperatures of the outer planets. **TEKS** 6.11(A); 6.2(E)

Planet	Surface Temperature
Neptune	−214°C
Uranus	−216°C
Jupiter	−148°C
Saturn	−178°C

What can you conclude about the outer planets based on the data table?

A If Neptune were closer to the Sun, it would be cooler.

B Saturn is closer to the Sun than any of the other outer planets.

C The coldest outer planet is Uranus.

D The surface temperature of Earth is between that of Neptune and Jupiter.

5 It was once thought that Earth was the center of the universe. Eventually it was proven that the planets orbit around the Sun. The illustration shows the path of Earth's orbit around the Sun.

TEKS 6.11(B) *supporting*

Describe the path of Earth if the pull of the Sun's gravity were to suddenly stop.

A Earth would continue to move within its orbit.

B Earth would move in a straight line towards the Sun.

C Earth would move in a straight line instead of a curve.

D Earth would stop moving and become suspended in one spot.

6 A student created a model of the solar system. **TEKS** 6.11(A); 6.3(C)

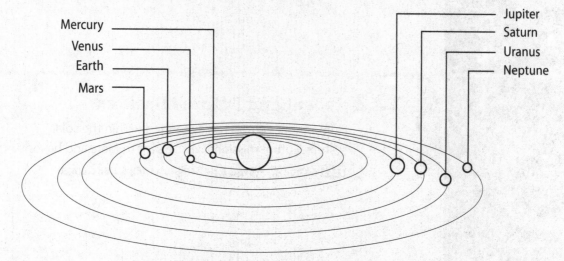

Which statement describes a limitation of the student's model?

A It does not show the correct order of the planets in the solar system.

B It does not show the correct scale among the inner and outer planets.

C It shows the path of the planets' orbits as they travel around the Sun.

D It shows the difference in characteristics between the inner and outer planets.

10 Space Exploration

The BIG Idea

Technology for space exploration has changed over time. Exploration of space is conducted by both human space-flight and robotic spacecrafts.

LESSON

10.1 Early History of Space Exploration

Rockets, satellites, space probes, and space stations have been used to explore space.

TEKS 6.11(C); Also covers 6.1(A); 6.2(A), (C), (E); 6.3(B), (D); 6.4(A), (B)

LESSON

10.2 Recent and Future Missions

Human space travel has expanded within the solar system. Future missions will be sent to Mars and beyond.

TEKS 6.11(C); Also covers 6.1(A); 6.2(A), (C), (E); 6.3(B); 6.4(A), (B)

How far have humans traveled?

In 1969, the *Apollo 11* astronauts were the first humans to land on the Moon. More than 50 years later, astronauts continue to travel in space. What do you think is the farthest distance humans have traveled from Earth since astronauts landed on the Moon in 1969?

☐ **A.** About 350 km above Earth

☐ **B.** About halfway to the Moon (191,250 km)

☐ **C.** To the Moon (about 382,500 km)

☐ **D.** About 10,000 km past the Moon

☐ **E.** Halfway to Mars (about 28,000,000 km)

☐ **F.** To Mars (about 56,000,000 km)

☐ **G.** Beyond Mars

Explain your thinking. What helped you decide how far humans have traveled in space?

Where is it headed?

Have you ever witnessed a rocket launch? Rockets produce gigantic clouds of smoke, long plumes of exhaust, and thundering noise. How are rockets used to explore space? What do they carry?

Write your responses in your interactive notebook.

 LAB Manager

Go to your Lab Manual or visit connectED.mcgraw-hill.com to perform the labs for this lesson.

MiniLAB: *How does lack of friction in space affect simple tasks?*

TEKS 6.1(A); 6.2(A), (C), (E); 6.4(B)

Explore Activity

TEKS 6.1(A); 6.2(A), (C), (E); 6.3(B); 6.4(A), (B); 6.11(C)

How do rockets work?

Space exploration would be impossible without rockets. Become a rocket scientist for a few minutes, and find out what sends rockets into space.

Procedure

1. Read and complete a lab safety form.

2. Use **scissors** to carefully cut a 5-m piece of **string.**

3. Insert the string into a **drinking straw.** Tie each end of the string to a stationary object. Make sure the string is taut. Slide the drinking straw to one end of the string.

4. Blow up a **balloon.** Do not tie it. Instead, twist the neck and clamp it with a **clothespin** or a **paper clip. Tape** the balloon to the straw.

5. Remove the clothespin or paperclip to launch your rocket. Observe how the rocket moves. Record your observations in your Lab Manual or interactive notebook.

Think About This

1. Describe how your rocket moved along the string.

_____

_____

2. How might you get your rocket to go farther or faster?

_____

_____

_____

3. How do you think rockets are used in space exploration?

_____

_____

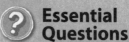

TEKS in this Lesson

6.11(C) Describe the history and future of space exploration, including the types of equipment and transportation needed for space travel

Also covers Process Standards: 6.1(A); 6.2(A), (C), (E); 6.3(B), (D); 6.4(A), (B)

Essential Questions

- What types of equipment was used in past space exploration missions?
- What type of transportation is used in space travel?

Vocabulary

rocket
satellite
space probe
lunar
Project Apollo
space shuttle

Rockes TEKS 6.11(C)

Figure 1 Exhaust gases ejected from the end of a rocket push the rocket forward.

Think about listening to a recording of your favorite music. Now think about how different it is to experience the same music at a live performance. This is like the difference between exploring space from a distance, with a telescope, and actually going there.

A big problem in launching an object into space is overcoming the force of Earth's gravity. This is accomplished with rockets. A **rocket** *is a vehicle designed to propel itself by ejecting exhaust gas from one end.* Fuel burned inside the rocket builds up pressure. The force from the exhaust thrusts the rocket forward, as shown in **Figure 1.** Rocket engines do not draw in oxygen from the surrounding air to burn their fuel, as jet engines do. They carry their oxygen with them. As a result, rockets can operate in space where there is very little oxygen.

Scientists launch rockets from Florida's Cape Canaveral Air Force Station or the Kennedy Space Center nearby. However, space missions are managed by scientists at several different research stations around the country. The Johnson Space Center in Houston, Texas, is an important center for design, development, and testing of spacecrafts used for human spaceflight. It is the home of astronaut training and mission control.

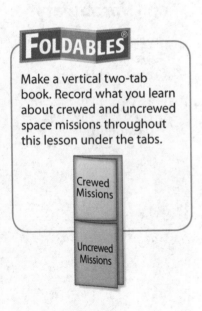

FOLDABLES

Make a vertical two-tab book. Record what you learn about crewed and uncrewed space missions throughout this lesson under the tabs.

Crewed Missions

Uncrewed Missions

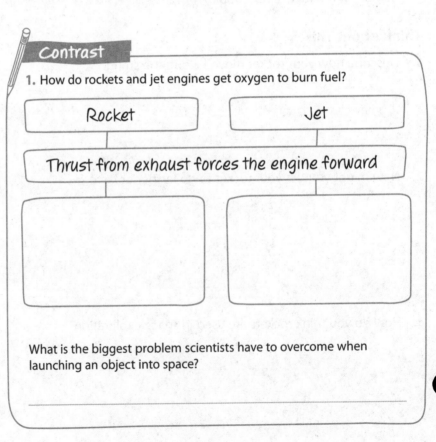

Contrast

1. How do rockets and jet engines get oxygen to burn fuel?

Rocket	Jet

Thrust from exhaust forces the engine forward

What is the biggest problem scientists have to overcome when launching an object into space?

Artificial Satellites TEKS 6.11(C)

Any small object that orbits a larger object is a **satellite.** The Moon is a natural satellite of Earth. Artificial satellites are made by people and launched by rockets. They orbit Earth or other bodies in space, transmitting radio signals back to Earth.

The First Satellites—*Sputnik* and *Explorer*

The first artificial, Earth-orbiting satellite sent into orbit was *Sputnik 1.* Many people think this satellite, launched in 1957 by the former Soviet Union, represents the beginning of the space age. In 1958, the United States launched its first Earth-orbiting satellite, *Explorer 1.* Today, thousands of satellites orbit Earth.

How Satellites Are Used

The earliest satellites were developed by the military for navigation and to gather information. Today, Earth-orbiting satellites are also used to transmit television and telephone signals and to monitor weather and climate. An array of satellites called the Global Positioning System (GPS) is used for navigation in cars, boats, airplanes, and even for hiking.

Early Exploration of the Solar System TEKS 6.11(C)

In 1958, the U.S. Congress established the National Aeronautics and Space Administration (NASA). NASA oversees all U.S. space missions, including space telescopes. Some early steps in U.S. space exploration are shown in **Figure 2.**

Word Origin

satellite from Latin *satellitem,* means "attendant" or "bodyguard"

Examine

2. How are Earth-orbiting satellites used?

_____

_____

_____

_____

_____

_____

_____

_____

_____

_____

Figure 2 Space exploration began with the first rocket launch in 1926.

Early Space Exploration

◀ **1926** First rocket: Robert Goddard's liquid-fueled rocket rose 12 m into the air.

1958 First U.S. satellite: In the same year NASA was founded, *Explorer 1* was launched. It orbited Earth 58,000 times before burning up in Earth's atmosphere in 1970. ▶

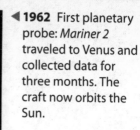

◀ **1962** First planetary probe: *Mariner 2* traveled to Venus and collected data for three months. The craft now orbits the Sun.

1972 First probe to outer ▶ solar system: After flying past Jupiter, *Pioneer 10* is still traveling onward, someday to exit the solar system.

Figure 3 Scientists use space probes to explore the planets and some moons in the solar system.

Orbiter	Lander	Flyby

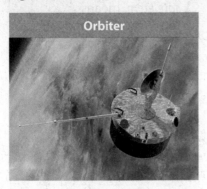  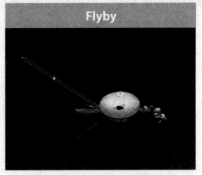

Once orbiters reach their destination, they use rockets to slow down enough to be captured in an object's orbit. How long they orbit depends on their fuel supply. The orbiter probe here, *Pioneer*, orbited Venus.

Landers touch down on surfaces. Sometimes they release rovers. Landers use rockets and parachutes to slow their descent. The lander probe here, *Phoenix*, analyzed the Martian surface for evidence of water.

Flybys do not orbit or land. When its mission is complete, a flyby continues through space, eventually leaving the solar system. *Voyager 1,* here, explored Jupiter and Saturn and has moved into interstellar space.

Copyright © McGraw-Hill Education   (l)AP Images, (c)NASA/JPL, (r)Atlas Photo Bank/Photo Researchers

Space Probes

Some spacecraft have human crews, but most do not. A **space probe** *is an uncrewed spacecraft sent from Earth to explore objects in space.* Space probes are robots that work automatically or by remote control. They take pictures and gather data. Probes are cheaper to build than crewed spacecraft, and they can make trips that would be too long or too dangerous for humans. Space probes are not designed to return to Earth. The data they gather are relayed to Earth via radio waves. **Figure 3** shows three major types of space probes.

Lunar and Planetary Probes

The first probes to the Moon were sent by the United States and the former Soviet Union in 1959. Probes to the Moon are called lunar probes. The term **lunar** *refers to anything related to the Moon.* The first spacecraft to gather information from another planet was the flyby *Mariner 2*, sent to Venus in 1962. Since then, space probes have been sent to all the planets.

> **Science Use v. Common Use**
>
> **probe**
> **Science Use** an uncrewed spacecraft
> **Common Use** to question or examine closely

Recognize

3. Why do scientists send uncrewed missions to space?

_____

_____

Human Spaceflight TEKS 6.11(C)

Sending humans into space was a major goal of the early space program. However, scientists worried about how radiation from the Sun and weightlessness in space might affect people's health. Because of this, they first sent dogs, monkeys, and chimpanzees. In 1961, the first human—an astronaut from the former Soviet Union—was launched into Earth's orbit. Shortly thereafter, the first American astronaut orbited Earth. Some highlights of the early U.S. human spaceflight program are shown in **Figure 4**.

The Apollo Program

In 1961, U.S. President John F. Kennedy challenged the American people to place a person on the Moon by the end of the decade. The result was **Project Apollo**—*a series of space missions designed to send people to the Moon.* In 1969, Neil Armstrong and Buzz Aldrin, *Apollo 11* astronauts, were the first people to walk on the Moon.

Identify

4. (Circle) the goal of Project Apollo.

Space Transportation Systems

Early spacecraft and the rockets used to launch them were used only once. **Space shuttles** *are reusable spacecraft that transport people and materials to and from space.* Space shuttles return to Earth and land much like airplanes. NASA's fleet of space shuttles began operating in 1981. As the shuttles aged, NASA retired the space shuttles and began encouraging private research companies to develop new transportation systems.

The *International Space Station*

The United States has its own space program. But it also cooperates with the space programs of other countries. In 1998, it joined 15 other nations to begin building the *International Space Station.* Occupied since 2000, this Earth-orbiting satellite is a research laboratory where astronauts from many countries work and live.

Research conducted aboard the *International Space Station* includes studying fungus, plant growth, and how human body systems react to low-gravity conditions. This type of research will be beneficial for planning future space missions.

U.S. Human Spaceflight

 Watch
 Go Online!

Figure 4 Forty years after human spaceflight began, people were living and working in space.

▲ Apollo moon walk

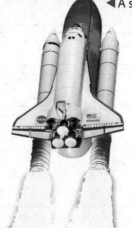

◄ A space shuttle piggyback on rockets

International Space Station orbiting Earth ▼

Figure 5 This scientist at the Marshall Space Flight Center is working on a mirror that will be used in the *James Webb Telescope*. The technology used to create this mirror could be used in everyday items in the future.

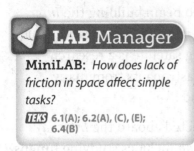

LAB Manager

MiniLAB: *How does lack of friction in space affect simple tasks?*
TEKS 6.1(A); 6.2(A), (C), (E); 6.4(B)

Space Technology TEKS 6.3(D)

The space program requires materials that can withstand the extreme temperatures and pressures of space. Many of these materials have been applied to everyday life on Earth. Technology that is used in space or on space materials, as seen in **Figure 5,** can be applied to items that we use every day.

New Materials

Space materials must protect people from extreme conditions. They also must be flexible and strong. Materials developed for spacesuits are now used to make racing suits for swimmers, lightweight firefighting gear, running shoes, and other sports clothing.

Safety and Health

NASA developed a strong, fibrous material to make parachute cords for spacecraft that land on planets and moons. This material, five times stronger than steel, is used to make radial tires for automobiles.

Medical Applications

Artificial limbs, infrared ear thermometers, robotic surgery, and orthodontic braces all have roots in the space program. Orthodontic braces contain ceramic material originally developed to strengthen the heat resistance of space shuttles.

Relate

5. Show how technology for the space program applies to everyday life using the graphic organizer below.

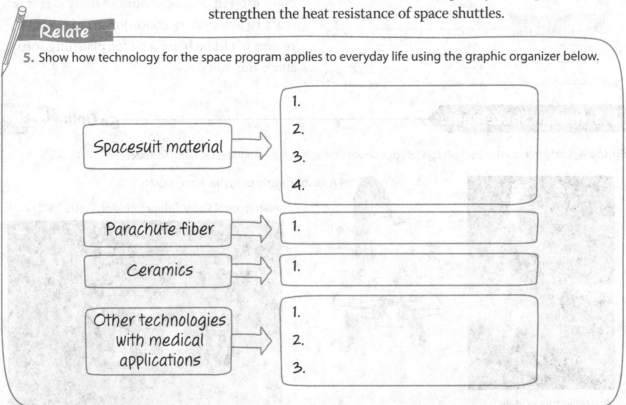

Spacesuit material →
1.
2.
3.
4.

Parachute fiber →
1.

Ceramics →
1.

Other technologies with medical applications →
1.
2.
3.

10.1 Review

Summarize it!

Construct a timeline in the space below that shows the history and progression of space exploration in the United States. Then create a comic strip to visually represent how space exploration has changed over time. **TEKS** 6.11(C)

 Connect it! Explain Imagine that you are a scientist planning a space mission. What factors must you consider when deciding whether to send humans or robots on the mission? Write your response in your interactive notebook.

Summarize it!

Early History of Space Exploration

Use Vocabulary

1. **Use** the term *space shuttle* in a sentence. **TEKS** 6.11(C)

_____

_____

_____

Apply the Essential Questions

2. **Distinguish** between how rockets and artificial satellites are used. **TEKS** 6.11(C)

_____

_____

_____

_____

_____

3. **Describe** the types of equipment used for space travel. **TEKS** 6.11(C)

_____

_____

_____

_____

_____

4. **Contrast** crewed and uncrewed space missions. **TEKS** 6.11(C)

_____

_____

_____

_____

_____

_____

_____

🔥 H.O.T. Questions (Higher Order Thinking)

5. **Predict** how your life would be different if all artificial satellites stopped working.

_____

_____

_____

_____

_____

_____

_____

_____

6. **Analyze** how space exploration would be different if Robert Goddard never created the first rocket in 1926. Write your response on a separate piece of paper. **TEKS** 6.11(C)

6.11(C)

Going Up !

Could a space elevator make space travel easier?

If you wanted to travel into space, the first thing you would have to do is overcome the force of Earth's gravity. So far, the only way to do that has been to use rockets. However, rockets are expensive. Many are used only once, and they require a lot of fuel. It takes a lot of resources to build and power a rocket. But what if you could take an elevator into space instead?

Space elevators were once science fiction, but scientists are now taking the possibility seriously. With the lightweight but strong materials under development today, experts say it could take only 10 years to build a space elevator. The image here shows how it might work.

It generally costs more than $100 million to place a 12,000-kg spacecraft into orbit using a rocket. Some people estimate that a space elevator could place the same craft into orbit for less than $120,000. A human passenger with luggage, together totaling 150 kg, might be able to ride the elevator to space for less than $1,500.

Counterweight: The spaceward end of the cable would attach to a captured asteroid or an artificial satellite. The asteroid or satellite would stabilize the cable and act as a counterweight.

Cable: Made of super-strong but thin materials, the cable would be the first part of the elevator to be built. A rocket-launched spacecraft would carry reels of cable into orbit. From there the cable would be unwound until one end reached Earth's surface.

Anchor Station: The cable's Earthward end would be attached to a movable platform. This would allow operators to move the cable away from space debris in Earth's orbit that could collide with it. The platform would be movable because it would float on the ocean.

Climber: The "elevator car" would carry human passengers and objects into space. It could be powered by Earth-based laser beams, which would activate solar-cell "ears" on the outside of the car.

It's Your Turn!

DEBATE Form an opinion about the space elevator and debate with a classmate. Could a space elevator become a reality in the near future? Would a space elevator benefit ordinary people? Should the space elevator be used for space tourism?

407

Copyright © McGraw-Hill Education   NASA/JPL/University of Arizona

INQUIRY

Blue moon? No, this is Mars! It is a false-color photo of an area on Mars where a future space probe might land. Scientists think the claylike material here might contain water and organic material. Could this material support life? Explain your answer.

Write your response in your interactive notebook.

 LAB Manager

Go to your Lab Manual or visit connectED.mcgraw-hill.com to perform the labs for this lesson.

MiniLAB: *What conditions are required for life on Earth?*
TEKS 6.2(A), (C), (E); 6.4(A); 6.11(C)

LAB: *Design and Construct a Moon Habitat* **TEKS** 6.1(A); 6.2(A), (C), (E); 6.3(B); 6.4(B); 6.11(C)

Explore Activity

TEKS 6.1(A); 6.2(A), (C), (E); 6.4(A), (B); 6.11(C)

How is gravity used to send spacecraft farther in space?

Spacecraft use fuel to get to where they are going. However, fuel is expensive and adds mass to the craft. Some spacecraft travel to far-distant regions with the help of gravity from the planets they pass. This is a technique called gravity assist. You can model gravity assist using a simple table-tennis ball.

Procedure

1. Read and complete a lab safety form.

2. Set a **turntable** in motion.

3. Gently throw a **table-tennis ball** so that it just skims the top of the spinning surface. You might have to practice before you are able to get the ball to glide over the surface.

4. Describe or draw a picture of what you observed. Record your observations in your Lab Manual or interactive notebook.

Think About This

1. Use your observations to describe how this activity is similar to gravity assist.

_____

_____

_____

_____

2. Describe why gravity assist is important for the transportation of spacecrafts such as rockets, satellites, and probes.

_____

_____

_____

_____

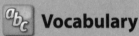

TEKS in this Lesson

6.11(C) Describe the history and future of space exploration, including the types of equipment and transportation needed for space travel

Also covers Process Standards: 6.1(A); 6.2(A), (C), (E); 6.3(B); 6.4(A), (B)

? Essential Questions

- What are the goals of future space exploration?
- What types of equipment and trasportation will be used in future space travel?

$^{a}b_{c}$ Vocabulary

extraterrestrial life
astrobiology

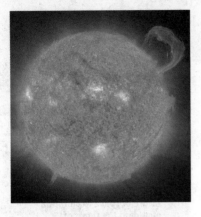

Figure 1 Storms on the Sun send charged particles far into space.

Missing to the Sun and Moon TEKS 6.11(C)

Missions to the Sun and Moon TEKS 6.11(C)

What is the future for space exploration? Scientists at NASA and other space agencies around the world have cooperatively developed goals for future space exploration. One goal is to expand human space travel within the solar system. Two steps leading to this goal are sending probes to the Sun and sending probes to the Moon and Mars.

Explain

1. What is a goal of future space exploration?

_____

_____

Solar Probes

The Sun emits high-energy radiation and charged particles. Storms on the Sun can eject powerful jets of gas and charged particles into space, as shown in **Figure 1.** The Sun's high-energy radiation and charged particles can harm astronauts and damage spacecraft. To better understand these hazards, scientists study data collected by solar probes that orbit the Sun. The solar probe *Ulysses*, launched in 1990, orbited the Sun and gathered data for 19 years.

Lunar Probes

NASA and other space agencies also plan to send several probes to the Moon. The *Lunar Reconnaissance Orbiter* (LRO), launched in 2009 and shown in **Figure 2,** has been mapping the lunar surface and studying the geological processes occuring on Earth's only natural satellite.

Figure 2 The *Lunar Reconnaissance Orbiter* is also studying the radiation that continuously bombards the astronauts.

Differentiate

2. What is the purpose of each type of probe?

Solar	Lunar

Cut out the Lesson 10.2 Foldables in the back of your book. Use it to compare and contrast information you will learn about space missions to the inner and outer planets.

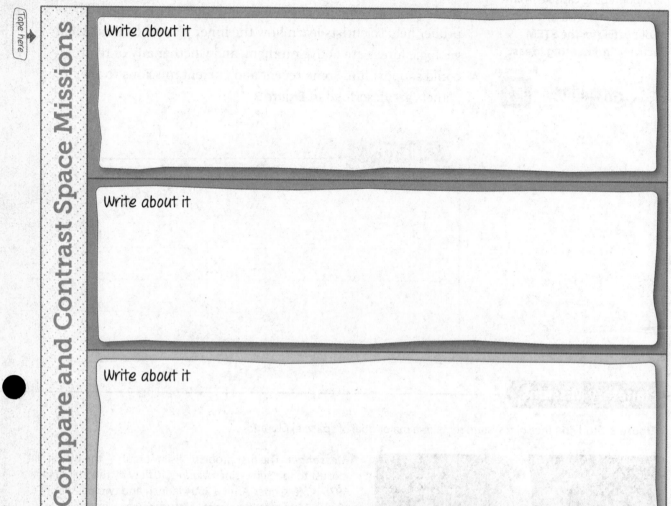

Tape here

Compare and Contrast Space Missions

Write about it

Write about it

Write about it

Connect it! Do you think the study of inner planets or the study of outer planets is more important for future space exploration? Explain your reasoning. **TEKS** 6.11(C)

STEM *online*

Design a mechanical arm that can successfully retrieve a model space capsule from land or water. Visit ConnectED for the **STEM** activity **Engineering Ideas.**

Resources

Go Online!

Missions to the Inner Planets *TEKS* 6.11(C)

The inner planets are the four rocky planets closest to the Sun—Mercury, Venus, Earth, and Mars. Scientists have sent many probes to the inner planets, and more are planned. These probes help scientists learn how the inner planets formed, what geologic forces are active on them, and whether any of them could support life. Some recent and current missions to the inner planets are described in **Figure 3.**

Identify

3. What do scientists want to learn about the inner planets?

_____

_____

_____

_____

_____

Planetary Missions

Figure 3 Studying the solar system remains a major goal of space exploration.

◀ **Messenger** The first probe to visit Mercury—the planet closest to the Sun—since *Mariner 10* flew by the planet in 1975 is *Messenger*. After a 2004 launch and two passes of Venus, *Messenger* flew past Mercury several times before it entered Mercury's orbit in 2011. *Messenger* collected data on Mercury's geology and chemistry. It sent images and data back to Earth for one Earth year. On its first pass by Mercury, in 2008, *Messenger* returned over 1,000 images in many wavelengths.

Spirit and **Opportunity** Since the first flyby reached Mars in 1964, many probes have been sent to Mars. One of them produced the spectacular photo shown at the beginning of this lesson. In 2003, two robotic rovers, *Spirit* and *Opportunity,* began exploring the Martian surface for the first time. These solar-powered rovers traveled more than 20 km and relayed data for over 5 years. They sent thousands of images to Earth. ▶

Missions to the Outer Planets and Beyond TEKS 6.11(C)

The outer planets are the four large planets farthest from the Sun—Jupiter, Saturn, Uranus, and Neptune. Pluto was once considered an outer planet, but it is now included with other small, icy **dwarf planets** observed orbiting the Sun outside the orbit of Neptune. Missions to outer planets are long and difficult because the planets are so far from Earth. Some missions to the outer planets and beyond are described in **Figure 3** below. *TESS*, set to launch in 2017, is a satellite that will use telescopes to search for habitable planets beyond our solar system.

Review Vocabulary

dwarf planet a round body that orbits the Sun but is not massive enough to clear away other objects in its orbit

Describe

4. Why are missions to the outer planets difficult?

_____

_____

_____

LAB Manager

MiniLAB: *What conditions are required for life on Earth?*
TEKS 6.2(A), (C), (E); 6.4(A); 6.11(C)

◄ *Cassini* The first orbiter sent to Saturn, *Cassini*, was launched in 1997 as part of an international effort involving 19 countries. *Cassini* traveled for 7 years before entering Saturn's orbit in 2004. When it arrived, it sent a smaller probe to the surface of Saturn's largest moon, Titan, as shown at left. *Cassini* is so large—6,000 kg—that no rocket was powerful enough to send it directly to Saturn. Scientists used gravity from closer planets—Venus, Earth, and Jupiter—to help power the trip. The gravity from each planet gave the spacecraft a boost toward Saturn.

New Horizons A much smaller spacecraft, *New Horizons*, is speeding toward Pluto. *New Horizons* is also using gravity assist for its journey, with a swing past Jupiter. Launched in 2006, *New Horizons* will not reach Pluto until 2015. It will leave the solar system in 2029. Without a gravity assist from Jupiter, it would take *New Horizons* 5 years longer to reach Pluto. ▶

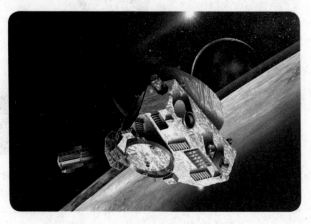

Future Missions TEKS 6.11(C)

Do you think there will ever be cities or communities built outside Earth? That is looking very far ahead. No person has ever been farther than the Moon. However, human space travel remains a goal of NASA and other space agencies around the world.

A New Era of Spaceflight

The *Orion* spacecraft, shown in **Figure 4,** is a human space flight system that is capable of missions to a variety of interplanetary destinations. The purpose of Orion is to take humans to places in deep space that have never been explored by humans. Future missions to the Moon and asteroids will help build our knowledge of human space travel with the ultimate goal of astronauts working and living on Mars. Human exploration missions greatly expand our scientific understanding of our solar system and the origins of life.

Studying and Visiting Mars

A visit to Mars will probably not occur for several more decades. To prepare for a visit to Mars, NASA plans to send additional probes to the planet. The probes will explore sites on Mars that might have resources that can support life. One of these probes is the *MAVEN* spacecraft. *MAVEN* will study the atmosphere of Mars and how it has evolved over time.

Astronauts will need secure housing once they establish a suitable landing area on Mars. The structure in **Figure 5** is one of those options.

Studying Jupiter

The largest planet in the solar system is going to be studied by the *Juno* spacecraft. It will take *Juno* 5 years to reach the gas giant. *Juno* will study Jupiter's atmosphere, gravity, magnetic fields, and atmosphere conditions.

Figure 4 The Orion spacecraft at Johnson Space Center in Houston, Texas, is modeled after the Apollo spacecraft. It can transport up to four crew members and provide a safe habitat from launch to landing. ▶

◀ **Figure 5** This structure, at the Johnson Space Center in Houston, Texas, could serve as housing for up to four astronauts. It has been evaluated to ensure safety for humans living on other planetary bodies.

Figure 7 The dark patches in the inset photo might represent areas where water from an underground ocean has seeped to Europa's surface. ▶

▲ **Figure 6** Bacteria live in the boiling water of this hot spring in Yellowstone National Park.

The Search for Life

No one knows whether life exists beyond Earth, but people have thought about the possibility for a long time. It even has a name. *Life that originates outside Earth is* **extraterrestrial** (ek struh tuh RES tree ul) **life.**

Conditions Needed for Life

Astrobiology *is the study of life in the universe, including life on Earth and the possibility of extraterrestrial life.* Investigating the conditions for life on Earth helps scientists predict where they might find life elsewhere in the solar system. Astrobiology also can help scientists locate environments in space where humans and other Earth life might be able to survive.

Life exists in a wide range of environments on Earth. Life-forms survive on dark ocean floors, deep in solid rocks, and in scorching water, such as the hot spring shown in **Figure 6.** No matter how extreme their environments, all known life-forms on Earth need liquid water, organic molecules, and some source of energy to survive. Scientists assume that if life exists elsewhere in space it would have the same requirements.

Water in the Solar System

A lunar space probe found water in a crater on the Moon. Enough frozen water was found in a single crater to fill 1,500 Olympic swimming pools. Evidence from other space probes suggests that water vapor or ice exists on many planets and moons in the solar system. NASA plans to launch the *Mars Science Laboratory* to sample a variety of soils and rocks on Mars. This mission will investigate the possibility that life exists or once existed on the planet.

Some of the moons in the outer solar system, such as Jupiter's moon Europa, shown in **Figure 7,** might also have large amounts of liquid water beneath their surfaces.

Connect

4. Highlight why it is important for scientists to investigate the conditions for life on Earth.

Understanding Earth by Exploring Space

Space provides frontiers for the human spirit of exploration and discovery. The exploration of space also provides insight into planet Earth. Information gathered in space helps scientists understand how the Sun and other bodies in the solar system influence Earth, how Earth formed, and how Earth supports life. Looking for Earthlike planets outside the solar system helps scientists learn if Earth is unique in the universe.

Searching for Other Planets

Astronomers have detected thousands of planet candidates outside the solar system. Most of these planets are much bigger than Earth and probably could not support liquid water—or life. To search for Earthlike planets, NASA launched the *Kepler* telescope in 2009. The *Kepler* telescope, illustrated in **Figure 8,** focuses on a single area of sky containing about 100,000 stars. However, though it might detect Earthlike planets orbiting other stars, *Kepler* will not be able to detect life on any planet.

Figure 8 *Kepler* is orbiting the Sun, searching a single area of sky for Earthlike planets.

Understanding Our Home Planet

Not all of NASA's missions are to other planets, to other moons, or to look at stars and galaxies. NASA and space agencies around the world also launch and maintain Earth-observing satellites. Satellites that orbit Earth provide large-scale images of Earth's surface. These images help scientists understand Earth's climate and weather. **Figure 9** shows a satellite image of Hurricane Ike. This storm was almost the same size as Texas and caused massive storm surges that led to power outages for most of east Texas.

Figure 9 Earth-orbiting satellites can collect data about Earth's surface. This is a satellite image of Hurricane Ike in 2008.

Create a graphic organizer to show how topics discussed in *Future Space Missions, The Search for Life, and Understanding Earth by Exploring Space* are related.

TEKS 6.11(C)

Connect it! **Plan** an imaginary trip to a future Martian outpost. What types of equipment and transporation would be needed to get to your destination? What equipment and transporation would be needed when you arrive? Write your response in your interactive notebook.

Summarize it!

Recent and Future Missions

Apply the Essential Questions

1. **Identify** the goals of future space transportation. **TEKS** 6.11(C)

   _____

   _____

   _____

   _____

2. **Discuss** a piece of equiment that might be needed for future space exploration missions.
   TEKS 6.11(C)

   _____

   _____

   _____

   _____

3. **Compare** past and future models of transporation in space. **TEKS** 6.11(C)

   _____

   _____

   _____

   _____

   _____

   _____

🔥 H.O.T. Questions (Higher Order Thinking)

4. **Write** In what different ways do humans observe and explore space? Why is the exploration of space important?
   TEKS 6.11(C)

   _____

   _____

   _____

   _____

   _____

   _____

   _____

   _____

   _____

   _____

5. **Debate** Write two arguments for and against human transportation in space. Prepare your arguments for a class discussion. **TEKS** 6.11(C)

   _____

   _____

   _____

   _____

   _____

   _____

Detecting Space Junk

Earth is surrounded by debris.

Since *Sputnik I*, the first human-made satellite, orbited Earth in 1957, humans have launched thousands of satellites into orbit around Earth. Many of these satellites are no longer used, yet they remain in orbit. Humans also have sent many other spacecraft into space. Parts of the rockets that launched these crafts, as well as parts of the crafts themselves, also remain in orbit around Earth. As a result, the space around our planet is becoming littered with junk.

Space junk, or orbital debris, is any piece of human-made material that orbits Earth and serves no function. It could be almost anything: an abandoned satellite, a chunk of old rocket, or a chip of paint. Whizzing through space at 26,000 km/h, even a tiny object could cause serious damage to a spacecraft or an astronaut. To avoid dangerous collisions, scientists at NASA and elsewhere track space junk. The U.S. Space Surveillance Network uses a variety of optical and radar-imaging tools across the globe to track over 13,000 Earth-orbiting objects with diameters greater than 10 cm. To detect smaller pieces of orbital debris, scientists rely mostly on the Haystack radar. How does it work?

The Haystack Long Range Imaging Radar in Massachusetts generally monitors objects smaller than 30 cm in diameter in low-Earth orbit. This is a region of space between 160 km and 2,000 km above Earth's surface, where it is most crowded with space junk.

▲ Millions of pieces of space junk circle Earth. Most are smaller than a marble. In this image, the dots represent Earth-orbiting objects larger than 10 cm in diameter. Of these, only 5 percent are working satellites.

AMERICAN MUSEUM of NATURAL HISTORY

1 The radar antenna focuses on one area in the sky and detects objects that pass through its field of view.

2 Radio waves sent out by the antenna bounce off objects and return to the antenna.

3 The radio-wave data are fed into computers and used by scientists to estimate the number, size, speed, and location of the objects.

4 To monitor small objects that orbit Earth, NASA relies mostly on the Haystack radar in Massachusetts.

It's Your Turn!

PROBLEM SOLVING With a group, research ideas for cleaning up Earth's orbit. Decide which one you think would be most effective. Draw a diagram of how the process would work. Share your research and diagram with the class.

Test-Taking Strategy

Compare and Contrast Some questions will ask you to compare and contrast two or more objects. This means you have to determine which characteristics make the objects similar and which characteristics make them different. Compare and contrast questions might not only ask you to describe multiple objects, but they might also have you compare and contrast different sets of data or texts.

Example

Use the photos to answer question 8.

② Carefully observe the images. Note the similarities between the two. Both are uncrewed space probes that transmit data back to Earth. A lander space probe lands on its destination, while a flyby space probe continues traveling through space.

8 Which of the following statements most accurately describes the relationship between a lander space probe and a flyby space probe? **TEKS** 6.11(C)

① Carefully read the question and determine what it is asking. This question asks you to identify similarities and differences between two types of space probes.

   A Both probes are used to gather data, but a lander is uncrewed.

   B Both probes are uncrewed, but a flyby orbits its destination.

③ The statement that most accurately describes the relationship between a lander space probe and a flyby space probe is **C**.

   C Both probes are used to gather data, but a flyby continues through space.

   D Both probes are uncrewed, but a lander will return to Earth

Tip: Try drawing a Venn diagram to organize your data. Draw two overlapping ovals. In each oval, list characteristics specific to that object. Where the ovals overlap, list characteristics that both objects have in common.

Multiple Choice

1   During the early years of NASA's space exploration program, several spacecraft programs launched. Three are listed in the table. **TEKS** 6.11(C); 6.2(E)

Year	Spacecraft Program	Number of astronauts in spacecraft	Number of Missions
1961–1963	Mercury	1	6
1965–1966	Gemini	2	10
1968–1972	Apollo	3	11

How many more astronauts flew in Apollo missions than flew in the Gemini and Mercury missions combined? Record and bubble in your answer on the answer document.

2   When a spacecraft enters a planet's atmosphere from space, friction creates heat. This heat can badly damage or even destroy the spacecraft. A new type of paint has been developed. It has been used to protect spacecrafts like the *International Space Station* and the Mars rover *Curiosity*. **TEKS** 6.11(C); 6.3(A)

What can you infer about Mars if heat-resistant paint was used when *Curiosity* landed on Mars?

A   Mars has an atmosphere.

B   Sunlight is very strong on Mars.

C   The paint is unaffected by space travel.

D   The surface of Mars is very hot.

3

> The first spacesuits were worn by the Mercury astronauts. These suits were pressurized and provided oxygen through a hose attached to the spacecraft. The Gemini astronauts also wore space suits that had a hose connecting them to the spacecraft. These astronauts did not have their own life support equipment. However, the Apollo astronauts wore spacesuits that had individual life support systems and boots. The orange spacesuits worn by the space shuttle astronauts had individual life support systems, a parachute, a pressurized helmet, and a flotation system.

Which spacesuit would provide the astronauts with protection in a wide variety of situations?
TEKS 6.11(C); 6.3(A)

A Apollo

B Gemini

C Mercury

D space shuttle

4

> *The International Space Station* (ISS) has no outside source of air and water. One problem in the ISS is the buildup of carbon dioxide (CO_2). With as many as six people living on the ISS, too much CO_2 can build up and become toxic to the crew. A new technology called the *Amine Swingbed* is being tested on the ISS. It removes excess CO_2 from the living spaces. This new system is smaller and uses less energy than the one the ISS is using now. Scientists hope that this new system can be used for long distance space travel when refilling the air and water supply is not possible.

Why should the *Amine Swingbed* be tested aboard the ISS before installing it and removing the existing system? **TEKS** 6.11(C)

A CO_2 cannot be removed without it.

B It does not need to be tested.

C There is no way to simulate the same situation on the ISS on Earth.

D If it malfunctions, there is a back-up cleaning system.

5 NASA has been sending exploration missions to Mars for almost 50 years. The length of time it has taken the different spacecrafts to reach Mars ranges from 150 days to 360 days. In order to make it possible for humans to travel to Mars, the travel time must be reduced.

TEKS 6.11(C); 6.2(E)

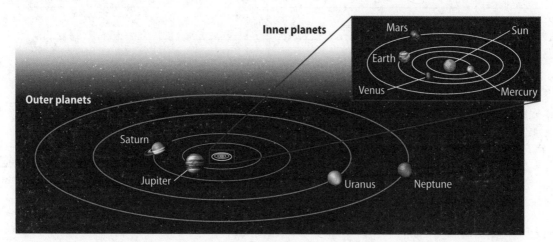

Assume the different spacecrafts were using same amount of fuel at the same rate. Why are there such large differences in travel time?

A The distance of Mars from the Sun changes.

B The distance from Earth to Mars changes.

C The position of Earth from the Sun changes.

D The shapes of both planets' orbits change.

TEKS Strand 5
Organisms and Environments

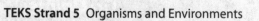

TEKS in this strand

✓ **6.12** The student knows all organisms are classified into Domains and Kingdoms. Organisms within these taxonomic groups share similar characteristics which allow them to interact with the living and nonliving parts of their ecosystem.

✓ Also includes the following Scientific Investigation and Reasoning strand TEKS: **6.1, 6.2, 6.3, 6.4**

Texas Fun Fact

Did You Know? Texas doesn't have one state flower—it has five! According to state law, any variety of bluebonnet is the state flower. Currently, five species of bluebonnets are known to grow in Texas, and each one is the state flower. If another species of bluebonnet is discovered, it will also be considered the state flower of Texas.

11 Interactions of Life

 The BIG Idea

Organisms are classified based on similar characteristics. These characteristics enable them to interact with the living and nonliving parts of their environments.

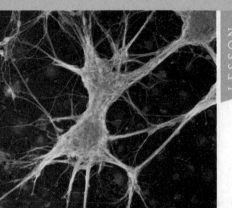

LESSON

11.1 Cells

Cells have specialized structures that enable them to survive in many different environments.

TEKS 6.12(A), (B); Also covers 6.1(A); 6.2(A), (C), (E); 6.3(B); 6.4(A)

LESSON

11.2 Classifying Living Things

All living things are organized, grow, develop, reproduce, use energy, and respond to changes in their environment. Living things are classified into groups based on similar characteristics.

TEKS 6.12(A), (C), (D); Also covers 6.1(A); 6.2(A), (C), (E); 6.3(D); 6.4(A), (B)

LESSON

11.3 Ecosystems

An ecosystem is all of the interactions among the living and nonliving things in a certain area.

TEKS 6.12(E), (F); Also covers 6.1(A); 6.2(A), (C), (E); 6.4(A), (B)

Ecosystems

Some people have different ideas about the word ecosystem. Here are some of the things people think about ecosystems.

A. Ecosystems are all the living things on land.

B. Ecosystems are all the living things on land and in water.

C. Ecosystems are all the living things on land, in water, and in air.

D. Ecosystems are all the nonliving things on land.

E. Ecosystems are all the nonliving things on land and in water.

F. Ecosystems are all the nonliving things on land, in water, and in air.

G. Ecosystems are all the living and nonliving things on land and in water.

H. Ecosystems are all the living and nonliving things on land, in water, and in air.

Which description best matches your thinking about ecosystems? Explain your ideas about ecosystems and what ecosystems include.

INQUIRY

Weird Web? This isn't a spider's strange web. These are nerve cells. The darker blue parts are the cell bodies. The pink threadlike parts carry electrical signals from one nerve cell to another. How do these parts help the cells?

Write your response in your interactive notebook.

🧹 LAB Manager

Go to your Lab Manual or visit connectED.mcgraw-hill.com to perform the labs for this lesson.

MiniLAB: *How do eukaryotic and prokaryotic cells compare?*

TEKS 6.1(A); 6.2(A), (C), (E); 6.3(B); 6.12(B)

Explore Activity

TEKS 6.2(A); 6.3(B); 6.4(A)
6.12(A)

Are all cells alive?

There are many bacteria that live on and in people. These single-celled organisms have all the characteristics of life and are alive. Are human cells, which the bacteria live on and in, also alive?

Procedure

1. In your Lab Manual or interactive notebook, draw a circle that takes up half of the page. The circle represents a human cell.

2. Draw and label the following things in your cell:

   A power plant to represent the need for and use of energy; label it *energy production*.

   A garbage truck to represent waste removal; label it *waste removal*.

   A city hall with a mayor to represent the organization and pro-cesses of the cell; label it *organization*.

   A road system to represent the transportation that occurs in the cell; label it *transportation*.

   A cement truck to represent the construction of new structures in the cell; label it *growth*.

   A fire truck to represent a cell's ability to respond to changes in its surroundings; label it *response to environment*.

   A copy machine in city hall to represent the cell's ability to follow instructions and make more cells; label it *reproduction*.

Think About This

1. Does the human cell you drew have all the characteristics of life? Explain your answer.

   _____

   _____

   _____

2. Based on your observations, what do you think is the basic unit of life?

   _____

   _____

TEKS in this Lesson

6.12(A) understand that all organisms are composed of one or more cells;

6.12(B) recognize that the presence of a nucleus determines whether a cell is prokaryotic or eukaryotic

Also covers Process Standards: **6.1(A); 6.2(A), (C), (E); 6.3(B); 6.4(A)**

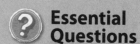

Essential Questions

- What is the basic unit of life?
- How do prokaryotic cells and eukaryotic cells compare?

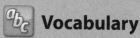

Vocabulary

prokaryotic cell
eukaryotic cell
cytoplasm
mitochondrion

431

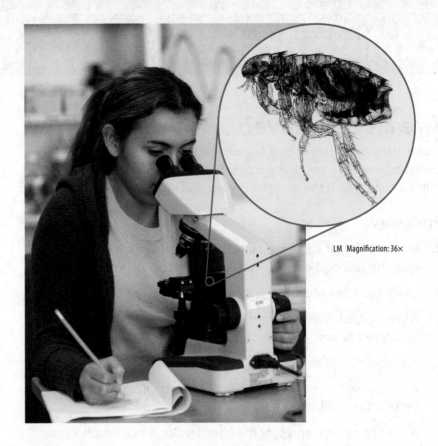

LM Magnification: 36×

Figure 1 Microscopes increase the size of an image so that a small thing, such as the flea shown here, can be observed.

What are cells? TEKS 6.12(A)

What is one thing all living things have in common? All living things have cells, the basic unit of an organism. Most organisms are unicellular—they are made up of only one cell. Other organisms are multicellular—they are made up of many cells. Humans have about 100 trillion cells! Most cells are so small that they cannot be seen without a microscope. Microscopes, such as the one shown in **Figure 1,** are used to view details of small objects or to view things that are too small to be seen by the unaided eye.

Scientists first used microscopes to look at cells over 300 years ago. Cells come in different shapes and sizes. Nerve cells are long and slender. Red blood cells are small and disk-shaped.

What are cells made of?

All cells are made of four macromolecules—nucleic acids, lipids, proteins, and carbohydrates. Cells also have many other characteristics. For example, all cells are surrounded by an outer structure called a cell membrane. The cell membrane keeps substances such as macromolecules inside the cell. It also helps protect cells by keeping harmful substances from entering. About 70 percent of the inside of a cell is water. Many of the substances inside cells are dissolved in water so they can move easily about the cell.

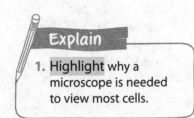

Explain

1. Highlight why a microscope is needed to view most cells.

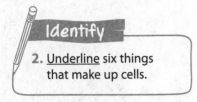

Identify

2. Underline six things that make up cells.

Types of Cells TEKS 6.12(B)

There are two main types of cells, as shown in **Figure 2.** **Prokaryotic** (pro kayr ee AH tihk) **cells** *do not have a nucleus or other membrane-bound organelles.* Organelles are structures in cells that carry out specific functions. A nucleus is a membrane-bound organelle that contains a cell's genetic material. The genetic material and the few organelles in prokaryotic cells are not surrounded by membranes. Organisms with prokaryotic cells are called prokaryotes. Most prokaryotes are unicellular organisms, such as bacteria.

Eukaryotic (yew ker ee AH tihk) **cells** *have a nucleus and other membrane-bound organelles.* Most multicellular organisms and some unicellular organisms are eukaryotes. The eukaryotic cell shown in **Figure 2** contains many structures that are not in a prokaryotic cell. In eukaryotes, membranes surround most of the organelles, including the nucleus.

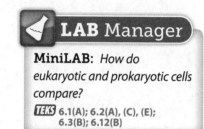
Figure 2 Prokaryotic cells do not have a nucleus. Eukaryotic cells, such as the animal cell below, have a nucleus and many other organelles.

Compare

3. On the prokaryotic cell, (circle) the names of the structures that are also in a eukaryotic cell.

Watch

Go Online!

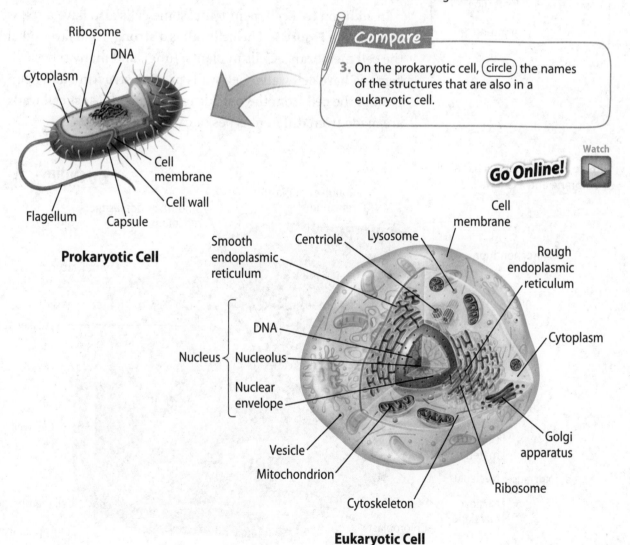

Prokaryotic Cell

Ribosome
DNA
Cytoplasm
Cell membrane
Cell wall
Flagellum
Capsule

Eukaryotic Cell

Smooth endoplasmic reticulum
Centriole
Lysosome
Cell membrane
Rough endoplasmic reticulum
DNA
Nucleus { Nucleolus
Nuclear envelope
Cytoplasm
Vesicle
Mitochondrion
Cytoskeleton
Golgi apparatus
Ribosome

The Outside of a Cell

As you have just read, the cell membrane surrounds a cell. Much like a fence surrounds a school, the cell membrane helps keep the substances inside a cell separate from the substances outside a cell. Some cells also are surrounded by a more rigid layer called a cell wall.

Cell Membrane

The cell membrane is made of lipids and proteins. Recall that lipids and proteins are macromolecules that help cells function. Lipids in the cell membrane protect the inside of a cell from the external environment. Proteins in the cell membrane transport substances between a cell's environment and the inside of the cell. Proteins in the cell membrane also communicate with other cells and organisms and sense changes in the cell's environment.

Cell Wall

In addition to a cell membrane, some cells also have a cell wall, as shown in **Figure 3.** The cell wall is a strong, rigid layer outside the cell membrane. Cells in plants, fungi, and many types of bacteria have cell walls. Cell walls provide structure and help protect the cell from the outside environment. Most cell walls are made from different types of carbohydrates.

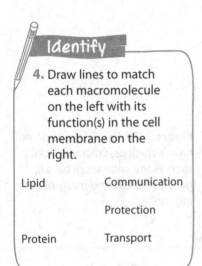

Identify

4. Draw lines to match each macromolecule on the left with its function(s) in the cell membrane on the right.

Lipid   Communication

             Protection

Protein   Transport

Figure 3 This plant cell has a cell membrane and a cell wall.

Watch

Go Online! ▶

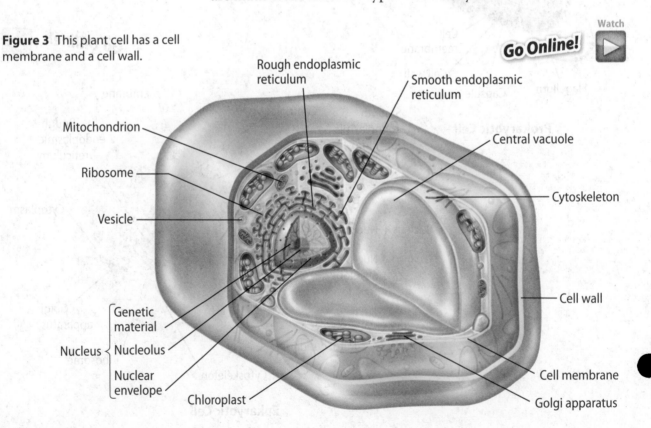

Rough endoplasmic reticulum

Smooth endoplasmic reticulum

Mitochondrion

Ribosome

Vesicle

Central vacuole

Cytoskeleton

Genetic material

Nucleolus

Nuclear envelope

Nucleus

Chloroplast

Cell wall

Cell membrane

Golgi apparatus

Organize it!

Characterize the makeup of cells.

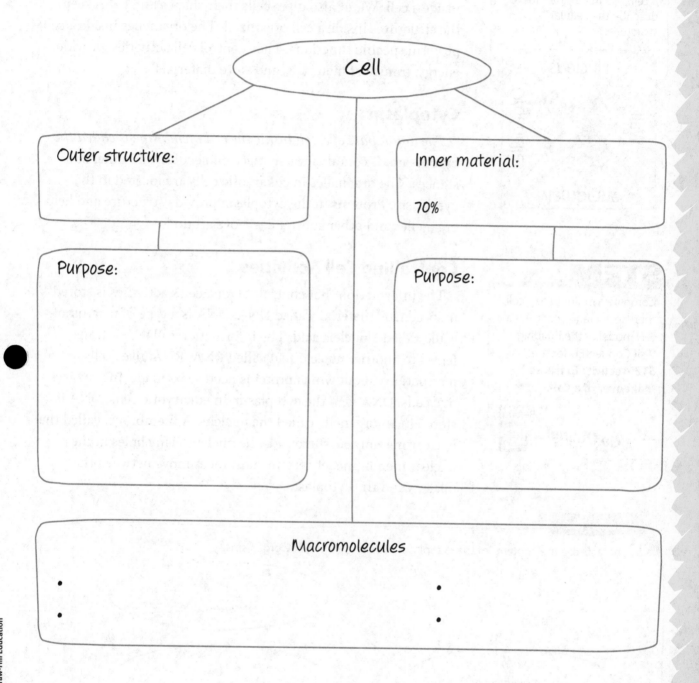

Cell

Outer structure:

Inner material:

70%

Purpose:

Purpose:

Macromolecules

- •
- •
- •
- •

 Connect it! **Infer** An organism's genetic material—DNA—is a nucleic acid. How can the structure of DNA be used to determine whether a cell is prokaryotic or eukaryotic? Write your response in your interactive notebook. **TEKS** 6.12(B)

Organize it!

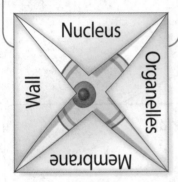

FOLDABLES®

Make an envelope book. Label it as shown. Use the center inside tab to illustrate a cell. Use the inside tabs to describe the cellular structures.

Nucleus

Organelles

Wall

Membrane

STEMonline

Compare a building to a cell, then design and construct a 3-D model of the building. Visit ConnectED for the **STEM** activity **Extreme Makeover of a Cell.**

Resources

Go Online!

The Inside of a Cell **TEKS** 6.12(B)

You might recall that the inside of a cell is mainly water. Many substances used for communication, energy, and growth dissolve in water. This makes it easier for the substances to move around inside a cell. Water also gives cells their shapes and helps keep the structures inside a cell organized. The organelles inside a cell perform specific functions. They control cell activities, provide energy, transport materials, and store materials.

Cytoplasm

The liquid part of a cell inside the cell membrane is called the **cytoplasm.** It contains water, macromolecules, and other substances. The organelles in eukaryotic cells are located in the cytoplasm. Proteins in the cytoplasm provide structure and help organelles and other substances move around.

Controlling Cell Activities

The information that controls all of a cell's activities is stored in its genetic material, called DNA. DNA is a type of macromolecule called a nucleic acid. The information in DNA is transferred to another nucleic acid called RNA. RNA gives cells instructions about which proteins need to be made. In prokaryotic cells, DNA is in the cytoplasm. In eukaryotic cells, DNA is stored in an organelle called the nucleus. A membrane, called the nuclear membrane, surrounds the nucleus. Tiny holes in the nuclear membrane let certain substances move between the nucleus and the cytoplasm.

Describe

5. Characterize the contents of the cytoplasm in cells of eukaryotic organisms.

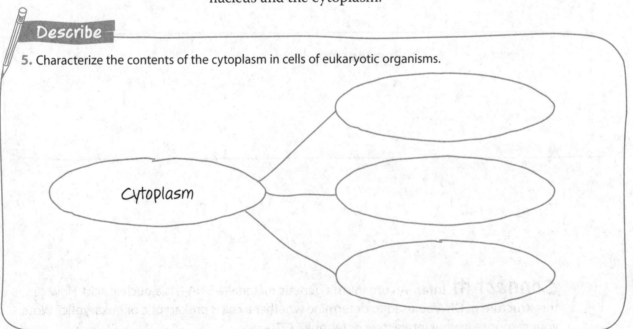

Cytoplasm

Copyright © McGraw-Hill Education

Plant Cell

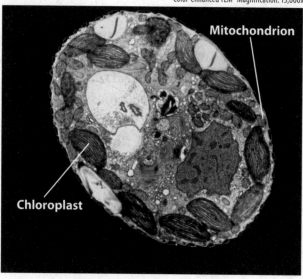

Color-enhanced TEM Magnification: 15,000x

Mitochondrion

Chloroplast

Animal Cell

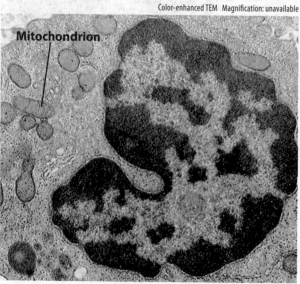

Color-enhanced TEM Magnification: unavailable

Mitochondrion

Figure 4 Plant cells have mitochondria and chloroplasts. Animal cells only contain mitochondria.

Energy for the Cell

All living things use energy. Proteins in the cytoplasm process energy in prokaryotes. Eukaryotes have special organelles, the chloroplasts and mitochondria (mi tuh KAHN dree uh; singular, mitochondrion) shown in **Figure 4,** that process energy.

Mitochondria Most eukaryotes contain hundreds of mitochondria. **Mitochondria** *are organelles that break down food and release energy.* This energy is stored in molecules called ATP—adenosine triphosphate (uh DEN uh seen • tri FAHS fayt). ATP provides a cell with energy to perform many functions, such as making proteins, storing information, and communicating with other cells.

Word Origin

mitochondrion
from Greek *mitos*, means "thread"; and *khondrion*, means "little granule"

Name

6. What energy molecule is made in a mitochondrion?

_____

Chloroplasts Energy also can be processed in organelles called chloroplasts, shown in **Figure 4.** Plants and many other autotrophs have chloroplasts and mitochondria. Chloroplasts capture light energy and convert it into chemical energy in a process called photosynthesis. Chloroplasts contain many structures that capture light energy. Like the reactions that occur in mitochondria, ATP molecules are produced during photosynthesis. However, photosynthesis also produces carbohydrates such as glucose that also are used to store energy.

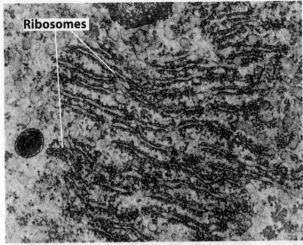

Figure 5 Ribosomes are attached to the endoplasmic reticulum.

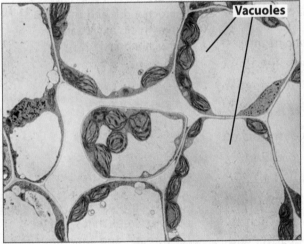

Color-enhanced TEM Magnification: 4,500×

Figure 6 Vacuoles are used by plant cells for storage and to provide structure.

Protein Production

You just read that cells use protein for many functions. These proteins are made on the surface of ribosomes that are in the cytoplasm of both prokaryotic and eukaryotic cells. In eukaryotic cells, some ribosomes are attached to an organelle called the endoplasmic reticulum (en duh PLAZ mihk • rih TIHK yuh lum), as shown in **Figure 5.** It is made of folded membranes. The proteins can be processed and can move inside the cell through the endoplasmic reticulum.

Cell Storage

What happens to the molecules that are made in a cell? An organelle called the Golgi (GAWL jee) apparatus packages proteins into tiny organelles called vesicles. Vesicles transport proteins around a cell. Other molecules are stored in organelles called vacuoles. A vacuole is usually the largest organelle in a plant cell, as shown in **Figure 6.** In plant cells, vacuoles store water and provide support. In contrast to all plant cells, only some animal and bacterial cells contain vacuoles. The vacuoles in animal and bacterial cells are smaller than the ones in plant cells.

Copyright © McGraw-Hill Education   (t)D Spector/Peter Arnold/Getty Images, (b)Biophoto Associates/Science Source

Understand

7. What are the roles of the cell structures listed in the table below?

Structure	Role
Ribosomes	
Golgi apparatus	
Vesicles	
Vacuoles	

Summarize it!

Summarize how the parts of a cell enable it to survive.

Cell membrane:

DNA:

Ribosomes:

Cell

Mitochondria/
Chloroplasts:

Vesicles:

 Connect it! **Generalize** how prokaryotic and eukaryotic cells relate to unicellular and multicellular organisms. Write your response in your interactive notebook. *TEKS* 6.12(B)

Summarize it!

Cells

Use Vocabulary

1. Water, proteins, and other substances are found in the _____ of a cell.

Apply the Essential Questions

2. **Explain** Why must all organisms be composed of one or more cells?
   TEKS 6.12(A)

   _____

   _____

   _____

   _____

3. **Describe** the structures that are found in both prokaryotic cells and eukaryotic cells. **TEKS** 6.12(B)

   _____

   _____

   _____

   _____

 **H.O.T. Questions** (Higher Order Thinking)

4. **Assess** how the classification of prokaryotes and eukaryotes relates to the structure of their cells. **TEKS** 6.12(B)

   _____

   _____

   _____

   _____

   _____

5. **Explain** the role of organelles in the functions of eukaryotic cells.
   TEKS 6.12(B)

   _____

   _____

   _____

   _____

   _____

   _____

   _____

6. **Assess** the role of water in cell function.

   _____

   _____

   _____

   _____

7. **Recognize** Is the cell below prokaryotic or eukaryotic? Explain how you determined your answer.
   TEKS 6.12(B)

   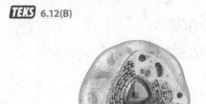

   _____

   _____

   _____

   _____

My Notes

INQUIRY

Living or Not? This roseate spoonbill and white ibis at the South Padre Island Birding and Nature Center are living. The sand and water are not living. How can you tell whether something is alive? With a partner take turns naming characteristics that make something alive.

Write your responses in your interactive notebook.

LAB Manager

Go to your Lab Manual or visit connectED.mcgraw-hill.com to perform the labs for this lesson.

MiniLAB: *Whose shoe is it?*
TEKS 6.1(A); 6.2(A), (C), (E); 6.12(D)

LAB: *How can living things be classified?*
TEKS 6.1(A); 6.2(A), (C), (E); 6.4(A), (B); 6.12(C), (D)

Explore Activity

How can you tell whether it is alive?

Living things share several basic characteristics. Think about what you have in common with other living things such as an insect or a tree. Do other things have some of those same characteristics?

Procedure

1. Read and complete a lab safety form.

2. Observe a **lit candle** for 1–2 min. Pay attention to both the candle and the flame.

3. Record your observations in your Lab Manual or interactive notebook.

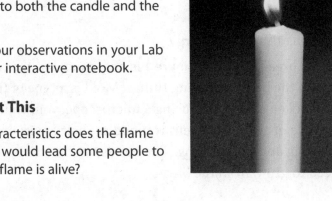

Think About This

1. What characteristics does the flame have that would lead some people to think the flame is alive?

   _____

   _____

   _____

2. What qualities did you think of earlier (that you share with other living things) that the candle does not possess?

   _____

   _____

   _____

3. What characteristics do you think something must have to be considered alive?

   _____

   _____

   _____

TEKS in this Lesson

6.12(A) understand that all organisms are composed of one or more cells;

6.12(C) recognize that the broadest taxonomic classification of living organisms is divided into currently recognized Domains

6.12(D) identify the basic characteristics of organisms, including prokaryotic or eukaryotic, unicellular or multicellular, autotrophic or heterotrophic, and mode of reproduction, that further classify them in the currently recognized Kingdoms

Also covers Process Standards: 6.1(A); 6.2(A), (C), (E); 6.3(D); 6.4(A), (B)

? Essential Questions

• How do unicellular and multicellular organisms compare?

• How are living things classified?

abc Vocabulary

autotroph
heterotroph
habitat
binomial nomenclature
taxon

Figure 1 Mold is a living thing.

What are living things? TEKS 6.12(A), (D)

It might be easy to tell whether a bird, a tree, or a person is alive. But for some organisms, it is harder to tell whether they are living things. Look at the moldy bread shown in **Figure 1.** Is the bread a living thing? What about the green mold and white mold on the bread? All living things have six basic characteristics in common:

• Living things are made of one or more cells.

• Living things are organized.

• Living things grow and develop.

• Living things respond to their environment.

• Living things reproduce.

• Living things use energy.

The bread shown in **Figure 1** is not living, but the molds growing on the bread are living things. Mold is a type of fungus. If you looked at the mold using a microscope, you would see that it is made of cells. Mold cells respond to their environment by growing and reproducing. The molds obtain energy, which they need to grow, from the bread.

Draw

1. Create a graphic organizer to describe the six characteristics of living things.

Living things are organized.

Marching bands are made up of rows of people playing different instruments. Some rows are made up of people playing flutes, and other rows are filled with drummers. Although marching bands are organized into different rows, all band members work together to play a song. Like marching bands, living things also are organized. Some living things are more complex than others, but all organisms are made of cells. In all cells, macromolecules are organized into different structures that help cells function. You might recall that there are four macromolecules in cells—nucleic acids, lipids, proteins, and carbohydrates. Nucleic acids, such as DNA, store information. Lipids are the main component of cell membranes and provide structure. Some proteins are enzymes, and others provide structure. Carbohydrates are used for energy.

Unicellular Organisms Some living things are unicellular, which means they are made up of only one cell. In fact, most living things on Earth are unicellular organisms. Unicellular organisms are the oldest forms of life. There are many groups of unicellular organisms, each with **unique** characteristics. Bacteria, amoebas (uh MEE buhz), and paramecia (per uh MEE see ah) are examples of unicellular organisms. Unicellular organisms have, inside one cell, everything needed to obtain and use energy, reproduce, and grow. Some unicellular organisms are tiny and cannot be seen without a microscope. Other unicellular organisms, such as the plasmodial (plaz MOH dee ul) slime mold shown in **Figure 2,** can be large.

Figure 2 A plasmodial slime mold is a huge cell formed by many cells that join together and form one cell.

Academic Vocabulary

unique
(adjective) without an equal, distinctive

Figure 3 Multicellular organisms, such as this ladybug, contain groups of cells that carry out special functions.

Identify

3. What structures can you identify in the ladybug that have specialized functions?

Multicellular Organisms Soccer teams are made up of many types of players, including goalkeepers, forwards, and fullbacks. Each team member has a specific job, but they all work together when playing a game. Many living things are made of more than one cell and are called multicellular organisms. Like the different types of players on a soccer team, multicellular organisms have different types of cells that carry out specialized functions. The ladybug shown in **Figure 3** has cells that form wings and other cells that form eyes.

Multicellular organisms have different levels of organization. Groups of cells that work together and perform a specific function are called tissues. Tissues that work together and carry out a specific function are called organs. Organs that work together and perform a specific function are called organ systems. Organ systems work together and perform all the functions an organism needs to survive.

Living things grow, develop, and reproduce.

During their lifetimes, living things grow, or increase in size. For a unicellular organism, the size of its cell increases. For a multicellular organism, the number of its cells increases. Living things also develop, or change, during their lifetimes. For some organisms, it is easy to see the changes that happen as they grow and develop. As shown in **Figure 4,** ladybug larvae grow into pupae (PYEW pee; singular, pupa) before developing into adults.

Once an organism is an adult, it can reproduce and form new organisms. Unicellular organisms, such as bacteria, reproduce asexually when one cell divides and forms two new organisms. Some multicellular organisms also can reproduce asexually; one parent organism produces offspring when body cells replicate and divide. Sexual reproduction occurs when the reproductive cells of one or two parent organisms join and form a new organism. Multicellular organisms such as humans and other mammals reproduce sexually. Some organisms, such as yeasts, can reproduce both asexually and sexually.

Larva   Pupa

Figure 4 A ladybug grows and develops from a larva to a pupa.

Living things use energy.

All living things need energy to survive. Some organisms are able to convert light energy to chemical energy that is used for many cellular processes. *Organisms that convert energy from light or inorganic substances to usable energy are called* **autotrophs** (AW tuh trohfs).

Many autotrophs use energy from light and convert carbon dioxide and water into carbohydrates, or sugars. Autotrophs use the carbohydrates for energy. Plants and the algae shown growing on the pond in **Figure 5** are autotrophs.

Other autotrophs, called chemoautotrophs (kee moh AW tuh trohfs), grow on energy released by chemical reactions of inorganic substances such as sulfur and ammonia. Many chemoautotrophs are bacteria that live in extreme environments such as deep in the ocean or in hot sulfur springs.

Heterotrophs (HE tuh roh trohfs) *are organisms that obtain energy from other organisms.* Heterotrophs eat autotrophs or other heterotrophs to obtain energy. Animals and fungi are examples of heterotrophs.

Living things respond to stimuli.

All living things sense their environments. If an organism detects a change in its external environment, it will respond to that change. A change in an organism's environment is called a stimulus (STIHM yuh lus; plural, stimuli). Responding to a stimulus might help an organism protect itself. For example, the octopus in **Figure 6** responds to predators by releasing ink, a black liquid. In many organisms, nerve cells detect the environment, process the information, and coordinate a response.

Figure 5 Algae are autotrophic because they use sunlight to produce energy.

Predict

4. Highlight how autotrophs and heterotrophs obtain energy. Predict what might happen if autotrophs were not present in an ecosystem. Write your response in your interactive notebook.

Figure 6 An octopus responds to potential harm by secreting ink. The ink hides the octopus while it escapes.

Copyright © McGraw-Hill Education   (t)Turner Forte/Botanica/Getty Images, (b)Jeff Rotman/Peter Arnold/Getty Images

Describe how the basic characteristics of living things enable them to perform the life functions listed below. **TEKS** 6.12(D)

Function	Description
Grow	Unicellular organism: Multicellular organism:
Develop	Example:
Reproduce	Asexual reproduction: Sexual reproduction:
Use energy	Autotrophs: Heterotrophs:
Respond to stimuli	Example:

 Connect it! Think of an organism that you see each day. **Explain** how it performs the functions listed above. Write your response in your interactive notebook.

What do living things need?

You just read that all living things need energy in order to survive. Some organisms obtain energy from food. What else do living things need to survive? Living things also need water and a place to live. Organisms live in environments specific to their needs where they are protected, can obtain food and water, and can get shelter.

A Place to Live

Living things are everywhere. Organisms live in the soil, in lakes, and in caves. Some living things live on or in other organisms. For example, bacteria live in your intestines and on other body surfaces. *A specific environment where an organism lives is its* **habitat.** Most organisms can survive in only a few habitats. The land iguana shown in **Figure 7** lives in warm, tropical environments and would not survive in cold places such as the arctic.

Food and Water

Living things also need food and water. Food is used for energy. Water is essential for survival. Water is in all cells and helps them function. The type of food that an organism eats depends on the habitat in which it lives. Marine iguanas live near the ocean and eat algae. Land iguanas, such as the one in **Figure 7,** live in hot, dry areas and eat cactus fruits and leaves. The food is processed to obtain energy. Plants and some bacteria use energy from sunlight and produce chemical energy for use in cells.

Figure 7 This Galápagos land iguana is eating the fruit of a prickly pear cactus.

FOLDABLES

Make a vertical three-column chart book. Label it as shown. Use it to organize your notes about living things, their needs, and classification criteria.

| Definition of a Living Thing | Survival Requirements | Classification Criteria |

Word Origin

habitat
from Latin *habitare,* means "to live or dwell"

Identify

5. What are three things all organisms, including this land iguana, need to survive?

_____

_____

_____

_____

_____

How are living things classified?

TEKS 6.3(D); 6.12(C), (D)

You might have a notebook with different sections for notes from different classes. This organizes information and makes it easier to find. Scientists use a classification system to group organisms with similar traits. This makes it easier to organize organisms and to recall how they are similar and how they differ.

Naming and Classifying Living Things

Scientists name living things using a system called binomial nomenclature (bi NOH mee ul • NOH mun klay chur). **Binomial nomenclature** *is a naming system that gives each living thing a two-word scientific name.* More than 300 years ago a scientist named Carolus Linnaeus created the binomial nomenclature system. All scientific names are in Latin. As shown in **Table 1,** the scientific name for an Eastern chipmunk is *Tamias striatus.*

Linnaeus classified organisms based on their behavior and appearance. Today, the branch of science that classifies living things is called taxonomy. *A group of organisms is called a* **taxon** (plural, taxa). There are many taxa, as shown in **Table 1.** Recall that all living things share similar traits. However, not all living things are exactly the same.

Recognize

6. (Circle) the name of the scientist who created the binomial nomenclature system. Underline how this scientist classified organisms.

Table 1 All species, such as the Eastern chipmunk, have a unique scientific name.

Table 1	Classification of the Eastern Chipmunk	Go Online!
Taxonomic Group	**Number of Species**	**Examples**
Domain Eukarya	About 4–10 million	
Kingdom Animalia	About 2 million	
Phylum Chordata	About 50,000	
Class Mammalia	About 5,000	
Order Rodentia	About 2,300	
Family Sciuridae	299	
Genus *Tamias*	25	
Species *striatus*	1	

Tutor

Taxonomy Using taxonomy, scientists divide all living things on Earth into three groups called domains. Domains are divided into kingdoms, and then phyla (FI luh; singular, phylum), classes, orders, families, genera (singular, genus), and species. A species is all organisms that can mate with one another and produce offspring that can reproduce.

Scientific Names Each species has a unique two-word scientific name. The first word in a scientific name is the organism's genus (JEE nus), and the second word might describe a distinguishing characteristic of the organism. For example, the nine-banded armadillo, *Dasypus novemcinctus*, belongs to the genus *Dasypus*. The second word of its scientific name, *novemcinctus*, means "nine bands."

Classifying Organisms Linnaeus used similar physical traits to group organisms. Today, scientists also look for other similarities, such as cell type. You might recall that there are two types of cells. A prokaryotic cell does not have a nucleus or other membrane-bound structures. A eukaryotic cell has a nucleus and other membrane-bound structures that are not in a prokaryotic cell.

To classify organisms, scientists also look at cell number (unicellular or multicellular), how an organism obtains energy (autotroph or heterotroph), and how it reproduces (asexually or sexually).

Dichotomous Keys A dichotomous (di KAH tah mus) key is a tool used to identify an organism. Dichotomous keys contain descriptions of traits that are compared when classifying an organism. Dichotomous keys are organized in steps. Each step might ask a yes or a no question and have two answer choices. Which question is answered next depends on the answer to the previous question. Based on the features, a choice is made that best describes the organism.

Math Skills   Math TEKS 6.1(A), (B); 6.3(E); 6.4(E), (G)

Use Ratios

A ratio expresses the relationship between two or more things. Ratios can be written in three ways:

$$3 \text{ to } 5,\ 3{:}5,\ \text{or } \frac{3}{5}.$$

Reduce ratios to their simplest form. For example, of about 3 million species in the animal kingdom, about 50,000 are mammals. What is the ratio of mammals to animals?

Write the ratio as a fraction.

$$\frac{50{,}000}{3{,}000{,}000}$$

Reduce the fraction to the simplest form.

$$\frac{50{,}000}{3{,}000{,}000} = \frac{5}{300} = \frac{1}{60}$$

(or 1:60 or 1 to 60)

Practice

Of the 5,000 species of mammals, 250 species are carnivores—heterotrophs that eat only meat. What is the ratio of carnivores to mammals? Write the ratio in all three ways.

Check   Tutor

Go Online!

LAB Manager

MiniLAB: *Whose shoe is it?*
TEKS 6.1(A); 6.2(A), (C), (E); 6.12(D)

LAB: *How can living things be classified?*
TEKS 6.1(A); 6.2(A), (C), (E); 6.4(A), (B); 6.12(C), (D)

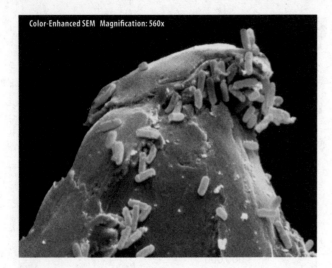

Color-Enhanced SEM Magnification: 560x

Figure 8 Bacteria are everywhere, even on surfaces that appear clean.

Figure 9 Archaea live in this geyser in Yellowstone National Park.

Figure 10 Although some algae are unicellular, these algae are multicellular.

Domains and Kingdoms

The three currently recognized domains are Bacteria, Archaea, and Eukarya. Domain Bacteria consists of Kingdom Bacteria, and Domain Archaea consists of Kingdom Archaea. Domain Eukarya consists of four kingdoms—Protista, Fungi, Plantae, and Animalia. Organisms are classified into kingdoms according to basic characteristics that they have in common.

Bacteria The organisms in Kingdom Bacteria, such as the bacteria in **Figure 8,** are unicellular prokaryotes. Because bacteria live in many different environments, they obtain food in various ways. Some are autotrophic. They use light energy or chemical energy and make food. Other bacteria are heterotrophic. They take in food and break it down to obtain energy. Bacteria reproduce asexually through a process called fission.

Archaea Like bacteria, archaea are unicellular prokaryotes. One key difference between bacteria and archaea is that archaea contain molecules in their cell walls that are not found in any other known organisms. Some archaea are autotrophic, and some are heterotrophic. Archaea often live in extreme environments, such as salt lakes, hot springs, or the geyser shown in **Figure 9.** Like bacteria, they reproduce asexually.

Protista All protists are eukaryotes. Some are unicellular, and some are multicellular. Members of the protist group share some characteristics with plants, animals, or fungi. Scientists classify protists as plantlike, animal-like, or funguslike based on which group they most resemble. Plantlike protists, such as the algae in **Figure 10,** make their own food. Animal-like and funguslike protists are heterotrophic and take in food. Most protists reproduce sexually. However, many can also reproduce asexually.

Fungi All fungi are eukaryotes, and most are multicellular. Only the fungi called yeasts are unicellular. Fungi are heterotrophs and cannot make their own food. Some fungi are parasites, obtaining nutrients from living organisms. Fungi dissolve their food by releasing chemicals that decompose organic matter. Fungi then absorb the nutrients.

Although fungi can reproduce sexually or asexually, almost all reproduce asexually by producing spores, as shown in **Figure 11.** Spores are small reproductive cells with a strong, protective covering. The spores can grow into new individuals.

Figure 11 A puffball mushroom releases a cloud of tiny spores. Each spore can grow into a new puffball fungus.

Plantae Plants are made of eukaryotic cells. They are multicellular. Plants are autotrophic and make their own food through a process called photosynthesis. Plants can reproduce asexually, sexually, or both ways. Plants can grow from spores or seeds. Plants that reproduce by spores often are called seedless plants. Most of the plants you see around you, such as pine trees, grasses, and bluebonnets, are seed plants. Some seed plants, such as the cactus in **Figure 12,** have flowers that produce fruit with one or more seeds. Others, such as pine trees, produce their seeds in cones.

Figure 12 The flowers of a prickly pear cactus produce fruits with many seeds.

Animalia All animals are multicellular eukaryotes. They are heterotrophs and get energy for their life processes by eating other organisms. Most animals reproduce sexually.

Animals can be grouped into two large categories: vertebrates (VUR tuh brayts) and invertebrates (ihn VUR tuh brayts). A vertebrate is an animal with a backbone. Fish, humans, and the Texas horned lizard shown in **Figure 13** are vertebrates. An invertebrate is an animal that does not have a backbone. Worms, spiders, snails, crayfish, and insects are examples of invertebrates. Invertebrates make up most of the animal kingdom—about 95 percent.

Figure 13 A backbone, or spine, is part of a vertebrate's internal skeleton.

Draw a graphic organizer to identify the basic characteristics of organisms that classify them in kingdoms. Include a brief description of each characteristic in your organizer. **TEKS** 6.12(D)

Summarize it!

Use Vocabulary

1. **Distinguish** between the terms *autotroph* and *heterotroph*.
   TEKS 6.12(D) *supporting*

   _____

   _____

   _____

Apply the Essential Questions

2. What is the smallest unit of all living things? **TEKS** 6.12(A)

   A. cell

   B. organ

   C. organelle

   D. tissue

3. **Identify** the broadest taxonomic classification of living organisms. Name the groupings within this taxonomic classification. **TEKS** 6.12(C)

   _____

   _____

   _____

   _____

 H.O.T. Questions (Higher Order Thinking)

4. **Evaluate** the contributions of Carolus Linnaeus to scientific thought.
   TEKS 6.3(D) *supporting*

   _____

   _____

   _____

   _____

5. **Infer** You are asked to classify an organism that is unicellular, makes its own food, reproduces asexually, and has membrane-bound cell structures. In which domain and kingdom would you place this organism? Explain.
   TEKS 6.12(C), (D) *supporting*

   _____

   _____

   _____

   _____

   _____

   _____

   _____

Math Skills | **Math** **TEKS** 6.1(A), (B); 6.3(E); 6.4(E), (G)

Use Ratios

6. Out of 300,000 plant species, 260,000 are flowering plants. What is the ratio of flowering plants to all plant species? Express the ratio in all three ways.

Check   Tutor

 Go Online! ✓ 💬

On a Quest for Leeches

How do you catch a leech? Let it bite you!

Mark Siddall travels the world searching for creatures that make most people cringe—leeches. He collects leeches to understand how they are related and how they evolved. This is a huge job since there are more than 600 known species of leeches!

Siddall is a scientist at the American Museum of Natural History. He travels to remote places, such as the jungles of Rwanda and the swamps of Argentina, to collect leeches. Once he's there, he lets the leeches find him. Barefoot, he treks through damp forests or wades in streams. Leeches attach to his skin, draw blood until they're full, and then fall off. That's when Mark adds them to the museum's collection.

Siddall identifies the leeches by their body parts. Some have jaws and teeth. Others have thin tubes for sucking in liquid. They use these parts to draw blood or fluids from animals, such as frogs, humans, snails, and other worms. Some even swallow their prey whole!

Through his research, Siddall is helping build a family tree for leeches to learn how they evolved. For example, leeches today live on land, in freshwater, and in the ocean. Siddall's research shows that leeches first appeared in freshwater and then moved onto land and into the ocean. Many species of leeches are being threatened by habitat destruction. Siddall hopes his research will help protect leeches and their habitats.

AMERICAN MUSEUM ᴼ NATURAL HISTORY

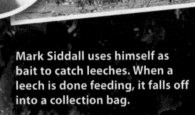

Mark Siddall uses himself as bait to catch leeches. When a leech is done feeding, it falls off into a collection bag.

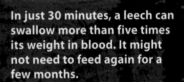

In just 30 minutes, a leech can swallow more than five times its weight in blood. It might not need to feed again for a few months.

It's Your Turn!

DIAGRAM Leeches are classified according to how they feed. Choose a jawed leech (*Hirudinidae*), a worm leech (*Erpobdellidae*), or a leech that uses a proboscis (*Glossiphoniidae*). Research how it feeds. Draw a diagram and present your findings.

INQUIRY

What lives here? Look at all the organisms in this picture. This coastal reef provides a place for many organisms to live. How do you think each of these organisms survives? How do you think they interact with each other and the environment?

Write your responses in your interactive notebook.

LAB Manager

Go to your Lab Manual or visit connectED.mcgraw-hill.com to perform the labs for this lesson.

MiniLAB: *How do you describe an ecosystem?*
TEKS 6.1(A); 6.2(A), (C), (E); 6.12(E), (F)

Skill Practice: *What can analyzing data reveal about predator-prey populations?*
TEKS 6.2(A), (E); 6.12(F)

LAB: *Design an Ecosystem*
TEKS 6.1(A); 6.2(A), (C), (E); 6.4(A), (B); 6.12(E), (F)

Explore Activity

TEKS 6.2(A), (C), (E); 6.12(E)

What is an environment?

Earth contains many different environments. What makes these environments different?

Procedure

1. Select a **postcard** from the ones provided. Look at the picture of the location on it.
2. Plan a vacation to that location. In your Lab Manual or interactive notebook, describe the clothing you will need to pack, and the types of activities you will participate in at the location.
3. On a separate sheet of paper, write a note to a friend describing the environment that you might visit on your vacation. Describe the living and nonliving things you might find.

Think About This

1. How is your vacation environment different from the one where you live?

2. Describe the types of organisms you will see in your vacation environment. How are these organisms suited to this environment? What organisms in your home environment are not suited to your vacation environment? Explain.

TEKS in this Lesson

6.12(E) Describe biotic and abiotic parts of an ecosystem in which organisms interact

6.12(F) Diagram the levels of organization within an ecosystem, including organism, population, community, and ecosystem.

Also covers Process Standards: 6.1(A); 6.2(A), (C), (E); 6.4(A), (B)

Essential Questions

- How can you describe an ecosystem?
- What are the similarities and differences between the abiotic and biotic parts of an ecosystem?
- What are the levels of organization within an ecosystem?

Vocabulary

ecosystem
abiotic factor
biotic factor
habitat
population
community

Figure 1 Ecosystems include the interactions among organisms and their environment.

What is an ecosystem? TEKS 6.12(E), (F)

Imagine that you visit a park. You sit on the grass in the warm sunshine. You watch a squirrel run down a tree trunk and chew an acorn. A robin pulls an earthworm from the soil. Traveling in a line, ants carry bits of dead insects to their underground nest. A breeze blows dandelion seeds through the air. These interactions are just a few of the many that can happen in an ecosystem, such as the park shown in **Figure 1.** *An* **ecosystem** *is all the living things and nonliving things in a given area.*

There are many kinds of ecosystems on Earth, including forests, deserts, grasslands, rivers, beaches, and coral reefs. Ecosystems that have similar climates and contain similar types of plants are grouped together into biomes. For example, the tropical rain forest biome includes ecosystems full of lush plant growth located near the equator in places where rainfall averages 200 cm per year and the temperature averages 25°C.

Characterize

1. Complete the graphic organizer at right to characterize ecosystems.

Ecosystems

Definition:

Examples:
- _____
- _____
- _____
- _____
- _____
- _____

When grouped together with others that have similar climates and plants, called

_____

Abiotic Factors

The nonliving parts of an ecosystem are called **abiotic factors.** They include sunlight, temperature, air, water, and soil. Abiotic factors provide many of the resources organisms need for survival and reproduction.

Sunlight and Temperature Sunlight is essential for almost all life on Earth. It supplies the energy for photosynthesis—the chemical reactions that produce sugars and occur in most plants and some bacteria and protists.

Sunlight also provides warmth. An ecosystem's temperature depends in part on the amount of sunlight it receives. In some ecosystems, such as the hot, dry desert shown in **Figure 2,** temperatures can be around 49°C during the day and below freezing at night.

Atmosphere The gases in Earth's atmosphere include nitrogen, oxygen, and carbon dioxide. Nitrogen is needed for plant growth. Some bacteria in the soil take nitrogen from the air and convert it to a form that plants can use. Oxygen is needed by most organisms for cellular respiration—the process that releases energy in cells. Air also contains carbon dioxide that is needed for photosynthesis.

Figure 2 Abiotic factors in an ecosystem determine what kinds of organisms can live there.

Desert life is limited to organisms that can survive with little water. Shade from plant life provides shelter from the heat of the Sun.

Stream life depends on a constant supply of water. Plants along stream banks provide shelter and food for hundreds of species.

Figure 3 Plant roots and soil-dwelling organisms need oxygen and water. Gophers, earthworms, and insects loosen the soil. This helps move air and water through soil.

LAB Manager

MiniLAB: *How do you describe an ecosystem?*
TEKS 6.1(A); 6.2(A), (C), (E); 6.12(E), (F)

Water Without water, life would not be possible. Water is required for all the life processes that take place inside cells, including cellular respiration, digestion, and photosynthesis. The stream ecosystem in **Figure 2** on the previous page can support many forms of life because water is plentiful. Areas with very little water support fewer organisms.

Soil If you ever have planted a garden, you might know about the importance of soil for healthy plants. Soil contains a mixture of living and nonliving things. The biotic part of soil is humus (HEW mus)—the decayed remains of plants, animals, bacteria, and other organisms. Deserts have thin soil with little humus. Forest soils usually are thick and fertile, with a higher humus content. Abiotic factors include minerals and particles of rock, sand, and clay. Many animals, including gophers, insects, and earthworms, such as those shown in **Figure 3,** make their homes in soil. Their tunnels help move water and air through the soil.

Biotic Factors

Living or once-living things in an ecosystem are called **biotic factors.** They include all living organisms—from the smallest bacterium (plural, bacteria) to the largest redwood tree. Biotic factors also include the remains of dead organisms, such as fallen leaves or decayed plant matter in soil.

Species are adapted to the abiotic and biotic factors of the ecosystems in which they live. Algae, fungi, and mosses live in moist ecosystems such as forests, ponds, and oceans. Many cactus species can survive in a desert because they have thick stems that can hold stored water. Gophers live in burrows underground. They have large front claws for digging and strong teeth for loosening soil and chewing plant roots.

Habitats TEKS 6.12(E), (F)

Every organism in an ecosystem has its own place to live. *A* **habitat** *is the place within an ecosystem that provides food, water, shelter, and other biotic and abiotic factors an organism needs to survive and reproduce.*

Organisms have a variety of habitats. For example, house martins such as the ones shown in **Figure 4** sometimes live in meadows or grasslands, but these birds have found a habitat under the eaves of a building. Crickets live in damp, dark places with plenty of plant material and fungi to eat. Skunks live in areas where they can find food such as mice, insects, eggs, and fruit. During the day, skunks take shelter near their food supply—in hollow logs, under brush piles, and underneath buildings.

Plants have their own habitats, too. You have read that cacti live in desert habitats. The wood sorrel is a plant species that grows in deep shade beneath trees.

When biotic or abiotic factors in an ecosystem change, habitats can change or disappear. A wildfire quickly can destroy the habitats of thousands of animals that live in forests or grasslands. Erosion or flooding can wash away soil, destroying plant habitats.

Figure 4 An organism's habitat provides shelter, food, and all the other resources it needs for survival.

FOLDABLES

Cut out the Lesson 11.3 Foldable in the back of the book. Use it to organize your notes about abiotic and biotic factors.

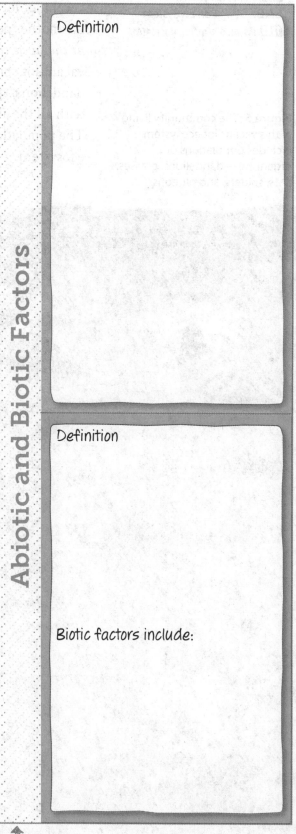

Abiotic and Biotic Factors

Definition

Definition

Biotic factors include:

Tape here

LAB Manager

Skill Practice: *What can analyzing data reveal about predator-prey populations?*

TEKS 6.2(A), (E); 6.12(F)

LAB: *Design an Ecosystem*

TEKS 6.1(A); 6.2(A), (C), (E); 6.4(A), (B); 6.12(E), (F)

Figure 5 The community living in this vacant-lot ecosystem includes populations of organisms—dandelions, grasses, ants, spiders, and pigeons.

Levels of Organization **TEKS** 6.12(E), (F)

An individual living thing is called an organism. *A* **population** *is all the organisms of the same species that live in the same area at the same time.* For example, all the dandelions growing in a vacant lot form a population. All the ants in the vacant lot make up another population. *All the populations living in the same area at the same time form a* **community.** As shown in **Figure 5,** a vacant-lot community might include populations of grasses, dandelions, spiders, ants, and pigeons. A community combined with all the abiotic factors in the same area forms an ecosystem. The populations that make up the community interact in the ecosystem.

Copyright © McGraw-Hill Education

Summarize it!

Diagram the levels of organization within an ecosystem that is familiar to you. To organize this diagram, draw a large triangle and use horizontal lines to divide it into four levels. Draw and label an organism from your ecosystem in the top level of the triangle. Fill in the other levels and illustrate them with appropriate biotic and abiotic examples from your ecosystem. **TEKS** 6.12(F)

Connect it! **Describe** the abiotic and biotic parts of the ecosystem you diagrammed above. Write your response in your interactive notebook. **TEKS** 6.12(E)

Ecosystems

Use Vocabulary

1. **Define** *biotic* in your own words.
   TEKS 6.12(E)

   _____

   _____

Apply the Essential Questions

2. **Describe** an ecosystem. **TEKS** 6.12(F)

   _____

   _____

   _____

3. **Explain** why soil is considered both
   an abiotic and a biotic factor.
   TEKS 6.12(E)

   _____

   _____

   _____

4. **Describe** the levels of organization within
   an ecosystem. **TEKS** 6.12(E)

   _____

   _____

   _____

   _____

   _____

H.O.T. Questions (Higher Order Thinking)

5. **Predict** how a squirrel population would
   be affected if a pine forest that had been
   cut down grew again. **TEKS** 6.12(E)

   _____

   _____

   _____

   _____

   _____

   _____

   _____

6. **Assess** Describe the ways in which the
   size of a fish population in an aquarium
   could be reduced by changes in the abiotic
   factors in its habitat. **TEKS** 6.12(E)

   _____

   _____

   _____

   _____

   _____

   _____

   _____

TEKS 6.12(E)

Abiotic Factors, Biotic Factors, and... BATS?

Now that you've learned about abiotic and biotic factors in an ecosystem, so what? Why do you need to know how living and nonliving things affect the ecosystems around you? Because you care about bats. That's right—bats!

There are approximately 1.3 million people living in San Antonio, Texas. However, there's a much larger population living in San Antonio—20 million bats! Bracken Cave near San Antonio houses the world's largest population of Mexican free-tailed bats (*Tadarida brasiliensis*).

Texas is also home to the largest urban population of bats in the world. Approximately 1.5 million Mexican free-tailed bats roost under the Ann W. Richards Congress Avenue Bridge in Austin, Texas. Both bat colonies spend March through October in Texas, and then migrate to Mexico for the winter.

Like all organisms, Mexican free-tailed bats require a place to live, water, and food to survive. Bracken Cave and the crevices under the Congress Avenue Bridge provide ideal living spaces for the bats. Both locations are near or over water, and water attracts insects. Mexican free-tailed bats can eat their body weight in insects every day. That means the 20 million bats living in Bracken Cave could eat 265 tons of insects every day!

With so many bats living in such small areas, a change in abiotic or biotic factors can affect the size of the bat populations.

Mexican free-tailed bat

So **WHAT?!**

Because bats eat insects that destroy crops and mosquitoes that can carry diseases, decreases in bat populations can result in the destruction of farm crops and more infections from mosquito-borne diseases.

THAT'S what!!

Test-Taking Strategy

Eliminate Choices When you are not sure about an answer, eliminate as many incorrect choices as possible. Then choose from the remaining choices.

Example

Use the table below to answer question 1.

Kingdom	Prokaryotic or Eukaryotic?	Unicellular or Multicellular?	Autotrophic or Heterotrophic?	Mode of Reproduction?
Bacteria	Prokaryotic	Unicellular	Either	Asexual
Archaea	Prokaryotic	Unicellular	Either	Asexual
Protista	Eukaryotic	Either	Either	Either
Fungi	Eukaryotic	Either	Heterotrophic	Either
Plantae	Eukaryotic	Multicellular	Autotrophic	Either or Both
Animalia				

1 Which sequence correctly completes the table to identify the characteristics of members of Kingdom Animalia? **TEKS** 6.12(D) *supporting*

A Eukaryotic, Multicellular, Heterotrophic, Asexual

B Eukaryotic, Unicellular, Heterotrophic, Sexual

C Eukaryotic, Multicellular, Autotrophic, Mostly Sexual

D Eukaryotic, Multicellular, Heterotrophic, Mostly Sexual

TIP: Trust your instincts! If you think that an answer is correct, it probably is. Do not go back and change answers unless you know that they are incorrect.

1 Read the answer choices. Cross off choices that you know are incorrect. You know that not all animals reproduce asexually. You also know that animals are not unicellular. Choices A and B are incorrect.

2 Make your best guess among the remaining choices. Use what you know to reason. For example, you know that the characteristics of animals are different from plants. You guess that choice D is correct, and it is! Heterotrophic means that animals must get their energy from other organisms.

Multiple Choice

1 A model of a eukaryotic cell is shown below. Which structures of the cell distinguish it from that of a prokaryotic cell? **TEKS** 6.12(B); 6.3(B)

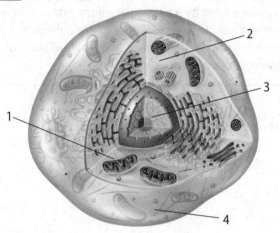

A 1 and 2

B 1 and 3

C 3 and 4

D 2 and 4

2 The illustration shows a thriving, interacting pond ecosystem. Which describes the abiotic factors in the pond environment? **TEKS** 6.12(E)

A ducks, frog, cattails, reeds, trees

B ducks, frog, cattails, soil, trees

C rocks, water, sunlight, air, reeds

D rocks, water, sunlight, air, soil

3

> *Euglena* is a genus of single-celled organisms. It is classified in one of the three domains and six kingdoms. A *Euglena* contains chloroplasts. It also has DNA contained in a nucleus. The organism moves itself by a single flagellum. Some species of *Euglena* have stiff cellulose walls. Others have a flexible covering called a pellicle. A *Euglena* can absorb food through its cell membrane and reproduces asexually.

In which domain and kingdom can *Euglena* be classified? **TEKS** 6.12(C); 6.3(A)

  A Archaea/Archaea

  B Bacteria/Bacteria

  C Eukarya/Animalia

  D Eukarya/Protista

---

4 The illustration below shows some of the interacting components of a desert. Which statement best describes this desert environment? **TEKS** 6.12(F)

  A The desert animals and cactus plants form a community.

  B The desert animals and cactus plants form an ecosystem.

  C The hares, cactus, snake, and lizard form a biome.

  D The hares, cactus, snake, and lizard form a population.

5

Three German scientists in the 1800s discovered much of what we now know about cells. Matthias Schleiden found that all plants are made of cells. Later, Theodor Schwann found that all animals are made of cells. A few years later, Rudolf Virchow stated that all cells come from other cells. Other scientists, working hundreds of years before these men, helped invent an instrument without which cells might never have been seen. Janssen, Hooke, and Leeuwenhoek worked to improve each other's version of the microscope. Leeuwenhoek's microscope could make images of objects look up to 266 times bigger.

Students are given a collection of objects. They have to use a microscope to determine which objects were once living and which are nonliving. How will they determine which objects were once living? **TEKS** 6.12(A); 6.3(D)

A Once-living objects will contain cells.

B Once-living objects will move.

C Once-living objects will be brown.

D Once-living objects will be larger than nonliving objects.

6 If a living organism contains a cell of this type, which identifies the basic characteristics of the organism? **TEKS** 6.12(D) *supporting;* 6.3(A)

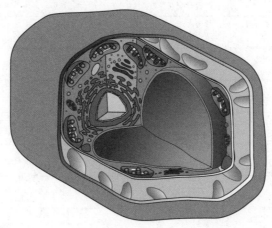

A autotrophic, eukaryotic

B autotrophic, prokaryotic

C heterotrophic, eukaryotic

D heterotrophic, prokaryotic

PERIODIC TABLE OF THE ELEMENTS

Element —— Hydrogen
Atomic number —— 1
Symbol —— **H**
Atomic mass —— 1.01

State of matter

- 🎈 Gas
- 💧 Liquid
- ▢ Solid
- ⊙ Synthetic

A column in the periodic table is called a **group.**

A row in the periodic table is called a **period.**

1

	1	2	3	4	5	6	7	8	9
1	Hydrogen 1 **H** 1.01								
2	Lithium 3 **Li** 6.94	Beryllium 4 **Be** 9.01							
3	Sodium 11 **Na** 22.99	Magnesium 12 **Mg** 24.31							
4	Potassium 19 **K** 39.10	Calcium 20 **Ca** 40.08	Scandium 21 **Sc** 44.96	Titanium 22 **Ti** 47.87	Vanadium 23 **V** 50.94	Chromium 24 **Cr** 52.00	Manganese 25 **Mn** 54.94	Iron 26 **Fe** 55.85	Cobalt 27 **Co** 58.93
5	Rubidium 37 **Rb** 85.47	Strontium 38 **Sr** 87.62	Yttrium 39 **Y** 88.91	Zirconium 40 **Zr** 91.22	Niobium 41 **Nb** 92.91	Molybdenum 42 **Mo** 95.96	Technetium 43 **Tc** (98)	Ruthenium 44 **Ru** 101.07	Rhodium 45 **Rh** 102.91
6	Cesium 55 **Cs** 132.91	Barium 56 **Ba** 137.33	Lanthanum 57 **La** 138.91	Hafnium 72 **Hf** 178.49	Tantalum 73 **Ta** 180.95	Tungsten 74 **W** 183.84	Rhenium 75 **Re** 186.21	Osmium 76 **Os** 190.23	Iridium 77 **Ir** 192.22
7	Francium 87 **Fr** (223)	Radium 88 **Ra** (226)	Actinium 89 **Ac** (227)	Rutherfordium 104 **Rf** (267)	Dubnium 105 **Db** (268)	Seaborgium 106 **Sg** (271)	Bohrium 107 **Bh** (272)	Hassium 108 **Hs** (270)	Meitnerium 109 **Mt** (276)

The number in parentheses is the mass number of the longest lived isotope for that element.

Lanthanide series	Cerium 58 **Ce** 140.12	Praseodymium 59 **Pr** 140.91	Neodymium 60 **Nd** 144.24	Promethium 61 **Pm** (145)	Samarium 62 **Sm** 150.36	Europium 63 **Eu** 151.96
Actinide series	Thorium 90 **Th** 232.04	Protactinium 91 **Pa** 231.04	Uranium 92 **U** 238.03	Neptunium 93 **Np** (237)	Plutonium 94 **Pu** (244)	Americium 95 **Am** (243)

Metal

Metalloid

Nonmetal

Recently discovered

18

Helium
2
He
4.00

13 **14** **15** **16** **17**

Boron	Carbon	Nitrogen	Oxygen	Fluorine	Neon
5	6	7	8	9	10
B	C	N	O	F	Ne
10.81	12.01	14.01	16.00	19.00	20.18

Aluminum	Silicon	Phosphorus	Sulfur	Chlorine	Argon
13	14	15	16	17	18
Al	Si	P	S	Cl	Ar
26.98	28.09	30.97	32.07	35.45	39.95

10 **11** **12**

Nickel	Copper	Zinc	Gallium	Germanium	Arsenic	Selenium	Bromine	Krypton
28	29	30	31	32	33	34	35	36
Ni	Cu	Zn	Ga	Ge	As	Se	Br	Kr
58.69	63.55	65.38	69.72	72.64	74.92	78.96	79.90	83.80

Palladium	Silver	Cadmium	Indium	Tin	Antimony	Tellurium	Iodine	Xenon
46	47	48	49	50	51	52	53	54
Pd	Ag	Cd	In	Sn	Sb	Te	I	Xe
106.42	107.87	112.41	114.82	118.71	121.76	127.60	126.90	131.29

Platinum	Gold	Mercury	Thallium	Lead	Bismuth	Polonium	Astatine	Radon
78	79	80	81	82	83	84	85	86
Pt	Au	Hg	Tl	Pb	Bi	Po	At	Rn
195.08	196.97	200.59	204.38	207.20	208.98	(209)	(210)	(222)

Darmstadtium	Roentgenium	Copernicium	Ununtrium	Flerovium	Ununpentium	Livermorium		Ununoctium
110	111	112	* 113	114	* 115	116		* 118
Ds	Rg	Cn	Uut	Fl	Uup	Lv		Uuo
(281)	(280)	(285)	(284)	(289)	(288)	(293)		(294)

* The names and symbols for elements 113, 115, and 118 are temporary. Final names will be selected when the elements' discoveries are verified.

Gadolinium	Terbium	Dysprosium	Holmium	Erbium	Thulium	Ytterbium	Lutetium
64	65	66	67	68	69	70	71
Gd	Tb	Dy	Ho	Er	Tm	Yb	Lu
157.25	158.93	162.50	164.93	167.26	168.93	173.05	174.97

Curium	Berkelium	Californium	Einsteinium	Fermium	Mendelevium	Nobelium	Lawrencium
96	97	98	99	100	101	102	103
Cm	Bk	Cf	Es	Fm	Md	No	Lr
(247)	(247)	(251)	(252)	(257)	(258)	(259)	(262)

Reference

Notebook Foldables

What are they and how do I create them?

Foldables are three-dimensional graphic organizers that help you create study guides for each lesson in your book.

Step 1 Go to the back of your book to find the Notebook Foldable for the lesson you are currently studying. Follow the cutting and assembly instructions at the top of the page.

Step 2 Find the Notebook Foldable page in the lesson. Match up the tabs and attach your Notebook Foldable to this page. Dotted tabs show where to place it on the page. Striped tabs indicate where to tape the Notebook Foldable.

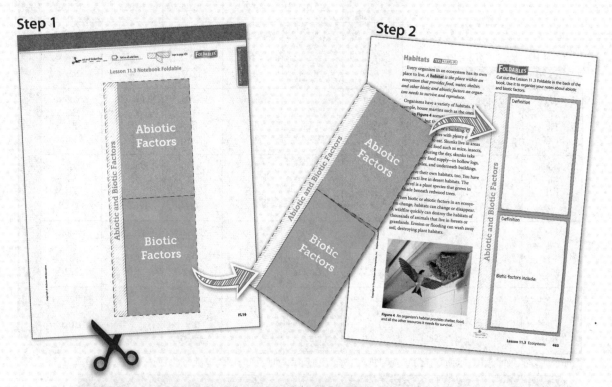

How do I complete my Notebook Foldable?

Each lesson's Notebook Foldable will be different. As you study the lesson, fill out the Notebook Foldable. Use it as a study guide as you learn the lesson material.

Meet Foldables Author Dinah Zike

Dinah Zike is known for designing hands-on manipulatives that are used nationally and internationally by teachers and parents. Dinah is an explosion of energy and ideas. Her excitement and joy for learning inspires everyone she touches.

Lesson 1.1 Notebook Foldable

Scientific Inquiry

Questions

Hypothesize and Predict

Test Hypothesis

Analyze Results

Draw Conclusions

Communicate Results

cut on all dashed lines   fold on all solid lines   tape to page 15   FOLDABLES

Lesson 1.1 Notebook Foldable

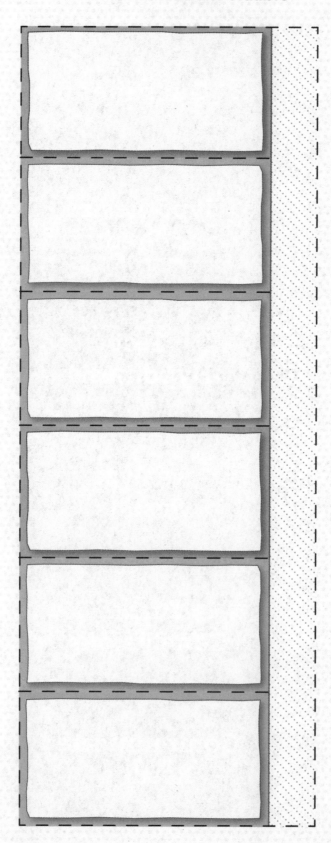

Lesson 2.1 Notebook Foldable

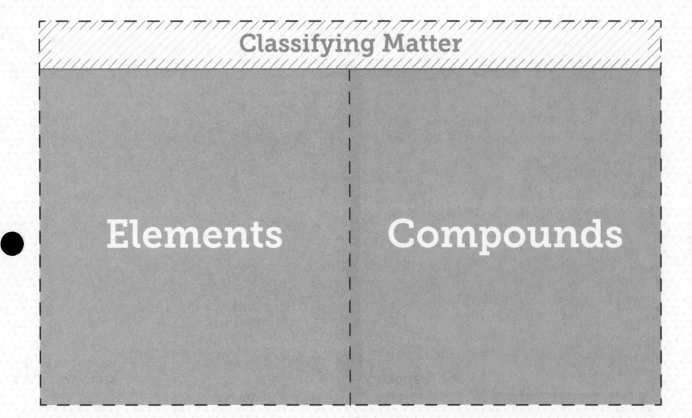

Classifying Matter

Elements | Compounds

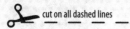 cut on all dashed lines   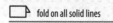 fold on all solid lines    tape to page 47   **FOLDABLES**

Lesson 2.1 Notebook Foldable

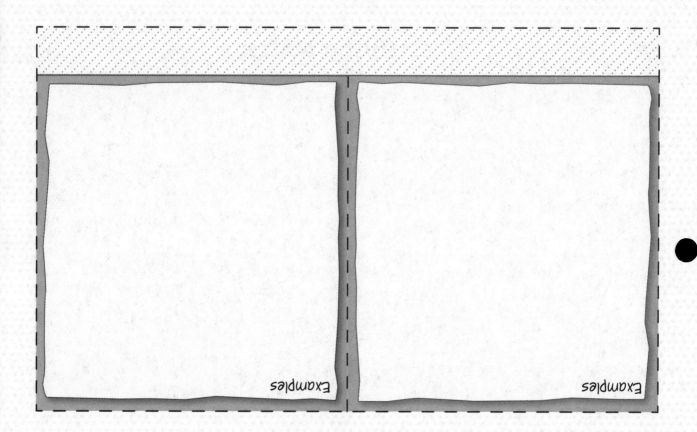

Examples

Examples

Lesson 3.3 Notebook Foldable

Nonmetals and Metalloids

Nonmetals

Metalloids

Lesson 3.3 Notebook Foldable

Uses

Uses

Lesson 4.1 Notebook Foldable

Energy Resources

Fossil Fuels

both

Nuclear Energy

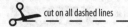 cut on all dashed lines 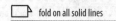 fold on all solid lines 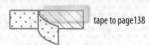 tape to page138

Lesson 4.1 Notebook Foldable

Write About It

Write About It

Write About It

Lesson 5.3 Notebook Foldable

Forces

contact	non-contact
balanced	unbalanced

Forces

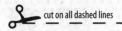 cut on all dashed lines 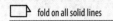 fold on all solid lines  tape to page 188 **FOLDABLES**

Lesson 5.3 Notebook Foldable

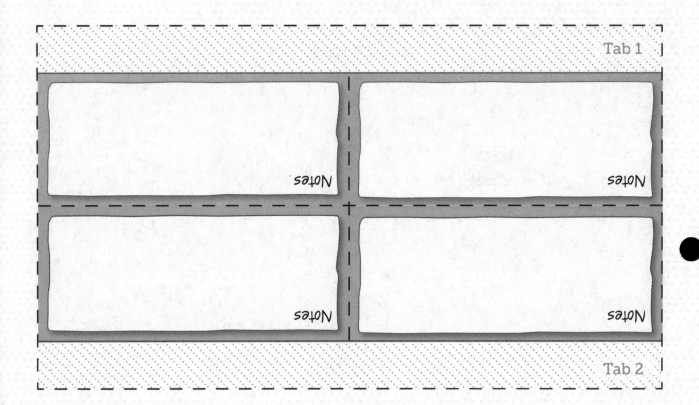

Tab 1

Notes

Notes

Notes

Notes

Tab 2

Lesson 6.2 Notebook Foldable

Type of Energy Transfer

| Conduction |
| Convection |
| Radiation |

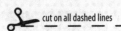 cut on all dashed lines   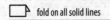 fold on all solid lines   tape to page 239   FOLDABLES®

Lesson 6.2 Notebook Foldable

Examples

Examples

Examples

Foldables® Library

Lesson 7.2 Notebook Foldable

Earth's Layers

Crust	Mantle
Outer Core	Inner Core

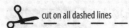 cut on all dashed lines   fold on all solid lines   tape to page 278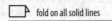

Lesson 7.2 Notebook Foldable

Write About It

Write About It

Write About It

Write About It

Tab 2

Tab 1

Lesson 8.2 Notebook Foldable

Types of Igneous Rocks

Extrusive	Intrusive

 cut on all dashed lines 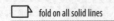 fold on all solid lines tape to page 315   FOLDABLES®

Lesson 8.2 Notebook Foldable

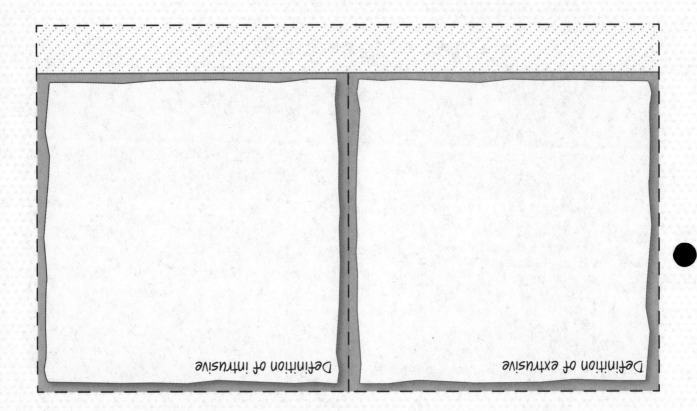

Definition of intrusive

Definition of extrusive

Lesson 9.3 Notebook Foldable

The Outer Planets

Jupiter

Saturn

Uranus

Neptune

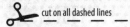 cut on all dashed lines   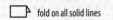 fold on all solid lines    tape to page 378   **FOLDABLES**

Lesson 9.3 Notebook Foldable

Composition and Location

Composition and Location

Composition and Location

Composition and Location

Lesson 10.2 Notebook Foldable

Compare and Contrast Space Missions

Space Missions to Inner Planets

both

Space Missions to Outer Planets

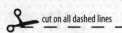 cut on all dashed lines   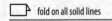 fold on all solid lines   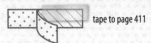 tape to page 411

Lesson 10.2 Notebook Foldable

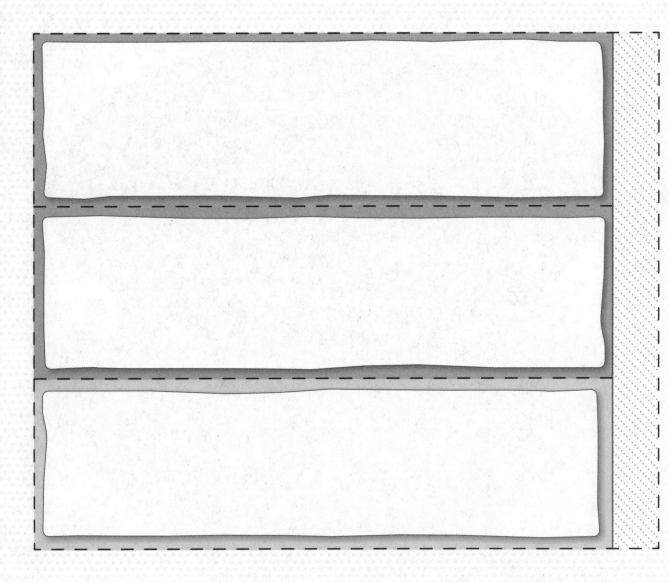

Lesson 11.3 Notebook Foldable

Abiotic and Biotic Factors

Abiotic Factors

Biotic Factors

 cut on all dashed lines   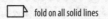 fold on all solid lines   tape to page 463   FOLDABLES®

Lesson 11.3 Notebook Foldable

Sunlight - Needed for:

Temperature - Needed for:

Air - Needed for:

Water - Needed for:

Soil - Needed for:

Examples

g **Multilingual Glossary**

A science multilingual glossary is available on the science website. The glossary includes the following languages.

Arabic	Hmong	Tagalog
Bengali	Korean	Urdu
Chinese	Portuguese	Vietnamese
English	Russian	
Haitian Creole	Spanish	

Cómo usar el glosario en español:
1. Busca el término en inglés que desees encontrar.
2. El término en español, junto con la definición, se encuentran en la columna de la derecha.

Pronunciation Key

Use the following key to help you sound out words in the glossary.

a	back (BAK)		**ew**	food (FEWD)
ay	day (DAY)		**yoo**	pure (PYOOR)
ah	father (FAH thur)		**yew**	few (FYEW)
ow	flower (FLOW ur)		**uh**	comma (CAH muh)
ar	car (CAR)		**u (+ con)**	rub (RUB)
e	less (LES)		**sh**	shelf (SHELF)
ee	leaf (LEEF)		**ch**	nature (NAY chur)
ih	trip (TRIHP)		**g**	gift (GIHFT)
i (i + com + e)	idea (i DEE uh)		**j**	gem (JEM)
oh	go (GOH)		**ing**	sing (SING)
aw	soft (SAWFT)		**zh**	vision (VIH zhun)
or	orbit (OR buht)		**k**	cake (KAYK)
oy	coin (COYN)		**s**	seed, cent (SEED)
oo	foot (FOOT)		**z**	zone, raise (ZOHN)

English Español

English

abiotic factor/asthenosphere

abiotic factor (ay bi AH tihk • FAK tuhr): a nonliving thing in an ecosystem (p. 461)

acceleration: a measure of the change in velocity during a period of time (p. 170)

air resistance: the frictional force between air and objects moving through it (p. 191)

alkali (AL kuh li) **metal**: an element in group 1 on the periodic table. (p. 105)

alkaline (AL kuh lun) **earth metal**: an element in group 2 on the periodic table. (p. 105)

asteroid: a small, rocky object that orbits the Sun (p. 353)

asthenosphere (as THE nuh sfir): the partially melted portion of the mantle below the lithosphere (p. 274)

Español

factor abiótico/astenosfera

factor abiótico: componente no vivo de un ecosistema. (pág. 461)

aceleración: medida del cambio de velocidad durante un periodo de tiempo. (pág. 170)

resistencia al aire: fuerza de fricción entre el aire y los objetos que se mueven a través de él. (pág. 191)

metal alcalino: elemento del grupo 1 de la tabla periódica. (pág. 105)

metal alcalinotérreo: elemento del grupo 2 de la tabla periódica. (pág. 105)

asteroide: objeto pequeño y rocoso que orbita el Sol. (pág. 353)

astenosfera: porción parcialmente fundida del manto debajo de la litosfera. (pág. 274)

astrobiology: the study of the origin, development, distribution, and future of life on Earth and in the universe (p. 415)

astronomical unit: the average distance from Earth to the Sun—about 150 million km. (p. 354)

atom: a small particle that is the building block of matter. (p. 42)

autotroph(AW tuh trohf): an organism that converts light energy to usable energy (p. 447)

astrobiología: estudio del origen, desarrollo, distribución y futuro de la vida en la Tierra y en el universo. (pág. 415)

unidad astronómica: distancia media entre la Tierra y el Sol, aproximadamente 150 millones de km. (pág. 354)

átomo: partícula pequeña que es el componente básico de la materia. (pág. 42)

autotrófo: organismo que convierte la energía lumínica en energía útil. (pág. 447)

B

binomial nomenclature (bi NOH mee ul • NOH mun klay chur): a naming system that gives each organism a two-word scientific name. (p. 450)

biochemical rock: sedimentary rock that was formed by organisms or contains the remains of organisms. (p. 327)

biomass energy: energy produced by burning organic matter, such as wood, food scraps, and alcohol (p. 146)

biotic factor (bi AH tihk • FAK tuhr): a living or once-living thing in an ecosystem (p. 462)

nomenclatura binomial: sistema de nombrar que le da a cada organismo un nombre científico de dos palabras. (pág. 450)

roca bioquímica: roca sedimentaria formada por organismos o que contiene restos de organismos. (pág. 327)

energía de biomasa: energía producida por la combustión de materia orgánica, como la madera, las sobras de comida y el alcohol. (pág. 146)

factor biótico: ser vivo o que una vez estuvo vivo en un ecosistema. (pág. 462)

C

cementation: a process in which minerals dissolved in water crystallize between sediment grains. (p. 324)

chemical change: a change in matter in which the substances that make up the matter change into other substances with different chemical and physical properties. (p. 67)

chemical property: the ability or inability of a substance to combine with or change into one or more new substances (p. 91)

chemical rock: sedimentary rock that forms when minerals crystallize directly from water. (p. 326)

clast: a broken piece or fragment that makes up a clastic rock. (p. 325)

clastic (KLAH stik) rock: sedimentary rock that is made up of broken pieces of minerals and rock fragments. (p. 325)

comet: a small, rocky and icy object that orbits the Sun (p. 353)

community: all the populations living in an ecosystem at the same time (p. 464)

cementación: proceso por el cual los minerales disueltos en agua se cristalizan entre granos de sedimento. (pág. 324)

propiedad química: capacidad o incapacidad de una sustancia para combinarse con una o más sustancias o transformarse en una o más sustancias. (pág. 67)

propiedad química: capacidad o incapacidad de una sustancia para combinarse con una o más sustancias o transformarse en una o más sustancias. (pág. 91)

roca química: roca sedimentaria que se forma cuando los minerales se cristalizan directamente del agua. (pág. 326)

clasto: pedazo partido o fragmentado que forma una roca clástica. (pág. 325)

roca clástica: roca sedimentaria formada por pedazos partidos de minerales y fragmentos de rocas. (pág. 325)

cometa: objeto pequeño, rocoso y helado que orbita el Sol. (pág. 353)

comunidad: todas las poblaciones que viven en un ecosistema al mismo tiempo. (pág. 464)

compaction: a process in which the weight from the layers of sediment forces out fluids and decreases the space between sediment grains. (p. 324)

compound: a substance made of two or more elements that are chemically joined in a specific combination. (p. 45)

conduction (kuhn DUK shun): the transfer of thermal energy by collisions between particles of matter. (p. 240)

contact force: a push or a pull on one object by another object that is touching it (p. 188)

contact metamorphism: formation of a metamorphic rock caused by magma coming into contact with existing rock. (p. 337)

convection: the transfer of thermal energy by the movement of particles from one part of a material to another (p. 240)

convection: the circulation of material caused by differences in temperature and density. (p. 290)

convergent plate boundary: the boundary between two plates that move toward each other (p. 286)

core: the dense, metallic center of Earth (p. 276)

critical thinking: comparing what you already know with the information you are given in order to decide whether you agree with it. (p. 14)

crust: the brittle, rocky outer layer of Earth (p. 273)

cytoplasm: the liquid part of a cell inside the cell membrane; contains salts and other molecules (p. 436)

compactación: proceso por el cual el peso de las capas de sedimento extrae los fluidos y reduce el espacio entre los granos de sedimento. (pág. 324)

compuesto: sustancia que contiene átomos de dos o más elementos diferentes unidos químicamente. (pág. 45)

conducción: transferencia de energía térmica debido a colisiones entre partículas. (pág. 240)

fuerza de contacto: empuje o arrastre ejercido sobre un objeto por otro que lo está tocando. (pág. 188)

metamorfismo de contacto: formación de roca metamórfica causada por el contacto del magma con la roca existente. (pág. 337)

convección: transferencia de energía térmica por el movimiento de partículas de una parte de la materia a otra. (pág. 240)

convección: circulación de partículas en el interior de un material causada por diferencias en la energía térmica y la densidad. (pág. 290)

límite convergente de placas: límite entre dos placas que se acercan una hacia la otra. (pág. 286)

núcleo: centro de la Tierra denso y metálico. (pág. 276)

pensamiento crítico: comparación que se hace cuando se sabe algo acerca de información nueva, y se decide si se está o no de acuerdo con ella. (pág. 14)

corteza: capa frágil y rocosa superficial de la Tierra. (pág. 273)

citoplasma: fluido en el interior de una célula que contiene sales y otras moléculas. (pág. 436)

density: the mass per unit volume of a substance (pp. 89, 264)

dependent variable: the factor a scientist observes or measures during an experiment. (p. 23)

displacement: the difference between the initial, or starting, position and the final position of an object that has moved (p. 165)

distance-time graph: a graph that shows how distance and time are related (p. 176)

divergent plate boundary: the boundary between two plates that move away from each other (p. 286)

ductility (duk TIH luh tee): the ability to be pulled into thin wires. (p. 104)

densidad: cantidad de masa por unidad de volumen de una sustancia. (pág. 89, 264)

variable dependiente: factor que el científico observa o mide durante un experimento. (pág. 23)

desplazamiento: diferencia entre la posición inicial, o salida, y la final de un objeto que se ha movido. (pág. 165)

gráfico distancia-tiempo: gráfico que muestra cómo se relacionan la distancia y el tiempo. (pág. 176)

límite divergente de placas: límite entre dos placas que se alejan una de la otra. (pág. 286)

ductilidad: capacidad para formar alambres delgados (pág. 104)

E

ecosystem: all the living things and nonliving things in a given area (p. 460)

electric energy: energy carried by an electric current (p. 211)

element: a pure substance made of only one kind of atom (p. 44)

energy: the ability to cause change (p. 206)

eukaryotic (yew ker ee AH tihk)cell: a cell that has a nucleus and other membrane-bound organelles (p. 433)

extraterrestrial life: life that originates outside Earth (p. 415)

extrusive rock: igneous rock that forms when volcanic material erupts, cools, and crystallizes on Earth's surface (p. 315)

ecosistema: todos los seres vivos y los componentes no vivos de un área dada. (pág. 460)

energía eléctrica: energía transportada por una corriente eléctrica. (pág. 211)

elemento: sustancia que consiste de un sólo tipo de átomo. (pág. 44)

energía: capacidad de causar cambio. (pág. 206)

célula eucariótica: célula que tiene un núcleo y otros organelos limitados por una membrana. (pág. 433)

vida extraterrestre: vida que se origina fuera de la Tierra. (pág. 415)

roca extrusiva: roca ígnea que se forma cuando el material volcánico sale, se enfría y se cristaliza en la superficie de la Tierra. (pág. 315)

F

foliated rock: rock that contains parallel layers of flat and elongated minerals (p. 336)

force: a push or a pull on an object (p. 188)

friction: a contact force that resists the sliding motion of two surfaces that are touching (pp. 191, 228)

roca foliada: roca que contiene capas paralelas de minerales planos y alargados. (pág. 336)

fuerza: empuje o arrastre ejercido sobre un objeto. (pág. 188)

fricción: fuerza de contacto que resiste el movimiento de dos superficies que están en contacto. (pág. 191, 228)

G

Galilean moons: the four largest of Jupiter's 63 moons discovered by Galileo (p. 375)

gas: matter that has no definite volume and no definite shape (p. 85)

geosphere: the solid part of Earth (p. 261)

geothermal energy: thermal energy from Earth's interior (p. 146)

grain: an individual particle in a rock (p. 304)

gravity: an attractive force that exists between all objects that have mass (pp. 189, 262)

greenhouse effect: the natural process that occurs when certain gases in the atmosphere absorb and reradiate thermal energy from the Sun (p. 364)

lunas de Galileo: las cuatro lunas más grandes de las 63 lunas de Júpiter; descubiertas por Galileo. (pág. 375)

gas: materia que no tiene volumen ni forma definidos. (pág. 85)

geosfera: parte sólida de la Tierra. (pág. 261)

energía geotérmica: energía térmica del interior de la Tierra. (pág. 146)

grano: partícula individual de una roca. (pág. 304)

gravedad: fuerza de atracción que existe entre todos los objetos que tienen masa. (pág. 189, 262)

efecto invernadero: proceso natural que ocurre cuando ciertos gases en la atmósfera absorben y vuelven a irradiar la energía térmica del Sol. (pág. 364)

H

habitat: the place within an ecosystem where an organism lives; provides the biotic and abiotic factors an organism needs to survive and reproduce (pp. 449, 463)

halogen (HA luh jun): an element in group 17 on the periodic table (p. 116)

heat: the movement of thermal energy from a region of higher temperature to a region of lower temperature (p. 239)

heterogeneous mixture: a mixture in which the substances are not evenly mixed (p. 52)

heterotroph (HE tuh roh trohf): an organism that obtains energy from other organisms (p. 447)

homogeneous mixture: a mixture in which two or more substances are evenly mixed, but not bonded together (p. 53)

hydroelectric power: electricity produced by flowing water (p. 145)

hypothesis: a possible explanation for an observation that can be tested by scientific investigations (p. 10)

hábitat: lugar en un ecosistema donde vive un organismo; proporciona los factores bióticos y abióticos de un organismo necesita para sobrevivir y reproducirse. (pág. 449, 463)

halógeno: elemento del grupo 17 de la tabla periódica. (pág. 116)

calor: movimiento de energía térmica desde una región de alta temperatura a una región de baja temperatura. (pág. 239)

mezcla heterogénea: mezcla en la cual las sustancias no están mezcladas de manera uniforme. (pág. 52)

heterótrofo: organismo que obtiene energía de otros organismos. (pág. 447)

mezcla homogénea: mezcla en la cual dos o más sustancias están mezcladas de manera uniforme, pero no están unidas químicamente. (pág. 53)

energía hidroeléctrica: electricidad producida por agua que fluye. (pág. 145)

hipótesis: explicación posible de una observación que se puede probar por medio de investigaciones científicas. (pág. 10)

 **I**

impact crater: a round depression formed on the surface of a planet, moon, or other space object by the impact of a meteorite (p. 387)

independent variable: the factor that you want to test; It is changed by the investigator to observe how it affects a dependent variable (p. 23)

inference: a logical explanation of an observation that is drawn from prior knowledge or experience (p. 10)

intrusive rock: igneous rocks that form as magma cools underground (p. 316)

cráter de impacto: depresión redonda formada en la superficie de un planeta, luna u otro objeto espacial debido al impacto de un meteorito. (pág. 387)

variable independiente: factor que el investigador cambia para observar cómo afecta la variable dependiente. (pág. 23)

inferencia: explicación lógica de una observación que se extrae de un conocimiento previo o experiencia. (pág. 10)

roca intrusiva: roca ígnea que se forma cuando el magma se enfría bajo el suelo. (pág. 316)

K

kinetic (kuh NEH tik) energy: energy due to motion (p. 207)

energía cinética: energía debida al movimiento. (pág. 207)

L

lava: magma that erupts onto Earth's surface (p. 306)

law of conservation of energy: law that states that energy can be transformed from one form to another, but it cannot be created or destroyed (p. 227)

law of conservation of mass: law that states that the total mass of the reactants before a chemical reaction is the same as the total mass of the products after the chemical reaction (p. 70)

liquid: matter with a definite volume but no definite shape (p. 85)

lithosphere (LIH thuh sfihr): the rigid outermost layer of Earth that includes the uppermost mantle and crust (p. 274)

lunar: term that refers to anything related to the Moon (p. 402)

luster: the way a mineral reflects or absorbs light at its surface (p. 104)

lava: magma que llega a la superficie de la Tierra. (pág. 306)

ley de la conservación de la energía: ley que plantea que la energía puede transformarse de una forma a otra, pero no puede crearse ni destruirse. (pág. 227)

ley de la conservación de la masa: ley que plantea que la masa total de los reactivos antes de una reacción química es la misma que la masa total de los productos después de la reacción química. (pág. 70)

líquido: materia con volumen definido y forma indefinida. (pág. 85)

litosfera: capa rígida más externa de la Tierra que incluye el manto superior y la corteza. (pág. 274)

lunar: término que hace referencia a todo lo relacionado con la luna. (pág. 402)

brillo: forma en que un mineral refleja o absorbe la luz en su superficie. (pág. 104)

M

magma: molten rock stored beneath Earth's surface (p. 306)

magnetosphere: the outer part of Earth's magnetic field that interacts with charged particles (p. 277)

malleability (ma lee uh BIH luh tee): the ability of a substance to be hammered or rolled into sheets (p. 104)

mantle: the thick middle layer in the solid part of Earth (p. 274)

mass: the amount of matter in an object (p. 88)

matter: anything that has mass and takes up space (p. 42)

mechanical energy: sum of the potential energy and the kinetic energy in a system (p. 211)

metal: an element that is generally shiny, is easily pulled into wires or hammered into thin sheets, and is a good conductor of electricity and thermal energy (p. 103)

metalloid (MEH tul oyd): an element that has physical and chemical properties of both metals and nonmetals (p. 118)

magma: roca derretida almacenada debajo de la superficie de la Tierra. (pág. 306)

magnetosfera: parte externa del campo magnético de la Tierra que interactúa con partículas cargadas. (pág. 277)

maleabilidad: capacidad de una sustancia de martillarse o laminarse para formar hojas. (pág. 104)

manto: capa delgada central de la parte sólida de la Tierra. (pág. 274)

masa: cantidad de materia en un objeto. (pág. 88)

materia: cualquier cosa que tiene masa y ocupa espacio. (pág. 42)

energía mecánica: suma de la energía potencial y la energía cinética en un sistema. (pág. 211)

metal: elemento que generalmente es brillante, fácilmente puede estirarse para formar alambres o martillarse para formar hojas delgadas y es buen conductor de electricidad y energía térmica. (pág. 103)

metaloide: elemento que tiene las propiedades físicas y químicas de metales y no metales. (pág. 118)

metamorphism: process that affects the structure or composition of a rock in a solid state as a result of changes in temperature, pressure, or the addition of chemical fluids (p. 334)

meteor: a meteoroid that has entered Earth's atmosphere and produces a streak of light (p. 387)

meteorite: a meteoroid that strikes a planet or a moon (p. 387)

meteoroid: a small rocky particle that moves through space (p. 387)

mitochondrion (mi tuh KAHN dree uhn): an organelle that breaks down food and releases energy (p. 437)

mixture: matter that can vary in composition (p. 52)

molecule (MAH lih kyewl): two or more atoms that are held together by chemical bonds and act as a unit (p. 44)

motion: the process of changing position (p. 166)

metamorfismo: proceso que afecta la estructura o composición de una roca en estado sólido como resultado de cambios en la temperatura, la presión, o por la adición de fluidos químicos. (pág. 334)

meteoro: meteorito que ha entrado a la atmósfera de la Tierra y produce un haz de luz. (pág. 387)

meteorito: meteoroide que impacta un planeta o una luna. (pág. 387)

meteoroide: partícula rocosa pequeña que se mueve por el espacio. (pág. 387)

mitocondria: organelo que descompone el alimento y libera energía. (pág. 437)

mezcla: materia que puede variar en composición. (pág. 52)

molécula: dos o más átomos que están unidos mediante enlaces covalentes y actúan como una unidad. (pág. 44)

movimiento: proceso de cambiar de posición. (pág. 166)

N

Newton's first law of motion: law that states that if the net force acting on an object is zero, the motion of the object does not change (p. 200)

Newton's second law of motion: law that states that the acceleration of an object is equal to the net force exerted on the object divided by the object's mass (p. 201)

Newton's third law of motion: law that states that for every action there is an equal and opposite reaction (p. 201)

noble gas: an element in group 18 on the periodic table (p. 117)

noncontact force: a force that one object applies to another object without touching it (p. 188)

nonfoliated rock: metamorphic rock with mineral grains that have a random, interlocking texture (p. 336)

nonmetal: an element that has no metallic properties (p. 114)

nonrenewable resource: a natural resource that is being used up faster than it can be replaced by natural processes (p. 132)

nuclear energy: energy stored in and released from the nucleus of an atom (pp. 136, 211)

primera ley del movimiento de Newton: ley que establece que si la fuerza neta ejercida sobre un objeto es cero, el movimiento de dicho objeto no cambia. (pág. 200)

segunda ley del movimiento de Newton: ley que establece que la aceleración de un objeto es igual a la fuerza neta que actúa sobre él divida por su masa. (pág. 201)

tercera ley del movimiento de Newton: ley que establece que para cada acción hay una reacción igual en dirección opuesta. (pág. 201)

gas noble: elemento del grupo 18 de la tabla periódica. (pág. 117)

fuerza de no contacto: fuerza que un objeto puede aplicar sobre otro sin tocarlo. (pág. 188)

roca no foliada: roca metamórfica con granos de mineral que tienen una textura entrelazada al azar. (pág. 336)

no metal: elemento que tiene propiedades no metálicas. (pág. 114)

recurso no renovable: recurso que se usa más rápidamente de lo que se puede reemplazar mediante procesos naturales. (pág. 132)

energía nuclear: energía almacenada en y liberada por el núcleo de un átomo. (pág. 136, 211)

O

observation: the act of using one or more of your senses to gather information and taking note of what occurs. (p. 10)

observación: acción de usar uno o más sentidos para reunir información y tomar notar de lo que ocurre. (pág. 10)

P

period of revolution: the time it takes an object to travel once around the Sun. (p. 354)

period of rotation: the time it takes an object to complete one rotation. (p. 354)

physical change: a change in the size, shape, form, or state of matter that does not change the matter's identity (p. 65)

physical property: a characteristic of matter that you can observe or measure without changing the identity of the matter (p. 88)

plastic deformation: the permanent change in shape of rocks caused by bending or folding (p. 335)

plate tectonics: theory that Earth's surface is broken into large, rigid pieces that move with respect to each other (p. 284)

population: all the organisms of the same species that live in the same area at the same time (p. 464)

position: an object's distance and direction from a reference point (p. 164)

potential (puh TEN chul) energy: stored energy due to the interactions between objects or particles (p. 207)

prediction: a statement of what will happen next in a sequence of events. (p. 10)

Project Apollo: a series of space missions designed to send people to the Moon (p. 403)

prokaryotic (pro kayr ee AH tihk)cell: a cell that does not have a nucleus or other membrane-bound organelles (p. 433)

período de revolución: tiempo que gasta un objeto en dar una vuelta alrededor del Sol. (pág. 354)

período de rotación: tiempo que gasta un objeto para completar una rotación. (pág. 354)

cambio físico: cambio en el tamaño, la forma o estado de la materia en el que no cambia la identidad de la materia. (pág. 65)

propiedad física: característica de la materia que puede observarse o medirse sin cambiar la identidad de la materia. (pág. 88)

deformación plástica: cambio permanente en la forma de las rocas causado por el doblamiento o el plegado. (pág. 335)

tectónica de placas: teoría que afirma que la superficie de la Tierra está dividida en piezas enormes y rígidas que se mueven una con respecto a la otra. (pág. 284)

población: todos los organismos de la misma especie que viven en la misma área al mismo tiempo. (pág. 464)

posición: distancia y dirección de un objeto según un punto de referencia. (pág. 164)

energía potencial: energía almacenada debido a las interacciones entre objetos o partículas. (pág. 207)

predicción: afirmación de lo que ocurrirá después en una secuencia de eventos. (pág. 10)

Proyecto Apolo: serie de misiones espaciales diseñadas para enviar personas a la Luna. (pág. 403)

célula procariota: célula que no tiene núcleo ni otros organelos limitados por una membrana. (pág. 433)

R

radiant energy: energy carried by an electromagnetic wave (p. 211)

radiation: the transfer of thermal energy by electromagnetic waves (p. 240)

reclamation: a process in which mined land must be recovered with soil and replanted with vegetation(p. 138)

energía radiante: energía que transporta una onda electromagnética. (pág. 211)

radiación: transferencia de energía térmica por ondas electromagnéticas. (pág. 240)

recuperación: proceso por el cual las tierras explotadas se deben recubrir con suelo y se deben replantar con vegetación. (pág. 138)

Glossary

Glossary

reference point: the starting point you use to describe the motion or the position of an object (p. 164)

regional metamorphism: formation of metamorphic rock bodies that are hundreds of square kilometers in size (p. 337)

renewable resource: a natural resource that can be replenished by natural processes at least as quickly as it is used (p. 132)

ridge push: the process that results when magma rises at a mid-ocean ridge and pushes oceanic plates in two different directions away from the ridge (p. 291)

rock: a naturally occurring solid composed of minerals, rock fragments, and sometimes other materials such as organic matter (p. 304)

rock cycle: the series of processes that change one type of rock into another type of rock (p. 307)

rocket: a vehicle propelled by the exhaust made from burning fuel (p. 400)

punto de referencia: punto que se escoge para describir la ubicación, o posición, de un objeto. (pág. 164)

metamorfismo regional: formación de cuerpos de rocas metamórficas que son del tamaño de cientos de kilómetros cuadrados. (pág. 337)

recurso renovable: recurso natural que se reabastece por procesos naturales al menos tan rápidamente como se usa. (pág. 132)

empuje de dorsal: proceso que resulta cuando el magma se levanta en la dorsal oceánica y empuja las placas oceánicas en dos direcciones diferentes, lejos de la dorsal. (pág. 291)

roca: sólido de origen natural compuesto de minerales, acumulación de fragmentos y algunas veces de otros materiales como materia orgánica. (pág. 304)

ciclo geológico: series de procesos que cambian un tipo de roca en otro tipo de roca. (pág. 307)

cohete: vehículo propulsado por gases de escape producidos por la ignición de combustible. (pág. 400)

S

satellite: any small object that orbits a larger object other than a star (p. 401)

science: the investigation and exploration of natural events and of the new information that results from those investigations (p. 8)

scientific law: a rule that describes a pattern in nature (p. 13)

scientific theory: an explanation of observations or events that is based on knowledge gained from many observations and investigations (p. 13)

sediment: rock material that forms when rocks are broken down into smaller pieces or dissolved in water as rocks erode (p. 306)

semiconductor: a substance that conducts electricity at high temperatures but not at low temperatures (p. 118)

slab pull: the process that results when a dense oceanic plate sinks beneath a more buoyant plate along a subduction zone, pulling the rest of the plate that trails behind it (p. 291)

satélite: cualquier objeto pequeño que orbita un objeto más grande diferente de una estrella. (pág. 401)

ciencia: la investigación y exploración de los eventos naturales y de la información nueva que es el resultado de estas investigaciones. (pág. 8)

ley científica: regla que describe un patrón dado en la naturaleza. (pág. 13)

teoría científica: explicación de observaciones o eventos con base en conocimiento obtenido de muchas observaciones e investigaciones. (pág. 13)

sedimento: material rocoso formado cuando las rocas se rompen en piezas pequeñas o se disuelven en agua al erosionarse. (pág. 306)

semiconductor: sustancia que conduce electricidad a altas temperaturas, pero no a bajas temperaturas. (pág. 118)

convergencia de placas: proceso que resulta cuando una placa oceánica densa se hunde debajo de una placa flotante en una zona de subducción, arrastrando el resto de la placa detrás suyo. (pág. 291)

solar energy: energy from the Sun (p. 144)

solid: matter that has a definite shape and a definite volume (p. 85)

solubility: the maximum amount of solute that can dissolve in a given amount of solvent at a given temperature and pressure (p. 90)

sound energy: energy carried by sound waves (p. 211)

space probe: an uncrewed spacecraft sent from Earth to explore objects in space (p. 402)

space shuttle: a reusable spacecraft that transports people and materials to and from space (p. 403)

speed: the distance an object moves divided by the time it takes to move that distance (p. 166)

speed-time graph: a graph that shows the speed of an object on the *y*-axis and time on the *x*-axis (p. 180)

sphere: a ball shape with all points on the surface at an equal distance from the center (p. 260)

subduction: the process that occurs when one tectonic plate moves under another tectonic plate (p. 286)

substance: matter with a composition that is always the same (p. 43)

energía solar: energía proveniente del Sol. (pág. 144)

sólido: materia con forma y volumen definidos. (pág. 85)

solubilidad: cantidad máxima de soluto que puede disolverse en una cantidad dada de solvente a temperatura y presión dadas. (pág. 90)

energía sonora: energía que transportan las ondas sonoras. (pág. 211)

sonda espacial: nave espacial sin tripulación enviada desde la Tierra para explorar objetos en el espacio. (pág. 402)

transbordador espacial: nave espacial reutilizable que transporta personas y materiales hacia y desde el espacio. (pág. 403)

rapidez: distancia que un objeto recorre dividida por el tiempo que éste tarda en recorrer dicha distancia. (pág. 166)

gráfico rapidez-tiempo: gráfico que muestra la rapidez de un objeto en el eje Y y el tiempo en el eje X. (pág. 180)

esfera: figura de bola cuyos puntos en la superficie están ubicados a una distancia igual del centro. (pág. 260)

subducción: proceso que ocurre cuando una placa tectónica se mueve debajo de otra placa tectónica. (pág. 286)

sustancia: materia cuya composición es siempre la misma. (pág. 43)

T

taxon: a group of organisms (p. 450)

technology: the practical use of scientific knowledge, especially for industrial or commercial use (p. 12)

temperature: the measure of the average kinetic energy of the particles in a material (p. 236)

terrestrial planets: Earth and the other inner planets that are closest to the Sun including Mercury, Venus, and Mars (p. 362)

texture: a rock's grain size and the way the grains fit together (p. 305)

thermal conductor: a material through which thermal energy flows quickly (p. 244)

thermal energy: the sum of the kinetic energy and the potential energy of the particles that make up an object (p. 211)

taxón: grupo de organismos. (pág. 450)

tecnología: uso práctico del conocimiento científico, especialmente para uso industrial o comercial. (pág. 12)

temperatura: medida de la energía cinética promedio de las partículas de un material. (pág. 236)

planetas terrestres: la Tierra y otros planetas interiores que están más cerca del Sol, incluidos Mercurio, Venus y Marte. (pág. 362)

textura: tamaño del grano de una roca y la forma como los granos encajan. (pág. 305)

conductor térmico: material en el cual la energía térmica se mueve con rapidez. (pág. 244)

energía térmica: suma de la energía cinética y potencial de las partículas que componen un objeto. (pág. 211)

Copyright © McGraw-Hill Education

thermal insulator: a material through which thermal energy flows slowly (p. 244)

transform plate boundary: the boundary between two plates that slide past each other (p. 286)

transition element: an element in groups 3–12 on the periodic table. (p. 106)

aislante térmico: material a través del cual la energía térmica fluye con lentitud. (pág. 244)

límite de placas transcurrente: límite entre dos placas que se deslizan una con respecto a la otra. (pág. 286)

elemento de transición: elemento de los grupos 3–12 de la tabla periódica. (pág. 106)

vaporization: the change in state of a liquid into a gas (p. 243)

variable: any factor that can have more than one value. (p. 23)

velocity: the speed and the direction of a moving object (p. 168)

volcanic rock: rock that forms when lava cools too quickly to form crystals (p. 315)

volume: the amount of space a sample of matter occupies. (p. 85)

vaporización: cambio de estado líquido a gaseoso. (pág. 243)

variable: cualquier factor que tenga más de un valor. (pág. 23)

velocidad: rapidez y dirección de un objeto en movimiento. (pág. 168)

roca volcánico: roca que se forma como resultado del enfriamiento muy rápido de la lava, formando cristales. (pág. 315)

volumen: cantidad de espacio que ocupa la materia. (pág. 85)

wind farm: a group of wind turbines that produce electricity (p. 145)

work: the amount of energy used as a force moves an object over a distance (p. 210)

parque eólico: grupo de turbinas de viento que produce electricidad. (pág. 145)

trabajo: cantidad de energía usada como fuerza que mueve un objeto a cierta distancia. (pág. 210)

Index

Index

Index

Index

Copyright © McGraw-Hill Education

Index